THE FASHION BOOK

Abbe James   Photographer

James Abbe's choice of a simple, uncluttered backdrop and soft use of lighting accentuates the seductiveness of Gilda Gray, a dancer in *Ziegfeld Follies* and other Broadway revues. Like many fashion photographs of its time, it promotes a feeling that we are privy to something intimate – as if Gray has been captured unawares, dreamily caught up in her own thoughts with her eyes turned away from the lens. Taken in Paris in 1924, the photograph seizes the essence of mid-1920s eveningwear – a plumb line dress, possibly by Lanvin or Patou, in filmy, sensuous fabric trimmed with fringed tiers. In the early twentieth century, American photographer James Abbe favoured taking portraits of stage and screen actresses. His well-mannered work for American *Vogue* represented what Alexander Liberman called '...an underlying dream of a world where people act and behave in a civilized manner'.

► Lanvin, Liberman, Patou

►e. b Alfred, ME (USA), 1883. d San Francisco, C∠ 'SA' 73. **Gilda Gray, Paris.** 1924

Abboud Joseph

Designer

A Mao jacket cut from rough linen is worn over a hand-knitted waistcoat and collarless shirt. The buttons on each garment have a natural, artisanal quality that defies the urban slant used by most American designers. Of Lebanese descent, Joseph Abboud makes clothes for men and women that are an unusual combination of American sportswear and North African colours and textures. In the 1960s Abboud collected Turkish kilims and these have inspired his natural palette and the stylized symbols that recur in his work. He began his career as a buyer and in 1981 joined Ralph Lauren, later to become associate director of menswear design. He emerged four years later with a similar philosophy to Lauren: that clothing is as much about lifestyle as it is about design. In 1986 Abboud launched his own label and found a niche for his understated clothes with their rich colours and unusually crafted textures.

► Alfaro, Armani, Lauren, Ozbek

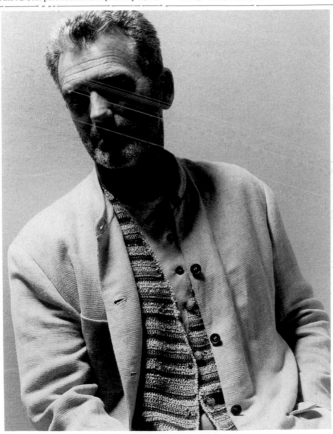

Joseph Abboud. b Boston, MA (USA) 1950. **Linen menswear, spring/summer 1995.** Photograph by Randall Mesdon.

Ackermann Haider

Designer

Reclining like a languorous odalisque in a Lord Leighton tableau, the model in this photograph exudes a dissolute air of exotic luxury, very much in keeping with the mood of Haider Ackermann's spring/summer 2011 collection presented at the Palazzo Pitti in Florence. A Silk-Road fantasy seen through a pipe-smoke haze, male and female silhouettes alike featured in rich silks and satins, dhoti pants and kimono collars. Born in Colombia, Ackermann had a peripatetic childhood, growing up in cities across Europe and Africa. Now based in Antwerp, his collections are often informed by a strong sense of place and what the designer describes as 'errance' – a kind of wandering sensibility. His garments for women are prized for their expert draping in soft leather and suede, heavy satins, jersey and silk, and for the sensual androgyny of his silhouettes, beautifully typified by the actress Tilda Swinton with whom the designer's style is strongly associated.

► Demeulemeester, Margiela, Owens, Swinton

ider Ackermann. b Santa Fé de Bogotá (COL), 1971. **Haider Ackermann Pitti Uomo Portfolio, 2011.** Photograph by s Madigan Heck.

Adolfo

Designer

This impromptu snap of society figures Mr and Mrs Wyatt Cooper is one of Adolfo's favourite pictures, and not just because both are wearing his refined clothes. He says, 'Getting dressed and going out is fun only because we don't do it often – it's good to feel glamorous once in a while.' But his glamour never strays into the realms of vulgarity. Adolfo worked first as a milliner, then trained at Chanel and Balenciaga, before setting up his New York salon. There, Adolfo provided his famous knitted suits,

one of which is worn here by Gloria Cooper (aka Gloria Vanderbilt). Inspired by Coco Chanel's jersey sportswear and iconic suits, they were bought by New York's old society. When his salon closed in 1993 his clientèle were distraught, not least Nancy Reagan, who had worn Adolfo's clothes for two decades. She, perhaps more than anyone, embodied his assertion that, 'An Adolfo lady should look simple, classic and comfortable.'

► Balenciaga, Chanel, Galanos, Vanderbilt

Adolfo (**Adolfo Sardina**). b Havana (CU), 1933. **Mr and Mrs Wyatt Cooper.** Photograph by Bill Cunningham, American *Vogue*, 1972.

Adrian Gilbert

Designer

Joan Crawford wears Adrian's famed 'coat hanger look': a suit with padded shoulders and slim skirt producing an 'inverted triangle' silhouette that has since intermittently returned to fashion – not least in the 1980s. Here that shape is exaggerated further by triangular lapels that reach over the shoulders and taper, pointing at the waist. As Adrian told *Life* magazine in 1947, 'American women's clothes should be streamlined in the daytime.' He is also known for long, elegantly draped dinner gowns, like those he designed for Joan Crawford in *Grand Hotel* (1932), and for his silver satin bias-cut dresses for starlet Jean Harlow. As a costume designer at Metro-Goldwyn-Mayer in the 1930s and 1940s, Adrian – born Adolphus Greenburg – found a vast audience for his work and became an influential fashion designer. In 1942 he retired as a costume designer to open his own fashion house, continuing to create his trademark suits and gowns.

▶ Garbo, Irene, Orry-Kelly, Platt Lynes

Gilbert Adrian (Adolphus Greenburg). b Naugatuck, CT (USA), 1903. d Los Angeles, CA (USA), 1959. **Joan Crawford.** c.1940.

Aghion Gaby (Chloé)   Designer

Chloé, a name synonymous with feminine modernity, was conceived by Egyptian-born designer Gaby Aghion, who established the label in 1952 with her business partner Jacques Lenoir. With a free-spirited and independent heroine in mind, Aghion rejected the structured silhouette of the time, approaching ready-to-wear with the finesse and detail of haute couture. Since then Chloé has seen a number of notable designers, but has always retained an ethereal, free-flowing style. Karl Lagerfeld, at the helm from 1965 to 1983, brought his 'Woodstock Couture' that evoked the flower-child mood of the era. Stella McCartney, as head designer from 1997, offered a similarly playful femininity in her design approach. Chloé is now an international brand owned by Richemont with a diffusion line and perfume ranges. With Clare Waight Keller joining in 2011 as creative director, the brand continues to grow.

► Bailly, Lagerfeld, McCartney, Paulin, Sitbon, Steiger

Gaby Aghion. b Alexandria (EG), 1921. (Chloé.) **'Rachmaninoff' dress, Chloé spring/summer 1973, as sketched by Karl Lagerfeld and on show at Restaurant Laurent, Paris.** Photograph by Jean-Luce Huré.

Agnès Madame   Milliner

During the 1930s, hats were literally the pinnacle of fashion, and a lady would no sooner go out without her hat than she would without her dress. In France millinery was an exclusively female occupation and Madame Agnès was the most popular milliner, famous for cutting her elegant brims while her clients were wearing them. Trained under Caroline Reboux, she established her own salon in 1917 on the rue du Faubourg Saint-Honoré in Paris among all the great couturiers. She worked in the same understated manner and combined this discrimination with an awareness of art and of the artistic trends of the 1930s. The remarkable designs shown here reflect the milliner's flair for the dramatic and surreal. The crown for each black suede hat is theatrically tweaked to a high point and, on the left, a tassel of fringes is looped elegantly around the neck.

► Barthet, Hoyningen-Huene, Reboux, Rouff, Talbot

Madame Agnès. b (FR), late 1800s. d (FR). (Active 1910s–1940s.) **Designs for black suede hats.** 1936.

Alaïa Azzedine

Designer

Amazonian models in skintight dresses and high-heeled shoes embody the slick sex appeal of the dress-to-kill 1980s. Each wears an outfit from Azzedine Alaïa's 1987 spring/summer collection. 'The base of all beauty is the body,' says Alaïa, who, inspired by Madeleine Vionnet, states 'there is nothing more beautiful than a healthy body dressed in wonderful clothes.' The 'King of Cling' is an expert manipulator of the female form, having studied sculpture when he was younger. He moved to Paris and worked briefly for Dior and Guy Laroche, and by the end of the 1960s had his own couture business on the Left Bank. In the early 1980s, his stretchy dresses and bodysuits, constructed from thick knitted panels, came to define the Lycra revolution. In 2008 he was made a *Chevalier* of the *Légion d'honneur*, and presented his autumn/winter 2011 *haute couture* collection in Paris after a long absence from the catwalk.

► Audibet, Dior, G. Jones, Laroche, Léger, Vionnet

Azzedine Alaïa. b Tunis (TUN), 1940. **Paris presentation.** Photograph by Arthur Elgort, British *Vogue*, 1987.

Albini Walter

Designer

Two women striking disco poses wear the Walter Albini hallmarks: fast, glamorous clothes that recall shapes from the 1930s. Albini started his luxury sportswear business in 1965 and became known for his fundamental allegiance to the early styles of Chanel and Patou, which were counterpointed by the global influences of the 1970s. Bold colours from Asian and African art, as well as bright tartans, were employed on the jackets, skirts and other basic silhouettes. As much as any 1970s designer, Albini energized anti-establishment hippie layering and ethnicity and mixed it with the sophistication of the urbane sportswear pedigree. Albini's motto was 'Enjoy today and leave unpleasant things for tomorrow'. Ironically, premature death obviated any tomorrows, but Albini's exuberant, aggressive and youthful sportswear was a significant contribution to the 1970s.

► Barnett, Bates, Chanel, Ozbek, Patou

b Busto Arsizio (IT), 1941. **d** Milan (IT), 1983. **Black crepe outfits.** Photograph by Chris von Wangenheim, 71.

Alexandre

Hairdresser

Alexandre de Paris, or 'Monsieur Alexandre', as he liked to be known, attends to Elizabeth Taylor's hair in 1962. Many legends surrounded the hairdresser, whose clients included the Duchess of Windsor, Coco Chanel and Grace Kelly. His parents, it is said, had wanted him to study medicine, but after a fortune teller predicted that 'the wife of a king will do everything for you', they relented and let him pursue his ambition. He was apprenticed to Antoine, the Parisian stylist who invented the urchin cut.

Alexandre took on his mantle and became the hairdresser of the European social set. Jean Cocteau designed his motif, a sphinx, for him in gratitude for the perm that restored to him 'the curly hair of a true poet'. In 1997, Jean Paul Gaultier persuaded Alexandre out of retirement to design the hair for his first couture show, as he had done for Coco Chanel, Pierre Balmain and Yves Saint Laurent.

► Antoine, Cocteau, Gaultier, Recine, Windsor, Winston

Alexandre (Louis Alexandre Raimon). b St Tropez (FR), 1922. **d** St Tropez (FR), 2008. **Alexandre de Paris with Elizabeth Taylor.** Photograph by Eric Adjani, 1962.

Alfaro Victor

Designer

Victor Alfaro's first collection, launched in 1991, was dubbed by *Cosmopolitan* magazine 'a series of heat-seeking glamour missiles'. Reputedly the heir to Oscar de la Renta and Bill Blass, Alfaro has never sought to philosophize through his offerings; on the contrary, his mission is as simple as making the wearer look beautiful. This image shows a quintessential Alfaro creation in which vulgarity is proscribed, leaving room for bare simplicity skilfully counterbalanced by sexy, luxurious

silk. The combination of a ball skirt and strapless top is typical of Alfaro's use of separates for cocktail and evening wear, acquired while working for American ready-to-wear designer Joseph Abboud. He uses slub silk as others use cotton, in keeping with the American sportswear tradition of evening clothes that quietly forgo decoration for practical statements, even on a ball gown. In 2008 he introduced his Victor by Victor Alfaro brand.

► Abboud, Blass, De la Renta, Tyler

Victor Alfaro. b Chihuahua (MEX), 1965. **Silk bustier and evening skirt, spring/summer 1996.** Photograph by Chris Moore.

Amies Sir Hardy

Designer

Her Majesty the Queen is photographed during the Silver Jubilee celebrations in 1977. She wears an eye-catching pink silk crepe dress, coat and stole by Sir Hardy Amies, dressmaker to Her Majesty since 1955 and the architect of her vivid, feminine and simple style. Amies, knighted in 1989, was designer and manager at Lachasse, a traditional British haute couture house, from 1934 to 1939. As well as being lieutenant-colonel in charge of special forces in Belgium, he designed clothes under the Utility rationing scheme. In 1946 he founded his own dressmaking business, designing for Princess Elizabeth and eventually holding the royal warrant. In 1950, Amies started ladies' ready-to-wear and in 1961 began working with menswear chain Hepworths. His remark 'A man should look as if he bought his clothes with intelligence, put them on with care, then forgot all about them' defines the Englishman's approach to fashion.

▶ Clements Ribeiro, Hartnell, Morton, Rayne, Stiebel

Sir Hardy Amies. b London (UK), 1909. **d** Langford, Oxfordshire (UK), 2003. **Her Majesty Queen Elizabeth II wears pink Royal Jubilee outfit.** 1977. 15

Antoine

Hairdresser

Josephine Baker was one of Antoine's many famous clients – she wore his wigs like skullcaps for her stage performances. Born in Russian Poland, Antoine moved to work in the Parisian salon of hairdresser Monsieur Decoux. He acquired a following and, cannily, Decoux took his star stylist to the fashionable seaside town of Deauville; there Antoine was introduced to the society he would coif for decades. On his return to Paris, Antoine set up his own salon, selling his own haircare and cosmetics range – the first to do so. Although he is famed for his 'Eton crop', he always maintained he could not claim it as his own. At the time he said he was simply carrying out the orders of a client who returned three times to have her short bobbed hair cut progressively shorter to suit the increasingly sporty lifestyle enjoyed by women of that era. The peak of Antoine's career was the coronation of George VI, when he supervised 400 coiffures in one night.

► Alexandre, G. Jones, Kenneth, De Meyer, Talbot

Antoine (Antak Cierplikowski). b Sieradz (POL), 1884. **d** Sieradz (POL), 1976. **Josephine Baker.** Photograph by Baron de Meyer, c.1925.

Antonio

Antonio's watercolour model embraces a deconstructed mannequin for Italian *Vogue* in 1981. This surreal element, a tradition created by Dalí, Cocteau and Bérard in the 1930s, was a theme used by Antonio throughout his career. Texan Jerry Hall was painted with Lone Star emblems and cacti growing from her Stetson, while Pat Cleveland was metamorphosed into a stiletto boot. Despite this visual play, Antonio worked from life, building sets as a photographer would. Antonio was inspired by the drawings of Boldini and Ingres, which becomes clear when looking at the fine finish on his pencil drawings. His work dominated fashion illustration for a decade, encouraging a discipline that had diminished throughout the 1950s. Antonio worked with a clique of international models and high-profile friends who converged on Paris in the 1970s. Tina Chow, Grace Jones and Paloma Picasso were regular sitters.

► Chow, Dalí, G. Jones, Khanh, Versace

Antonio (Antonio Lopez). b (PR), 1943. **d** (PR), 1987. **Gianni Versace editorial.** Italian *Vogue*, 1981.

Apfel Iris

Icon

'Rare Bird', the title of the popular 2005 Metropolitan Museum of Art exhibition featuring Iris Apfel's couture collection, summarizes the style icon's character perfectly. The Queens (New York) native, textile entrepreneur and former *Women's Wear Daily* staffer has become a figure in pop culture revered for her honest intelligence and witty style. The only child of a clothing boutique owner and mirror manufacturer, Apfel possessed an affinity for fashion at an early age. Her lauded wardrobe, assembled with care over the course of her life, is a rare combination of haute couture and flea-market gems, showcasing her eclectic taste and individuality. Seen here modelling Rei Kawakubo's designs for Comme des Garçons for the cover of *Dazed & Confused* magazine in 2012, her irreverent personality and distinctive sense of style is ever apparent. Apfel has stated 'the worst fashion faux pas is looking in the mirror and seeing somebody else'.

▶ Blow, Cunningham, Guinness, Kawakubo, Wintour

Iris Apfel. b New York (USA), 1921. **Iris Apfel wears Comme des Garçons autumn/winter 2012, for *Dazed & Confused*.** Photograph by Jeff Bark.

Arai Junichi

Textile designer

Junichi Arai has been described as the 'truly *enfant terrible* of Japanese textiles... a naughty boy playing with high-tech toys'. His favoured toys are the jacquard loom and digital computer. The fabric illustrated here is typical of his work, which commonly uses metallic fibres and turns them into exquisite works of art destined only to be admired. The son and nephew of weavers, Arai was born in Kiryu, a historic centre for textiles. He initially worked with his father on kimono and obi cloths, which he developed, eventually acquiring three-dozen patents for new fabrics. From 1970 Arai worked experimentally and began long-standing collaborations with Rei Kawakubo and Issey Miyake, who would suggest phrases such as 'like clouds', 'like stone' or 'driving rain' for Arai to magic into a representative fabric by using his idiosyncratic weaving techniques.

► Hishinuma, Isogawa, Jinteok, Kawakubo, Miyake

Junichi Arai. b Kiryu (JAP), 1932. **Crush-pleated fabric, spring/summer 1990.** Photograph by Masanao Arai.

Arden Elizabeth

Cosmetics creator

In one of Baron de Meyer's famous advertisements for Elizabeth Arden, a model resembling a figure from a Modigliani painting wears the Arden face. The name behind one of the century's greatest cosmetic houses was inspired by Tennyson's poem *'Enoch Arden'* and a love of the name Elizabeth. Her real name was Florence Nightingale Graham and she worked as a beauty treatment girl for Eleanor Adair in New York where, in 1910, she opened her own salon on Fifth Avenue with her signature red door. One of the first beauty gurus to encourage exercise, she opened a spa and health retreat in Maine in 1934, and was passionate about horses. Arden developed a range of make-up for Hollywood that would not melt under the lights and was later used by women when they were out dancing. In 1935 she launched the legendary Eight Hour Cream, which remains to this day a cult beauty product.

► Bourjois, C. James, De Meyer, Revson, Uemura

den (**Florence Nightingale Graham**). **b** Woodbridge, ONT (CAN), 1878. **d** New York (USA), 1966. **Advertising** otograph by Baron de Meyer, *c.*1927.

Armani Giorgio   Designer

A man and woman wear the hallmarks of a great modernist: tailoring that trades stiff formality for assured relaxation. Giorgio Armani laid the groundwork for the easy, minimalist working uniform of emancipated 1980s women and blazed the trail for designers such as Calvin Klein and Donna Karan. His menswear was equally mould-breaking: taking the stuffing and stiffness out of the suit, he made the laid-back style of southern Europe coveted around the world. Armani was assistant to Nino Cerruti before starting his own business in 1973. His name came to the fore when he dressed Richard Gere for the film *American Gigolo* (1980). Every scene was choreographed to work for Armani's clothes, prompting Gere to ask, 'Who's acting in this scene, me or the jacket?' In 2005 Armani made his début in haute couture with his Giorgio Armani Privé collection. The same year the Guggenheim Museum, New York, dedicated an exhibition to him.

▶ Alboud, Cerruti, Dominguez, Klein, Prada, Valentino

Giorgio Armani. b Piacenza (IT), 1934. **Unstructured tailoring, spring/summer 1995.** Photograph by Peter Lindbergh.

Arnold Eve

Photographer

Eve Arnold's camera captured the gold beaded skullcap, glossed lips and lacquered nails of a model backstage at a Lanvin show in 1977. Arnold rarely used studios; relying instead on natural light and her hand-held Nikon. Her work was always respectful and sympathetic to its subject, background details were never an afterthought – Arnold insisted, 'You have to take advantage of the variables. It might be the smile, the gesture, the light. None of which you can predict.' She took pictures of black women modelling in Harlem fashion shows in 1948 and continued the project for two years, until *Picture Post* published her story. As a result, she was offered a job as the first female stringer for the Magnum Photos agency. A long friendship with Marilyn Monroe produced some of her best-known images. But Arnold's work covered a broad spectrum – 'everything from serious disaster to Hollywood hoop-la'.

► Lanvin, Lapidus, L. Miller, Stern

b Philadelphia, PA (USA), 1913. d London (UK), 2012. **Lanvin model at Mappins, Paris.** French *Vogue*, 1977.

Ascher Zika

Textile designer

In the long tradition of artists turning fabric designers, such as Dufy and Cocteau, the unmistakable sketches of Henry Moore are applied to silk by Zika Ascher. This design, which combines screen printing with batik painting, was selected for use by Nina Ricci. When *Vogue* asked in 1962, 'Which comes first, the chicken or the egg? The fabric or the fashion?', it could have had Ascher in mind. His innovative approach to fabrics revolutionized fashion from the 1940s. He started his own production company and silk-screen print works in London in 1942. In 1948 he approached artists such as Moore and Henri Matisse to design prints. His own inventive approach to textiles acted as a catalyst for fashion designers of that time: in 1952 his highly original large-scale floral prints were used by Dior and Schiaparelli, and in 1957 his shaggy mohair inspired Castillo to create huge enveloping coats.

► Castillo, Etro, Pucci, Ricci, Schiaparelli

Zika Ascher. b Prague (CZ), 1910. **d** London (UK), 1992. **Detail of textile designed by Henry Moore, 1945.** Photograph by Daniel McGrath.

Ashley Laura

Designer

A Victorian-inspired, white cotton dress worn under a floral pinafore sums up the mood of romantic rural idyll that made Laura Ashley a household name. She once said that she designed for women who wanted to look 'sweet': 'I sensed that most people wanted to raise families, have gardens and live as nicely as they can.' She used puffed sleeves, sprig prints, pin-tucking, lace trims and high collars to make romantic references to a pastoral lifestyle, which in reality was a hard one for most. In a way that only fashion can, the look reinvented history and enabled women to dress for a role. It precipitated a movement known as 'milkmaidism'. In 1953, Ashley and husband Bernard began silk-screen printing textiles by hand in a small workshop in Pimlico, making table mats and napkins. In 1968 they opened their first shop, selling the basic Laura Ashley dress for £5. By the 1970s, it had become a symbol of femininity.

▶ Ettedgui, Fratini, Kenzo, Liberty

Laura Ashley. b Merthyr Tydfil, Wales (UK), 1926. **d** Coventry, West Midlands (UK), 1985. **Dress with pinafore.** *c.*1970.

Audibet Marc

Designer

This design is entirely about 'stretch'. There are no hooks, no eyes, no buttons and no zippers. It is a seamless, asymmetrical creation that clings to the body, following the lines of the model's figure. Audibet is both a fashion designer and an industrial designer, and is celebrated in the fashion world for his research into stretch fabrics. His expertise was acquired working as an assistant for Emanuel Ungaro and then as a designer for Pierre Balmain, Madame Grès and Nino Cerruti. An admirer of the work of Madame Vionnet and Claire McCardell, Audibet believes that fashion is a matter of anatomy and that innovation starts with fabrics. In 1987 he became textile adviser to the fabric and fibre company DuPont and together they created and launched single- and two-way stretch fabrics made from DuPont's 'Lycra' – the most important development in fashion in the 1980s.

► Alaïa, Bruce, Godley, Grès, Ungaro, Zoran

Marc Audibet. b Boulogne-sur-Seine (FR), 1958. **Model wears stretch column.** Photograph by Tyen, American *Elle*, 1987.   25

Avedon Richard

Photographer

Penelope Tree is suspended in space, frozen in a joyful leap by Richard Avedon. It is an image that epitomizes the motion and emotion Avedon introduced into fashion photography, resisting the prevailing tradition of static poses. Instead he preferred the mood of street reality; a woman glimpsed on a busy pavement or the unexpectedness of his famous 'Dovima With Elephants'. Influenced by photographer Martin Munkácsi, who explored the principle of the fashion figure in motion,

Avedon established his images of dancing and swinging frenzy, which have retained their freshness to this day. Avedon joined *Harper's Bazaar* in 1945, moving to *Vogue* in 1965. He never deserted fashion but, through his keen political convictions and intense interest in subcultures, Avedon became a photographer in service to a vision larger than fashion *per se*. His work was exhibited at the Metropolitan Museum of Art, New York, in 2002.
▶ D. Bailey, Brodovitch, Dovima, Moss, Parker, Tree, Ungaro

Richard Avedon. b New York (USA), 1923. **d** San Antonio, TX (USA), 2004. **Penelope Tree in Ungaro suit, Paris studio.** 1968.

Bailey Christopher

Designer

Christopher Bailey's brilliance at Burberry lies in his ability not only to respect the brand's traditions but also to update them with an understanding of modern dressing. The iconic trench, always represented in the collections, retains original features – epaulettes, D-ring buckles and gun flaps – but has a tighter, sharper silhouette. Bailey has made the Burberry name synonymous with cool, British style, whilst creating innovative collections without losing Burberry's distinctive heritage. A graduate from London's Royal College of Art in 1994, he immediately stepped into a role at Donna Karan womenswear. From there he moved to Gucci, before joining Burberry as creative director in 2001, and becoming chief creative officer in 2009. In 2005 and 2009 he won Designer of the Year at the British Fashion Awards and was appointed a Member of the Order of the British Empire (MBE) for services to the British Fashion Industry in 2009.

► Brooks, Burberry, Gucci, Kane, Karan

Christopher Bailey. b Halifax, West Yorkshire (UK), 1971. **Burberry spring/summer 2012 campaign.** Photograph by Mario Testino.

Bailey David

Jean Shrimpton, the face of the early 1960s, shares a confidence with Cecil Beaton, photographer, illustrator, costume designer and writer, whose influence on fashion spanned forty years. The photograph is by David Bailey. His shots of Jean Shrimpton, who he first met in 1960 and with whom he had a relationship for four years, let the world into an intimate bond between photographer and model. Bailey, who was regarded as a bad boy, used few models and developed long working relationships with them. His reluctance to be categorized as a fashion photographer is justified by time: those fashion shots now stand as legendary portraits in themselves. As Marie Helvin, model and former wife, put it, '...the very essence of Bailey's style is his refusal to allow his models to be simply clothes hangers or his pictures moments of fashion. He photographs women wearing clothes.'

► Beaton, French, Horvat, Shrimpton, Twiggy

David Bailey. b London (UK), 1938. **Jean Shrimpton and Cecil Beaton.** British *Vogue*, 1965.

Bailly Christiane

Designer

Christiane Bailly was part of the *prêt-à-porter* revolution of the 1960s. Her radical methods included experimenting with synthetic fabrics such as silver plastic and 'cigarette paper'. She took the stiff interlinings out of jackets for a suppler silhouette, and cut close-fitting clothes from black ciré in 1962. Bailly began her career as a model for Balenciaga, Chanel and Dior in 1957. Her interest in fashion developed and she entered design, working on more approachable clothes than those she had been modelling at the grand haute couture houses. In 1961 she started designing for Chloé and, after two years, moved on to work with Michèle Rosier. In 1962 Bailly formed a company with Emmanuelle Khanh, and both were assisted by a young Paco Rabanne. Their label, Emma Christie, produced revolutionary designs to critical acclaim and poor commercial success, but their role in the birth of French *prêt* was an important one.

► Bousquet, Betsey Johnson, Khanh, Lenoir, Rabanne

Christiane Bailly. b Lyon (FR), 1932. **Bouclé jacket and black wool skirt.** Photograph by Tim Jenkins, *Women's Wear Daily*, 1979.

Bakst Léon

Illustrator / Designer

The overall effect of this costume is both classical and oriental. It reflects the current fashionable silhouette in its long, columnar shape. However, this severe line is softened by the lavish surface decoration, reminiscent of the East. Léon Bakst's contribution to the history of fashion came through the theatre. He collaborated with Sergei Diaghilev in the creation of the Ballets Russes, which came to Paris in 1909. As its artistic director, Bakst designed the vibrantly coloured and exotic costumes. It was his designs for *Schéhérazade* that caused a sensation when it was performed in Paris in 1910. Orientalism in haute couture had already been successfully promoted by Paul Poiret. It was given further impetus by Bakst's sensual costumes, which had an extraordinary impact on Parisian fashion houses such as Worth and Paquin, who used his designs from 1912 to 1915. Bakst, like Erté, was a designer and an illustrator.

► Barbier, Brunelleschi, Dœuillet, Erté, Iribe, Poiret

Léon Bakst. b St Petersburg (RUS), 1866. **d** Paris (FR), 1924. **Design for Paquin.** 1912.

Balenciaga Cristóbal

Layered bells form the sleeves of this cape, worn over a matching dress. They exemplify the shapely simplicity that made Cristóbal Balenciaga a great couturier. His genius lay in cut. The sack dress, the balloon dress, the kimono-sleeve coat and a collar cut to elongate the neck were a few of his fashion innovations, although his clothes also came with a disclaimer: 'No woman can make herself chic if she is not chic herself,' Balenciaga once said. His Spanish severity contrasted with the light femininity of French designers; his favourite fabric was silk gazar, diaphanous but stiff, which satisfied his instinct for the sculptural. As early as 1938, Balenciaga's modern vision was influential, explained by *Harper's Bazaar* thus, 'Balenciaga abides by the law that elimination is the secret of chic.' In 1968, after a battle against what he saw as the tide of vulgarity flowing through fashion, Balenciaga bowed out with the words, 'It's a dog's life.'

► Chow, Ghesquière, Penn, Rabanne, Saint Laurent, Snow

Cristóbal Balenciaga. b Guetaria (SP), 1895. **d** Valencia (SP), 1972. **Dress and cape, autumn/winter 1964.** Photograph by Kublin.

Balla Giacomo   Designer

Although flat on the surface, this suit fuses movement, line and colour in a representation of the excitement of speed. Intrinsically forceful, the jagged strokes on the jacket, like storm-strewn palm leaves, mark high velocity and transmit energy. It gives us an image of an experimentalist at work. Balla, like fellow Futurists Severini and Boccioni, felt a positive need to extend his interests from the canvas to his environment, in this case exploring the subject of dress as a medium for expressing his Futurist ideas. Focusing more on male clothing, he stated the tenets of modernity in his 'Manifesto of Anti-Neutral Clothing', which aimed to bring disorder to the logic and communication of clothing. His ideas were based on asymmetry, clashing colours and juxtaposed forms that opposed tradition and convention. 'The past I so fiercely reject,' he said, embracing the industrial dynamics of modern art in his perception of fashion.

► Delaunay, Exter, Warhol

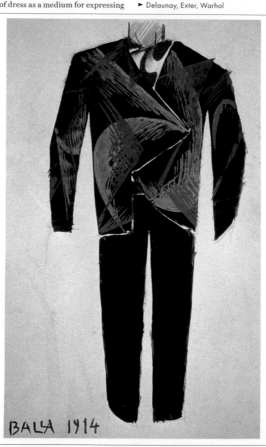

BALLA 1914

Giacomo Balla. b Turin (IT), 1871. d Rome (IT), 1958. **Sketch for men's suit, 1914.** Photograph by Giuseppe Schiavinotto.

Bally Carl Franz

Shoe designer

The continuity of fashion is illustrated by two examples of Bally's 'Mary Jane' shoes, separated by fifty years: the delicacy of red suede, gold leather trim and diamond button was replaced by serviceable leather for the 1990s. Carl Franz Bally decided to mass-produce high-quality footwear after falling in love with a pair of shoes he found for his wife in Paris. The son of a silk ribbon weaver, Franz had taken over the family business, expanding the company to include an elastic tape that was used by shoemakers. While visiting one of his clients in Paris, he saw the inspirational shoes and bought the entire stock, and began manufacturing his own shoe collections in his factory. Today the house of Bally remains a classic one, albeit expanded into a global company. Graeme Fidler and Michael Herz, creative directors since 2010, maintain the traditional craftsmanship and Swiss luxury heritage that the brand was founded on.

► Chéruit, Hermès, Steiger, Vivier

Carl Franz Bally. b Schönenwerd (SW), 1821. **d** Schönenwerd (SW), 1898. **Scarlet evening shoe, 1930, and brown leather reinterpretation, 1998.**

Balmain Pierre

Designer

Mlle Laure de Noailles wears her debutante gown, with foaming tulle skirt, by Pierre Balmain. *Vogue* declared that 'eventful skirts' were his speciality; they were often embellished with embroidered motifs such as leaves, cherries or scrolls. Trained as an architect, Balmain believed that both professions worked to beautify the world, declaring haute couture to be 'the architecture of movement'. In 1931 he was appointed junior designer at Molyneux. He then worked at Lucien Lelong where he was joined by Christian Dior; they collaborated for four years, nearly going into partnership together, but in 1945 Balmain left to establish his own house. Like Dior's New Look of 1947, Balmain's full-skirted silhouette was part of the new postwar luxury. Upon the designer's death in 1982, Balmain's assistant and close friend Erik Mortensen took over the brand, which today, helmed by Olivier Rousteing, continues to have contemporary relevance.

▶ Cavanagh, Dior, Lelong, Molyneux, Piguet, De la Renta

Pierre Balmain. b St-Jean-de-Maurienne (FR), 1914. **d** Paris (FR), 1982. **Mlle Laure de Noailles.** Photograph by Cecil Beaton, American *Vogue*, 1945.

Bandy Way

Make-up artist

Model Gia wears the perfect work of Way Bandy. Her light, translucent make-up was delivered with very few products. Usually working with liquid cosmetics, Bandy would mix his colours at home and tie them up in two small Japanese baskets. He was visionary in the formulations he used: his foundations were blended with eye drops that would tighten the pores, promoting the flawlessness he worked for. Blending was also very important to his work and Bandy named his dog Smudge after his refining technique. He was always perfectly made-up himself, turning up for fashion shoots wearing inconspicuous base and powder. For one night, however, Bandy demonstrated his skill by arriving at a Halloween party thrown by his friend Halston wearing the full, traditional *kabuki* face. As a friend remembered, 'He loved beauty and from those little bottles could come perfection in the form of lightness or the bizarre'.

► Halston, Saint Laurent, Uemura

Way Bandy. b Birmingham, AL (USA), *c.*1941. **d** New York (USA), 1986. **Gia.** Photograph by Arthur Elgort, 1978.

Banton Travis

Designer

Travis Banton's costume for Marlene Dietrich is from the film *Shanghai Express* (1932). He disguised her as a black swan in a costume of feathers, veiled and hung with ropes of crystal beads. Her handbag and gloves were specially made for her by Hermès; the hat was a John P. John creation. Banton regularly visited Paris; on one occasion, he bought up an entire stock of bugle beads and fish-scale paillettes reserved for Schiaparelli. In reparation, he sent her enough trim to complete her line for the season.

Banton worked in couture in New York; his break came when he designed the costumes for Paramount's *The Dressmaker from Paris* (1925), after which he became Paramount's head designer. He designed for Dietrich, Mae West, Claudette Colbert and Carole Lombard. One of his signatures was dressing women in men's clothes. He continued to run his successful couture business alongside costume designing.

► Carnegie, Hermès, John, Schiaparelli, Trigère

Travis Banton. b Waco, TX (USA), 1894. **d** Los Angeles, CA (USA), 1958. **Marlene Dietrich.** Still from *Shanghai Express*, 1932.

Barbier George

Illustrator

George Barbier was, together with Paul Iribe and Georges Lepape, one of the great fashion artists of his day. Commissioned by designer Paul Poiret to illustrate his fashions, Barbier here portrays two of Poiret's models in a moonlit rose garden. The evening coat on the right has a long train that falls from the shoulders and drops back at the sides like huge wings. It has an intricate Art Deco design of a stylized tree. A similar coat designed by Paul Poiret and called 'Battick' was photographed by Edward Steichen and appeared in *Art et Décoration* in April 1911. The required headwear to be worn with the coat and equally exotic dress (with its high waistline reminiscent of the 'Directoire' line of late eighteenth-century France) was the turban, trimmed with pearls and surmounted by an aigrette. Barbier has united Poiret's simple classical line with the bold colours and design elements of his oriental style.

► Bakst, Drian, Iribe, Lepape, Poiret, Steichen

George Barbier. b Nantes (FR), 1882. **d** Nantes (FR), 1932. **Exotic coat and dress by Paul Poiret.** Cover of *Les Modes*, April 1912.

Barbieri Gian Paolo

Photographer

A woman in full, glamorous make-up wears the uniform of a meat market trader. It could be a reference to the model's work, but in a practical sense it is advertising a mesh vest that parodies the string version worn by working men. It is a typically dramatic example of Gian Paolo Barbieri's work. In 1997, he directed Vivienne Westwood's first-ever campaign, which was based on the work of the sixteenth-century painter Holbein. For Barbieri this was more than fashion work. It was the creation of a filmic tableau that indulged all his passions: proportion, minute detail and a desire to seal the moment. In 1965 Barbieri photographed the first cover of Italian *Vogue*. His work for that magazine and others opened doors to advertising work for designers such as Valentino, Armani, Versace and Yves Saint Laurent. Barbieri's work continues to have influence well into the digital age, blurring the line between art and fashion.

► Bourdin, Valentino, Westwood

Gian Paolo Barbieri. b Milan (IT), 1938. **Meat Market.** 1982.

Bardot Brigitte

Icon

Actress Brigitte Bardot sits under a tree, smoking moodily, her *deshabille* hair and *au naturel* appearance the epitome of amoral French sensuality. British *Vogue* called her 'the sensuous idol, a potent mixture of the sexy and the babyish, a seething milky bosom below a childish pout'. She was known simply as 'BB' (the French pronounced it *'bébé'* – French for 'baby'), and the phrase 'sex kitten' was invented to describe her. Her narrow trousers and tight black sweater reflect the nonchalant beat style. She also popularized flat ballet pumps in the 1950s, setting a trend for not wearing socks in her film *And...God Created Woman* (1956), and for ruffles and ringlets, petticoats and prettiness in *Les Grandes Manoeuvres* (1955), and for Edwardian dress in *Viva Maria* (1965). Jeanne Moreau wrote that Bardot 'was the real modern revolutionary character for women'.

► Bouquin, Esterel, Féraud, Frizon, Heim

Brigitte Bardot. b Paris (FR), 1934. **Bardot during the filming of** *Vie Privée.* 1961.

Barnett Sheridan　　　Designer

A cool bride is transported to the church on a Harley-Davidson. Her wedding outfit is by Sheridan Barnett, who graced the 1970s with lean, uncontrived fashion. Her cream jacket and skirt are spare of any detail other than Perspex buttons to fasten her jacket and patch pockets to carry her handkerchief. Barnett was almost architectural in his approach to clothes, demanding function and purity of line at a time when all around him were making additions – with embroidery, printing and appliqué fighting for space on dresses everywhere. Because function is more commonly found on menswear, Barnett often used it as a central theme. Although the bride's cloche hat is trimmed with net, a black pussy-cat bow is tied at her neck and her stockinged legs end in a pair of wedge sandals, that clean, masculine theme comes through in a jacket modelled on a classic, double-breasted blazer.

► Albini, Bates, Wainwright

Sheridan Barnett. b Bradford, West Yorkshire (UK), 1951. **Cream blazer and skirt.** Photograph by Peter Knapp, *Vogue*, 1971.

Baron Fabien   Art director

Fabien Baron's clean, clear layouts, allowing tangled graphics to float luxuriantly in vast areas of space, recall the power of Alexey Brodovitch's work and have set new standards in modern design. Starting his career at *New York Woman* in 1982, Baron moved quickly to Italian *Vogue*, and a stint at *Interview* magazine, before he was appointed creative director at Brodovitch's old home, *Harper's Bazaar*. His style has been widely influential and Baron acknowledges, 'the look doesn't belong to me any

more'. He directed Madonna's *Erotica* video and designed her metal-covered book, *Sex*. The frosted bottle for Calvin Klein's unisex CK One perfume was also his creation. Klein says, 'We are on the same wavelength, except Fabien goes way beyond my capabilities of aestheticism.' From 2003 to 2008 he was creative director at French *Vogue* alongside his art direction and marketing agency Baron + Baron which he founded in 1990.

► Brodovitch, C. Klein, Madonna

Fabien Baron. b Antony (FR), 1959. **Collage of spreads from *Harper's Bazaar, Interview* and Italian *Vogue*.** 1998.

Barrett Slim

Jewellery designer

In this swathe of chain links by Slim Barrett, jewellery becomes a garment with a piece that suggests both a draped necklace and a hood. Pierre Cardin and Paco Rabanne both used this theme by expanding dresses to become hybrids of fashion and jewellery, and here Barrett has done the same from his perspective as a jewellery designer. He returns intermittently to medieval themes – he helped Karl Lagerfeld by developing silver wire so fine that it could be knitted – and in the 1990s Barrett was responsible for the tiara's rise in popularity. In his quest to extend the realm of costume jewellery, other catwalk collaborations (including those for Chanel, Versace, Montana and Ungaro) have resulted in the creation of plated armour, waistcoats and skullcaps as vehicles for Barrett's work. In 2000 he won the De Beers Diamond International Award and his work can be seen in the Victoria & Albert Museum, London.

► Lagerfeld, Morris, Rabanne

Slim Barrett. b Galway (IRE), 1960. **Chainmail torso in sterling silver.** Photograph by Philip Newton, British *Elle*, 1990.

Barthet Jean   Milliner

While he often designed in the traditional manner of the great French hat makers such as Caroline Reboux, who placed the emphasis on purity of line and structure, Parisian Jean Barthet also embellished his creations with trimmings that reflected his own imagination. In this case, inspired by existentialist ideas of the period, Barthet created a hat that symbolized the hovering hands of fate. Two rose satin hands, one adorned with a diamond studded ring and bracelet from Boucheron, decorate the shallow black velvet calotte. Barthet showed his first collection in 1949 and rose to become the most successful milliner in Paris, dressing the heads of Sophia Loren and Catherine Deneuve. His success was underlined by his membership of the Chambre Syndicale de la Couture Parisienne and he collaborated throughout his career with his colleagues Claude Montana, Sonia Rykiel, Emanuel Ungaro and Karl Lagerfeld.

► Deneuve, Hirata, Paulette, Reboux

Jean Barthet. b The Pyrénées (FR), 1930. **d** 2000. **'Hands of Fate' hat.** 1948.

Bartlett John

Designer

A shirt is laid open at the throat and left untucked in the style of the 1950s. John Bartlett's aesthetic is a relaxed one. He thinks about clothing pictorially and his fashion shows have profound themes and narratives, often becoming essays in style. Bartlett trained at Willi Smith, a label historically known for its democratic attitude towards fashion, and he has developed a natural feel for sportswear. He began his menswear collections in 1992, adding womenswear five years later, when he told *People*,

'My mission is to make women look sexy,' just as it is for men. He is said to be the American version of Thierry Mugler in sexy stories, but Bartlett adds something extra with his relish for the rhetoric of fashion – he introduced his menswear collection in 1998 with, 'Imagine a world where *Forrest Gump* is directed by Otto Fassbinder...' a reference to the subversive filmmakers Otto Preminger and Rainer Werner Fassbinder.

► Matsushima, Mugler, Presley, W. Smith

John Bartlett. b Cincinnati, OH (USA), 1963. **White open-neck shirt.** Photograph by Enrique Badulescu, *Arena*, 1997.

Bassman Lillian

Photographer

'I almost always focus on a long, elegant neck,' said Bassman of this photograph featured in *Harper's Bazaar*. Her shadowy, sensual pictures are known for their gentle intimacy, 'Women didn't have to seduce me the way they did male photographers. There was a kind of inner calm between the model and myself.' Her images were created by innovative printing techniques such as bleaching areas to give results that resembled charcoal drawings, recalling Bassman's early career as a fashion illustrator before being apprenticed to Alexey Brodovitch. Bassman's work is more evocative of moods than subjects and has not always been understood. Carmel Snow, former editor of *Harper's Bazaar*, once berated Bassman for photographing a diaphanous Piguet gown to resemble butterfly wings, saying, 'You are not here to make art, you are here to photograph buttons and bows' – a landmark in the debate about the purpose of fashion photography.
► Brodovitch, Parker, Piguet, Snow

Lillian Bassman. b New York (USA), 1917. **d** New York (USA), 2012. **Barbara Mullen.** *Harper's Bazaar, c.*1950.

Bates John

Designer

John Bates is photographed with two dramatic outfits from a 1979 collection. They both use silk cut away to reveal the torso – a charismatic theme based on shapes from the 1930s and 1940s. The black dress uses a geometrically bared midriff in a modern take on Carmen Miranda's trademark – a feature Bates had used in 1965 with his 'bikini dress', the halves of which were joined with transparent netting. These squared-off shoulders minimize the hips, and spaghetti ties are used as suggestively available fastenings. Decorative cocktail hats finish both outfits and lend them the highly co-ordinated, polished look of the 1930s. In the 1960s, Bates created 'the smallest dress in the world' and the black leather wardrobe for *The Avengers* television series. His wide range of eveningwear, much of it ethnically inspired in the 1970s, was skilfully made and had a sophisticated youthfulness.

▶ Albini, Barnett, Burrows, N. Miller, Wainwright

John Bates. b Ponteland, Northumberland (UK), 1938. **John Bates with models, spring/summer 1979.** Photograph by Chris Moore.

The Beatles

The Beatles are credited with marketing the 'youthquake' look around the world. In 1962, while touring Germany, Stuart Sutcliffe's photographer girlfriend Astrid Kirchherr gave the group a co-ordinated image: matching 'moptop' haircuts like her own beatnik-style gamine cut. The following year, The Beatles' manager Brian Epstein contacted Soho tailor Dougie Millings, who recalled, 'I'd been experimenting with round collars. I did a sketch of one, showed it to Brian, and that was that. I've never claimed to have entirely "invented" it, I just came up with the suggestion.' In fact, the neat, collarless, high-neck, grey jackets with black trim had been inspired by Pierre Cardin. They became a trademark for The Beatles, worn with whip ties and pointed 'Chelsea' boots. The Beatles hit the USA the following year and their girlfriends were credited with introducing America to the miniskirt.

► Cardin, Leonard, McCartney, Sassoon, Vivier

John Lennon. b Liverpool (UK), 1940. **d** New York (USA), 1980; **Ringo Starr. b** Liverpool (UK), 1940; **Sir Paul McCartney. b** Liverpool (UK), 1942; **George Harrison. b** Liverpool (UK), 1943. **d** Los Angeles, CA (USA), 2001. **The Beatles.** 1963.

Beaton Sir Cecil

Photographer

Eight models in a spectacular neoclassical interior are wearing ball gowns by Charles James in this 1948 American *Vogue* editorial by Cecil Beaton. Its mood of elegant grandeur captures the spirit of Dior's New Look, which revolutionized fashion with its feminine romanticism and state-of-the-art construction. Dior claimed James had inspired the New Look and Beaton and James were lifelong friends. Beaton – photographer, illustrator, designer, writer, diarist and aesthete –

captured the nuances of fashion and the fashionable from the 1920s until his death. In 1928 he began a long relationship with *Vogue*. Always in touch with the zeitgeist, he developed accordingly, photographing the Rolling Stones, Penelope Tree and Twiggy in the 1960s. He was as much a part of Swinging London as they were. 'Fashion was his cocaine. He could make it happen. He sought the eternal in fashion,' wrote a friend after his death.

► Campbell-Walter, Coward, Ferré, Garbo, C. James

Sir Cecil Beaton. b London (UK), 1904. **d** Broadchalke, Wiltshire (UK), 1980. **Dresses by Charles James, 1948.**

Beckham David

Icon

David Beckham's immense fame and fortune boil down to his world-class football skills, a daring fashion sense and commercially viable sex appeal. Already the star of major endorsements, he launched a permanent collection of bodywear with H&M in 2012, accompanied by a Super Bowl ad and a gigantic, hand-painted mural in midtown Manhattan. He began his career with Manchester United at only seventeen, later playing with Real Madrid and Los Angeles Galaxy. In 1997 he met 'Posh Spice' (now better known as fashion designer Victoria Beckham), and 'Posh and Becks' became a media sensation. Despite the occasional fashion misstep, he has inspired many male trends, from cornrows to diamond studs. Both athlete and lucrative sex object, he epitomizes a contemporary breed of man: in 1994 the term 'metrosexual' was coined and he was subsequently identified as its archetype.

► V. Beckham, Bikkembergs, Dean, Knight & Bowerman, Madonna

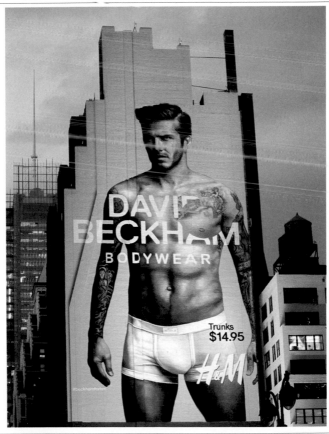

David Beckham. b Leytonstone (UK), 1975. **220-foot tall H&M Bodywear mural, New York City.** February 2012.

49

Beckham Victoria

Designer

Victoria Beckham took the pop world by storm in the 1990s as a member of the chart-topping Spice Girls, and alongside her football and fashion icon husband David (or 'Posh and Becks' as they have become unavoidably known) she is half of one of the most powerful couples in fashion, gracing the pages of high-fashion magazines and tabloids alike. In more recent years Beckham has also shown herself to be a shrewd businesswoman in the fashion industry. Having modelled for runway shows and editorials, Beckham launched her womenswear label in 2008 to wide acclaim, her structured, body-conscious silhouette an evident hit. Beckham's modern aesthetic – which emphasizes form, colour and female contours – is fast becoming a staple on the red carpet. In 2012 Beckham added an eyewear collection to her increasingly successful brand.

► D. Beckham, Berardi, Dolce & Gabbana, McCartney, Mouret

Victoria Beckham. b Harlow, Essex (UK), 1974. **Victoria Beckham.**

Beene Geoffrey

Designer

The model's pleated trousers are 'not too wide, not too narrow' and the perfect coat to throw over it is a 'trench coat in beige cotton'. With their soft wrapping and pared-down functionality, Beene's creations were the epitome of simple elegance. While his dresses were sometimes seen as the American version of couture, Beene was ultimately a designer with a sportswear sensibility and a focus on comfort. Comfort was paramount and had been since his label was launched in 1963. His first collections used an easy fit for clothes designed for active women – he often worked with humble materials, including cotton piqué and sweatshirt fleece. Beene freely borrowed from menswear – collections included vests and ties – whilst the West met the East in his use of quilting, obi belts and layering. In honour of his legacy, the Council of Fashion Designers of America created the Geoffrey Beene Lifetime Achievement Award.

► Blass, Miyake, Mizrahi, Vionnet

Geoffrey Beene. b Haynesville, LA (USA), 1927. **d** New York (USA), 2004. **Geoffrey Beene with model wearing stone mac and silk trousers.** Photograph by Deborah Turbeville, American *Vogue*, 1975.

Van Beirendonck Walter   Designer

Hovering somewhere in the aesthetic territory between a video game, tribal costume and sexual fetishism, this outfit expresses the all-embracing futuristic hedonism of W&LT, the club-wear label designed by Walter Van Beirendonck during the 1990s. Graduating from Antwerp's Royal Academy of Fine Arts in 1980, he was one of the 'Antwerp Six' who broke onto the international scene in 1987. His roving imagination is fed by his interest in contemporary art, anthropology, historical costume and current affairs. After leaving W&LT in 1999 he turned his attention to beautifully realized experimental high fashion, using bespoke textiles and materials such as raffia, printed tablecloths and techniques not usually associated with menswear. A great supporter and promoter of young designers, he has taught fashion at the Royal Academy of Fine Arts in Antwerp since 1985, becoming head of the fashion department in 2006.

► Bikkembergs, Bowery, Mugler, Royal Academy of Fine Arts

Walter Van Beirendonck. b Brecht (BEL), 1957. **Printed T-shirt and rubber trousers, W&LT autumn/winter 1995.** Photograph by Jean-Baptiste Mondino.

Benetton Luciano

Retailer

Unusually for fashion advertising, the clothes in this photograph can barely be seen and are not the central focus of the picture. Two people of different races are handcuffed together but it is not clear who is handcuffed to whom, and why. 'I am not asked by Benetton to sell clothes', claims the photographer and former creative director Oliviero Toscani. 'The communication is a product in itself.' Such advertisements were an iconoclastic method of selling fashion. Previously Benetton's adverts had featured young people of all nationalities, the 'United Colors of Benetton' tagline referring to both their worldwide customers and the rainbow spectrum of knitwear and clothing. Luciano Benetton, the family-run company's founder, admits these 1990s images contrast with its design philosophy: 'It is true our clothes are not at all extreme or controversial'.

► Fiorucci, Fisher, Strauss, Topshop

Luciano Benetton. b Treviso (IT), 1935. **Handcuffed campaign.** Photograph by Oliviero Toscani, 1985.

Benito

Benito, one of the masters of fashion illustration of the Art Deco period, captured through his simple, supple strokes the statuesque women in their extravagant gowns who epitomized the 1920s. His outstanding characteristic was the extreme elongation of the figure to emphasize the elegance of the silhouette. His style was reminiscent of sixteenth-century Mannerist painting and of the Cubist paintings of Picasso and the sculptures of Brancusi and Modigliani. Benito was also noted for his inventive vignettes. The close links between fashion and interior decoration are shown with perfect clarity and create an Art Deco harmony of design, colour and line. Born in Spain, Benito went to Paris at the age of nineteen, where he established himself as a fashion artist. Along with Lepape, his illustrations for *Vogue* reflected the *haut monde* of the Jazz Age.

▶ Bouché, Lepape, Patou, Poiret

Benito (Eduardo García Benito). b Valladolid (SP), 1892. **d** Paris (FR), 1953. **Afternoon dress by Paul Poiret.** Illustration from *La Gazette du Bon Ton*, 1922.

Bérard Christian

Illustrator

As his painted caption reports, Bérard's subject in this rich watercolour sketch wears the train of her ruby velvet gown draped over a medieval chain slung around her hips. Like his close friend Cocteau, Bérard was a master of many artistic media. He designed the stage sets and costumes for several of Cocteau's plays. During the 1930s he turned his artistry to designing fabrics and to fashion illustration, becoming associated with Schiaparelli and Surrealism in fashion. His drawings appeared in *Vogue*

for the first time in 1935. They were so well received that he worked for *Vogue* until his death in 1949. Also like Cocteau, Bérard's draughtsmanship is immediately recognizable by its very stumpy, spidery line that is liberally imbued with vivid colours. It was this lush style, enhanced by his vision of fashion as a kind of theatre, that he brought to his graphic work for *Vogue*. It was defined as romantic expressionism.

▶ Bouché, Cocteau, Creed, Dalí, Rochas, Schiaparelli

At Patou's Opening
Velvet draped low on a chain

Christian Bérard. b Paris (FR), 1902. **d** Paris (FR), 1949. **Dress by Jean Patou.** American *Vogue*, 1938.

Berardi Antonio

Designer

Antonio Berardi's woman is a goddess-like heroine – an attitude reflected in his clothes, which are structured, empowering and true to the female form. His cutting techniques and decorative detailing have led him to be compared to John Galliano, with whom he trained for three years before finally being accepted as a student at Central Saint Martins in London (on his fourth attempt). The designer's Italian roots manifest themselves in his love of traditionally crafted leather and hand-worked lace and macramé. His stunning leather pieces are decorated with embroidery and pierced with cutwork, specialist techniques that were reintroduced at a time when simplicity was being championed elsewhere. His light-as-air, lingerie-style eveningwear is intended to be flirtatious rather than vulgar. He describes his style as 'sensual, sexy and thought provoking – and intrinsically feminine.'

► V. Beckham, Galliano, Mouret, Pearl

Antonio Berardi. b Grantham, Lincolnshire (UK), 1968. **Antonio Berardi spring/summer 2012 collection, London Fashion Week.**

Beretta Anne-Marie   Designer

In an abstract, graphic, red, white and black scheme, two leather coats are trimmed with Bs to signify the work of Anne-Marie Beretta. Her trademark is a play on proportions, from wide-collared coats to mid-calf-length trousers and asymmetrical lines, used here to break the conformity of these coats. The upper part of each letter is larger, throwing the emphasis onto the shoulders and thereby minimizing the widths of the models' hips. Beretta has used these techniques for many different collections, including ski-wear, but when she opened her own boutique in 1975 it was with business-like tailoring, similar in style to those collections she has since designed for the Italian label MaxMara. Beretta wanted to pursue a career in fashion from an early age – by the time she was eighteen she was designing for Jacques Esterel and Antonio Castillo. In 1974 she established her own label.

► Castillo, Esterel, Maramotti

Anne-Marie Beretta. b Béziers (FR), 1937. **Leather 'B' coats.** Photograph by Gilles Serrand, *L'Officiel*, 1980.

Bergère Eric

Designer

These spare wrap dresses represent the self-assured work of Eric Bergère. Briefly apprenticed to Thierry Mugler, he arrived at Hermès aged just seventeen. It was Bergère who gave modernity to Hermès' luxury, using the then passé snaffle and H logo to add wit. In doing so, he famously created a camp, mink jogging suit. Bergère blends European humour and respect for tradition with the American sportswear sensibility. He has said, 'I like the work of Americans, like Anne Klein...very simple clothes, very elegant,' and he keeps detail to a minimum, using a thin tie belt or a tiny bow on a knitted camisole top. His first collection under the Bergère label was tightly edited: twelve pieces of knitwear in three colours and one jacket in three different lengths. 'I want the jackets to be like cardigans, I try to make everything lighter – the finishings, the linings, the foundations – but they must still have a definite shoulder.'

► Evangelista, Von Fürstenberg, Hermès, A. Klein, Testino

Eric Bergère. b Troyes (FR), 1960. **Shalom Harlow and Linda Evangelista wear black dresses.** Photograph by Mario Testino, *Visionaire*, 1997.

Bernard Augusta (Augustabernard)   Designer

During the 1930s there was a revival of interest in classical art and an evening gown was an especially suitable garment for re-creating the flowing movement of the draperies of Ancient Greek statues. It is this sculptural form and the long, floating line billowing out at the bottom that Man Ray captures in his photograph. Augusta Bernard enjoyed a successful career during the first half of the 1930s. A neoclassical evening gown she designed in 1932 was chosen by *Vogue* as the most beautiful dress of that year. Augusta Bernard belonged to that eminent band of couturières between the two World Wars, which included Chanel, Vionnet, Schiaparelli, Louiseboulanger and the Callot Sœurs. Like Vionnet, she was a technician with a mastery of the bias cut. By cutting the fabric of the dress on the cross-grain, she achieved a fluidity that gave the evening gown great elasticity and a refined, draping quality.

▶ Boulanger, Callot, Chanel, Man Ray, Schiaparelli, Vionnet

Augusta Bernard. b Provence (FR), 1886. **d** 1946. **Bias-cut dress.** Photograph by Man Ray, *Harper's Bazaar*, 1934.

Berthoud François

Illustrator

François Berthoud's startling illustration presents a woman in a stovepipe hat, her demonic eyes watching from the shadows. Berthoud uses linocuts and woodcuts for his melodramatic work. They are brave and unusual methods for fashion illustration, which usually demands flowing lines. But these approaches can often suit the sharp contours of contemporary fashion, lending strength and drama to the simplest garment. Berthoud studied illustration in Lausanne and, after receiving his diploma in 1982, moved straight to Milan where he worked for Condé Nast. He later became heavily involved in the visual appearance of *Vanity* magazine, a publication that showcased illustration, designing many of their covers. In the 1990s Berthoud's enduring illustrations have appeared in the New York-based style quarterly *Visionaire*.

► Delhomme, Eric, Gustafson, S. Jones

François Berthoud. b Lausanne (SW), 1961. **Woman with hat.** Woodcut, *Mondi*, 1993.

Bettina

Model

Wearing a sharply constructed black dress by Christian Dior, the French model gives a pose of polished *froideur*. Bettina's gamine beauty is unique in having inspired three designers over two generations. Born in Brittany, the daughter of a railway worker, Simone Bodin dreamed of becoming a fashion designer. She took her drawings to the couturier Jacques Costet, who took her on as his model and assistant. When the house closed, she moved to Lucien Lelong, employer of Christian Dior, who then invited her to join him in his own house. She refused, choosing to work for Jacques Fath instead. He renamed her Bettina and made her 'the face' of his scent Canasta, which was launched in 1950. Her fame took her to America where *Vogue* loved her 'Gigi looks, and 20th Century Fox offered her a seven-year contract, which she declined. In 1955 she left modelling, returning three decades later as muse (and best friend) of Azzedine Alaïa.

► Alaïa, Dior, Fath, Lelong

Bettina (Simone Bodin). b Laval (FR), 1925. **Christian Dior cocktail dress, autumn/winter 1952.** Photograph by Frances McLaughlin-Gill.

Biagiotti Laura　　　　　Designer

The fluid spirit of Italy's 'Queen of Cashmere' is illustrated by René Gruau in 1976. His easy lines imitate the composed chic for which Laura Biagiotti is known: the sweater worn with lean tailoring and an open-necked shirt. Biagiotti read archaeology at university in Rome and worked in her mother's small clothing company after graduation. In 1965 she founded her company, with partner Gianni Cigna. It manufactured and exported clothing for the eminent Italian fashion designers Roberto Capucci and Emilio Schuberth. As the company grew, so did Biagiotti's aspiration to design. She presented a small but successful womenswear collection for the first time in 1972. Designing with comfort as a priority, Biagiotti became known for working with fabrics of exceptional quality, especially cashmere in the most subtle colours – a blueprint later used by Rebecca Moses.

► Capucci, Gruau, Moses, Schuberth, Tarlazzi

Laura Biagiotti. b Rome (IT), 1943. **Daywear.** Illustration by René Gruau, 1976.

Bikkembergs Dirk

Designer

These muscular sportsmen present a very different image from the moody and conceptual menswear that made Dirk Bikkembergs' name as one of the 'Antwerp Six' in the 1990s. In 1999 Bikkembergs changed his approach to fashion. After seeing a teenage boy's bedroom plastered with posters of footballers, he was inspired to take a new direction, focusing his entire output and brand image around sport, and football in particular. In 2000, Bikkembergs started using FC Fossombrone, the local football team, as a testing ground for his high-performance designs. In 2006 Bikkembergs purchased a majority stake in the team, dressing the players on and off the field, from boots to suits, making them a walking advertisement for the world's first 'sports couture' brand. Since then, the Bikkembergs label has evolved along the axes of luxury and athleticism, reflecting the ever-increasing status of sports stars as icons of contemporary style.

► D. Beckham, Demeulemeester, Fonticoli, Van Noten

Dirk Bikkembergs. b Bonn (GER), 1959. **Bikkembergs spring/summer 2010 advertising campaign.** Photograph by Luc Williame.

Birtwell Celia

Textile designer

Actress Jane Asher sits amidst the jumble of accessories and kooky paraphernalia of a London boutique in 1966. She wears a printed paper minidress by Ossie Clark, another variation of which hangs on the wall behind her. The print is by Celia Birtwell, who decorated the fabric used by her husband Clark, and the 'paper' is a prototype of that used by Johnson & Johnson for J-cloths. Birtwell's stylized, sometimes psychedelic, florals with striped borders were also used for flowing fabrics resurrected

from the 1930s, such as crepe and satin. Her lavish, two-dimensional style, which suited the fantastical and semi-historical fashion of the late 1960s and early 1970s, was part of a print explosion. Birtwell's bohemian mixture of Indian and traditional English themes was an expression of the wealthy, young Chelsea society around her, which was exploring the trail to Goa at the same time as inheriting the English countryside.

► Clark, Gibb, Pollock

Celia Birtwell. b Bury, Greater Manchester (UK), 1941. **Jane Asher wears screen-printed paper minidress.** Photograph by Brian Duffy, 1966.

Blahnik Manolo

Shoe designer

Rude and nude, but executed with as much refinement as a queen's coronation slipper, Manolo Blahnik's sexy sandal is made out of black leather. The transforming powers of Blahnik's shoes are legendary. They are said to lengthen the leg from the hip all the way to the toe. The secret lies in balance and taste; neither proportion nor degree of fashionability ever stray into vulgarity, thereby upsetting Blahnik's careful blend of style and function. He left the Canary Islands to study at the University of Geneva and at the École du Louvre in Paris. During a trip to New York in 1973, an appointment with American *Vogue* editor Diana Vreeland inspired him to settle in London and open his first shop. Blahnik's influential shoe designs are the sole choice for catwalk collections for many designers. His shoes were immortalized in TV's *Sex and the City* and in 2012 he received the Outstanding Achievement Award at the British Fashion Awards.

► Coddington, Field, Galliano, Hardy, Vreeland

Manolo Blahnik (Manuel Blahnik Rodriguez). b Santa Cruz (CI), 1942. **'Lara' heel, autumn/winter collection 1997.** Illustration by Manolo Blahnik.

Blair Alistair

Designer

With deftness, Alistair Blair turns satin and velvet into a gracious evening outfit. The jacket rolls outward with the help of quilted facings and is cut to follow the waist inwards. Blair trained with Marc Bohan at Christian Dior, before moving on to assist Hubert de Givenchy and Karl Lagerfeld at Chloé. After six years in Paris, his ready-to-wear had taken on the quality and glamour of continental couture. Of his first own-label collection in March 1989, Blair said, 'The designing was absolutely the easiest part –

it's what I enjoy'. He provided grown-up glamour during the eccentric streetwear boom of the 1980s. His use of luxurious fabrics such as cashmere, duchesse satin, grey flannel and kid leather brought a nostalgic quality to his carefully edited designs. Since 1995 he has designed for Louis Féraud, claiming, 'Today women want more than adoration from a designer – they want insight'. He was designer at Laura Ashley until 2004.

► Ashley, Bohan, Cox, Féraud, Tran

Alistair Blair. b Helensburgh, Argyll & Bute (UK), 1956. **Quilted satin evening jacket.** Photograph by Ian Thomas, *Harpers & Queen*, 1987.

Blass Bill

Three distinctly American graces capture the essence of Blass's high-style sportswear. Urbane and Europe-aware, but definitely easy to wear and pared-down in ornament, Blass's separates for day and evening, and his dresses for the 'cocktail hour' captured the American spirit in functional, elegant clothing. Blass perpetuated the traditions of Norman Norell and Hattie Carnegie in providing smart sophistication for American women. Sweater dressing, even for evening gowns, was a Blass signature; layering and the harmony of rich materials, from silk to cashmere, are favoured. Witty references to menswear or vernacular dress were also frequent in Blass. Often referred to as the 'dean of American designers', Blass was one of the last of the designers consistently delivering classic good taste, filtering fashion's fluctuations through a fine sieve. He finished his autobiography *Bare Blass* in 2002 but died before it was published.

► Alfaro, Beene, Roehm, Sieff, Underwood

Bill Blass. b Fort Wayne, IN (USA), 1922. **d** New Preston, CT (USA), 2002. **Heavy, white, silk crepe dresses with bugle beads, spring/summer 1984.** Photograph by Gideon Lewin.

Blow Isabella

Editor

With her passion for emerging talent and fostering creative potential, fashion icon Isabella Blow launched the careers of some of the biggest names in the industry. She purchased Alexander McQueen's entire graduate collection in 1992, and championed Philip Treacy's work from 1986 when he brought his hats to the office of *Tatler*, where she was style editor. Renowned for her personal style and flair for dress up, Blow was rarely seen with a bare head. Originally a student of ancient Chinese art in New York, she went on to a career in fashion after working for the house Guy Laroche. She returned to London in the mid-1980s to take up a position at *Tatler* and from 1997 she continued to influence the industry as fashion director of the *Sunday Times Style* magazine, before leaving the position in 2001 to focus on her styling and consulting work. Throughout her career Blow remained a style icon as well as being a true creative talent in her own right.

► Baron, Guinness, McQueen, Tennant, Treacy, Wintour

Isabella Blow (Isabella Delves Broughton). b London (UK), 1958. d Gloucester, Gloucestershire (UK), 2007. **Isabella Blow with Philip Treacy behind the scenes at a *Harper's Bazaar* shoot.** Photograph by Kevin Davies, 2002.

Blumenfeld Erwin

Legs are wrapped in damp muslin; this is not a fashion image but a beauty one. This photograph by Erwin Blumenfeld is reminiscent of his first art success, a suite of collages and altered images in the style of Berlin Dada. His late work in New York was equally cryptic, often obscuring the nude with smoke, mirrors and shadows, and implying spiritual forms through reference to the body. In between, in a series of photographs in *Vogue* and *Harper's Bazaar* in the 1930s through to the 1960s, he addressed fashion, but often subjected icons of beauty to his own obscurities and emendations. He allowed body parts to stand for the whole (most famously in a cover image of lips and eye for *Vogue* in January 1950), rendering fashion misty and mystical. Blumenfeld came to fashion at the age of forty-one. He was an experimenter who reserved his admiration, and film, for the work of great designers such as Balenciaga and Charles James.

► Dalí, Hoyningen-Huene, Man Ray

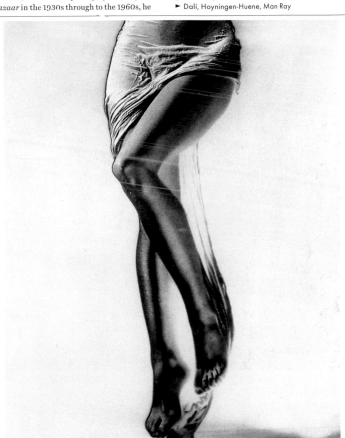

Erwin Blumenfeld. b Berlin (GER), 1897. d Rome (IT), 1969. **Solarized Legs.** Paris, *c*.1937.

Bohan Marc

Designer

In the preamble to Marc Bohan's show for Christian Dior, the designer and his model, wearing a slim cardigan jacket over a belted dress, pose for American *Vogue*. Bohan won plaudits for restoring haute couture to the tradition set by the grand couturiers, when he was appointed chief designer and artistic director of the house of Dior in succession to Yves Saint Laurent in 1960. He was of his time, however, and was able to communicate a youthful spirit. His collection for winter 1966, influenced by the film *Doctor Zhivago* (1965), started the craze for fur-trimmed, belted tweed coats worn with long, black boots. Marc Bohan gained valuable practical experience in fashion from his mother, who was a milliner. Between 1945 and 1958 he worked for the fashion houses of Piguet, Molyneux and Patou. Having left Dior in 1989, he moved to London where he was enlisted in an attempt to revive the house of Norman Hartnell.

► Blair, Dior, Ghesquière, Hartnell, Molyneux, Patou

Marc Bohan. b Paris (FR), 1926. **Marc Bohan and model.** Photograph by Deborah Turbeville, American *Vogue*, 1975.

Bouché René

Illustrator

Working in pen and ink, Bouché was a master at blending fashion and society. Two attenuated figures are silhouetted against an empty background like a *tableau vivant*. They are linked by their large, fur muffs. With his vivacious and witty line, Bouché has revealed these fashionable women and their elegant clothes and has expressed their character, their manner and a sense of occasion. It is a throwaway style but the informal virtuosity of Bouché as a fashion illustrator was combined with a skilful training in painting, drawing and portraiture. Bouché illustrated the pages of *Vogue* during the 1940s, 1950s and early 1960s, and had a particular flair for communicating the relationship between clothes and wearers with accuracy and humour. The prestige of *Vogue* was due in large measure to the revival of fashion illustration by artists of the calibre of Benito, Eric, Christian Bérard, René Gruau and René Bouché.

► Balmain, Benito, Bérard, Eric, Gruau

René Bouché. b Prague (CZ), 1905. d (UK), 1963. **Two suits by Pierre Balmain.** Illustrated in American *Vogue*, 1945.

Boué Sylvie & Jeanne (Boué Sœurs)   Designers

A delicate lace and embroidered lawn tea gown is caught up on the hips with a threaded silk sash. Roses decorate the shoulders and, as was customary, the hem dips either side to create the impression of swags. The Paris haute couture house of the Boué Sœurs flourished at the beginning of the twentieth century, together with those of Paul Poiret, the Callot Sœurs and Madame Paquin. During the First World War the Boué Sœurs moved to New York, where John Redfern and Lucile had already opened branches of their businesses. The Boué Sœurs, who contributed much to the city's high fashion, were renowned for their romantic designs, which often borrowed details from costume found in historical paintings. Their garments, sometimes reminiscent of underwear as here, were made in luscious fabrics such as paper taffetas and silk organdies and were ornately decorated.

▶ Callot, Duff Gordon, De Meyer, Paquin, Redfern

Boué. Sylvie. b (FR), 1880; Jeanne. b (FR), 1881. (Active 1910s–1930s.) (Boué Sœurs.) Tea dress. c.1920.

Boulanger Louise (Louiseboulanger)   Designer

Lace and tulle is projected as the backdrop for a dress whose bodice is so fine that it appears almost gaseous. Louise Boulanger was very much influenced by the work of her contemporary, Madeleine Vionnet. She imitated with finesse Vionnet's use of the bias, cutting diagonally across the grain of the fabric to achieve a seamless, flowing movement. She was noted for launching graceful evening gowns that had skirts which were knee-length in front and reaching to the ankles at the back. Another of her trademarks was elegantly tailored suits worn with hats designed by Caroline Reboux. Louise Boulanger learned her craft as a thirteen-year-old apprentice with Madame Chéruit. In 1923 she opened her own fashion house, whose name was an amalgam of her first and last names, With her svelte figure, she was a couturière in the manner of Coco Chanel.

► Bernard, Chéruit, Reboux, Vionnet

Louise Boulanger. b Paris (FR), 1878. d 1950. **Black tulle and corded silk dress.** Photograph by Cecil Beaton, British *Vogue*, 1935.

Bouquin Jean

Designer

'Hippie deluxe' is the phrase that will forever be linked with Jean Bouquin's clothes and lifestyle. Although he dabbled in fashion for just seven years, Bouquin captured the bohemian spirit of St Tropez's jet-set society at the end of the 1960s. This photograph from French *Vogue* epitomizes Bouquin's vision: a natural woman, draped with beads, who lives an ironically privileged hippie life wearing a luxurious interpretation of the nonconformist's uniform, all sold in Bouquin's boutique. Her printed panne velvet minidress uses drawstrings, borrowed from Indian pyjamas, at the cuffs, and ends just shy of the bikini bottoms she might have worn underneath it. After his success in St Tropez, Bouquin opened a second shop in Paris called Mayfair, which continued his theme of relaxed 'non-dressing'. He retired from the fashion business in 1971 to enjoy his social life.

► Bardot, Hendrix, Hulanicki, Porter, Veruschka

Jean Bouquin. b Paris (FR), 1936. **Panne velvet dress with beads.** French *Vogue*, **1970.** Photograph by Henry Clarke.

Bourdin Guy

Photographer

An exercise of self-satisfaction, stimulated by the looks of John Travolta, mirrors the 1970s obsession with sex, individuality and status. The glamour of sheer fabrics and flashing make-up serves as a canvas for Guy Bourdin's cold yet unmistakably sexual vision. Daringly showing the symbiosis between savvy disco decadence and stardom, this image is finely in tune with the psyche of Bourdin's times. A Pop-Surrealist, he began to work for French *Vogue* in 1960, recommended by photographer Man Ray and couturier Jacques Fath. He concentrated on editorial work for this publication alongside advertising campaigns for Charles Jourdan shoes and Bloomingdales' lingerie range. An obsessive master colourist, Bourdin is said to have left actress Ursula Andress lying naked on a glass table for six hours while searching Paris for the right shade of rose petals to match her skin.

► Barbieri, Fath, Jourdan, Man Ray, Mert & Marcus, Newton

Guy Bourdin. b Paris (FR), 1928. **d** Paris (FR), 1991. **Advertising campaign for Charles Jourdan.** 1979.

Bourjois Alexandre Napoléon   Cosmetics creator

The fashionably blanched face of the 1920s is given colour by one of the first cosmetics companies, Bourjois, which was launched in Paris in 1863. Alexandre Napoléon Bourjois originally created his powders with the theatre in mind, and he sold them from a barrow. The dusty texture of his Rouge Fin de Théâtre was completely different from the greasepaint available at the time, and soon he was the official supplier to the Imperial theatres. Fashionable Parisiennes, taking their cue from actresses and courtesans, began to use his cosmetics. Bourjois repackaged his rice powder, Fard Pastels, in little card pots stamped with the legend *Fabrique Spéciale pour la Beauté des Dames*. Bourjois set a precedent for printing phrases and quotes on the boxes; famously, in 1947 it was 'Women Will Vote'. One of the original colours, Cendre de Roses Brune, is still a bestseller, and the distinctive rose-water scent remains unchanged.

► Brown, Factor, Lauder, Uemura

Alexandre Napoléon Bourjois. b Tours (FR), 1845. **d** Paris (FR), 1893. **Pastel face.** Illustration, 1927.

Bousquet Jean (Cacharel)   Designer

In a scene created by photographer Sarah Moon, a plaid pinafore by Cacharel is worn by a doll-like figure who lies on a vast sewing machine. The designer, Jean Bousquet, founded his company Cacharel in 1958 with an aim to represent a wild, free image; rejecting the formality of clothing favoured by older generations. As such, Bousquet was part of the new ready-to-wear scene in Paris along with Christiane Bailly, Michèle Rosier and Emmanuelle Khanh. In 1961 the company produced a blouse constructed without bust darts; the result was a best-selling fitted shirt that became an icon for the brand. A collaboration with Liberty in the late 1960s also became a commercially successful and iconic partnership. Bringing the brand into the new millennium, husband and wife design team Clements Ribeiro were appointed as artistic directors in 2000, a position that is now held by Ling Liu and Dawei Sun, who took over in 2011.

► Bailly, Clements, Khanh, Liberty, Moon, Rosier, Troublé

Jean Bousquet. b Nîmes (FR), 1932. **Fashion show invitation, spring/summer 1982.** Photograph by Sarah Moon.

Bowery Leigh

Icon

Leigh Bowery approached dressing as a creative, artistic act, although whether his 'Redbeard with Aerosol Tops' from winter 1987 is 'art' or not is a matter of opinion. Part voodoo, part clown, Bowery's surreal and often disturbing costumes were always highly creative. 'I am in this odd area between fashion and art,' he said. He described his work as 'both serious and very funny'. Bowery arrived in London in 1980 during the New Romantic era. He dressed up for the first time at an Alternative Miss World contest, and was delighted to find himself the centre of attention. Later he hosted the gay nightclub Taboo, continually reinventing himself and always trying to 'improve' on his previous outfit. An expert tailor, Bowery collaborated with Rifat Ozbek, although posterity will remember him as a sitter for the painter Lucian Freud.

► Van Beirendonck, Boy George, G. Jones, N. Knight, Ozbek

Leigh Bowery. b Melbourne (ASL), 1962. **d** London (UK), 1994. **Leigh Bowery.** Photograph by Nick Knight, *i-D* magazine, 1987.

Bowie David

Icon

Wearing a glittering knitted unitard, David Bowie plays Aladdin Sane. He used clothes as costumes for his stage personae, each one representing a phase and an album from *Ziggy Stardust's* tight metallic spacesuits and wild plastic quilted bodysuits by Kansai Yamamoto to a sleek suit and tie for his 'plastic soul' disco album, *Young Americans*. He said of his inventions, 'The important fact is that I don't have to drag up. I want to go on like this long after the fashion has finished... I've always worn my own style of clothes. I design them. I don't wear dresses all the time either. I change every day. I'm not outrageous. I'm David Bowie.' At times he was a sexually ambiguous figure, using make-up and hair dye to achieve these characters and in doing so inspiring the New Romantic movement, Bowie's interest in fashion continued in the 1990s with his slightly less theatrical outfits designed by Alexander McQueen and his marriage to model Iman.

▶ The Beatles, Boy George, Iman, McQueen, K. Yamamoto

David Bowie (David Jones). b London (UK), 1947. **David Bowie.** Photograph by Bill Orchard, 1973.

Boy George

Icon

Boy George holds a doll given to him by a Japanese fan. Like him, it wears a theatrical outfit from 1984. With his Hasidic Jew's hat, dreadlocks, face of a geisha, loose-fitting Islamic-style shirt, checked trousers and hip-hop shoes by Adidas, George represented an eclectic, home-styled approach invented in the squats and clubs around London. It was a fashion born of necessity. Students and the unemployed spent their days making ever-more exotic outfits to wear at night. The clubs, such as Taboo, had

rigorous door policies – issuing humiliating rejections for those who had not made the effort – and they became a spawning ground for designers such as Body Map, John Galliano and John Flett. George, who was a central character, had been inspired by the androgynous costumes of David Bowie. He styled himself 'Boy George' to clear the confusion his dresses created amongst the wider public.

► Bowie, Dassler, Flett, Forbes, Stewart, Treacy

Boy George (George O'Dowd). b Bexleyheath, Bexley (UK), 1961. **Boy George wears Dexter Wong.** Photograph by Brian Aris, 1984.

Branquinho Veronique   Designer

Like a storyteller, Veronique Branquinho's designs play on the tension between suggestion, concealment and teasing revelation, a style embodied by these girls poised conspiratorially on a staircase. Inspired by the complex heroines and troublesome sexuality of films ranging from *Story of O* (1975) and *Emmanuelle* (1974) to *Rosemary's Baby* (1968) and the TV series *Twin Peaks* (1990), her garments create an evocative image. Launching her first collection in Paris in 1997, only two years after graduating from Antwerp's Royal Academy, Branquinho rose to rapid prominence, winning the VH1 Best Newcomer Award the following year for her impeccable tailoring. Soft layering, like the petals of a rose, hints at the moving body within; while heavy knits and tweed trenches offer a sense of protection. Branquinho offers a vision that embraces strength and fantasy, softness and sexual empowerment.

▶ Demeulemeester, Margiela, Simons, Sitbon, Theyskens

Veronique Branquinho. b Vilvoorde (BEL), 1973. **Heavy knitwear and tweed trench coats in Veronique Branquinho's autumn/winter 2000 collection.** Photograph by Annick Geenen.

Brodovitch Alexey

Art director

Two cotton dresses are made exciting by placing them against a speeding foreground and background, like lambs playing amongst the rush-hour traffic. Alexey Brodovitch, who commissioned and laid out these pictures, brought a new informality and spontaneity to magazine design. Based on European graphic modernism, his years as art director of *Harper's Bazaar* (1934 to 1958), brought life to fashion photography. By creating complementary typographic images to put next to a picture, producing two-page spreads and using multiple images (a single woman photographed several times running across the page), he invented the modern lexicon of art directors. His credo was 'Astonish me!' Richard Avedon, Hiro and Lillian Bassman were a few of his favoured photographers and his Design Laboratory in Philadelphia was a workshop 'for studying new materials, new ideas...in order to establish new devices for the future'.

► Avedon, Baron, Bassman, Hiro, Snow

Uncommon Cottons–Embroidered and Marbled

• It takes an uncommonly knowing eye, these days, to know what's cotton and what isn't. The coat on our Junior escort, for instance: cotton looking uncommonly like tweed. And here, cotton embroidered so thickly it stands by itself or, alone, cotton piqué, waffled and printed in marbly whorls. There's more here than just two surfaces, too: these cottons are ready to start spring now, ride on through fashion summer.
• The overall dress, opposite, is peppery red, encrusted with embroidery. About $25. And the properly workmanlike striped shirt that goes with it, about $7. Both by Lemringer. Wamsutta cotton, Abraxas; Harzfeld's; Joseph Magnin; Sakowitz. Hat by Madcaps; M M satchel. The loafers are 1955 Hodges.
• Print in three dimensions, above, black and white waffle piqué ironed off in wishy satin. By Lanz Originals; cotton piqué by Everfast. About $35, Bonwit Teller; L. S. Ayres; Sakowitz. Hat by Madcaps.

Brooks Daniel, John, Elisha & Edward (Brooks Brothers)   Retailers

From Wall Street to Capitol Hill, the oldest retail clothing company in America has been catering to the establishment since 1818. Brooks Brothers pioneered men's ready-to-wear, with an emphasis on soft construction and ease. Its unmistakable air of traditionalism has not prevented Brooks Brothers from introducing some of the principal innovations in American men's clothing. Bermuda-length shorts and the classic pink shirt first hit the American shores through their stores. Brooks also brought over the button-down shirt collars worn by polo players in England, instituted madras fabric for shirts (originally designed for British officers in India), and introduced the Brooks Shetland sweater and their trademark Polo coat in white, camel or grey with mother-of-pearl buttons and a full belt. Ralph Lauren's early work experience for Brooks Brothers was a crucial influence in shaping his own label's style.

▶ Burberry, Hilfiger, Lauren

Brown Bobbi

Cosmetics creator

In the early 1990s, Bobbi Brown provided an antidote to the exotic colours used throughout fashion. From beige to bitter chocolate, her earthy colours reflect natural beauty. They are achieved through a whole range of cosmetic products, without camouflaging ethnicity, age or skin tone. It is a method that looks to the skin for its lead: eye shadow that does exactly that, and lipstick that accentuates rather than masks natural colour. Brown is simple, straightforward and basic. 'Make-up is not rocket science,' she says, downplaying the hype of make-up as an art form. With her degree in theatrical make-up and extensive catwalk and editorial work, Brown started on a small scale with ten neutral-toned lipsticks. While the beauty colourscape has radically altered, Brown remains true to her plain-spoken philosophy and has published numerous books and manuals on the subject.

► Bourjois, Lauder, Page, Toskan & Angelo

Bobbi Brown. b Chicago, IL (USA), 1957. **Bridget Hall.** Photograph by Walter Chin, 1995.

Browne Thom

Designer

Thom Browne has made models walk on stilts, don astronaut suits and glide across an ice rink. For his autumn/winter 2011 collection, male models seated around an exaggerated banquet table in a gilded salon picked at the elaborate dishes in front of them, intermittently rising to lap the table at a geriatric pace. As always, the clothes were a mix of the commercially viable and the outright outré: knitted wigs and crested skirts, corduroy blazers and John Lennon-style sunglasses.

Despite his theatrical flair, since 2001 Browne has made a name for himself with a single, spotless silhouette: a shrunken grey flannel suit, accessorized with chunky black shoes and a clipped skinny tie. He is credited with reintroducing classicism to menswear, reimagining preppy tradition with a twist. Now also producing womenswear and eyewear lines, Browne won CFDA Menswear Designer of the Year in 2006.

► Van Beirendonck, Lauren, Pugh, Simons

Thom Browne. b Allentown, PA (USA), 1965. **Thom Browne autumn/winter 2011 show at the Salon Impérial of the Westin Paris, Vendôme.** Photograph by Dan and Corinna Lecca.

Bruce Liza

Designer

Lisa Lyon, bodybuilding champion of 1979 and inspiration for Liza Bruce, braces herself in a strongwoman pose. Stretched across her muscular form is 'Liza', a black Lycra bikini that uses futuristic, graphic shapes to section her body. From the outset, Bruce determined to make experimentation a central theme of her work, and her career has been punctuated by innovations that have found their way onto the high street. Initially a swimwear designer, she made a thick lustre crepe, designed by textile specialist Rosemary Moore, her signature material. They later developed a 'crinkle' crepe fabric which was widely copied throughout the swimwear business. Bruce is also credited with introducing leggings in the 1980s. Sport has been an enduring theme for Bruce, with function conspicuously dominating the design of everything from cycling shorts in the 1980s to an evening dress in 1998.

► Audibet, Godley, Di Sant'Angelo

Liza Bruce. b New York (USA), 1955. **Lisa Lyon wears 'Liza' bikini.** Photograph by Robert Mapplethorpe, 1984.

Brunelleschi Umberto　Illustrator

Around the time of this drawing, a Paris critic wrote of Brunelleschi, 'His art has nothing realistic about it. He would not know how to evoke modern life with its huge factories and streets full of people. But the world of fiction, which is so much more beautiful than the world of men, that he makes real.' Parisian by adoption, Brunelleschi worked as a costume and set designer in the theatre, where the effects of the innovations made by Bakst and Poiret were still very much alive. The hallmarks of a Brunelleschi theatrical costume drawing are clear, strong, calligraphic lines, derived from his sound training at the Accademia di Belle Arti in Florence, and brilliant, jewel-like colours that bring a fairy-tale world to life, the influence of Bakst and Poiret. Like Bakst and Erté, Brunelleschi was both a designer and illustrator, making him a leading figure in the history of twentieth-century fashion.

► Bakst, Erté, Poiret

Umberto Brunelleschi. b Montemerio (IT), 1879. d Paris (FR), 1949. 'Danseuse Orientale.' c.1920.

Bruyère Marie-Louise   Designer

The model wears a windbreaker coat from the Bruyère salon in the Place Vendôme. It has a more feminine look than the simple, tailored styles seen in London in 1944. The shoulders have a softened, draped line, the waist is narrow and the sleeves are full as is the hemline, which has a swing to it. She is photographed outside the salon, opened in 1937 and decorated by Bruyère herself. The window has been strafed with bullets and temporarily mended with brown paper, a detail that places this photograph between fashion photography and wartime reportage. Lee Miller, the photographer and journalist, was one of the first people to arrive in Paris on the liberation of the city in August 1944. Recording her impressions in *Vogue*, she wrote that, 'The French concept of civilized life has been maintained.' Bruyère trained with the Callot Sœurs and worked as an apprentice with Jeanne Lanvin.

► Callot, Von Drecoll, French, Lanvin, L. Miller

Marie-Louise Bruyère. b (FR). (Active 1920s–1950s.) **Bruyère windbreaker coat.** Photograph by Lee Miller, 1944.

Bulgari Sotirio

Jewellery designer

A Bulgari collar and earrings modelled by Tatjana Patitz makes a statement worthy of a Medici, although the jewellery is a blend of traditional Italian forms and contemporary style. Warhol once called the Bulgari store on Rome's via Condotti 'the best gallery of contemporary art'. The company was founded in Rome by silversmith Sotirios Voulgaris (Sotirio Bulgari in Italian), who honed his skills in his native Greece before moving to Italy where he founded the now world-famous brand in 1884. His

sons, Constantino and Giorgio, developed the jewel and precious stone side of the business in the early twentieth century. In the 1970s, Bulgari drew on their Art Deco themes, in particular the rectangle-cut baguette work, to develop modern, graphically spare jewellery that put diamonds in geometric settings. Precious jewellery was thus placed in the domain of young, fashionable society. The company was purchased by the LVMH group in 2011.

► Cartier, Lalique, Warhol

Sotirio Bulgari. b Epirus (GR) 1857. d Rome (IT) 1932. **Tatjana Patitz wears a diamond collar and earrings.** Photograph by Fabrizio Ferri, 1989.

Burberry Thomas

Designer

A geometric layout illustrates all the features that have made the Burberry check as British as the Liberty print or Scottish tartan. Thomas Burberry, a country draper, developed a water- and wind-proof fabric he called gabardine; his first raincoat went on sale in the 1890s. Designed for field sports, it was later used by officers in the trenches of the First World War and dubbed the 'trench coat'. Many of the original features, from epaulettes and storm flaps to the metal D-rings, still appear on the coat today. The coat's shape evolves to keep pace with fashion movements. The distinctive beige and red check lining was first used in the 1920s and Hollywood stars of the 1940s invested it with an aura of glamour. Given new life by the Japanese Burberry-fever of the 1980s, it has since been applied to everything from umbrellas to bags. In 2001 Christopher Bailey became creative director and in 2009 was appointed chief creative officer.

► C. Bailey, Brooks, Creed, Hermès, Jaeger

Thomas Burberry. b Dorking, Surrey (UK), 1835. **d** Hook, Hampshire (UK), 1926. **Classic trench coat.** 1995.

Burrows Stephen   Designer

A matte jersey dress by Stephen Burrows is decorated with his trademark 'lettuce' edging. Deliberately created by closely spaced zig-zag stitching on raw seams, it is an example of how Burrows sparingly used machine techniques to decorate his fluid, sexy vision of modern femininity. The full cut of this dress will have produced a wake of rippling fabric, giving it sinuous movement. Customers who visited his store-within-a-store, Stephen Burrows' World at Henri Bendel, in the 1970s, came for simple jersey and chiffon outfits that then defined New York style. In 1971, Halston told *Interview* magazine that Burrows was 'one of the unrecognized geniuses of the fashion world... Stephen gives the most original cut in America today. And the thing is really the cut. One of Burrows' favourite cuts is the asymmetric (where the hem is cut on the diagonal), about which he said, 'There's something nice about something wrong.'

▶ Bates, Halston, Munkacsi, Torimaru

Stephen Burrows. b Newark, NJ (USA), 1943. **Electric blue jersey wrap and matching pants.** Photograph by Oliviero Toscani, American *Vogue*, 1974.

Burton Sarah

Designer

The Duchess of Cambridge's wedding dress unites the old and the new. The ivory satin bodice is narrow at the waist and slightly padded at the hips, drawing upon the Victorian tradition of corsetry so beloved of Alexander McQueen. Sarah Burton's cutting technique and tactile exploration of the fabric create an elegant, streamlined, modern silhouette, while hand-cut English and Chantilly lace (another McQueen trademark) embellish the dress. Burton had not yet finished her degree at London's

Central Saint Martins when she began an internship at Alexander McQueen. Appointed head of womenswear in 2000, she took up the position of creative director after McQueen's death in 2010. In 2011 Burton won Designer of the Year at the British Fashion Awards and the International Designer of the Year Award from Elle UK in 2012. Burton was awarded an Order of the British Empire (OBE) in 2012 for services to the British fashion industry.

► Central Saint Martins, McCartney, McQueen, Treacy

Sarah Burton. b Macclesfield, Cheshire (UK), 1974. **Kate Middleton wears Alexander McQueen to marry Prince William on 29 April 2011 at Westminster Abbey, London.**

Butler Nicky & Wilson Simon (Butler & Wilson) Jewellery designers

A face is framed by glittering diamanté jewellery, one eye obscured by an amusing lizard. Recognizing the potential for antique costume jewellery in the late 1960s, antique dealers Nicky Butler and Simon Wilson started selling Art Deco and Art Nouveau treasures at London's most fashionable markets. By the time they opened their first shop in 1972, Butler and Wilson had themselves started designing. Their eponymous period-inspired and often witty creations raised the profile of costume jewellery. The change in conventional attitudes towards genuine fakes, however, was never more conspicuous than in the opulently ornamental 1980s, when glamorous ambassadors of Butler & Wilson's style included Jerry Hall, Marie Helvin, Lauren Hutton and the Princess of Wales, who often wore their bejewelled designs for formal evening occasions.

► Diana, Hutton, Lane, Winston

Nicky Butler. b (UK), *c.*1950; Simon Wilson. b Glasgow (UK), 1950. Twenty-first birthday celebratory cover from *Rough Diamonds: The Butler & Wilson Collection.* Photograph by John Swanell, 1989.

Callot Marie, Marthe, Regina & Joséphine (Callot Sœurs)   Designers

This panniered taffeta evening dress represents the exotic work of the Callot Sœurs. Its sheer vest is wrapped over a taffeta bodice and caught into a rose on the hip. The petalled skirt, inspired by an eighteenth-century dress, is appliquéd with green billows reminiscent of designs painted by Erté. The sisters worked with exquisite and unusual materials, including antique lace, rubberized gabardine and Chinese silks, with *Orientalisme* a favourite theme. They are remembered for introducing the fashion for the gold and silver lamé evening dresses popular in the 1910s and 1920s. They were influential into the 1920s when Madame Marie Callot Gerber, the eldest sister, was referred to as the backbone of the fashion world of Europe. Madeleine Vionnet said of her training at Callot Sœurs, 'Without the example of the Callot Sœurs, I would have continued to make Fords. It is because of them that I have been able to make Rolls-Royces.'

► Bernard, Boué, Bruyère, Dinnigan, Duff Gordon, Erté, Vionnet

Callot. Marie, Marthe, Regina, Joséphine. (Active 1890s–1920s.) **Ivory and chartreuse evening dress.** *c.*1920s.

Campbell Naomi

Model

Herb Ritts casts Naomi Campbell as Pan, representing eternal spring. Her athletic frame is regarded as being as near perfect as it is possible to be – even in the fashion industry. Azzedine Alaïa realized her potential early, and dressed Campbell in his clothes, which are as equally demanding of perfection. She sought stardom from an early age, attending stage school in London, and has rarely been out of the news since she was hailed as a supermodel. Known for her diva-like qualities, she has a star-like ability to dominate a picture or catwalk. She was dubbed 'the black Bardot' for her full lips and sexy demeanour, although she claims to have encountered prejudice, saying 'This is a business about selling – and blonde, blue-eyed girls are what sells.' However, her success has contributed to a broader conception of the feminine ideal. After many decades, she is still in demand and in 2007 appeared in Dior's 60th anniversary show at Versailles.

► Crawford, Evangelista, Moss, Ritts, Schiffer

Naomi Campbell. b London (UK), 1970. **Campbell in Norma Kamali bikini bottoms.** Photograph by Herb Ritts, *Vogue*, 1990.

Campbell-Walter Fiona   Model

Fiona Campbell-Walter wears the duchesse satin ball gown, stole and gloves of an aristocrat, the society she represented in the 1950s. Born the daughter of an admiral in the Royal Navy, she was encouraged by her mother to become a model at eighteen, and was photographed by Henry Clarke, John French, Richard Avedon and David Bailey. She attended modelling school and soon became a *Vogue* regular, chosen for her aristocratic looks. She was also Cecil Beaton's favourite. Always in the gossip columns, Campbell-Walter married Baron Hans Heinrich Thyssen-Bornemisza, an industrialist. Together they were prolific art collectors, living mainly in Switzerland. They had two children but divorced in 1964. A high point of the Baroness's career in 1952 was to feature on the front cover of *Life* magazine – a surprising but understandable source of aspiration for fashion models, given its intellectual gravitas.

► Beaton, Clarke, McLaughlin-Gill

Fiona Campbell-Walter. b Auckland (NZ), 1932. **Duchesse satin ball gown, Salle des Glaces, Versailles.** Photograph by Frances McLaughlin-Gill, 1952.

Capasa Ennio (Costume National)   Designer

Described as a 'mix of couture and the street', Ennio Capasa's dress uses cutaway armholes to reveal the shoulders, and a simple tie at the neck. These are its only details. Its focus is the fabric: shimmering Lurex highlights the curves of the body. Capasa's work is dictated by material. 'I always start designing a collection from the fabrics,' he says. 'I love the interplay between matt and shine. The fabrics are where you really experiment in fashion.' He trained with Yohji Yamamoto

in Japan in the early 1980s, where the practice was to pare details away from a design and to take inspiration from traditional cutting techniques. On his return to Milan in 1987, Capasa started his own label, Costume National. It combines his perception of Japanese purism with a sexier, more close-fitting silhouette influenced by street fashion – a 1990s imperative epitomized by Helmut Lang and Ann Demeulemeester.

► Demeulemeester, Lang, Prada, Y. Yamamoto

Ennio Capasa. b Lecce (IT), 1960. **Lurex dress, spring/summer 1997.** Photograph by Nathaniel Goldberg.

Capucci Roberto

Designer

Two immense ball gowns are assembled from an acre of pleated rainbow taffeta. The backs are constructed in such a way that they appear to be shoulder-to-floor bows. They are an example of engineering from Roberto Capucci who, in 1957, was called the 'Givenchy of Rome' by fashion writer Alison Adburgham. She continued, 'He designs as though for an abstract woman, the woman we never meet.' Such is the extravagance of some experiments that the wearer becomes secondary to the gown. For ten years

Capucci showed in Rome before decamping for six years to Paris in 1962, and showing alongside fashion's other architect, Cristóbal Balenciaga, with whom he is often compared. The purity of Capucci's work extended to his selling technique. His fashion shows would be conducted in silence and he refused to replicate an outfit, so that any woman buying from him would have to do so from the show collection.

▶ Biagiotti, Exter, Givenchy, W. Klein

Roberto Capucci. b Rome (IT), 1930. **Pleated gowns, 1985.** Photograph by Fiorenzo Niccoli.

Cardin Pierre

Designer

In what could be a still from *Star Trek*, men, women and even a boy strike poses to accentuate their tomorrow's wardrobe. In the mid-1960s Pierre Cardin spun off into deep space with Courrèges and Paco Rabanne. He offered utopian clothes to a new generation. Graphic symbols were cut from his jersey tunics; men's jackets were given military epaulettes. The silver shine of asymmetric zips, steel belts and buckles brought haute couture into the space age. Cardin's training had been a traditional one, at the houses of Paquin, Schiaparelli and Dior, but his mind was on the future. In 1959 he was the first couturier to design ready-to-wear and was expelled from the Chambre Syndicale. He became fashion's scientist, developing his own material, Cardine, a bonded fibre that would rigidly hold his geometric shapes, and experimenting with metals to produce dresses. In later years, Cardin put his name to everything from pens to frying pans.

► The Beatles, De Castelbajac, Courrèges, Rabanne, Schön

Pierre Cardin. b Sant'Andrea di Barbarana (IT), 1922. **'Space' collection, autumn/winter 1967.** Photograph by Yoshi Takata.   99

Carnegie Hattie   Retailer

C.Z. Guest, an American social figure, wears a simple gown by Hattie Carnegie. Although she has a reputation as a revered designer, Carnegie never actually made a dress. She was a retailer who delivered a current look, such as this strapless, wasp-waisted silhouette derived from Dior, a shape that formed the hourglass figure of the 1950s. Carnegie's reputation was legendary. She employed designers of the calibre of Norman Norell, Travis Banton, Jean Louis and Claire McCardell; the 'Carnegie look' was a sophisticated simplification of European design that was favoured by American society and high-profile clients such as the Duchess of Windsor. In 1947, *Life* declared Carnegie (née Kanengeiser, but she took the name of the richest American of the time) to be the 'undisputed leader' of American fashion, with more than one hundred stores selling her product, and her imprimatur the keenest sign of prestige in American clothing.

► Banton, Daché, Louis, Norell, Trigère, Windsor

Hattie Carnegie. b Vienna (AUS), 1889. **d** New York (USA), 1956. **C.Z. Guest.** Photograph by Cecil Beaton, 1952.

Cartier Louis François

Jewellery designer

This brooch, designed as a flamingo in characteristic pose, has plumage set with calibré-cut emeralds, rubies and sapphires. Cabochon citrine and sapphire are used for the beak, a sapphire for the eye, with the head, neck, body and legs pavé-set with brilliant-cut diamonds. It was created in 1940 by Jeanne Toussaint for the jewellery firm Cartier, founded in Paris in 1847 by Louis François Cartier. This jewel was designed for the Duchess of Windsor, who owned one of the finest jewellery collections of the 1940s.

It was chosen for her by the Duke of Windsor, who spent a great deal of time choosing jewels to adorn her clothes, often designed as a setting for a particular gem. Pieces such as this one (resold in 1987 for $470,000) were still considered avant-garde many years after their design and were the precursors of a new vocabulary in *bijouterie* after the Second World War.

► Bulgari, Butler, Tiffany, Windsor

Louis François Cartier. b (FR), 1819. **d** Paris (FR), 1904. **Flamingo brooch created for the Duchess of Windsor, 1940.**
Photograph by Louis Tirilly.

101

Cashin Bonnie

Designer

A capacious, grey cashmere poncho trimmed in leather typifies Bonnie Cashin's distinctive contribution to American sportswear. Attuned to dancers and their motion, the variable weather and outdoor life of California, and to Hollywood and the movies (she was a designer for Twentieth Century Fox), Cashin created ingenious sportswear. She often used global references but always remained faithful to the pragmatic and contemporary woman. Separates were versatile and luxurious; sizing was easy, given that most tops, dresses, skirts and trousers wrapped or tied, allowing for accommodation for many body types. Cashin used layering before it became an accepted and expected part of women's lives. Toggles and luggage hardware became practical fastenings for her bags and leather-trimmed wools. Cashin is regarded, along with Claire McCardell, as the mother of American sportswear.

► Karan, A. Klein, McCardell, Maxwell, Schön

Bonnie Cashin. b Oakland, CA (USA), 1915. **d** New York (USA), 2000. **Cashmere shawl.** Photograph by Francesco Scavullo, 1966.

Cassini Oleg

Designer

In the 1960s, Cassini was the American designer most identified with Jacqueline Kennedy as First Lady, an evening dress for whom is illustrated here. Stung by criticism of her costly wardrobe (largely from Balenciaga and Givenchy), even before her husband was elected president, she chose to consider Cassini her official designer. Although her mother-in-law and aides secretly helped her to continue to acquire clothes by Grès, Chanel and Givenchy, Cassini's sleek minimalism supplemented that elite wardrobe and the American designer was publicly acclaimed. By the conspicuous association with Kennedy, Cassini became a powerful figure in 1960s style, offering youthful, smooth modernity; his A-line dresses and suits of a semi-fitted top over a slim skirt corresponded to Parisian designs. Cassini respected Mrs Kennedy's demureness, while letting each garment stand out in a manner appropriate for a First Lady.

▶ Givenchy, Grès, Kennedy

Oleg Cassini. b Paris (FR), 1913. **d** Manhasset, NY (USA), 2006. **Evening dress for Jacqueline Kennedy.** 1961.

De Castelbajac Jean-Charles   Designer

The deadpan expression on the model's face contradicts Jean-Charles de Castelbajac's joke: a square-cut dress that imitates the front-opening of a huge pair of blue jeans. His simple, enveloping clothes remain true to the uncut cloth. Thick, felt-like fabrics have preoccupied him since he was at boarding school, where he cut his first garment out of a blanket. He was one of France's new age of ready-to-wear designers in the 1960s and has worked with Pop Art themes such as Warhol's Campbell's soup can, which he printed onto a cylindrical dress in 1984. Inspired by the work of Paco Rabanne and Pierre Cardin, which he said surpassed the work of artists working on the theme of futurism, he has been called 'the space-age Bonnie Cashin'. In 2006 the Victoria & Albert Museum, London, featured a display that showed the variety of his work, including jackets made from toys, parachute ballgowns and Pop Art dresses.

► Cardin, Ettedgui, Farhi, Rabanne, Warhol

Jean-Charles de Castelbajac. b Casablanca (MOR), 1950. **'Jeans' dress.** Photograph by Denis Malerbi, 1984.

Castillo Antonio

Designer

The risqué potential of the black lace used in Castillo's A-line dress is at once removed by its stately aura. A black hat, moulded into the shape of a mantilla comb, lends grace, while the model maintains an imperial pose, turning her back to the camera as if to shake hands with foreign heads of state. Born of a noble Spanish family, regality and dignity surround every one of Antonio Castillo's designs – his training was as accessory designer for Chanel and as designer at the distinguished fashion houses Piguet and Lanvin. Castillo left Spain for France in 1936 at the onset of the Spanish Civil War. He was no Courrèges, indulging in avant-garde couture for the younger generation of customers in the 1960s; instead, he subtly instilled a sense of innovation into mature seemingly classic looks, which resulted in a quiet, exceedingly tidy style.

► Ascher, Beretta, Lanvin, Piguet, G. Smith

Antonio Castillo. b Madrid (SP), 1908. d c.1984. **Lace Cage.** Photograph by Seeberger Brothers, 1965.

Cavanagh John   Designer

John Cavanagh is photographed with a model wearing his full, yet immaculately tailored coat. Its black cuffs, plain collar and geometric configuration of buttons are its only details beyond top-stitched, princess-line seams into which the pockets disappear. His was an international training, firstly with Molyneux on his return from Paris and then at Pierre Balmain. In 1952 Cavanagh opened his own couture house in London, making clothes with international appeal. He noted, 'A couturier worth his name must design in the world-stream of design change, but direct it to the lives of his clients that make this business exist.' Cavanagh was at the centre of London's small made-to-measure society that continued to dress the English season, despite becoming engulfed by cheap imitations. In 1964 he said, 'Couture will and must continue. It is the lifeblood of the ready-to-wear.'

▶ Balmain, Dior, French, Molyneux, Morton

John Cavanagh. b County Mayo (IRE), 1914. **d** 2003. **John Cavanagh and model wearing cream wool coat.** Photograph by John French, 1962.

Central Saint Martins   School

London's increasingly sophisticated reputation within the fashion industry in recent decades is thanks in no small part to the ferocious training ground that is the CSM fashion department, formed in 1989 when the Central School of Art and Design merged with Saint Martins School of Art. The MA course (under the direction of the highly demanding and formidably straight-talking Louise Wilson since 1992) has garnered a prestigious reputation. Maintaining strong ties with industry power players and an impressive graduate show at London Fashion Week, the fashion department encourages original vision, tempered with an understanding of the tough realities of the modern business. As a result, CSM graduates are some of the most recognizable names in the industry; internationally celebrated alumni include John Galliano, Alexander McQueen, Stella McCartney and Christopher Kane.

► Parsons The New School for Design, Royal Academy of Fine Arts

Central Saint Martins College of Art and Design. est. London (UK), 1989. **BA fashion graduation show.** Photograph by John Sturrock, 2012.

Cerruti Nino

Designer

Jack Nicholson wears loose linen separates by Cerruti in the film *The Witches of Eastwick* (1987). 'Fashion, ultimately, is a way of describing the world we live in,' says Cerruti, a philosophy that applies itself not only to the world of fashion but also to film – he has designed costumes for over sixty movies. Cerruti initially studied philosophy and wanted to become a writer, but in 1950 he took over the family textile business in northern Italy. His launch of a menswear range, Hitman, in 1957 was the start of the company's transformation into a luxury label. A women's ready-to-wear collection followed in 1977. Epitomizing the aspirational dressing of the 1980s, the Cerruti label was used in films such as *Wall Street* (1987). In the 1990s, Cerruti's womenswear enjoyed a period of success while it was designed by Narciso Rodriguez, who introduced contemporary themes such as transparent, embroidered fabrics worn with precise tailoring.

► Armani, Von Etzdorf, Gucci, Rodriguez

Nino Cerruti. b Biella (IT), 1930. **Jack Nicholson in *The Witches of Eastwick*.** Directed by George Miller, 1987.

Chalayan Hussein

Designer

Moulded from a fibreglass and resin composite, the hard shell of the 'Remote Control Dress' opens to reveal a contrasting mass of soft tulle. Operated by a boy on the catwalk with a radio control, this playful counterpoint speaks of the relationship between technology and nature, and our attempts to use one to control the other. Highly inventive collections and conceptual projects have become Hussein Chalayan's trademark since his debut collection in 1994, with pieces including furniture that transforms into garments and a dress made of 200 lasers. Chalayan is celebrated for the complex, almost architectural rigour of his pattern-cutting, which results in structured, geometric designs. Coming to prominence in the 1990s, Chalayan was one of a generation of designers, including Alexander McQueen, responsible for the cutting-edge style associated with London's cultural boom in that decade.

► Berardi, Cardin, Kawakubo, McQueen, Pugh, Y. Yamamoto

Hussein Chalayan. b Nicosia (CYP), 1970. **'Remote Control Dress', spring/summer 2000.** Photograph by Chris Moore.

Chanel Gabrielle (Coco)

Designer

Coco Chanel is strolling in the Tuileries in Paris, a short distance from the rue Cambon where she lived and had her *maison de couture*, which she closed in 1939 and re-opened in 1954. She is wearing all the hallmarks of her signature style: suit, blouse, pearl jewellery, scarf, hat, gloves and handbag with gilt chains. She was a perfectionist, and the way she gestures to Alexander Liberman with her right arm manifests one of her fixations – a comfortable arm movement. She would rip off the sleeves of her suit time and again to achieve a perfect fit. The basic idea for her suits came from the concept of military uniforms. As the mistress of the Duke of Westminster, she had taken many trips on his yacht where the crew wore uniforms. The essence of her style was rooted in a masculine model of power, a direction that has dominated twentieth-century fashion.

► Cocteau, Dalí, Lagerfeld, Liberman, Parker, Di Verdura

Gabrielle (Coco) Chanel. b Saumur (FR), 1883. **d** Paris (FR), 1971. **Coco Chanel wearing Chanel suit.** Photograph by Alexander Liberman, 1951.

Charles Caroline

Designer

In an early design, Caroline Charles uses a chequerboard pattern jacket, worn with long socks. During the 1960s, Charles also worked as a broadcaster and journalist but she stayed with fashion. 'Does it fit? Is it useful? Does it create the feeling that someone wants to get close to you?' These practical questions are considered for every piece of Caroline Charles clothing. Charles recalls wanting to be a dress designer from an early age. After graduating from Swindon Art School, she headed to London, which was in full 1960s swing. Following a spell at Mary Quant, she launched her own collection in 1963. Charles's occasion- and eveningwear were an instant hit with the entertainment trendsetters of the day, including Cilla Black and Barbra Streisand. However, it has been her knack of creating very British clothes – and, latterly, accessories and interiors – that has allowed her career to span three decades.

▶ Courrèges, Foale & Tuffin, Quant

Caroline Charles. b Cairo (EG), 1942. **Check weave wool jacket and black wool skirt.** *Tatler*, 1964.

Chéruit Madeleine

Designer

Monochromes forge a vintage ambience, illuminated by porcelain skin set against dazzling sequins under transparent organza. Marion Morehouse wears a deep V neckline, then considered risqué, that runs to a beltless waist, indicating the move away from the curvaceous prewar silhouette to a relaxed contour. Trained in the 1880s at the couture house Raudnitz, Chéruit was a Parisian designer who, like Lelong and Louise Boulanger, transformed high fashion into the reality of ready-to-

wear. She refined the excessiveness of couture for her aristocratic Parisian clientele, who favoured her richly ornamented dresses. Fascinated by the effect of light on fabric, she worked with taffeta, lamé and gauze. With Chanel's move towards simple fashions in the 1920s, her opulent taste lost appeal. She retired in 1923, but her design house continued until 1935 when Schiaparelli famously took over her premises.

► Bally, Boulanger, Lelong, Morehouse

Madeleine Chéruit. b (FR), c.1880s. **d** 1935. **Marion Morehouse.** Photograph by Edward Steichen for American *Vogue*, 1927.

Choo Jimmy

Shoe designer

A powder-blue suede sandal is trimmed with feathers, an example of the dainty, seductive work of Jimmy Choo, who was born into a family of shoemakers and made his first pair aged eleven. Previously all Choo shoes were handmade; he has recently adapted his perfectionist craftsmanship for an additional ready-to-wear line. Choo attended London's Cordwainers Technical College with a fresh generation of cobblers, including Patrick Cox and Emma Hope. Of his style, Choo says, 'There is an

elegance, a femininity, maybe a sexiness.' It was one that came to be favoured by the Princess of Wales, who would buy one style in several colours for eveningwear and to co-ordinate with her day suits. Choo's Malaysian roots account for his signature palette: a range of crystalline colours that includes aqua blue, fuchsia pink and bright orange. Since 1999 he has also been designing men's shoes.

► Blahnik, Cox, Diana, Hardy, Hope

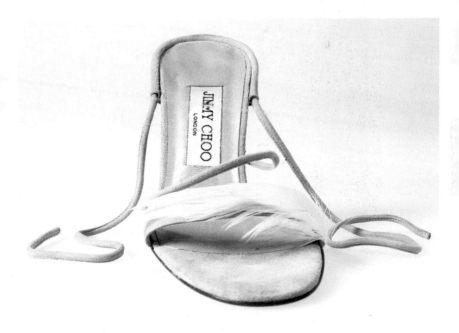

Jimmy Choo. b Penang (MAL), 1961. **Feathered sandal, spring/summer 1997.** Photograph by Simon Archer, *E.S.* magazine, 1998.

Chow Tina

Icon

Tina Chow strikes an elegant, demure pose. A supreme model in the 1970s, she went on to become one of the great fashion connoisseur-collectors of the twentieth century. An Asian-American, Chow represented the new diversity and universalism of modern beauty, but her fashion intelligence was even greater than her beauty. One of the most important collectors of couture clothing, Chow's practised eye is still regarded as the paradigm of collecting and connoisseurship. Chow knew the great designers of her time, but demonstrated her interest in the past by choosing works by Madeleine Vionnet, Cristóbal Balenciaga and Christian Dior for her astute collection. Her initial collecting interest was Mariano Fortuny, whose 'Delphos' dresses, capes and mantles were a syncretist interpretation of East and West.

▶ Antonio, Balenciaga, Fortuny, Vionnet

Tina Chow. b Cleveland, OH (USA), 1950. **d** New York (USA), 1992. **Tina Chow.** Photograph by Arthur Elgort, 1982.

Clark Ossie

Designer

In this wild scene photographed at London's Chelsea Town Hall in 1970, Ossie Clark shows his clothes under the name Quorum, a company set up by Alice Pollock. It was, according to *Vogue*, 'more a spring dance than a show'. The spaced-out models wear Clark's chiffon dresses (each with a secret pocket into which a key and a £5 note would fit – his trademark), both printed by his wife, textile designer Celia Birtwell. The couple were immortalized in a portrait entitled *Mr and Mrs Clark and Percy* by their friend, painter David Hockney, who can be seen on the far right of this picture. 'I'm a master cutter. It's all in my brain and fingers,' Clark had said, and that talent became one of the most sought after in the late 1960s and early 1970s. Singer Marianne Faithfull and Anita Pallenberg, then the girlfriend of the Rolling Stones guitarist Keith Richards, shared an 'Ossie' snakeskin suit, now one of the most precious reminders of the age.

► Birtwell, Fratini, Hulanicki, Pollock, Sarne

Ossie Clark. b Liverpool, Merseyside (UK), 1942. **d** London (UK), 1996. **Printed chiffon dresses.** Photograph by Annette Green, 1970.

Clarke Henry

Photographer

The citrus colours of summer are given a fresh, literal interpretation. Photographer Henry Clarke was first drawn to fashion photography by watching Cecil Beaton photograph Dorian Leigh. He created animated photographs, but Clarke was also naturally inclined to elegance, and his images of French fashion in the 1950s, in particular, exemplify the balance he sought between the formal, almost statuesque, dress of the epoch and the casual effect of snapshot instantaneity. Artful and artless at the same time, Clarke's photographs benefited from the licence given him by Diana Vreeland at *Vogue* and the exotic locations they used for photo shoots. Skilfully moving from 1950s high style to the dazzling colours and layering of the 1960s, he made the flamboyant and ethnographic clothes come alive in the context of Mayan archaeological sites and various settings in India, Sicily and around the world.

► Campbell-Walter, Goalen, Pertegaz, Vreeland

Henry Clarke. b Los Angeles, CA (USA), 1918. **d** Le Cannet (FR), 1996. **Fruit sweaters.** French *Vogue*, 1957.

Clements <small>Suzanne &</small> Ribeiro <small>Inacio (Clements Ribeiro)</small> Designers

Clements Ribeiro's graphically patterned cashmere has become its trademark: from rainbow stripes to this striking Union Jack insignia, which symbolized the 1990s upswing in British fashion fortunes known as 'Cool Britannia'. Ribeiro said, 'We do simple cuts with strong fabrics; we call it clumsy couture.' Bright prints define the themes of each collection; from traditional tartans and windowpane checks to bohemian paisleys and mottled florals. Luxurious materials are used for daywear – dusty-coloured suedes, cashmere, silk taffeta and sequins. They met at Central Saint Martins College of Art and Design, married and moved to Brazil after graduating. They designed their first joint collection in London in 1993. The success of their womenswear collections led in the late 1990s to the launch of a cashmere menswear line. In 2000 they revived the house of Cacharel in Paris where they were creative directors until 2007.

► Amies, Cacharel, Campbell, Chalayan, Van Noten

Suzanne Clements. b London (UK), 1969; **Inacio Ribeiro. b** São Paulo (BR), 1963. **Union Jack cashmere sweater, autumn/winter 1997.** Photograph by Chris Moore.

Cobain Kurt

Icon

Cobain was to grunge what Johnny Rotten was to punk. His greasy, bleached hair, pale waif-like body and thrift-shop clothes created the image of a strung-out, moody adolescent. The garments of grunge bands such as Cobain's Nirvana, Pearl Jam and Alice in Chains were cheap and casual; washed-out jeans and rock T-shirts. It started as an anti-fashion formula that dressed a generation of disaffected youth known as Generation X, but, predictably, was 'cleaned up' to become a mainstream movement known as 'Heroin Chic': an affected representation of an addict's wardrobe. Rebelling against his upbringing among homophobic lumberjacks in his home town, Cobain would sometimes try harder by wearing his partner's flowery dress and painting his nails red. That partner, Courtney Love, came to personify a feminized version of the look that inspired Marc Jacobs to create his 'grunge' collection of 1993.

▶ Dell'Acqua, Jacobs, McLaren, Rotten

Kurt Cobain. b Hoquiam, WA (USA), 1967. **d** Seattle, WA (USA), 1994. **Kurt Cobain and daughter, Frances Bean.** Photograph by Stephen Sweet, 1994.

Cocteau Jean

Illustrator

The legend on this fashion drawing reads, 'Paris 1937'. Schiaparelli made this tapering sheath dress for dining and dancing; Jean Cocteau drew it for *Harper's Bazaar*. Cocteau was a writer, film-maker, painter, print-maker, stage-, fabric- and jewellery-designer and fashion illustrator. His *entrée* into the world of fashion came through the theatre. Cocteau met Diaghilev when the Ballets Russes came to Paris in 1910 and he designed posters for him. Some of Cocteau's most important work

for the theatre and fashion included his collaborations with Chanel. Between 1922 and 1937 she designed costumes for a whole cycle of his plays, including *Le Train Bleu* of 1924. He often sketched her and her fashions in his characteristic form of outline drawing with its sharp line and elegant simplicity. Cocteau was also closely associated with Surrealism and fashion. For Schiaparelli he designed fabrics, embroideries and jewellery.

▶ Bérard, Chanel, Dessès, Horst, Rochas, Schiaparelli

Jean Cocteau. b Paris (FR), 1889. d Paris (FR), 1963. **Schiaparelli dress.** Illustration for *Harper's Bazaar*, 1937.

Coddington Grace

Editor / Stylist

'Grace Coddington is the eye – the eye... I never saw a wrong dress she chose... Grace was without a doubt the fashion editor,' says Manolo Blahnik. Coddington has influenced fashion in many different ways. In 1959 'The Cod', photographed here wearing all-over prints by Jacques Heim, was spotted by Norman Parkinson. She constantly reinvented her image by changing her distinctive red hair from a chunky Vidal Sassoon bob to a halo of frizzy curls – a formula that would later be used by

Linda Evangelista. In 1968 she moved to British *Vogue*, taking Calvin Klein's modern aesthetic to a 1970s European audience. Her style inspired designers such as Kenzo and Pablo & Delia and she later championed the talents of Azzedine Alaïa and Zoran. Coddington moved to American *Vogue* in 1987. She said of her time there, 'You're either having dinner with 300 people or grovelling on the floor with pins in your mouth.'

► French, Heim, Menkes, Nast, Walker, Wintour

Grace Coddington. b Holyhead, Gwynedd (UK), 1941. **Coddington wearing Jacques Heim.** Photograph by John French, 1965.

Coffin Clifford

Photographer

For the June 1949 issue of American *Vogue*, Clifford Coffin photographed four models wearing swimsuits as polka-dots on a sand dune in a customarily strong composition. Coffin's main contribution to fashion photography in the 1950s was his use of ring-flash lighting – a circular bulb that wraps around the lens and casts a directional light onto the model, thereby creating an indistinct shadow. A technique that 'blasts' light onto the subject, highlighting shiny fabric and make-up, it

was widely used in tandem with a wind machine in the 1970s and 1990s. Coffin was a fashion personality whose early ambition was to be a dancer. He was also an 'out' homosexual, who was close to society writer Truman Capote. His work for American, British and French *Vogues* secured his own position in that society and he was described as 'the first photographer to actually think fashion, sometimes more than fashion editors'.

► Gattinoni, Gernreich, Goalen

Clifford Coffin. b IL (USA), 1913. **d** Pasadena, CA (USA), 1972. **Swimsuits.** American *Vogue*, 1949.

Colonna Jean

Designer

Imagine the dark backstreets of Paris, a flashing neon sign and a hidden door opening to an underground world inhabited by women who sleep during the day and dress for the night in leopard prints, stretchy sheer lace and little else. This is the world of French designer Jean Colonna, whose fashion shows conjure up the world of the Pigalle district after dark. He came to prominence during the 'deconstruction' trend of the early 1990s, upsetting the establishment by creating clothes that people could actually afford. His manufacturing methods included overlocked hems and edges, doing away with the need for finishing. Colonna trained in Paris and spent two years at Balmain, before launching his own label in 1985. Colonna's philosophy has always been that 'a piece of clothing must be simple – to make, to sell and to wear'. He was also among the first to attempt to dispense with the catwalk and to present his collections through catalogues.

► Balmain, Dolce & Gabbana, Topolino

Jean Colonna. b Oran (ALG), 1955. **Backstage, spring/summer 1998.** Photograph by Thierry Ledé.

Connolly Sybil

Designer

Photographed in her Dublin home, Sybil Connolly wears a dress made from her famous pleated linen. The tailored shawl covers a simple bodice and typically understated skirt. The doyenne of Irish fashion in the 1950s, Connolly specialized in adapting traditional Irish fabrics for modern, easy dressing. Her forward-thinking designs transformed thick mohair, Donegal tweed and linen, which she hand-pleated for delicate blouses and dresses. Like her American contemporary, Claire McCardell, she was a pioneer in the creation of smart shapes that used informal fabrics and a relaxed attitude during the 1950s and 1960s. Connolly moved to London to learn dress design, but returned to Ireland upon the outbreak of the Second World War. At the age of twenty-two she became design director of the Irish fashion house Richard Alan, going on to launch her own couture label in 1957 at the age of thirty-six.

▶ Leser, McCardell, Maltézos

Sybil Connolly. b Swansea, West Glamorgan (UK), 1921. **d** Dublin (IRE), 1998. **Sybil Connolly at home, Merrion Square, Dublin.** Photograph by Perry Ogden, 1987.

Conran Jasper

Designer

In an exercise in contrast, a scarlet poppy hat, designed by Jasper Conran and made by Philip Treacy for a production of *My Fair Lady*, explodes above an unadorned Conran black dress. Conran regarded Jean Muir as his mentor and his own work carries her hallmarks of modern sophistication. Having studied at Parsons School of Design in New York, Conran set up his own label at the age of nineteen. He relies on a monochrome palette interspersed with stimulating bursts of striped fabric or salvos of colour: bold orange, cerise or cobalt blue. He likes his clothes to have, 'speed and life... For me it's always about the cut and the shape.' Conran's work is also wearable. In 1996 he launched the J by Jasper Conran womenswear line for the British department store Debenhams. The collection has expanded to include women's accessories, lingerie, hosiery, menswear, men's accessories, childrenswear and homewares.

► Muir, Parsons The New School for Design, Treacy

Jasper Conran. b London (UK), 1959. **'Poppy' hat designed for *My Fair Lady* stage production.** Photograph by Tessa Traeger, 1992.

Courrèges André Designer

A former civil engineer, André Courrèges placed the meticulous cut of fashion he had practised in Balenciaga's atelier in the 1950s in the service of the 1960s idealism of youth and the future. Along with Pierre Cardin and Paco Rabanne, Courrèges led the cult of visionary fashion design in Paris. It was a movement that cut away superfluous material, banned decoration and established geometry and new materials for fashion. 'I think the women of the future, morphologically speaking, will have a young body,' said Courrèges at the time. His miniskirts were stiff and square and advocated a minimum of body coverage, enjoying those 'young' bodies that became visible in the 1960s. His most characteristic symbol, often covering his dresses and bare body parts, was the youthful daisy. Unisex was another Courrèges theme. He predicted that womenswear would become at least as practical as menswear.

► Cardin, Charles, Frizon, Quant, Rabanne, Schön

André Courrèges. b Pau (FR), 1923. **Space-age designs.** Photograph by William Klein, 1964.

Coward Noël

The playwright and entertainer Noël Coward strikes a classic pose in this photograph by Horst. A flawless Prince of Wales check, accessorized with polka-dot silk and woven checks, epitomizes his peerless sophistication. After his first theatrical success in 1924, Coward remarked, 'I was unwise enough to be photographed in bed wearing a Chinese dressing gown as an expression of enhanced degeneracy. I indulged in silk shirts, pyjamas and underclothes...coloured turtleneck jerseys...and started a fashion.' It was the look for the glamorous, brittle 1920s aesthete. For the first time since Oscar Wilde, a writer's appearance seemed as important as what he wrote. 'All sorts of men suddenly wanted to look like Coward – sleek and satiny, clipped and well groomed,' observed Cecil Beaton. Cary Grant was one of them, remarking that he based his own urbane style on, 'a combination of Jack Buchanan and Noël Coward'.

► Beaton, Horst, Wilde

Noël Coward. b London (UK), 1899. **d** Blue Harbour (JAM), 1973. **Noël Coward, Paris, 1934.** Photograph by Horst P. Horst.

Cox Patrick

Shoe designer

A model wears the python-skin 'Wannabe' shoe that became an icon in 1993, when Patrick Cox realized that his collection needed a lightweight summer shoe. His answer was the 'Wannabe': a moccasin-constructed loafer. In 1995 his Chelsea shop was besieged by customers wanting a pair, some of whom attempted bribery. When he launched the range in 1993, Cox acknowledged his debt to the white loafers worn by the American comedian Pee-Wee Herman. An indispensable accessory of the rave culture, the Wannabe is one half of Cox's shoe business – the other comprises a collection of styles that develops with fashion trends. Born in Canada, Patrick Cox moved to London in 1983 to study at Cordwainers Technical College. His first success was a customized Dr Martens shoe in 1984, and he went on to work with a long list of designers. In 2008, Cox relinquished ownership of his business while remaining on the board.

► Blair, Choo, Flett, R. James, Maertens, Westwood

Patrick Cox. b Edmonton, AB (CAN), 1963. **Python 'Wannabe' loafer autumn/winter 1995.** Photograph by François Rotger.

Crahay Jules-François

Designer

Jules-François Crahay poses with Jane Birkin who wears a matte jersey dress pulled into a lazy handkerchief knot at the shoulder. Crahay learned the techniques of dressmaking at his mother's shop in Liège and at the fashion house of Jane Régny in Paris. After these apprenticeships he became a designer at Nina Ricci in 1952, then at the house of Lanvin in 1963. While he was fêted for his refined eveningwear, Crahay was also one of the leading fashion designers to promote the peasant and gypsy styles that dominated fashion at the end of the 1960s. As early as 1959, his collections contained full, flounced skirts worn with low-cut, elasticated blouses and scarves worn around the head, neck and waist. All were made in vividly coloured, lightweight materials that produced the light, feminine style for which Crahay is remembered. He characterized his own work by saying that he wanted to have fun making his dresses.

► Lanvin, Pipart, Ricci

Jules-François Crahay. b Liège (BEL), 1917. **d** Monte Carlo (MON), 1988. **Jules-François Crahay and Jane Birkin.** Photograph by Jacques-Henri Lartigue, French *Vogue*, 1976.

Crawford Cindy   Model

Cindy Crawford works on her multi-million-dollar body, the marketing of which is still controlled by its owner, who says, 'I see myself as a president of a company that owns a product that everybody wants.' Her defined physique, honed in the fitness market, welded the connection between health and beauty for a generation of women. A shoot for *Playboy* was also part of the business strategy, 'I wanted to reach a different audience...let's face it, most college guys don't buy *Vogue*.' While conservative in the fashion sense (she kept the same hairstyle for ten years), Crawford was a commercial supermodel. Her popularity is attributable to her clean sex appeal and 'multicultural' appearance. It adds up to the perfect cover face: a beauty that alienates nobody. Crawford remains a pragmatist, an example of the new model breed that has learned to separate fact from fantasy.

► Campbell, Evangelista, Lindbergh, Schiffer

Cindy Crawford. b De Kalb, IL (USA), 1966. **Cindy Crawford in a still from *Shape your Body* workout video.** Photograph by Tim Rooke, 1992.

Creed Charles

Designer

This outfit is typical of the 1930s. The suit has a boxy-style jacket with a broad shoulder line and wide lapels, while the skirt is straight and the hemline stays well below the knees. It foreshadows the masculine, military style of the Second World War, but details such as the buttons and the hat anchor the outfit firmly in the prewar era. Charles Creed belonged to an English family of tailors who were known for their understated tweeds, popular in nineteenth-century Paris. The family established a tailoring firm in London in 1710 and in Paris in 1850, launching womenswear in the early 1890s. During the Second World War, Creed designed women's suits and coats while on leave from the army and was also involved in the Utility scheme. He set up his own fashion house in London in 1946 and enjoyed success in America where his restrained English tailoring found a ready market.

► Bérard, Burberry, Jaeger, Morton

Charles Creed. b Paris (FR), 1906. **d** London (UK), 1966. **Travel coat.** Illustration by Christian Bérard, 1935.

Crolla Scott

Designer

Using rich colours, opulent brocade and blooming prints, Scott Crolla's early work was a historical fantasy. Crolla trained in art and sculpture, but grew bored of the discipline, moving to fashion because it is, 'the honest side of the whole artistic discourse'. In 1981 he formed a partnership with fellow artist Georgina Godley. This tableau, styled by Amanda Harlech, who went on to work for John Galliano and Chanel, suggests the ecstasy of an eighteenth-century poet – a scene that epitomizes Crolla's fanciful work. Brocade trousers worn with silk stockings and tail coats dominated a time when fashion became costume and men rediscovered the vain pleasure of peacockery – a historical tendency that puts this outfit into context. Despite its fancy-dress connotations, Crolla's work was instrumental in encouraging men and women to wear ruffled shirts and brocade trousers.

► Godley, Hope, Wilde

Scott Crolla. b Edinburgh (UK), 1955. **Ruffled shirt.** Photograph by Andrew Macpherson, *The Face*, 1984.

Cunningham Bill

Photographer

The grandfather of street-style photography, Bill Cunningham has chronicled fashion for *The New York Times* since the late 1970s. He can be spotted – most likely in his signature cobalt blue jacket – on a trusty Schwinn bike heading towards 5th Avenue and 57th Street, his preferred corner for shooting. Born in 1929, Cunningham dropped out of Harvard to move to New York City. Initially working in advertising, he went on to write for *Women's Wear Daily* – where he picked up his first camera.

His first *New York Times* photos depict Greta Garbo (whose coat he captured before recognizing its owner) and Farrah Fawcett (who, as he didn't own a TV, he didn't know). Today, the private-minded photographer lives in a studio brimming with filing cabinets of his photos, which he develops at a one-hour lab. The 2010 documentary *Bill Cunningham New York* captured the life of one of the city's most endearing and enduring fixtures.

► Grand, Menkes, Schuman, Wintour

Bill Cunningham. b. Boston, MA (USA), 1929. **Cunningham at work in *Bill Cunningham New York*.** Directed by Richard Press (First Thought Films), 2010.

Daché Lilly

Milliner

Lilly Daché decorates a half-hat with feathers, autumnal berries and dried flowers for American *Vogue*. Towering turbans, draped toques and snoods, and knitted or openwork nets that enclosed the hair at the back of the head were other millinery confections characteristic of Daché. Trained at Caroline Reboux's atelier in Paris, she emigrated to the United States and in 1924 became, like Hattie Carnegie before her, an assistant in the millinery department at Macy's. Two years later she set up her own establishment in New York and became one of the most eminent milliners in America, challenging Paris for the title of millinery capital. She adorned the heads of New York high society and of Hollywood stars such as Betty Grable and Marlene Dietrich – as well as Carmen Miranda. Her most outstanding discovery was Halston, who designed pillbox hats for Jacqueline Kennedy before moving into fashion.

► Carnegie, Kennedy, Sieff, Talbot

Lilly Daché. b Bégles (FR), 1907. **d** Louveciennes (FR), 1989. **'Autumnal Berry' hat.** Photograph by Edward Steichen, American *Vogue*, 1946.

Dahl-Wolfe Louise

Photographer

Beneath the Cairo sun, model Nathalie shades herself in a cotton robe by Alix Grès. Louise Dahl-Wolfe, the photographer, often cast her images in bright sunlight. Beaches, deserts and sunny plains were her natural domain, first for compositions in black and white and later for some of the most sumptuous photographs ever taken of swimwear, playsuits and the exoticism of modern fashion. Her most frequent editor-stylist was Diana Vreeland. The unpretentious Dahl-Wolfe and the extravagant Vreeland were an odd couple in style, but together they became collaborator-adventurers in seeking out an ambient naturalism for the modern woman. Vreeland's flamboyance and artifice were sweetly tempered by Dahl-Wolfe's interest in portraiture and in landscape. Even in the most glamorous image, Dahl-Wolfe displays her inquiring mind and analytical insight, giving photography character and idiosyncrasy.

▶ Grès, McCardell, Maxwell, Revillon, Snow, Vreeland

Louise Dahl-Wolfe. b San Francisco, CA (USA), 1895. **d** New York (USA), 1989. **Grès coat, Egypt.** 1950.

Dalí Salvador

Illustrator

In this dream sequence by Salvador Dalí, the spectator's attention is fixed on the figure wearing a bold red dress very fashionably cut on the bias, the fabric falling in smooth, vertical folds from the hips. Dalí described his pictures as 'hand-painted dream photographs' and his juxtaposition of the real and unreal presented fashion in a new way, bringing out its elegance and seduction. During the 1930s, with economic and political pressures mounting, fashion and fashion illustration took an

escapist route, venturing into Surrealism, the dominant art movement of the decade. Cecil Beaton, Erwin Blumenfeld and George Hoyningen-Huene captured Surrealism's bizarre elements in their work. *Vogue* also commissioned artists such as Dalí, who collaborated with Schiaparelli in the design of fabrics and accessories, to make 'photo-paintings', presenting fashion's relationship with Surrealism.

► Bérard, Blumenfeld, Cocteau, Man Ray, L. Miller, Schiaparelli

Salvador Dalí. b Figueres (SP), 1904. **d** Figueres (SP), 1989. **'I Dream about an Evening Dress.'** Illustration for American *Vogue*, 1937.

Dassler Adi (Adidas)

Designer

Sport met fashion and music in 1986 when hip hop group Run DMC recorded its devotion to streetwear on the track 'My Adidas'. Sweatshirts, track pants and trainers were appropriated by a generation of men and women who threw away the laces and decorated themselves with heavyweight gold jewellery. In the 1970s, Adidas trainers had been an anti-establishment fashion statement worn with jeans, but in the defiant, label-aware 1980s branding took over and an unsuspecting sportswear company found itself at the heart of a fashion movement. At the 1936 Olympics, Jesse Owens, a black American runner, won four gold medals wearing a pair of trainers made by cobbler Adi Dassler and his brother, Rudolf. They had seen a gap in the market for high-performance athletic shoes in 1920 and they started to build what was to become a label as important to street fashion as it was to sport.

► Hechter, Hilfiger, Knight & Bowerman, McCartney,
   Y. Yamamoto

Adi (Adolf) Dassler. b Herzogenaurach (GER), 1900. **d** Herzogenaurach (GER), 1978. **Run DMC in 'Superstar' shoes.**
Photograph by Michael E. Heeg, 1986.

Day Corinne

Photographer

In this picture, from the series that introduced Kate Moss to the world, Corinne Day aimed to capture, 'a teenage sexuality which I love. I want to make my images as documentary as possible, an image of life that is real.' Day's style rejects everything that fashion photography has traditionally stood for – glamour, sexiness, sophistication – by shooting skinny girls in cheap nylon amidst squat-like squalor. Her anti-fashion attitude exemplified the mood of the 1990s. Herself an ex-model,

Day discovered her subjects in the street. She launched the career of Kate Moss when the model was just fifteen. Day is credited with starting the trend for pre-pubescent-looking waifs. *Vogue* editor Alexandra Shulman, however, defended her work as 'a celebration of vulnerability and joyousness'. In 2011 Gimpel Fils Gallery, London, mounted the exhibition 'Corinne Day. The Face', the first solo exhibition of her work since her untimely death in 2010.

► Moss, Page, Sims, Teller

Corinne Day. b London (UK), 1965. d London (UK), 2010. **Kate Moss.** 1990.

Deacon Giles   Designer

In 2012 the Victoria & Albert Museum, London, celebrated the reopening of its renovated fashion galleries with the exhibition 'Ballgowns: British Glamour Since 1950'. Giles Deacon's stunning spring/summer 2007 ballgown appeared as the poster image for the exhibition. As the catalogue stated, Deacon's 'structured big-entrance dresses, aimed at women who want to be noticed' reflected an elegant and classic side of the designer more often known for his tongue-in-cheek approach. Before starting his own label in 2003, Deacon worked for revered fashion houses such as Jean-Charles de Castelbajac, Bottega Veneta and Gucci. In 2004 he was named Best New Designer after launching his first collection at London Fashion Week, which was styled by his friend Katie Grand. In 2009 Deacon won the ANDAM (Association Nationale pour le Développement des Arts de la Mode) Fashion Award Grand Prix.

► De Castelbajac, Ford, Grand, Gucci, Kane, Worth

Giles Deacon. b Darlington, County Durham (UK), 1969. **Coco Rocha wears Giles Deacon, spring/summer 2007.** Photograph by Tim Walker.

Dean James

Icon

James Dean, the original teenage rebel, leans against a wall, smoking. Dean was the role model for generations of disaffected youth who immediately related to his portrayal of lost adolescence and emulated his wardrobe because of it. Andy Warhol called him, 'the damaged but beautiful soul of our time'. His status as a handsome movie star far outshone his acting talents, and in his short-lived career he made only three films: *East of Eden* (1955), *Rebel Without a Cause* (1955) and *Giant* (1956).

Dean said, 'Being a good actor isn't easy; being a man is even harder. I want to do both before I'm done.' But, tragically, he was killed at the age of twenty-four, crashing his Porsche Spyder on the way to a race meeting. He is now suspended forever in adolescence. The basics that Dean wore are still popular today as the uniform of youth: Levi's jeans, white T-shirt and zip-up bomber jacket.

▶ Presley, Strauss, Warhol

James Dean. b Fairmount, IN (USA), 1931. **d** Cholame, CA (USA), 1955. **Bomber jacket and Levi's.** *Rebel Without a Cause* publicity shot, 1955.

Delaunay Sonia

Designer

Brilliantly coloured and sharply patterned geometric designs are lavishly displayed on this 'simultaneous' coat. Sonia Delaunay, a leading Parisian artist of Orphism, a movement that developed out of Cubism and made colour the primary means of artistic expression, has here merged art with fashion. In 1912 she began a series of non-figurative paintings called *Contrastes simultanés*, combining geometric forms with bright, prismatic hues. This work was based on the theory of the simultaneous contrast of colours of the nineteenth-century chemist Michel-Eugène Chevreul. Her simultaneous fashions had their origins in these paintings, since she moulded the fabric to the shape of the garment to ensure that the application of the colours remained intact. Her new concept of fabric pattern, whereby the cut and decoration of the garment were created at the same time, perfectly complemented the unstructured clothes of the 1920s.

▶ Balla, P. Ellis, Exter, Heim

Sonia Delaunay. b Odessa (RUS), 1884. **d** Paris (FR), 1979. **Embroidered 'Simultaneous' coat created for Gloria Swanson.** 1923.

Delhomme Jean-Philippe   Illustrator

The supermodel, the hairstylist, the photographer and the assistant interact in a familiar scene from the fashion world. Such familiarity, however, becomes a novelty when painted in the form of a comic-style strip. An accessory to Jean-Philippe Delhomme's wit, fashions are blurred in favour of visually comforting satires of the affectations of those who lead their everyday lives in this industry. This bright, hand-painted gouache, which belongs to Delhomme's own one-page column published monthly in French *Glamour* since 1988, reveals a knowing artist. While drawing inspiration from his friends in the fashion trade, he claims to operate in, 'a *décalage*, a kind of jet lag, that appears between life written up in magazines and what's happening in the real world'. Delhomme's highly stylized and spontaneous caricatures recall the work of Marcel Vertès who, in the 1930s, fondly satirized the foibles of fashionable society.

► Berthoud, Gustafson, Lerfel, Vertès

Jean-Philippe Delhomme. b Nanterre (FR), 1959. **Modes de Vie.** Illustration for *Glamour*, 1993.

Dell'Acqua Alessandro   Designer

How to make something delicate and romantic appear hard-edged and punky: this dilemma is at the centre of Alessandro Dell'Acqua's work. While his clothes have a softness and sensuality defined by materials such as chiffon, shown here on a T-shirt with fluted, bias-cut sleeves, his outfits are often styled with aggression. Long leather gloves and broad sweeps of violet eye shadow lend edge to what would otherwise be a dainty shirt. He claims rock star Courtney Love as his heroine and her own style reflects his blend of aggressive femininity. His mix-and-match, layered pieces are modern in their versatility and wearability. His signature palette is contrasting colours (nude and black for example). Initially he specialized in knitwear, working with a small group of artisans in Bologna, and his collections carry reminders of this period through fragile knits of delicate, lacy mohair. In 1998 he presented his first men's collection at Pitti Immagine.

► Berardi, Chalayan, Cobain, Ferretti, Sarne

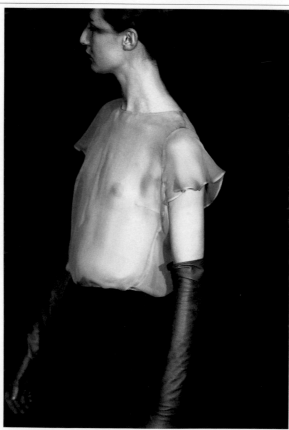

Alessandro Dell'Acqua. b Naples (IT), 1963. **Silk chiffon T-shirt, autumn/winter 1997.** Photograph by Chris Moore.

Dell'Olio Louis

Designer

Dogtooth check and black leather is a blend of fashion and function, ease and shrewdness by Louis Dell'Olio, called 'the designer for everywoman'. The fitted, single-breasted jacket follows a body-conscious line without alienating his conservative clientele. This outfit was created under Anne Klein's label that he had taken over with Donna Karan, a friend from college, after Klein's death in 1974. Dell'Olio said of the experience, 'We didn't know enough to be terrified' but together they forged a style that suited the working women of America. In 1984 Karan left to set up her own label and Dell'Olio continued what they had started until Richard Tyler took over the company in 1993. One fan of Dell'Olio's work told *Vogue*, 'I don't want to be gussied up to the ears... the jackets hide a multitude of sins, the pants have a fabulous fit, the clothes are clean.'

► Karan, A. Klein, Tyler

Louis Dell'Olio. b New York (USA), 1948. **Dogtooth check and black leather for Anne Klein.** Photograph by Chris Moore, 1988.

Demarchelier Patrick

Photographer

Patrick Demarchelier catches Nadja Auermann mid-spin, her aigrette adding to an aura of costume history. Though relentlessly modern, Demarchelier's work also has a grand quality usually associated with the great haute couture photographers of the 1950s. He left Paris for New York in 1975 and started a long relationship with America's magazines, in particular the Condé Nast titles *Vogue*, *Glamour* and *Mademoiselle*. In 1992 he joined *Harper's Bazaar*, recruited by Liz Tilberis for his clear,

graphic photographs. It was the perfect material for the spreads designed by creative director Fabien Baron. Though dealing largely with the vicissitudes of fashion, Demarchelier's work has also explored other territories. With a highly successful and prolific career, Demarchelier remains in demand, regularly shooting for titles like *Vogue*, *Interview*, *Vanity Fair* and *W*.

► Baron, Chanel, Lagerfeld, Wainwright

Patrick Demarchelier. b Le Havre (FR), 1943. **Nadja Auermann wears Karl Lagerfeld for Chanel haute couture.** *Harper's Bazaar*, 1994.

Demeulemeester Ann   Designer

Resembling a well-accoutred rock band, these models wear pieces from collections spanning fifteen years, illustrating the remarkable consistency of Ann Demeulemeester's vision. Founding her label for women in 1987, with menswear following in 1996, the Antwerp-based designer has remained true to a darkly romantic aesthetic, a combination of fragile-but-tough Northern poeticism, gypsy elegance and punk rebellion. Her silhouettes are typically long and layered, with lean jackets, waistcoats, tailored knitwear and flowing shirts. Her palette is restrained – often monochrome – with richly textured fabrics accented by totemic embellishments of ribbon and feathers. The success of this apparent stylistic asceticism rests on her talent for cutting close to the body yet barely touching it, with panels of her garments curving subtly around the contours of the wearer to create an empowering, yet seductive, carapace.

▶ Ackermann, Bikkembergs, Capasa, Thimister, Van Noten

Ann Demeulemeester. b Waregem (BEL), 1959. **Ann Demeulemeester menswear retrospective 1996–2009.** Photograph by Erik Madigan Heck, 2009.

Deneuve Catherine

Icon

Catherine Deneuve leaps for Francesco Scavullo's camera, a consummate model as well as an icon of French elegance, *froideur* and sensibility. Deneuve is also a long-term muse to Yves Saint Laurent, whom she met when he dressed her for *Belle de Jour*. Saint Laurent says of her, 'She is a woman who makes me dream... As a friend she is the most delightful, warmest, sweetest and most protective.' As French *Vogue*'s most featured cover face, Deneuve represents the legendary chic femininity of French womanhood and as such was also the face of Chanel No.5. Here, she wears a suit made of calfskin printed with cheetah spots and trimmed with mink, a powerful combination brought together by Arnold Scaasi. When she talks about the de-feminized roles played by actresses in modern films, Deneuve outlines her own style, 'Superficially, it may appear that the women now are stronger, but they are not stronger, only more masculine.'

► Barthet, Chanel, Saint Laurent, Scaasi, Scavullo

Catherine Deneuve. b Paris (FR), 1943. **Calfskin and mink cheetah print suit by Arnold Scaasi.** Photograph by Francesco Scavullo, 1970.

Dessès Jean

Designer

The roses at the hem of this chiffon dress were only usually exposed as the wearer walked. They are a charming addition to a classically inspired gown. The fashions of Dessès were inspired by his Greek heritage and Egyptian place of birth. He was a master of draped chiffon and muslin evening dresses derived from ancient robes. He was also noted for dresses made in the form of fitted jackets in plain colours with voluminous skirts in a contrasting patterned print. He established his own *maison de couture* in Paris in 1937. Dessès participated in the 'Théâtre de la Mode', the fashion doll exhibition organized by the Chambre Syndicale de la Couture Parisienne under its president, Lucien Lelong. Some forty couturiers designed haute couture in miniature for these little mannequins made of wire. They were placed in sets depicting scenes of Parisian life designed by artists involved in fashion, such as Cocteau and Bérard.

► Cocteau, Laroche, Lelong, McLaughlin-Gill, Valentino

Jean Dessès. b Alexandria (EG), 1904. **d** Athens (GR), 1970. **Black chiffon dress with pink silk roses on underskirt.** Photograph by Frances McLaughlin-Gill, American *Vogue*, 1952.

Diana Princess of Wales

Icon

'Clothes are now not as essential to my work as they used to be,' Diana, Princess of Wales, told *Vogue* in 1997. It was a confident statement from a woman who had come to realize that a pair of jeans wouldn't compromise her effectiveness. And it showed. Towards the end of her life, Diana's wardrobe finally took a back seat to the person she was and the work she did; an utterly modern concept. Here she wears an artfully uncomplicated navy lace dress by Catherine Walker for a charity film premiere in 1997.

From the day Lady Diana Spencer was first caught on film in the early 1980s wearing archetypal British upper-class clothing, the ensuing developments in her wardrobe and the colour of lipstick she chose were closely watched and copied. Particular attention was given to her hair, sleeked and simplified in the 1990s by Sam McKnight. In 1999 *Time* magazine named Diana one of the '100 Most Important People of the Twentieth Century'.

► Choo, Emanuel, Fratini, Oldfield, G. Smith, Testino

Diana, Princess of Wales. b Sandringham, Norfolk (UK), 1961. **d** Paris (FR), 1997. **Catherine Walker dress.** Photograph by Kelvin Bruce, 1997.

Dinnigan Collette   Designer

Collette Dinnigan's dress has the charm of an antique gown, yet possesses a modern sensuality, suspended as it is from two spaghetti straps. Its lace tiers and train belong to the romantic, early twentieth-century designers such as Paquin, Lucile and Dœuillet. Dinnigan launched her career designing and selling lace and chiffon lingerie. Her success allowed her to open a shop in Sydney in 1992, and begin designing a ready-to-wear line. Her use of womanly fabrics and attention to the female form resulted in

clinging slip dresses that gave sophistication to the trend for wearing underwear as outerwear. The preciousness of her designs is reminiscent of haute couture detailing and was a contrast to the prevailing use of undecorated fabrics cut into graphic forms. The simple shapes of underwear are wrought in lace and placed over contrasting satins to achieve the luminescence illustrated here.

► Dœuillet, Duff Gordon, Isagowa, Moon, Oudejans, Sarne

Collette Dinnigan. b Durban (SA), 1965. **Satin dress overlaid with lace.** Photograph by Gerald Jenkins, *Australian Style*, 1997.   149

Dior Christian

Designer

Reading the faces of this salon audience, it is possible to gauge the breadth of reaction that greeted Christian Dior's first collection, which was dubbed the 'New Look' after this show by Carmel Snow, editor of *Harper's Bazaar*. As they gaze at an hourglass jacket of cream tussore over a skirt constructed from a decadent yardage of black wool, the audience registers shock, disapproval and deep yearning. At a time of postwar austerity, the New Look tempted women back into the nostalgic femininity of corsets and, most controversially, flowing skirts that would use up to fifty yards of material. Dior, who had wanted to be an architect but turned to fashion, working for Piguet, Lelong and Balmain, said that it was one of the happiest moments of his life, 'I created flower women with gentle shoulders and generous bosoms, with tiny waists like stems and skirts belling out like petals.'

► Bettina, Bohan, Galliano, Ghesquière, Molyneux, Saint Laurent

Christian Dior. b Granville (FR), 1905. **d** Montecatini (IT), 1957. **New Look parade, 1947.** Photograph by Bellini.

Dœuillet Georges

Designer

The exquisite work of Georges Dœuillet is captured here in the fashion plates of André Marty. Fastidiously stylish, Marty has created a pictorial witticism to depict the character of the dress. Here the delicacy and fragility of Dœuillet's *robe de lingerie* is juxtaposed against the foreboding figure of Cupid. It is an example of haute couture providing a stimulating atmosphere for the rejuvenation of fashion illustration, a combination of luxurious design and texture with artistic excellence that captured the spirit of the times. Dœuillet's Paris couture house was founded in 1900, creating exquisitely intricate workmanship very much of its time. Noted for his use of magnificent fabrics, Dœuillet was a prestigious fashion house that provided the *bon ton* with some of the most opulent clothes of the early years of the twentieth century. It merged with the salon of Jacques Doucet on his death in 1929.

► Bakst, Dinnigan, Doucet, Poiret

Georges Dœuillet. b Oise (FR), 1865. **d** (FR), 1929. **Broderie anglaise boudoir dress.** Illustration by André Marty, *La Gazette du Bon Ton*, 1913.

Dolce Domenico & Gabbana Stefano (Dolce & Gabbana) Designers

This photograph of Italian icon Isabella Rossellini could almost be a still from one of her father, Roberto Rossellini's, black-and-white films of the 1940s. This cinematic sensuality is typical of Dolce & Gabbana's style. Their idealistic vision of Italy revolves around specific themes: silver screen sirens (leopard prints and corsetry *à la* Sophia Loren), Catholicism (Sunday best suits and rosary beads) and various Italian stereotypes, from Mafioso machismo (pinstripe suits and trilbys) to the simplicity of Sicilian widows (little black dresses, headscarves, fishing village baskets). But beneath this puritanical patriotism there are also hints of playful subversion: suits cut with integral corsetry or lace panels are favourites. Successfully integrating these sensibilities into a global brand, Dolce & Gabbana launched their first couture show in Taormina, Sicily, in 2012.

► V. Beckham, Colonna, Fendi, McGrath, Matsushima, Meisel

Domenico Dolce. b Palermo (IT), 1958; **Stefano Gabbana. b** Milan (IT), 1962. **Isabella Rossellini wears leopard-print coat, autumn/winter 1994.** Photograph by Michel Comte.

Dominguez Adolfo

Designer

Adolfo Dominguez is Spain's answer to Giorgio Armani, growing his label from the beginnings of his small tailoring business. In the 1980s he was famously called 'King of the Wrinklies' for his tailored but unpressed, crinkled suits for men; during this time he also designed the uniforms for the TV series *Miami Vice*. Today he has a much sleeker image, still maintaining, like Armani, a use of fabrics that direct his work and lend themselves to a simpler, softer look. These visual preoccupations come from the fact that Dominguez is not a traditionally trained designer, but a tailor, originally studying cinematography in Paris before returning to his father's drapery shop in northern Spain. He launched his first men's ready-to-wear collection in Madrid in 1982, and followed it with womenswear in 1992. In 2001 he entered the American market, opening a boutique in Miami – one of many, in what has become a successful retail business worldwide.

► Armani, Marant, Matsuda, Del Pozo

Adolfo Dominguez. b Orense (SP), 1950. **Adolfo Dominguez spring/summer 2012 collection presented at Madrid Fashion Week.** 2011.

Doucet Jacques

Designer

Doucet's gown is beautifully illustrated by Magnin for *La Gazette du Bon Ton* in 1914. The illustration reflects not only the high-waisted style in vogue before the First World War but also the way Doucet worked with artists. Together with his contemporary Poiret, he helped revive the art of fashion illustration in France. He was also a patron of the fine arts and in 1909 bought Picasso's avantgarde painting *Les Demoiselles d'Avignon*, installing it at the head of a crystal staircase in a specially built wing of

his house. The grandson of a lace merchant, Doucet expanded the family business by opening a couture department in 1871. With his gowns of rare *gros-point de Venise*, bodices of paper-thin ivory chamois and opera capes lined with swans' down or chinchilla, Doucet's style epitomized the opulent femininity of the *belle époque*.

▶ Dœuillet, Iribe, Paquin, Poiret

Jacques Doucet. b Paris (FR), 1853. **d** Paris (FR), 1932. **Afternoon dress.** Illustrated by J. Magnin for *La Gazette du Bon Ton*, 1914.

Dovima

Model

Dovima, made-up with the painted kohl lids and expressive pencilled brows of the 1950s, strikes an artful pose from behind white tulle. She and Richard Avedon broke new ground in fashion photography. Modelling with elephants or in front of the pyramids, they took fashion out of the whitewashed studio and into the 'real' world for the first time. Dovima was talent-spotted on the street outside the offices of *Vogue* in New York and was soon in front of Irving Penn's lens. She told him her name was Dovima (the first letters from her real names, Dorothy Virginia Margaret) because that was how she signed her paintings. Charging an hourly rate of $60, she became known as the dollar-a-minute girl. After twelve years at the top, she appeared alongside Audrey Hepburn in one of the most famous fashion films, *Funny Face*. Dovima's graceful, arch poses are now regarded as the *sine qua non* of haute couture presentation.

► Avedon, Beaton, Lauder, Penn

Dovima (Dorothy Virginia Margaret Juba). b New York (USA), 1927. **d** Fort Lauderdale, FL (USA), 1990. **Dovima behind tulle.** Photograph by Sir Cecil Beaton, 1950s.

Von Drecoll Baron Christoff Designer

The house of Drecoll spanned the years from 1905 to 1929 and shows two distinct styles. During the *belle époque*, Drecoll specialized in promenade gowns and evening dresses with boned bodices, tight waists and full skirts, which produced the S-shaped figure of the period. Photographs in *Les Modes* show that Drecoll ensembles were fussier and trimmed with more confection than comparable outfits from other couture houses. In the 1920s the house was known for chic, short, low-waisted gowns teamed with the cloche, a tight-fitting hat shaped like a bell and pulled low over the forehead. These flapper outfits were illustrated in luxury fashion magazines such as *Art*, *Goût* and *Beauté*. The house of Drecoll was founded by Christoff von Drecoll in Vienna. It opened in Paris in 1905 under the ownership of M and Mme de Wagner, a Belgian couple, who also supported Marie-Louise Bruyère.

► Bruyère, Gibson, Poiret, Redfern, Rouff

Baron Christoff von Drecoll. (Active 1890s–1920s.) **Afternoon dress.** *Les Modes*, 1914.

Drian Etienne

Illustrator

'Evening dress in moon-blue sequined silk' is the caption accompanying this watercolour illustration by Drian. His loose and simple technique successfully conveys the soft and fluid texture of silk. Drian was an artist who worked in Paris for the illustrated fashion magazine *La Gazette du Bon Ton*, from its foundation in 1912 until its closure in 1925. He illustrated articles and also produced fashion plates. His graphic style was brisk and clear, with the *bon ton* depicted in fluid movement in anecdotal settings, giving a picture of contemporary life. He was very adept at bringing out the intricate workmanship of the haute couture of the period, in the fashions, for example, of Paul Poiret. Among his contemporaries at *La Gazette du Bon Ton* were Georges Barbier and Georges Lepape. Drian was also well known in the 1920s and 1930s for his sanguine portrait drawings and for his decorative murals.

► Barbier, Lepape, Poiret, Sumurun

Duff Gordon Lady (Lucile) Designer

Lucile, who started out in 1890 by dressmaking for her friends, opened her own fashion house in 1891. Her marriage to Sir Cosmo Duff Gordon in 1900 catapulted her into designing for the upper echelons of international society, with branches in New York (1909), Chicago (1911) and Paris (1911). Like the Callot Sœurs, she designed romantic dresses made of silk and lace. Her speciality was picturesque tea gowns in pastel shades worn with mild corsetry, the fitting of which is being conducted here. Like her countryman Charles Frederick Worth, she held fashion shows for her clients. Like Poiret, she was an innovator, designing clothes that were startling for the time – such as draped skirts that revealed the legs. She was also involved in the entertainment world, designing costumes that became popular fashion, such as those for Lily Elsie, star of *The Merry Widow* (1934). Her other clients included the dancer Irene Castle and actress Sarah Bernhardt.

► Boué, Callot, Dinnigan, Molyneux, Poiret, Worth

Lady Duff Gordon (Lucy Sutherland; Lucile). b London (UK), 1863. **d** London (UK), 1935. **Lucile with client and mannequin at a fitting.** 1912.

Dufy Raoul

Textile designer

This lush silk is decorated with silver lamé work. The oriental motifs in sky blue, royal blue and rose reflect the imagery of the woodcuts Dufy executed for Guillaume Apollinaire's *Le Bestiaire* of 1911. Rose-coloured horses frolic amongst waves, scallops, dolphins and froth, all spectacularly taking on silver highlights. This fabric was chosen by Poiret for an evening dress he displayed at the Exposition des Arts Décoratifs in Paris in 1925. It was produced by the textile company Bianchini Férier,

with whom Dufy had an exclusive contract from 1912 to 1928. His use of colour came from his association with the Fauves (a group of artists who developed a new style of painting characterized by a bold handling of vivid colours). Dufy collaborated with Poiret in establishing the Petite Usine for fabric-printing. Even though it closed at the end of 1911, it had a great impact on Dufy's career as a fashion artist.

► Lesage, Patou, Poiret, Rubinstein

Raoul Dufy. b Le Havre (FR), 1877. **d** Forcalquier (FR), 1953. **'Shells and Marine Horses' fabric detail.** Produced by Bianchini Férier, 1925.

Eisen Mark

Designer

Jodie Kidd is picked out in a catwalk line-up at the end of Mark Eisen's show. She is wearing a mix of animal skin, wool and shiny silk. Born in South Africa, Eisen studied at the University of Southern California, where he learned business and achieved fame by designing a football helmet for 'Trojans' fans, and also gained the sensibility for streamlined, no-nonsense dressing that stresses contemporary materials. Eisen's flirtatious, but simple, silhouettes and intense materials are relaxed versions of contentious European fashion, giving wearability to otherwise challenging schemes. He has shown 'couture denim' and other signs of the street in a style former *New York Times* journalist Amy Spindler called, 'driven by the spirit of techno music, repetitive, strong and stripped down'. He was a key sponsor of the Africa Designs Fashion Competition in 2000, and although he closed his brand in 2009 he continues to work as a consultant.

► Kors, Oldham, Rocha

Mark Eisen. b Cape Town (SA), 1960. **Catwalk line-up, autumn/winter 1998.** Photograph by Chris Moore.

Elbaz Alber

Designer

Casablanca-born Alber Elbaz is undoubtedly a breath of fresh air in fashion. The designer grew up in Tel Aviv, where he studied fashion at Shenkar College, before moving to New York to work with Geoffrey Beene, followed by stints with Guy Laroche and Yves Saint Laurent in Paris. In 2001 Elbaz was appointed artistic director at Lanvin, bringing with him his distinctive take on elegance: a simplicity of form putting visual emphasis on colour and luxurious, humorous details such as his trademark bow. Elbaz is a realist in the fashion world, saying, 'I think that for me commercial is not a bad word.' This philosophy carries through to his innovative campaigns and press material, working with illustrators and photographers – here with Steven Meisel – hinting wittily at Surrealism in the designer's characteristic high-fashion playfulness that has made Lanvin, once again, a highly coveted brand.

► Beene, Lanvin, Laroche, Meisel, Pilati, Viktor & Rolf

Alber Elbaz. b Casablanca (MOR), 1961. **Lanvin autumn/winter 2011 campaign art direction by Alber Elbaz and Ronnie Cooke Newhouse.** Photograph by Steven Meisel.

Ellis Perry

Designer

Ellis, who launched his own label in 1978, created a strong brand of American sportswear by emphasizing colour, often in stripes and blocks, and by using the textures of natural fibres. Here, linen is used for a T-shirt and skirt, joined in the middle by an outsize belt. His inspirations included Sonia Delaunay, Patou and Chanel in the 1920s and contemporary culture. Capacious summer linen trousers and skirts were often matched with cotton sweaters or blouses. Sweaters were a staple for Ellis throughout the year. Winter wools were luxurious and, like all the clothes, cuddly and easy to wear. Ellis began in fashion sales; his design was conceptual and often devoted to stories or ideas that readily translated to the consumer: the winter 1985 sweaters seized unicorns, decorative foliage and sleek greyhounds from medieval tapestry, and his slouchy looks of the 1980s were exaggerated to create the look of a picturesque hobo.

► Delaunay, Jackson, Jacobs, Patou

Perry Ellis. b Portsmouth, VA (USA), 1940. **d** New York (USA), 1986. **Blue linen dress with scarlet belt, spring/summer 1983.** Photograph by Erica Lennard.

Ellis Sean

Photographer

In a fashion shoot for *The Face*, Sean Ellis re-creates a fantasy based on a supernatural storyline about voyeurism and death. It gives meaning to the phrase 'fashion story', which is used by magazines to explain a theme that runs through a **multi-page** shoot. In this case, the angelic character's eyes are made luminous to signify contact lenses that allow her tormentor to see himself as she would. The red dye that stains her snowy chiffon top signifies blood. Such stories put fashion into an anomalous context rather than simply showcasing clothes. It is a challenging method of fashion photography, which came to the fore in the 1990s, although other photographers such as Guy Bourdin and Helmut Newton developed sophisticated story-telling techniques around sex and death themes in the 1970s. Ellis explains his narrative pictures as 'not necessarily fashion pictures – they just happen to be fashionable'.

► N. Knight, McDean, Macdonald, Meisel, Sims, Tennant

Sean Ellis. b Brighton, East Sussex (UK), 1970. **'White Dragon' shirt by Tristan Webber.** *The Face*, 1998.

Emanuel David & Elizabeth   Designers

A spontaneous moment is snapped on 31 July 1981. The Princess of Wales is dressed in the romantic counterpoint to her husband's uniform. The flashlight throws into relief the yards of silk taffeta ruffles at her neck and the delicate, specially made Nottingham lace cuffs at her wrist. Unseen is the eight-metre train decorated with pearls. It was called 'a dress for a real fairy princess'. David and Elizabeth Emanuel, who designed the dress for the Princess, had created a popular movement in womenswear that reflected the moment it was designed for – one that reached a record television audience around the world. The Emanuels originally met at the Royal College of Art. They graduated in 1978, the year they also launched their Mayfair boutique. They garnered a celebrity following, with Joan Collins and Bianca Jagger among those who wore their extravagant and quixotic visions of femininity.

► Diana, Fratini, Tappé

Emanuel. David. b Bridgend, Mid Glamorgan (UK), 1952; **Elizabeth. b** London (UK), 1953. **The Prince and Princess of Wales on their wedding day.** 1981.

Enninful Edward

Stylist

An impeccably styled Linda Evangelista is led through the halls of a hotel wearing facelift bandages. The tongue-in-cheek post-operative narrative is the concept of fashion editor Edward Enninful and photographer Steven Meisel. The bandages become high fashion accessories in a witty and hyperbolic take on plastic surgery. Enninful's innate flair for fashion led to an early discovery by photographer Nick Knight, modelling for fashion magazine *i-D* before later becoming their fashion director at only eighteen years old – the youngest ever appointed to an international publication. Positions as contributing fashion editor with American and Italian *Vogue* followed before Enninful landed at fashion powerhouse *W* magazine as fashion and style director. Beyond editorial assignments, Enninful has collaborated on advertising campaigns with major houses such as Comme des Garçons, Christian Dior, Céline, Lanvin and Valentino.

► Evangelista, Grand, N. Knight, McGrath, Meisel, Wintour

Edward Enninful. b (GHA), 1973. **Linda Evangelista styled for Italian *Vogue* in 'Makeover Madness' by Edward Enninful, 2005.** Photograph by Steven Meisel.

Erdem

Designer

Unusually for Erdem Moralıoğlu (better known simply as Erdem), often celebrated for his signature floral prints, there were no flowers in his autumn/winter 2011 collection. Instead he turned to art. The life and work of American painter Jackson Pollock gave rise to a striking palette of bright red fabric overprinted with digital abstract splashes that appear to drip like a Pollock painting. Still, the designer's expertly cut, structured, feminine silhouettes harked back to the 1950s. Their elegantly slim, straight clean lines, fitting close to the body, were feminine classics with a modern twist. Erdem says his ideal client is, 'a clever person who doesn't care about seasons'. Originally studying fashion in Toronto, Erdem moved to London to intern at Vivienne Westwood, going on to complete his MA at the Royal College of Art. His collection debut in 2005 won him the prestigious Fashion Fringe prize.

▶ Katrantzou, Kirkwood, Pilotto, Saunders, Williamson

Erdem Moralıoğlu. b Montreal, QC (CAN), 1977. **Abstract print satin dresses, autumn/winter 2011.** Photograph by Morgan O'Donovan.

Eric

Illustrator

Using the broad mirror of a powder room, Eric is able to describe the jewelled details of Jean Patou's evening dress from both front and rear. He had a deft, calligraphic style whereby the model and the clothes she was wearing were minutely examined. To get such accuracy of observation, Eric drew from life and insisted the models remain static in their settings for long periods. To him, fidelity to detail was all-important. Born in America to Swedish parents, Carl Erickson studied at the Academy of Fine Arts in Chicago, where he acquired the training and discipline required for working with the figure. His first fashion illustrations for *Vogue* appeared in 1916. By 1925 he was settled in France, and, apart from the period during the Occupation of Paris (when he returned to America), he provided *Vogue* with fashion illustrations on the modes and manners of the Parisian *beau monde* right up to the mid-1950s.

► Antonio, Berthoud, Bouché, Patou

Eric (**Carl Erickson**). **b** Joliet, IL (USA), 1891. **d** Senlis (FR), 1958. **Dress by Jean Patou.** American *Vogue*, 1933.

Erté

This illustration was accompanied by the provocative words, 'Nature changes her costume each season, but quite without cost, whereas with the fairer sex...' Erté had a highly personal concept of women and fashion. He portrayed the female form in a very stylized manner. Women were exotic goddesses for whom money was no object. As for fashion, he himself said that he did not follow its trends but that from his creations each woman could select something that suited her without strictly adhering to the mode. His love of accessories, especially jewellery, is displayed here, in a picture that exemplifies his mastery of precise detail and lavish ornamentation, hallmarks for which he became known as the father of Art Deco. Erté had two major influences, which came from his native and adopted countries: Léon Bakst and the Ballets Russes and Paul Poiret, for whom he worked on fashionable and theatrical dress.

► Bakst, Brunelleschi, Callot, Poiret

Erté (Romain de Tirtoff). b St Petersburg (RUS), 1892. **d** Paris (FR), 1990. **'La Toilette de la Nature'.** Design for *Harper's Bazaar* cover, 1920.

Esterel Jacques

Designer

Seen here during her 1959 wedding to Jacques Charrier, Brigitte Bardot looks both demure and sensual in her pink-and-white, Vichy check linen dress, edged in broderie anglaise lace and designed by Jacques Esterel. The first celebrity endorsement for Esterel, the dress was the source of worldwide gossip following the secret visits he made to Bardot's Parisian hotel prior to the wedding. It was also the start of an association that led the multimillionaire Jean-Baptiste Doumeng to rename the

house Benoit Bartherotte on the designer's death in 1974. Esterel was an unlikely fashion convert: previously he presided over a foundry and was an exporter-importer of machine tools. A visit to Louis Féraud's Cannes house persuaded him to try fashion in 1950, but lack of formal training forced him to employ two of Féraud's salespeople before he finally launched his label in Paris in 1958.

► Bardot, Beretta, Féraud, Gaultier

Jacques Esterel. b Bourne-Argental (FR), 1917. **d** Paris (FR), 1974. **Brigitte Bardot and Jacques Charrier on their wedding day.** 169
Photograph by Garofalo, 1959.

Etro Gimmo

Textile designer

This family group of outfitted wildlife illustrates the *haute* bohemian spirit of the Italian label Etro. Capturing its hallmark jewel colours and rich textiles, this portrait, entitled 'Animen', portrays curious hybrids of man and animal. The family-run company was set up by patriarch Gimmo Etro in 1968. Returning from his travels with fabrics from the Far East and North Africa, he replicated these designs onto sumptuous cashmere, silk and linen. These he supplied to top couture houses and designers

Armani, Mugler and Lacroix, earning himself the title of 'Grand Man of Italian Textiles'. Joined by his offspring, he launched his menswear collection in the 1980s, deploying his signature paisley motif and vivid velvets as lining on tweed coats, bright flashes on collars and cuffs, and even in an all-over paisley suit for David Bowie. The brand remains in the Etro family with all four of Gimmo Etro's children handling various aspects of the business today.

► Armani, Ascher, Benetton, Kenzo, Lacroix

Gimmo (Gerolamo) Etro. b Milan (IT), 1940. **'Animen', Etro autumn/winter 1997.** Photograph by Christopher Griffith.

Ettedgui Joseph

A knitted column and scarf are a conceptual notion of menswear. The Joseph Ettedgui style was a moveable one, but the basic tenets of an urban designer lifestyle have remained since he opened his first boutique, selling Kenzo, Emmanuelle Khanh and Jean-Charles de Castelbajac. Antipathetic to the chintz world of Laura Ashley, Ettedgui admired the young vision of the designers he stocked. This interest developed into a modernistic theme for his boutiques, which used steel and concrete colours as the background to contemporary collections. He also nurtured the careers of Margaret Howell, Katherine Hammett and John Galliano. In 1983, Joseph introduced his own label, Joseph Tricot, with a sloppy Joe sweater that has sold in various guises since. In 1984, the concept expanded to include tailoring. Men and women of the same mindset used Joseph's basic wardrobe as the building blocks of their style.

► De Castelbajac, Galliano, Hammett, Howell, Kenzo, Khanh

Joseph Ettedgui. b Casablanca (MOR), 1936. **d** London (UK), 2010. **'Red Indians', Joseph Tricot.** Photograph by Michael Roberts, 1986.

Von Etzdorf Georgina

Textile designer

Colour and texture meet on an outfit by the textile design partnership, Georgina von Etzdorf. Golden sunbursts are embroidered onto a woollen gauze vest and devoré velvet is used to give a shadowy, raised pattern to a bias-cut skirt. Foliage and flower motifs, evoking the atmosphere of rural England, typify the work of a company that is inspired by natural imagery. In 1981 Georgina von Etzdorf entered into a partnership with two art school contemporaries: Martin Simcock and Jonathan Docherty. The hand-printing method they developed involves screen-printing supplemented by hand-applied paint strokes, a process that lends individuality to each garment. The designer's contribution to fashion has been to stimulate the use of handmade fabrics, especially for scarves. Velvet and silk is printed with abstract shafts and blocks of colour, the result being a wearable piece of conceptual textile design.

► Cerruti, Lloyd, Mazzilli, Williamson

Georgina von Etzdorf. b Lima (PER), 1955. **Hand-embroidered camisole and velvet devoré skirt, autumn/winter 1998.** Photograph by Howard Sooley.

Eula Joe

Illustrator

Free, vivid colour captures a woman mid-step in a sketch that typifies the art of modern fashion illustration. Eula was a keeper of the graphic tradition of fashion at a time when photography dominated. His fashion illustrations for Italian and French *Harper's Bazaar*, from 1979, used impressionistic watercolour. Eula began his career in the 1950s on the fashion and social pages of the *Herald Tribune*, then worked for *The Sunday Times* in London. Back in New York in the 1960s, he worked on fashion stories for *Life* and designed sets and costumes for the New York City Ballet under George Balanchine. He diversified into television, directing 'fashion specials' for movie stars such as Lauren Bacall. In the 1970s he also worked with Halston, illustrated fashion for *Vogue* and assisted Diana Vreeland, who was then head of the Costume Institute at the Metropolitan Museum of Art in New York.

► Halston, Missoni, Vreeland

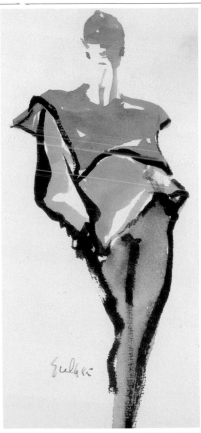

Joe Eula. b Norwalk, CT (USA), 1925. d Kingston, NY (USA), 2004. **Knitwear by Missoni, spring/summer 1985.** Illustration for *Harper's Bazaar.*

Evangelista Linda   Model

Linda's haircut transformed a model into not just a supermodel, but *the* supermodel. In October 1988 *Vogue* photographer Peter Lindbergh persuaded her to have her hair cut short. Evangelista cried throughout, but the crop made her career. Over the following six months, she appeared on the covers of every edition of *Vogue*. Linda knew that the key to longevity was versatility, so she continued to change her haircut and colour every couple of months – and fashion followed. Evangelista's professionalism put her at the top and she became famous for her audacious statements. 'We don't *Vogue* – we are *Vogue*,' was surpassed by a comment that defined the supermodel era: 'We don't wake up for less than $10,000.' While the 'supers' were inevitably equalled by the 1990s beauty cult – that of Stella Tennant and Kate Moss – Evangelista's fame gave her the longevity she was looking for. She has featured on more than 600 magazine covers.

► Bergère, Campbell, Enninful, Garren, Lindbergh, Moss, Twiggy

Linda Evangelista. b St Katherine, ONT (CAN), 1965. **Velvet tank by Kenar, autumn/winter 1997.** Photograph by Rocco Laspata.

Exter Alexandra

Designer

Alexandra Exter, an artist/fashion designer, brings the two disciplines together with *Dama al Ballo*, the painting of a dress that lives somewhere between both. After studying art in Kiev, she went to Paris where she met Pablo Picasso, Georges Braque and Filippo Marinetti. From 1900 to 1914 she travelled between Paris, Moscow and Kiev, spreading the doctrines of Cubism and Futurism among the Russian avant-garde. By 1916 she was working in theatrical costume design in Moscow and in 1921 she became a teacher at the Higher Artistic and Technical Workshops there. She promoted the idea that art and fashion could enhance everyday life and began working in fashion design. She designed proletarian dresses in brightly coloured geometric patterns analogous to the work of her friend Sonia Delaunay. In the traditions of haute couture, she made sumptuously embroidered dresses inspired by peasant art.

► Balla, Capucci, Delaunay

Alexandra Exter. b Kiev (RUS), 1882. d Paris (FR), 1949. **'Dama al Ballo', costume design for a Russian production of the ballet *Romeo and Juliet*.** 1921.

Factor Max

Cosmetics creator

Known as 'Hollywood's make-up wizard', Max Factor oversaw Jean Harlow's *maquillage* – he created a star and started a beauty revolution when he dyed her hair platinum blonde. Harlow's heavy scheme of oily, blackened lids and lips was typical of that used for black-and-white films, which required strong contrasts. Pancake make-up base was created to even out skin tone as films were transformed in the age of colour. It was cosmetics that created the glamorous images of the movie stars and, as they testified to the quality of the products they were using on a daily basis, the general public clamoured for them. Factor's products coincided with an acceptance of coloured cosmetics for women. The studios sent their budding starlets to him for grooming, and in 1937 the Max Factor Hollywood Make-Up Studio opened and Max Factor set about bringing the make-up of the stars to the public.

► Bourjois, Lauder, Revson, Uemura

Max Factor. b Lodz (POL), 1872. **d** Los Angeles, CA (USA), 1938. **Max Factor with Jean Harlow.** 1931.

Farhi Nicole

Designer

Easy, wearable, comfortable linen is the fabric most associated with the work of Nicole Farhi. When she launched her label in 1983, Farhi's clothes became the epitome of understated fashion for women – all based on what she likes to wear. They are not intended to make major fashion statements. Instead, they drift with the differing times, staying in touch with them but always bearing the wearer in mind. Farhi described herself in the *Guardian* as 'a feminist in a soft way', and her clothes appeal to women who are looking for approachable tailoring and casual clothes that have Farhi's own dressed-up European attitude. Farhi studied fashion in Paris and freelanced for de Castelbajac before moving to Britain in 1973 to design for the French Connection chain. In 1989 she introduced menswear to the Farhi label, blending British tailoring and her European unstructured style.

▶ De Castelbajac, Kerrigan, Marant

Nicole Farhi. b Nice (FR), 1946. **Elasticized linen dress, spring/summer 1998.** Photograph by Kelly Klein.

Fath Jacques

Designer

A negative image accentuates a perfect hourglass figure created on a soft line with a curving, structured shape. This evening dress evokes the heady exuberance and gaiety of the early 1950s, when Jacques Fath, called the 'couturier's couturier', was in the same haute couture firmament as Christian Dior. He was famed for his feminine evening dresses, whipped up for royalty and movie stars. This golden era was described by his muse, Bettina, in an interview in 1994. She recalled the extremely creative atmosphere when he worked with assistants who were to succeed in their own right, such as Guy Laroche and Hubert de Givenchy. Fath worked in tandem with the model. He moulded the fabric directly onto her body without any preliminary drawing. Standing in front of a mirror, he would ask her to strike a pose, creating a *théâtre de la mode*, which became the source for the design in the collection.

▶ Bettina, Bourdin, Head, Lagerfeld, Maltézos, Perugia, Pipart

Jacques Fath. b Maisons-Lafitte (FR), 1912. **d** Paris (FR), 1954. **Cocktail dress.** Photograph by Maurice Tabard, *Jardin des Modes*, 1950s.

Fendi Adele & Edoardo

Designers

Fendi's greatest achievement was to update fur's traditional image by giving it a contemporary edge. Here, fox is seen transformed into a punky coat. Adele Casagrande founded the company in 1918, changing its name when she married Edoardo Fendi in 1925. Since then Fendi has remained a family-run business, now managed by granddaughter Silvia after she inherited it from Adele's five daughters. Karl Lagerfeld became creative director in 1965 and introduced the family's now-iconic double-F motif in 1969. Under Lagerfeld the brand continues to make innovations in fur, combining a high-fashion aesthetic with high-tech developments, such as tiny perforations that make the coats lighter to wear. Also renowned for their bags; Fendi's 'Baguette' handbag has become somewhat of an icon, and as such was widely copied when it was reintroduced in the late 1990s.

► Lagerfeld, Léger, Prada, Revillon

Fendi. Adele. b Rome (IT), 1897. **d** Rome (IT), 1978; **Edoardo. b** Rome (IT). (Active 1920s–1950s.) **d** Rome (IT), 1954. **'Feather fox' coat, autumn/winter 1997.** Photograph by Jerome Esch.

Féraud Louis

Designer

Sunny, heavily embroidered clothes are Louis Féraud's métier. The designer says of his work, 'I live in the joy of being surrounded by women, of somehow directing their destiny, in so far as their destiny depends on a note of excess'. In 1955, Féraud opened a boutique in Cannes. He had dressed the young star Brigitte Bardot in an off-the-shoulder, white piqué frock; 600 copies of this dress were sold and Féraud's success was established. Grace Kelly, Ingrid Bergman and Christian Lacroix's mother were also customers. He opened a boutique in Paris where he began to produce couture alongside ready-to-wear, and he and his wife were dubbed 'The Gypsies' because of their bright, Midi-inspired look. In the 1960s, Féraud's work was characterized by simple, architectural shapes with graphic detailing; Twiggy modelled the collections. Féraud designed the costumes for the cult television serial *The Prisoner*.

► Bardot, Blair, Esterel, Ley

Louis Féraud. b Arles (FR), 1920. **d** Paris (FR), 1999. **'Golden Sun' dress, haute couture spring/summer 1997.** Photograph by Sylvie Lancrenon.

Ferragamo Salvatore Shoe designer

This shoe, which marries glamour with imagination, is made of gilded glass mosaic, satin and kid leather. Salvatore Ferragamo was a shoemaker of great originality whose choice of materials made him unique. When leather was in short supply during the Second World War, he experimented with cellophane for the body of his shoes. For soles he revived the use of cork and wood. Amongst his other cobbling innovations were wedge heels, platform soles and the steel shaft that stabilizes spike heels.

Ferragamo's heyday was after the war, when Italian fashion was recovering and film production was booming. Film stars, rich tourists and socialites such as the Duchess of Windsor flocked to his Florence shop. He also earned himself the sobriquet 'shoemaker to the stars' by decorating the feet of two Hollywood generations, stretching from Gloria Swanson in the 1920s to Audrey Hepburn in the 1950s.

► Gucci, Levine, Louboutin, Pfister, Windsor

Salvatore Ferragamo. b Naples (IT), 1898. **d** Flumetto (IT), 1960. **Golden wedge shoe in gilded glass mosaic, satin and kid leather.** 1935.

Ferré Gianfranco

Designer

The dramatic play on proportions of this white taffeta shirt – exaggerated sleeves and cuffs and carefully structured corset – link fashion with Gianfranco Ferré's training as an architect. 'I use the same approach to clothes as I did when I designed buildings,' he says. 'It is basic geometry: you take a flat form and revolve it in space.' Ferré originally worked as a jewellery and accessories designer, before launching a ready-to-wear label in Milan in 1978. In 1989 he was appointed artistic director at Christian Dior; his first collection was inspired by Cecil Beaton's black-and-white costumes for *My Fair Lady* (1964), preferring a neutral palette with dashes of his signature bright red. A perfectionist, his technical skill is shown in his precision tailoring, with a love of proportion-play revealed in his constant reinvention of the white shirt, worn with jodhpurs and evening skirts, but under Ferré's direction it is always glamorized.

► Beaton, Dior, Dolce & Gabbana, Turlington

Gianfranco Ferré. b Legnano (IT), 1944. **d** Milan (IT), 2007. **Taffeta shirt, spring/summer 1994.** Photograph by Kazuo Oishi.

Ferretti Alberta

Designer

Two women recline on a chaise longue in ethereal chiffon dresses. The overall effect is one of old-fashioned prettiness, yet their gaze and pose are self-assured, undermining any sense of passivity that prettiness might imply. 'I like to think I design feminine clothes,' says Ferretti. 'Everything is created by a woman for women, understanding what they want.' That vision is a particularly delicate one. Ferretti developed a special appreciation of textiles, especially daintily beaded or embroidered chiffons and sari silks, through watching her couturière mother at work. A young entrepreneur, she opened her own designer clothes shop at the age of seventeen. At the end of the twentieth century, Ferretti was one of the most powerful businesswomen in Italy, manufacturing not only her own collections but those of Narciso Rodriguez and Jean Paul Gaultier.

► Von Etzdorf, Fendi, Prada, Rodriguez, Roversi

Alberta Ferretti. b Riccione (IT), 1950. **Chiffon dresses, autumn/winter 1997.** Photograph by Paolo Roversi.

Field Patricia

Stylist

Patricia Field, a native New Yorker, began her career with the opening of her Greenwich Village boutique in 1966. For over forty-five years her eclectic designs have been a defining factor in the urban style of New York fashion. More recently Field was propelled into the limelight during her time as costume designer on the television series *Sex and the City*. The show – set and filmed in the atmospheric streets of New York City – became famous for its sharp, well-written episodes and fashion-forward heroines. Field's approach took outfits that would be attention-grabbing but not seasonal; luxury brands like Prada, Louis Vuitton and Gucci were given a witty street edge in Field's hands, worn by Sarah Jessica Parker as the central character, Carrie Bradshaw. Winning an Emmy Award in 2002 for her work on the show, Field was also nominated for an Oscar for her designs for the film *The Devil Wears Prada* (2006).

▶ Apfel, Grand, Lady Gaga, Wintour

Patricia Field. b New York (USA), 1941. **Sarah Jessica Parker filming the title sequence to *Sex and the City*.** 1998.

Fiorucci Elio

Designer

Oliviero Toscani's colourful, sexy images for Fiorucci defined the disco era of the 1970s and early 1980s. The label's skintight Buffalo '70 jeans, worn here by Manhattan modelling queen Donna Jordan, were popular with New York's clubbing crowd. Jackie Kennedy, Diana Ross and Bianca Jagger were all fans. Elio Fiorucci is credited with inventing the concept of designer denim, a theme taken up by Gloria Vanderbilt, Calvin Klein and virtually every label-aware designer since. Fiorucci refused to design for women above a size 10, claiming his clothes suited smaller sizes better. Fiorucci also set out to make fashion fun, creating glittery Plexiglas jewellery and strawberry-scented carrier bags. His cheeky graphics included Vargas-style pin-ups and cherubs wearing sunglasses. He made his name in 1962 with rainbow-coloured Wellington boots. This was Fiorucci's forte: turning function into fashion without losing a sense of fun.

► Benetton, Fisher, Kennedy, T. Roberts

Elio Fiorucci. b Milan (IT), 1935. **Donna Jordan in 'Buffalo '70' advertising campaign.** Photograph by Oliviero Toscani, 1973.

Fisher Donald & Doris (Gap)

Retailers

Born in 1969 during the disillusioned post-hippie era, Gap offered a reactionary-chic approach to the cultural phenomenon of the time. Immaculate, harmonious and unpretentious, it bridged societal fissures, notably the generation gap from which it drew its name. Founded by Donald and Doris Fisher, the company initially sold Levi's jeans and records before creating their own label of basic, modest merchandise in an extensive array of colours and sizes. Serving the homogeneous American masses with its brand of modernism cast in neatly piled, prismatic shades, Gap has become a widely copied retail phenomenon. In recent decades, it has developed the idea of gender integration, selling wardrobe basics with few differences between the men's and women's lines and pioneering the concept of 'androgynous chic'. The company has five primary brands: Old Navy, Banana Republic, Piperlime, Athleta and the namesake Gap.

► Benetton, Fiorucci, Strauss, Topshop

Fisher. Donald. b San Francisco, CA (USA), 1928. **d** San Francisco, CA (USA), 2009. **Doris. b** San Francisco, CA (USA), 1932. **'Khaki' campaign, spring/summer 1998.** Photograph by Walter Chin.

Fish Michael (Mr Fish) Designer

Matching shirt, tie and waistcoat exemplify the work of Michael Fish. He was Swinging London's fey fashion boy and image-maker, whose camp, outrageous style defined 'flower power'. In 1965 he dressed the actor Terence Stamp in matching Liberty prints for the cult movie *Modesty Blaise*. One-inch ties were fashionable; Fish made Stamp's four inches wide. The following year he opened his men's boutique, Mr Fish, in London's Clifford Street near the heartland of tailoring, Savile Row. The clothing ranged from outfits cut from voile, sequins and brocade to flower-printed hats and 'mini-shirts' (as famously worn by Mick Jagger for the Rolling Stones' Hyde Park concert). Other clients included Lord Snowdon and the Duke of Bedford. 'The people in my shop don't dress to conform to any given image,' said Fish. 'They dress as they do because they're confident in themselves. They're blowing their minds.'

► Gilbey, Liberty, Nutter, Snowdon, Stephen

Michael Fish. b Essex (UK), 1940. **Chevron striped waistcoat and giant peaked cap.** Photograph by Bill King, *Queen*, 1970.

Flett John

Designer

A wide-shouldered business jacket, sliced at the chest, is worn over a shirt and gauze skirt and the shoes are turned inside-out. John Flett's clothes were known for their complexity of cut: circular seams, abundant drapes and cavalier shapes that made theatrical figures of those who wore them. Widely respected and admired for his work, Flett was a central figure in the 1980s club scene in London, where he partied with other designers of the time including his former boyfriend John Galliano. They both created theatrical fashion that challenged the status quo but matured into distinctive, directional styles. Flett started his own label in 1988 but closed it down a year later to go freelance. He moved to Europe to work with Claude Montana at Lanvin in Paris and then at Enrico Coveri in Milan, but died of a heart attack, aged twenty-seven, before his promise could be fulfilled.

► Boy George, Cox, Galliano, Montana

John Flett. b London (UK), 1964. **d** Florence (IT), 1991. **Tailored jacket and gauze trousers.** Photograph by Jill Furmanovsky, *The Face*, 1985.

Foale Marion & Tuffin Sally (Foale & Tuffin)   Designers

Wearing a miniskirt, the uniform of the time, Twiggy swings her fringed sleeves for Cecil Beaton in 1967. 'We made Swinging Sixties clothes,' says Marion Foale of the fashion company she set up in 1961 with Sally Tuffin. The pair were taught at the Royal College of Art by Janey Ironside, who was an influential force in British fashion. After graduating in 1961 and deciding that they didn't want to make 'elderly clothes', the two designers set to work in their bedsits on a range of bright, fun dresses, skirts and tops. They were picked up by a London store that had just established a 'young' department, and David Bailey photographed Foale and Tuffin's clothes for *Vogue* just as London's 'youthquake' movement took hold. They opened a shop on Carnaby Street and became allied to a group of British designers, including Mary Quant, dedicated to producing affordable fashion for teenage and twenty-something customers.

▶ D. Bailey, Charles, Betsey Johnson, Quant, Twiggy

Marion Foale. b London (UK), 1939; **Sally Tuffin. b** London (UK), 1938. **Twiggy wears a white minidress.** Photograph by Sir Cecil Beaton, 1967.

Fonssagrives Lisa   Model

Photographed by her husband Irving Penn, Lisa Fonssagrives wears a 'harlequin' opera outfit from 1950. Once described as 'the highest paid, highest praised, high-fashion model in the business', Fonssagrives used to call herself simply 'the clothes hanger'. In the 1930s she moved to Paris from Sweden to train for the ballet. Here she met and married another dancer, Fernand Fonssagrives, who took some pictures of her to *Vogue*. She was immediately sent to see Horst; his assistant, Scavullo, later recalled,

'She had a marvellous profile and moved like a dream.' Fonssagrives was famous for her grace and poise, learnt from her ballet background. She called modelling 'still-dancing' and referred to her poses as 'arrested dance movements'. She became one of the most sought-after models in Paris in the 1930s and 1940s and in New York in the 1950s.

▶ Bettina, Horst, Penn, Scavullo

Lisa Fonssagrives. b Gothenburg (SWE), 1911. **d** New York (USA), 1992. **Harlequin dress.** Photograph by Irving Penn, 1950.

Fontana Zoe, Micol & Giovanna (Sorelle Fontana) Designers

A monkishly simple, white satin dress, with half-sleeves, boat neck and gently belled skirt, is decorated with embroidery formed from cord. It plays on the cotton dresses worn by gamines such as Audrey Hepburn and Brigitte Bardot but the Fontana sisters were always associated with the aristocracy and society figures such as Jackie Kennedy, for whom they provided evening gowns and tailored suits. Roman couture also appealed to movie stars. Their most famous client was the film actress Ava Gardner, whom they dressed for *The Barefoot Contessa* (1954). One of their most memorable outfits was the impish Cardinal outfit, which featured a black hat and black dress with a white collar set off by a jewelled cross. The fashion house of the Fontana family was founded in Parma, Italy, in 1907. The three Fontana sisters, Zoe, Micol and Giovanna, moved to Rome in the 1930s. There they established their own house in 1943.

► Galitzine, W. Klein, Schuberth, Watanabe

Fontana. Zoe. b Parma (IT), 1911. d Rome (IT), 1978; Micol. b Parma (IT), 1913; Giovanna. b Rome (IT), 1915. d 2004. Dorothy McGowan wears Fontana, Rome. Photograph by William Klein, 1962.

Fonticoli Nazareno & Savini Gaetano (Brioni)   Tailors

This 1971 high-waisted, double-breasted dinner suit, together with a car coat, describes the progressive tailoring of Rome's extrovert menswear house, Brioni. From the 1954 futuristic space-age suit to the Maharajah styles, which were popular in mid-1960s London, and the elegant tailoring devised for Pierce Brosnan's role as James Bond, Brioni left no avenue unexplored in men's couture. Its colourful silks and metallic threads, rarely seen since the eighteenth century, heralded the 'male peacock revolution' in the late 1950s. Even though the use of tunics, bolero jackets, lace and macramé clearly contrasts with the Anglo-Saxon tradition, a Brioni blazer epitomized elegance and flaunted wealth in preppie, early 1980s California. Having been responsible for the first ever men's catwalk show in 1952, Brioni inaugurated prêt-couture six years later, resolving flow production methods within a made-to-measure system.

▶ Bikkembergs, Brooks, Gilbey, Nutter, G. Versace

Nazareno Fonticoli. b Penne (IT), 1906. **d** Penne (IT), 1981; **Gaetano Savini. b** Rome (IT), 1910. **d** Rome (IT), 1987. **Evening suit and car coat.** 1971.

Forbes Simon

Hairdresser

This stark, androgynous image of hair fashion is the work of Simon Forbes, owner of Antenna, the salon famous for developing hair extensions. The picture represents hair as sculpture and created a cutting-edge, 'anti-beauty' statement that followed from the punk and new wave proclivity for making hair an intrinsic part of the costume. Forbes invented the Monofibre Extensions technique, which allowed greater creativity for stylists to do this. Synthetic hair was grafted onto real hair to give it instant and dramatic length. It was often dyed with vivid colours and wrapped with rags. With this and his electric clippering and precision razoring, Forbes became the directional hairdresser of the early 1980s and his salon became a fashion venue. Extensions, which were inspired by the urban street style of Rastafarians, were sported by musicians such as Boy George and Annie Lennox.

► Boy George, Ettedgui, Recine, Stewart

Simon Forbes. b London (UK), 1950. **Fibre dreadlocks for Antenna.** Photograph by Mike Owen, 1982.

Ford Tom

Designer

Pinstripes for a man and woman, body-conscious shirts and a shining G: all elements that contributed to Tom Ford's unmistakable image for Gucci. As creative director he took styling from the 1970s and created a culture of seasonal icons: handbags and shoes that shine brightly for six months but become redundant through their high-fashion visibility. Ford's success is rooted in his American blend of sexy, market-aware commercialism married with Italian craftsmanship. As John Fairchild, owner of the

fashion trade paper *Women's Wear Daily*, wrote in 1989, the year before Ford joined Gucci, 'If American designers were working in Europe with the…eagerness to be different for novelty's sake…they could be better style leaders than anyone.' In 2004 Ford left Gucci to launch his own label with his colleague Domenico de Sole. The designer has also branched out of fashion, enjoying praise as a film director with his debut film *A Single Man* (2009).

► Gucci, Halston, Lagerfeld, Pilati, Saint Laurent, Testino

Tom Ford. b Austin, TX (USA), 1962. **Evening outfits for Gucci, autumn/winter 1996.** Photograph by Mario Testino.

Formichetti Nicola

Designer / Stylist

Digital media-obsessed Nicola Formichetti discovered Rick Genest – starring here in Mugler's autumn/winter 2011 campaign – via his Facebook page, and exposed the tattoo devotee to the international limelight. Formichetti had just been appointed creative director of Thierry Mugler and was charged with resuscitating the brand. The designer enlisted Genest – aka Zombie Boy – to personify its bold resurrection. Raised in both Tokyo and Rome, Formichetti first delved into fashion working at London shop The Pineal Eye. He is now a global fashion phenomenon, from styling friend and collaborator Lady Gaga, to his role as fashion director for Japanese mass-market retailer Uniqlo. Formerly editor-in-chief of *Vogue Hommes* Japan, Formichetti regularly contributes to *V*, *VMAN* and *Dazed & Confused* magazines. His experimental and playful vision has won him the status of guru to some of today's most influential fashion players.

► Blow, Lady Gaga, Mugler, Toskan & Angelo

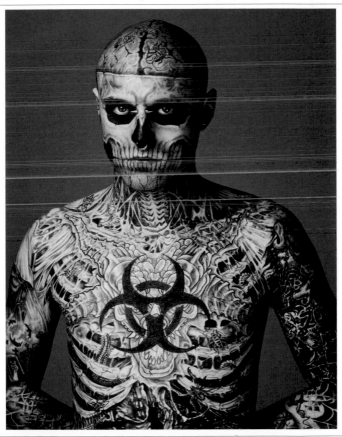

Nicola Formichetti. b Tokyo (JAP), 1977. **Rick Genest in Mugler's autumn/winter 2011 campaign.** Photograph by Mariano Vivanco.

Fortuny Mariano

Designer

The Delphos was constructed from four to five widths of silk that were sewn into a tubular shape and secured at the shoulder, as Lillian Gish demonstrates. The cord around her neckline added finish to the gown and also served to adjust the fit. Fortuny started to design his Delphos around 1907 when a nostalgia for Classical Greece was beginning to be felt in fashion, art and theatre. However, what made Fortuny's Delphos unique was its pleating, a secret process he patented in 1909. Named after the Ancient Greek sanctuary of Delphi, Fortuny's garment derived from the *chiton*, a tunic worn by Classical Greek charioteers that focused on the natural shape of the body. Since the Delphos emphasized the female form in movement, it was popular among actresses and dancers such as Isadora Duncan. Trained as an artist, Fortuny advocated a timeless form of dress and continued to create the Delphos right up to his death.

► Chow, Lester, McFadden, Miyake, Poiret

Mariano Fortuny. b Granada (SP), 1871. **d** Venice (IT), 1949. **Lillian Gish wears a Delphos dress.** *c.*1920.

Fratini Gina

Designer

The range of Byronic details used on this gown distinguishes it as the work of Gina Fratini. Unafraid of romantic themes, she trimmed cuffs with rosebuds and edged frills with lace on her chiffon, lawn and silk gauze dresses. Historical references, such as off-the-shoulder 'Winterhalter' necklines and pin-tucked bodices usually seen on Victorian nightgowns, added to that charm. For this reason her wedding dresses were particularly popular. Fratini's romanticism came to the fore in 1971 when Norman Parkinson delivered samples of her work to Princess Anne in preparation for her twenty-first-birthday portrait. She chose a classic Fratini gown with a lace-trimmed ruff that co-ordinated with her pretty, tawny pink make-up. After her own business closed, Fratini designed lingerie with Ossie Clark as well as collections for Norman Hartnell and for private clients, including the Princess of Wales.

► Ashley, Clark, Diana, Emanuel, Hartnell, Parkinson

Gina Fratini. b Kobe (JAP), 1931. **Cream chiffon dress.** Photograph by Sir Norman Parkinson, British *Vogue*, 1973.

French John

Photographer

A formal velvet coat is given a surreal treatment by John French. Originally a graphic designer, he believed, 'You have to compose a picture in the view-finder exactly as if it were an artist's picture on the canvas.' His black-and-white portraits were always perfectly arranged. 'Fill in the space. The space round the subject is as important as the subject itself,' he would say. French's apparently impromptu style contrasted with the posed formality of fashion photography in the early 1950s. One of Britain's first model talent-spotters, he encouraged Barbara Goalen and others to develop their own personalities in front of the lens. The hand intruding at the bottom of the picture doesn't belong to French. He never actually released the camera shutter himself; instead he would direct set, lighting and model, then tell his assistant (at times David Bailey or Terence Donovan) to take the photograph.

► D. Bailey, Bruyère, Goalen, Morton

John French. b London (UK), 1907. **d** London (UK), 1966. **Fur-trimmed velvet coat by Digby Morton.** *Daily Express*, 1955.

Frissell Toni

Photographer

Toni Frissell's fashion photographs of the 1930s through to the 1950s captured the idyllic sense of the rich at play. Here, a model swims in her gown to illustrate its flowing material. With the innate nonchalance of an aristocrat, Frissell documented her world of wealthy playgrounds. Some of her vivid fashion images were of the beach, featuring playful swimwear and recreation dresses, and crisp tennis outfits. Frissell loved the outdoor setting and sunlight's play at least as much as the clothes or model,

and let that casual naturalism permeate photographs for *Vogue* and *Harper's Bazaar*. Frissell's images appear effortless, whether of dogs, children, fox-hunting, war or fashion. She mingled the snapshot's vitality and compassion with traditional composition. Frissell recorded a charmed life in every way, including radiant photographs of the 1953 wedding of John F. Kennedy and Jacqueline Bouvier.

► Horst, Kennedy, McLaughlin-Gill, Vallhonrat

Toni Frissell. b New York (USA), 1907. **d** New York (USA), 1988. **Weeki Wachee Spring, Florida.** *Harper's Bazaar*, 1947.

Frizon Maud

Shoe designer

Maud Frizon is known for her shoes with cone-shaped heels, a black suede pair of which are the only garments worn in this picture. The role of the man is to communicate the sexual intention of Frizon's work. 'A shoe has to make you look beautiful. You can be wearing a simple dress, but if you have something exquisite on your feet, it becomes a perfect look,' said Frizon, who gained this understanding as a model for Courrèges, Nina Ricci, Jean Patou and Christian Dior. She decided to design shoes when she was unable to find styles to go with the designers' clothes on her modelling assignments (in the 1960s models were expected to provide their own shoes). In 1970 she created her first collection of witty, sexy shoes, all hand-cut and finished. There were queues outside her tiny shop on Paris's rue Saint Germain. Brigitte Bardot was a fan, particularly of Frizon's innovative, zipless, high-heeled Russian boots and simple girlie pumps.

► Bardot, Courrèges, Jourdan, Kélian, Patou, Ricci

Maud Frizon (Maud Frizon De Marco). b Paris (FR), 1941. **Heeled pumps.** Photograph by Dominique Issermann, 1989.

Von Fürstenberg Diane   Designer

Diane von Fürstenberg wears her own fashion phenomenon for the cover of *Newsweek*. The real appeal of her wrap dress was its wearable shape and endless versatility. Smart yet sexy, it looked as good at the disco as it did at the office. The designer called it 'Simple one-step dressing. Chic, comfortable and sexy. It won't become dated after one season. It works around the clock, travels across the world and fits all a woman's priorities.' An ex-model, von Fürstenberg partied at Studio 54 and was briefly married to Fiat heir Prince Egon von Fürstenberg. The glamorous divorcée's jet-set lifestyle contributed to the cachet of her dresses. Originally launched in 1972, the DVF wrap dresses contrasted with the unisex trouser suits of the time and the swing tickets attached made this point with the words, 'Feel like a woman. Wear a dress.' Her clothes have been worn by many celebrities, including Michelle Obama and the Duchess of Cambridge.

▶ Bergère, Karan, De Ribes, Scavullo, Vanderbilt

Diane von Fürstenberg. b Brussels (BEL), 1946. **Wrap dress.** Photograph by Francesco Scavullo, *Newsweek* cover, 1976.

Galanos James

Designer

With this perfectly plain, wool dress, Galanos displays the reason why he was dubbed 'America's couturier'. 'I never deviated from what was most important, which was quality,' said Galanos, who actually produced the highest class of ready-to-wear. Nancy Reagan claimed, 'You can take one of Jimmy's dresses and just wear it inside out, they're so beautifully made.' The simplicity of his designs was deceptive and he used couture-standard dressmaking techniques, which made his pieces expensive. Galanos worked in Hollywood with John Louis, head of costume design at Columbia, who soon found his fledgling designer's clothes were as popular with the stars as his own. Having later trained with Robert Piguet in Paris, Galanos opened a small shop in Los Angeles in 1951. His designs were discovered by a senior buyer at Neiman Marcus, who claimed she had found 'a young designer from California who would set the world on fire'.

► Adolfo, Louis, Piguet, Simpson

James Galanos. b Philadelphia, PA (USA), 1925. **Black wool dress.** Photograph by Kourken Pakchanian, American *Vogue*, 1973.

Galitzine Irene   Designer

William Klein arranges a party of variously uniformed men as accessories for Irene Galitzine's evening trouser outfits. They are variations of her famous wide-leg trouser suits which were dubbed 'palazzo pyjamas' by Diana Vreeland, then at *Harper's Bazaar*. Galitzine's aristocratic Russian family fled the Revolution in 1918. She studied art in Rome, English at Cambridge and French at the Sorbonne. Galitzine finished her broad education as an assistant to the Fontana sisters in Rome.

Her own collection, first designed in 1959, suggested an international, yet easy way of dressing. It blurred the distinction between day- and eveningwear and made a relaxed alternative to formal cocktail dresses. It was a look that immediately appealed to the Italian aristocracy. Her draped sari-style tunics could be worn for day or evening, and were favoured by Elizabeth Taylor, Greta Garbo and Sophia Loren.

► Fontana, Garbo, W. Klein, Pulitzer, Vreeland

Irene Galitzine. b Tiflis (RUS), 1916. **d** Rome (IT), 2006. **'Palazzo pyjamas.'** Photograph by William Klein, 1962.   203

Galliano John

Designer

This show-stopping creation is a fitting example of designer John Galliano's trademark flamboyance and cheeky wit. A prodigious talent, Galliano caught the fashion world's attention with 'Les Incroyables', his graduation collection from Saint Martins School of Art in 1984. Launching his own label in the same year, he quickly made a name for himself as a master of intricate couture techniques and expert bias cuts. In 1995 he was appointed creative director of Givenchy, the first British designer to head a French couture house. A year later he moved to Dior, where his romantic sensibility produced spectacular collections, referencing *Madame Butterfly*, Napoleon and Josephine and *A Streetcar Named Desire*. In 2011 he was dismissed from Dior, a victim of what journalist Suzy Menkes described as the 'perfect storm' of increasing commercial pressure and the ruthless commodification of talent that bedevils the fashion industry.

► Dior, Gaultier, Givenchy, LaChapelle, Poiret

John Galliano. b Gibraltar (SP), 1960. **John Galliano spring/summer 1992 hat collection.** Photograph by Julio Donoso, 1991.

Garbo Greta

Icon

Called the 'greatest star of all', Greta Garbo wears a masculine jacket, cut with sexual ambiguity, in a portrait by Cecil Beaton. Beaton wrote of his subject, 'Perhaps no other person has had such an influence on the appearance of a whole generation...the secret of her appeal seems to lie in an elusive and haunting sensitivity... Garbo has created a style in fashion which is concerned with her individual self.' Garbo arrived in Hollywood aged nineteen in the entourage of Mauritz Stiller from Sweden.

Signed up by Metro-Goldwyn-Mayer, she went on to star in *Queen Christina* (1933), *Camille* (1936) and *Anna Karenina* (1935), dressed by Adrian. Famed as a recluse, she said in 1932, 'I am awkward, shy, afraid, nervous and self-conscious about my English. That is why I built a wall of repression about myself and lived behind it.' The director George Cukor said that she reserved 'her real sensuousness for the camera'.

► Adrian, Beaton, Galitzine, Sui

Greta Garbo. b Stockholm (SWE), 1905. **d** New York (USA), 1990. **Greta Garbo.** Photograph by Sir Cecil Beaton, 1946.

Garren

Hairdresser

From the strawberry-red, Sophia Loren bouffant to the boyish, platinum, Andy Warhol bob, Garren has been the architect behind all of supermodel Linda Evangelista's publicized, chameleon-like hairstyle changes. His directional approach has been witnessed not only in the high-glam look he achieved in collaboration with photographer Steven Meisel in the late 1980s, but also in the spiky 'chicken do' (his trademark punk-inspired style seen earlier that decade), which he modified in the softer, more feminine gamine cut seen in the wake of the waif look. His extreme work in editorial and on the catwalk for Marc Jacobs and Anna Sui is tempered in the salon where he gives reality a chance. As he told American *Vogue*, 'As soon as a client comes in…I'm checking out the way she moves, her shoes, her handbag and body language. That tells me what her needs are.'

▶ Evangelista, Jacobs, Meisel, Recine, Warhol

Garren Defazio). b 1948. **Garren with Linda Evangelista.** Photograph by Peter Lindbergh, *Harper's Bazaar*, 1997.

Gattinoni Fernanda   Designer

The serene allure of Gattinoni's brilliant green, brocade evening coat is captured by Clifford Coffin in a photograph for American *Vogue* in 1947. Hinting at Imperial Chinese influences, its Zen-like dignity anticipates the refined ethnicity of Romeo Gigli. Gattinoni trained at the Rome fashion house Ventura, before opening her own atelier. Here she attracted the likes of Audrey Hepburn, Ingrid Bergman and Anna Magnani – film-star clients renowned for their highly

photogenic mix of thoroughbred grace and soft femininity. In the 1950s, with the great success of films such as *Roman Holiday* (1953), Rome became synonymous with the glamour of cinema and Gattinoni came to epitomize cultured European sophistication and romance. She also offered indulgent escapism – twenty-five full-time embroiderers were employed to decorate wedding dresses – for a clientele weary of postwar realities.

► Coffin, Gigli, Molyneux

Fernanda Gattinoni. b Cocquio (IT), 1907. **d** Rome (IT), 2002. **Brocade evening coat.** Photograph by Clifford Coffin, American *Vogue*, 1947.

207

Gaultier Jean Paul   Designer

The Breton stripe, modelled here by Hannelore Knuts, is given iconic status by *l'enfant terrible* fashion designer Jean Paul Gaultier. Since establishing his label in 1978, he has taken inspiration from a variety of influences, from the traditional ethnic textiles and techniques of historic costume, to the dishevelled garb of London's punks. Playing with sexual iconography – from the ambiguity of men in skirts, to the overtly erotic costumes of Madonna's 'Blonde Ambition' tour – has become his trademark. His menswear uses camp clichés of macho bodybuilders and butch sailors, simultaneously celebrating and challenging archetypal gender roles. His skillful ability to adapt pop culture has given success on and off the runway, designing costumes for films such as *The Fifth Element* (1997). As with most of his work, his style is a humorous, energetic and eclectic challenge to the French establishment.

▶ Alexandre, Van Beirendonck, Galliano, Madonna, Margiela, Pita

Jean Paul Gaultier. b Arcueil (FR), 1952. **Gaultier's 'Les Indes Galantes' (Romantic India) spring/summer 2000 haute couture collection.** Photograph by Patrice Sable.

Gernreich Rudi

Designer

The topless bathing suit, worn here by Peggy Moffitt, Rudi Gernreich's favourite model, was developed to meet the trend for topless bathing. It was also intended to be something of a feminist statement, as was his no-bra bra of 1964, which was the first to allow the natural shape of a woman's breasts. Gernreich also invented the high-cut, buttock-baring, thong bathing suit. His radical body-based clothes of the 1960s and 1970s reflected the social revolution of women's liberation and his early designs provided unprecedented freedom of movement. In the 1950s he produced knitted swimwear without the usual boning and underpinning and he developed the concept into tube dresses. It was Gernreich's early influences that helped to develop our relationship between stretch and comfort; Rudi joined several modern dance companies and became fascinated by the leotards and tights of the dancers.

► Coffin, Heim, Rabanne, Sassoon

Rudi Gernreich. b Vienna (AUS), 1922. **d** Los Angeles, CA (USA), 1985. **Peggy Moffitt wears a topless swimsuit.** Photograph by William Claxton, 1964.

Ghesquière Nicolas   Designer

After serving an internship with agnès b and assisting Jean Paul Gaultier, Nicolas Ghesquière was plucked from relative obscurity to become the creative director at Balenciaga in 1997. He reinvigorated the brand with electrifying, cutting-edge collections, mixing minimalism with technology to design clothes 'for a woman who is looking to the future'. His spring/summer 2007 collection for Balenciaga was just that. Ghesquière produced a vision of fashion's future. The model is as sharp, slick and cool as the black-and-white printed silk dress and black leather waistcoat she wears, cut around the body with a laser precision. Her jointed leggings in gleaming silver, gold and black metal are astonishingly delicate pieces of armour, while her scraped-back hair and gargantuan goggles complete the silhouette of a futuristic fashion android. Ghesquière's fifteen-year tenure at Balenciaga ended in 2012.

► Balenciaga, Gaultier, Kane, Simons, Tisci

Nicolas Ghesquière. b Comines (FR), 1971. **Ghesquière's metallic leggings for Balenciaga spring/summer 2007.** Photograph by Chris Moore.

Gibb Bill

Designer

'Miles of untouched forest hand-printed onto silk… the Bill Gibb environment, rich fabrics with richer decorations – marbled, hand-painted, feathered, piped… flower-faced beauty.' As it is, the words that accompanied this editorial picture left out a few of the techniques used on Gibb's lavish, layered and fantastical dress. He claimed to have an aversion to 'the tailored thing' and his grand vision was an alternative to the lean trouser suits of the 1970s. Gibb came from a farming family, but was encouraged by his grandmother, a painter, to enjoy his hobby of copying pictures of historical costume, especially that of the Renaissance era. This influence has affected his most spectacular work. He often incorporated knitwear into his collection by collaborating with Missoni and knitting specialist Kaffe Fassett, saying, 'What women want to wear in the daytime is beautiful knits.'

► Birtwell, Mesejeán & Cancela, Missoni, Porter

Bill Gibb. b Fraserburgh, Aberdeenshire (UK), 1943. **d** London (UK), 1988. **'Forest' dress.** Photograph by Gianni Penati, British *Vogue*, 1972.

Gibson Charles Dana

Illustrator

Before television and movies, Gibson identified an essential character as deftly and as unforgettably as any novelist. His 'Gibson Girl' was the personification of America's modern woman. Probably seen wearing the fashionable shirtwaist (a masculine-styled blouse of the early twentieth century), her S-curve figure and loosely constructed mound of hair gave shape to the new woman. Her face varied slightly, but she was the icon of twentieth-century fashion embodied in an active life in such Gibson

books on the middle and upper-middle classes as *The Education of Mr Pipp* (1899), *The Americans* (1900) and *The Social Ladder* (1902). Gibson had studied at the Art Students' League in New York and worked for late nineteenth-century magazines that required illustrations for news and stories, but ultimately he invented his own story of the fashionable, independent woman of the twentieth century.

▶ Von Drecoll, Paquin, Redfern

Charles Dana Gibson. b Roxbury, MA (USA), 1867. **d** New York (USA), 1944. **Gibson Girls on the beach.** 1901.

Gigli Romeo

Designer

Benedetta Barzini is photographed enjoying Romeo Gigli's extravagant coat. Gold flowers and embroidered leaves collect around the shawl collar, cuffs and hem. Gigli's childhood was saturated in art history. It gave him an appreciation of beauty, and history and travel underly his work – playing with elements from historical costume and non-European dress. The Gigli look was, and still is, one of the most distinctive in fashion. In the 1980s, Gigli's vision had a grandeur only equalled by that of Christian Lacroix. Silk suits, with either stovepipe trousers or long, narrow skirts, were worn with shirt collars that framed the wearer's face (as here) and placed under velvet coats that enveloped the figure in luxury. The impression was similar to that created by Poiret: a decorated bloom growing from a narrow stalk. A large collection of Gigli's most representative clothes and accessories are held by the Metropolitan Museum of Art, New York.

► Gattinoni, Iribe, Meisel, Poiret, Roversi, Vallhonrat

Romeo Gigli. b Faenza (IT), 1949. **Benedetta Barzini wears an embroidered coat.** Photograph by Steven Meisel, French *Vogue*, 1989.

Gilbey Tom

Designer

This is classic Tom Gilbey. With his trademark simplicity and an almost militaristic neatness, Gilbey was an important force in menswear in the 1960s. Here, he uses both traditionally masculine details and softer, experimental methods, such as sleeves gathered into cuffs. Despite their feminized aspects, these outfits are strong, angular examples of the new wave of British tailoring. Gilbey began designing for John Michael and in 1968 opened his own shop, in London's Sackville Street.

Gilbey is one of fashion's visionaries. In 1982 he launched a waistcoat collection that suited the aspirational yuppie. Around the same time, and pre-dating the transatlantic sportswear boom by fifteen years, he said, 'I'm influenced by the American campus look, it's so classic and immaculate. Jeans and a T-shirt, big bumper shoes, Bermuda shorts... I hate fuss. I love things to be clean, strong and aggressive.'

► Brioni, Fish, Fonticoli, Nutter, Stephen

Tom Gilbey. b London (UK), 1938. **Winter coats.** 1971.

De Givenchy Hubert   Designer

Snap! Audrey Hepburn, playing a model, is captured in a still from the film *Funny Face* (1957). Her dress, a floral cotton gown, is by the man who became a lifelong friend and collaborator. 'It was as though I was born to wear his clothes,' said Hepburn of Hubert de Givenchy. When she was first sent to his house, Givenchy was expecting the other 'Miss Hepburn' – Katharine. His disappointment gave way to adoration. He had already worked at Lelong, Piguet, Fath and Schiaparelli, before opening his couture house at the age of twenty-five. Encouraged by Balenciaga, he specialized in clothes for the new era of air travel and grand eveningwear. In 1956 Givenchy banned the press from his shows, saying, 'A fashion house is a laboratory which must conserve its mystery.' He retired in 1995, making way for two of the most publicity-aware designers – John Galliano and Alexander McQueen – to design under his name.

► Horvat, Lelong, Pipart, Tiffany, Venet

Hubert de Givenchy. b Beauvais (FR), 1927. **Audrey Hepburn.** Still from *Funny Face*, 1957.

Goalen Barbara

Model

The archetypal 1950s aloof and haughty mannequin, the well-bred Goalen was chauffeur-driven to assignments in a Rolls-Royce. Careful to protect her image, she said, 'I always did high fashion and I never touched anything that wasn't high quality.' The photographer Henry Clarke said, 'You put the dress on Barbara and she made it sing.' At one time she was almost exclusively photographed by John French and was Coffin's favourite model. She was the first British model to be sent to the Paris shows by British *Vogue*. At the height of her fame, she toured Australia and was mobbed in the North of England. Like many models in the 1950s, she married well – to Lloyd's underwriter Nigel Campbell. Her hips were too slender for sample sizes, so she rarely did catwalk modelling. She only worked for five years, before retiring while still very much in demand.

► Bettina, Clarke, Coffin, French

Barbara Goalen. b (MAL), 1921. **d** London (UK), 2002. **Strapless evening dress.** Photograph by John French, 1954.

Godley Georgina

Designer

An otherwise utterly plain, jersey T-shirt dress springs away from the average with the introduction of organza into the hem and neck. An experimental purist, Georgina Godley uses sculpture to introduce avant-garde shape into her work. 'We are dealing with a woman who is an individual now,' she told *Vogue*. 'Fashion is so retrograde, putting people down. It's not a designer's personality you're buying, it's yours. I believe in a reappraisal of sexual roles.' Her contemporary work is in contrast to the historicism explored during her partnership with Scott Crolla. Their cult shop, Crolla (opened in 1981), stocked romantic men's clothes in velvet and brocade, which matched the New Romantic mood. After parting from him in 1985, Godley developed her own line, favouring a one-to-one relationship with the client, in which her creativity could be displayed by women who relish her individual experiments.

▶ Audibet, Bruce, Crolla

Georgina Godley. b London (UK), 1955. **Cotton jersey body-and-soul dress.** Photograph by Alex Chatelain, British *Vogue*, 1986. 217

Grand Katie

Stylist

Fashion in the new millennium has seen the birth of the 'superstar stylist', a title for which Katie Grand is undoubtedly the poster girl. A student of Central Saint Martins in London, Grand honed her skills in the 1990s at *Dazed & Confused*, later becoming fashion director of style bible *The Face* in 1999, and launching her own magazine *POP* in 2000. Now Grand is in high demand for her freelance styling for fashion houses such as Louis Vuitton, Proenza Schouler and her friend Giles Deacon,

alongside editorials for *W, Vogue* and *Interview* where she is contributing style director in addition to her own magazine, *LOVE*. Her emphasis is on strong image-led content and lyrical – sometimes controversial – covers, often featuring famous faces. Here Kate Moss, shot by Mert & Marcus, appears to defy gravity perched in the bathtub, semi-submerged in glistening, foaming water.

► Deacon, Enninful, Formichetti, McGrath, Mert & Marcus, Moss

Katie Grand. b Leeds, West Yorkshire (UK), 1971. *LOVE* **magazine issue nine, featuring Kate Moss, styled by Katie Grand.** Photograph by Mert & Marcus, 2013.

Grès Madame

Designer

The white, silk jersey fabric of this evening gown has been moulded onto the figure as if it had the properties of the piece of sculpture standing next to the model. Even the play of light and shade in its deep pleats echoes the sculpture. Silk jersey is a material that lends itself to pleating in precise, fluid folds and it was a mainstay in the classicism of Madame Alix Grès, one of the great couture artists. *Harper's Bazaar* proclaimed in 1936 that, 'Alix stands for the body rampant, for the rounded, feminine

sculptural form beneath the dress'. She had been trained as a sculptress and it was her feeling for Classical Greek sculpture that enabled her to capture its timeless elegance in her evening gowns. Hers was an individualistic, uncompromising style where the sculptural cut of her gowns had the liquid effect of the 'wet' drapery of Classical Greek sculpture that turned fashionable women into living statues.

▶ Audibet, Cassini, Lanvin, Pertegaz, Toledo, Valentina

Madame Alix Grès (Germaine Krebs). b Paris (FR), 1903. **d** Provence (FR), 1993. **Grecian column dress.** Photograph by Eugène Rubin, *Femina*, 1937.

Griffe Jacques

Designer

In a picture from an American *Vogue* sitting in 1952, the model's seated pose makes a display of Jacques Griffe's diaphanous pin-tucks. The entire evening dress grows from a flamboyant pink tulle bow which uses the fabric of both bodice and skirt. It finishes ten inches from the floor – a younger look for ball gowns at the time and known as the ballet length. Griffe trained with Vionnet where he learned the techniques of draping and cutting fabrics, such as this luscious chiffon, from the Lyons textile firm Bianchini-Férier, noted for its fluid materials in brilliant colours. After the Second World War, Griffe worked for Molyneux before opening his own *maison de couture* in 1946. Like Vionnet, he worked directly with the material, modelling it on a wooden dummy. Griffe's tailoring work was distinguished by the use of seams and darts as decorative details and by his invention of the boxy jacket.

► McLaughlin-Gill, Molyneux, Vionnet

Jacques Griffe. b Carcassonne (FR), 1917. **d** 1996. **Tulle dress.** Photograph by Frances McLaughlin-Gill, American *Vogue*, 1952.

Gruau René

Illustrator

In this suggestive advertisement for Christian Dior, the sinuous lines of a woman's hand are placed on a panther's paw, reflecting a spirit of graceful worldliness and glamour. Noted for his strong silhouettes and tonalities of colour, Gruau's images became prestigious icons of elegance. He was an outstanding graphic artist of the period after the Second World War, when his swift, expressive line was chosen by Dior's couture and perfume company to illustrate their perfume advertisements.

Together with Bouché, Gruau also brilliantly illustrated haute couture of the era in French *Vogue*. Influenced by the posters of Toulouse-Lautrec, he used strong outlines – a technique that perfectly accentuates fashion's shape and form. He was one of the last grand magazine illustrators before the creative possibilities of fashion photography made it equal to the fantasy of illustration.

► Berthoud, Biagiotti, Bouché, Dior, Gustafson

René Gruau. b Rimini (IT), 1908. **d** Rome (IT), 2004. **Panther Paw.** Advertisement for 'Miss Dior' perfume, 1949.

Gucci Guccio

On a terrace in Cannes, Romy Schneider caresses the classic Gucci loafers worn by Alain Delon. The snaffle loafer has been an icon of wealth and European style since it was designed in 1932 by Guccio Gucci. After rebelling against joining his family's ailing business, Gucci ran away to London. He found a job as maître d'hôtel at the Savoy where he looked after the wealthy guests, paying particular attention to their baggage. He returned to Florence and opened a small shop selling saddlery, later expanding into leather bags and shoes that were decorated with a horse's snaffle. In 1933 Aldo, his son, joined the business and designed the iconic Gucci logo using the interlocking double Gs of his father's initials. Intermittent periods of great success were counterpointed with family squabbles and even murder, marring the Gucci story. The business enjoyed a renaissance under Tom Ford, who was its creative director from 1994 to 2004.

► Fendi, Ferragamo, Ford, Hermès

Guccio Gucci. b Florence (IT), 1881. **d** Milan (IT), 1953. **Alain Delon wears Gucci loafers.** *c.*1959.

Guinness Daphne   Icon

Daphne Guinness, heiress, artist, muse and fashion's rare bird, is captured here by theatrical photographers Markus and Indrani. The elaborately styled Guinness is a stunning and unmistakable sight. Guinness has worked with many designers and photographers during her career – including Tom Ford, Karl Lagerfeld, Philip Treacy, David LaChapelle and her close friend, the late Alexander McQueen – but she is also a creative force in her own right. In particular many of Guinness's designs are inspired by her fascination with armour and fashion's protective qualities. In 2012, Christie's in London held an auction of The Daphne Guinness Collection to benefit the Isabella Blow Foundation, which Guinness founded in memory of her friend. Guinness is an exceptional icon; the very image of personal, individual style, she was celebrated in 2011 in an exhibition devoted to her at the Museum of the Fashion Institute of Technology, New York.

► Blow, Ford, LaChapelle, Lady Gaga, McQueen, Treacy

Daphne Guinness. b London (UK), 1967. **Daphne Guinness on the set of** *Legend of Lady White Snake,* **with creative direction by GK Reid.** Photograph by Markus & Indrani, 2012.

Gustafson Mats

Illustrator

It's difficult to overstate the elegance and artistry of this beautiful Yohji Yamamoto watercolour. The silhouetted figure displays a relaxed posture and easy gait as it strides ahead, echoing the characteristic serenity of the watercolour's muted tones. Illustration had long been eclipsed by photography for showcasing designer collections by the time the illustrator Mats Gustafson began his career in the late 1970s. Nearly single-handedly reinvigorating the medium, his exquisite aquarelle

sketches and cut-out works on paper recast illustration as a conceptual tool, extending its relevance and broadening its expressive possibilities. Early editorial illustration assignments led him to hone his focus on fashion leading to an impressive roster of editorial clients such as *Vogue* and *Visionaire*. His work in advertising has also resulted in stunning collaborations with eminent brands such as Hermès, Tiffany, Dior and Comme des Garçons.

▶ Antonio, Berthoud, Gruau, Roberts, Y. Yamamoto

Mats Gustafson. b Mjölby (SWE), 1951. **Yohji Yamamoto silhouette.** Watercolour illustration, 1997.

Halston

Halston is surrounded by eleven models for a 1972 *Vogue* sitting. Their fluid, silk jersey dresses and svelte clothes made from Ultrasuede are pure Halston: utterly simple and an eternal antidote to fussy dressing. These are the hallmarks of classic American design, and Halston was recognized as a master of the art. His popularity in the 1970s made him a social figure, most famously among the set that frequented Manhattan's Studio 54 club. Bianca Jagger and Liza Minnelli were friends and clients, and both were Concorde-class models for his draped jersey dresses and lean trouser suits. Halston designed for his friends, saying in 1971, 'Fashion starts with fashionable people… No designer has ever made fashion alone. People make fashion,' Although he died in 1990, Halston's influence has continued to grow. Tom Ford, designer at Gucci, acknowledged his Studio 54 look as crucial to uncluttered fashion in the 1990s.

▶ Bandy, Daché, Ford, Maxwell, Peretti, Warhol

Hamnett Katharine

Designer

'At last! An original,' was Prime Minister Margaret Thatcher's response to Katharine Hamnett's anti-missile message when the two met at a British government reception in 1984. Such an easily copied idea (deliberately so, claimed Hamnett, who wanted her messages to be read by as many people as possible) meant that her slogan T-shirts became a symbol of the 1980s. Hamnett has since fostered the connection between cloth and politics, most notably by using and helping with the development of organic cotton. Practicality and youth have always been important to the label – parachute silk, cotton jersey and denim are some of the relaxed and functional fabrics that have been trademarks for Hamnett over the years. She has said of her clothes, 'There is a real utility in them... they're functional, they're easy to look after and they last a long time.'

► Stiebel, Teller, Von Unwerth

Katharine Hamnett. b Gravesend (UK), 1948. **Katharine Hamnett with Margaret Thatcher, 10 Downing Street.** 1984.

Hardy Pierre

Shoe designer

A student of dance as well as fine arts, Pierre Hardy's theatrical background shows in his approach to design. Since his first collection for Christian Dior in 1988, Hardy has demonstrated an affinity not only with fashion, but with broader principles of design and form, be it his own label (launched in 1999) or his collaboration with Nicolas Ghesquière at Balenciaga from 2001 and 2012. Creating a range of strikingly modern footwear – such as his renowned Lego shoes, with geometric, sculptural shapes and primary colours, for autumn/winter 2007 – cemented his reputation, and Balenciaga's, for progressive design. Hardy's influences are drawn from a broad spectrum, including the Abstract Expressionists, renaissance painter Botticelli and the Milan-based Memphis group of designers and architects, with his shoes more resembling miniature buildings than footwear, with their pointed shapes and razor-sharp heels.

► Chalayan, Ghesquière, Jourdan, Kirkwood

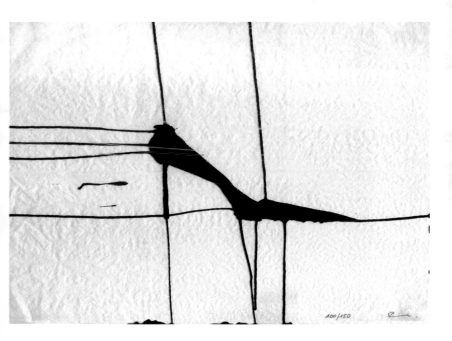

Pierre Hardy. b Paris (FR). **A Hardy stiletto captured in a serigraph print by Pierre Hardy, edition of 150.** 2007.

Hartnell Sir Norman

Designer

Princess Margaret's picturesque white evening gown, with its scooped neckline, tight bodice and full skirt, recalls the gowns Charles Frederick Worth made for the Empress Eugénie, immortalized in the portraits of her painted by Winterhalter. This distinctively British romantic revival interpretation was the creation of the royal couturier, Sir Norman Hartnell. Its origins can be traced back to the royal visit to Paris in 1938, when King George VI specifically requested Hartnell to design a wardrobe for his queen based on the royal portraits painted by Winterhalter in the 1860s that hung in Buckingham Palace. Hartnell exquisitely used white silk, satin, chiffon and tulle for evening gowns and decorated them sumptuously with embroidered and beaded motifs. This style of evening dress gained an international reputation as a British fashion classic. It remained a constant in the royal wardrobe throughout the postwar period.

► Bohan, Rayne, Sumurun, Worth

Sir Norman Hartnell. b London (UK), 1901. **d** Windsor, Berkshire (UK), 1979. **HRH Princess Margaret wears sequined butterfly gown for her nineteenth birthday.** Photograph by Sir Cecil Beaton, 1949.

Head Edith

Designer

Perhaps the most honoured of Hollywood's costume designers, Edith Head was also the most versatile. She excelled at recognizing the trends in contemporary fashion and in creating movie costumes realistic for their age, as in Elizabeth Taylor's wardrobe, inspired by Christian Dior and Jacques Fath, for *Elephant Walk* (1954). In her years at Paramount Pictures, Head designed for Mae West, created the sarong for Dorothy Lamour and made Barbara Stanwyck *The Lady Eve* (1941), but her real gift was an 'eye' – a keen sense for what was happening in contemporary fashion. She wrangled with fashion designers (most notably, Hubert de Givenchy) over design credits, and she gave her films a timely sense of fashion, unlike the grand picturesque of Hollywood Golden Age fashions, and anticipating 1980s and 1990s films where fashion is chosen from the marketplace.

► Fath, Givenchy, Irene, Louis, Travilla

Edith Head. b Los Angeles, CA (USA), 1907. **d** Hollywood, CA (USA), 1981. **Elizabeth Taylor.** Still from *Elephant Walk*, 1954.

Hechter Daniel

Designer

Daniel Hechter's leaping tracksuit represents the age of performance fashion. His reality-check womenswear emerged in the 1960s, with function dominating style. Hechter is realistic about his role: 'Fashion is not art. It can be artistic, but it is not art. I'm really a stylist. I respect designers who create fashion, like Chanel, Poiret. Or Levi's...[but] if you dress a billion people, that's phenomenal.' The first ready-to-wear womenswear collection, co-designed with friend Armand Orustein,

was launched in 1963, and was perfectly pitched for the 'youthquake' market. He persuaded Twiggy to model clothes that were targeted at young women who aspired to a designer lifestyle and integrated pop culture into his scheme, creating accessible clothes designed to be worn out and then replaced. His maxi coats, trouser suits and divided skirts were counterpointed with menswear that mixed separates in the 1970s.

▶ Dassler, Kamali, Knight & Bowerman, Strauss, Twiggy

Daniel Hechter. b Paris (FR), 1938. **Tracksuit**. Photograph by Jim Greenberg, *L'Officiel*, 1980.

Heim Jacques

Designer

Heim will be forever known as the couturier who promoted the bikini. He featured it in his 1946 collection under the name '*atome*'. When, in the same year, atomic bomb tests were conducted by the United States at Bikini Atoll, the swimsuit's name was changed to bikini. This bathing suit shot to fame when Brigitte Bardot was photographed in 1956 wearing one made of gingham adorned with frills. Heim entered the world of fashion through his parents' fur business, founded in 1898. He also collaborated with Sonia Delaunay, designing dresses, coats and sportswear that were exhibited at the Art Deco exhibition in Paris in 1925. He established his own fashion house in the 1930s, his forte being beachwear and sportswear. Between 1946 and 1966 he opened a series of boutiques that specialized in these garments. Heim was president of the Chambre Syndicale de la Couture Parisienne from 1958 to 1962.

► Bardot, Coddington, Delaunay, Gernreich, Jantzen

Jacques Heim. b Paris (FR), 1899. **d** Paris (FR), 1967. **Slip-over top and cotton bikini.** 1950.

Hemingway Wayne (Red or Dead)   Designer

Loud and opinionated, just like this line-up of his team's work, Wayne Hemingway doesn't care about high fashion. Beyond showing his collections at the expected times, Hemingway's company, Red or Dead, rejoices in its desire to please nobody but its young, clubby customers. It started life in 1982 as a second-hand clothing and shoe stall at London's Camden Market. In 1995 it demanded press reaction when models wielding bloody knives and knitting needles prowled along the catwalk in a pastiche of Alfred Hitchcock thrillers. Hemingway's fashion philosophy is based around the desire to reinterpret youth culture, using socio-political sloganeering as a hook. 'I design for a free-thinking British youth culture,' he has said. In other words, he gives them what they want, be it Bollywood, Punk, Mod, Britpop, Grandad or 1980s trash. In 2002 Red Or Dead published *The Good, the Bad, and the Ugly*, a chronicle of twenty years of the brand.

► Hamnett, Leroy, Mazzilli, Rotten

Wayne Hemingway. b Morecambe (UK), 1961. **Catwalk montage, 1989–96.** Photograph by Chris Moore and Suresh Karadia.

Hendrix Jimi   Icon

Hendrix was as individualistic in his stage wardrobe as he was in his stage act. His clothes, old mixed with new, clothes of war mixed with the tie-dye fabrics of war protesters, were as loud and chaotic as his electric guitar playing. His own sense of style was manifest at eight years old when he was ordered out of a Baptist church for being dressed too extravagantly. Expelled from school at fifteen, he drifted into juvenile delinquency, stealing flashy clothes from stores. He wore his hair in a wild, unkempt version of the Afro hairstyle adopted by the 'Black Pride' movement of the late 1960s. His clothes were often an eclectic mix of almost fop-like finery and hippie ethnicity. He often wore his trademark black felt fedora. His psychedelic clothing – multicoloured patchwork shirts flower-print jackets and swirly scarves – was reminiscent of the drug-induced hallucinations that inspired the lyrics of his songs.

► The Beatles, Bouquin, Bowie, Ozbek, Presley

Jimi Hendrix (James Marshall Hendrix). b Seattle, WA (USA), 1942. **d** London (UK), 1970. **Jimi Hendrix.** Photograph by Gered Mankowitz, 1967.

Hermès Thierry

Accessory designer

Princess Grace of Monaco carries a handbag big enough for a mother, yet courtly enough for any member of royalty. On the occasion of her marriage to Prince Rainier, Hermès renamed the bag in her honour. The 'Kelly bag' has been desired ever since and involves a three-month waiting list. Modelled on a '*sac haut à courroie*' or 'high-handle', which was used as a carrying case for saddles, the flap is fastened with horizontal straps and a twisting clasp. Hermès was founded in 1837 by Thierry Hermès. In 1920 his grandson

Emile brought modern design and luxurious clothes to the label, but Hermès continues to prosper from its image as a high-quality saddler, using snaffles and stirrups as themes for its printed silk scarves. From 1997 to 2003 avant-garde designer Martin Margiela oversaw women's ready-to-wear, and the following year Jean Paul Gaultier, as head designer, debuted his first collection for autumn/ winter 2004.

► Banton, Bergère, Gaultier, Gucci, Loewe, Margiela

Thierry Hermès. b Crefeld (GER), 1797. **d** Paris (FR), 1878. **Princess Grace with 'Kelly' bag and her daughter Caroline in Monaco.** 1958.

Van Herpen Iris

Designer

Recalling a skilled medieval woodcarving, the Cathedral dress from Iris van Herpen's 'Hybrid Holism' collection from 2012 is in fact the product of cutting-edge technology. The one single intricate piece is manufactured using a 3D-printing process called stereolithography. An interest in structure – be it architectural, anatomical or atomic – lies at the heart of much of this Dutch designer's work, as her complex couture pieces are often compared to sculpture. As a student, Van Herpen felt limited by the structural possibilities of fabric, exploring other materials and calling in architectural and manufacturing collaborators. The technology-conscious themes of her collections have included scanning electron microscopy and synaesthesia, matched by a fascination for ancient handcrafting techniques. Popular as they are as museum and gallery exhibits, van Herpen insists that the beauty of her garments can be fully realized only on the moving body.

► Guinness, Lady Gaga, McQueen, Viktor & Rolf

Iris van Herpen. b Wamel (NL), 1984. **'Cathedral' dress from the 'Hybrid Holism' collection, 2012.** Photograph by Ronald Stoops.

Hilfiger Tommy

Designer

'Check it out...check out Tommy...Tommy Hilfiger...' raps Treach as he models for a Hilfiger catwalk show in 1997. Hilfiger's name dominates his streetwise sportswear and turns his customers into advertisements. The distinctive red, white and blue logo came about after he noticed that counterfeiters were taking the discreet insignia of his competitors and enlarging them on T-shirts and caps. It was effortless advertising. Thus Hilfiger sold the idea back to those who invented and bought it. He started producing his logo-aware designs and was soon being name-checked in hip-hop songs – and worn by those who listen to them. In the 1970s Hilfiger's New York shop, People's Place, became a celebrity draw. In the 1980s his clothing assumed a preppie style similar in feel to that of Ralph Lauren's, but it was his mastery of the street market that made an impact on fashion. Hilfiger won the Geoffrey Beene Lifetime Achievement Award in 2012.

► Beene, Brooks, Dassler, Lauren, Moss

Tommy Hilfiger. b Elmira, NY (USA), 1952. **Rapper Treach and Kate Moss, spring/summer 1997.** Photograph by Chris Moore.

Hirata Akio

Milliner

With its delicate sculptural form and body-encompassing loops circling the shoulders, this hat challenges our preconceived ideas about millinery work. Akio Hirata, Japan's most influential milliner, has collaborated with many avant-garde Japanese designers including Yohji Yamamoto, Comme des Garçons and Hanae Mori. His passion for European fashion magazines encouraged him to tour France in 1962. There he met French milliner, Jean Barthet, with whom he trained for three years at his Paris salon and perfected his craft. He returned to Japan and founded his own house, Haute Mode Hirata, in 1965. Every design in his boutique, Salon Coco in Hiroo, was handmade. He worked on commissions for Pierre Balmain and Nina Ricci and designed for the wives of Japanese heads of state, who brought his work to the attention of a wider international audience during state visits abroad.

► Barthet, Kawakubo, Mori, Ricci, Sieff, Y. Yamamoto

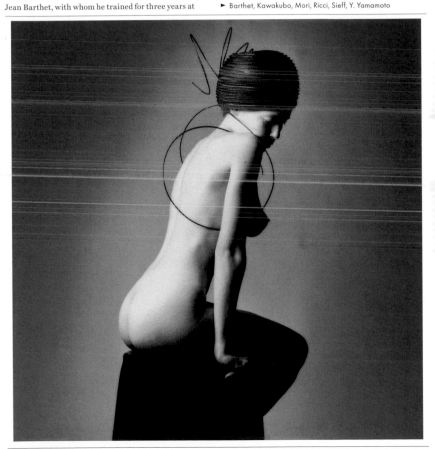

Akio Hirata. b Nagano Prefecture (JAP), 1925. **Black cord hat.** Photograph by Jeanloup Sieff, 1992.

Hiro

In a stunning removal of fashion from its accepted context, Harry Winston's diamond and ruby necklace is placed on a cloven hoof. Attention is centred on the contrast between bestial nature and the glamour of Winston's work – usually associated with Hollywood – with all its amusing connotations. Hiro has applied the same humour to other subjects, including a silver bangle by New York society's favourite fashion jeweller, Elsa Peretti, which he placed on a bleached bone. Taken for the December 1963 issue of *Harper's Bazaar*, this image exemplifies both the technical and artistic brilliance of the photographer known as Hiro. Born in Shanghai to Japanese parents, he moved to New York in 1954, working with Richard Avedon and becoming a member of Alexey Brodovitch's Design Laboratory. In 1958 he became a photographer at *Harper's Bazaar*, where he defined the decade through his still-life compositions.

► Avedon, Brodovitch, Penn, Peretti, Winston

Hiro (Yasuhiro Wakabayashi). b Shanghai (CHN), 1930. **Harry Winston necklace.** New York, 1963.

Hishinuma Yoshiki

Textile designer

Using a mixed technique known as *shibori*, Yoshiki Hishinuma creates a negative silhouette in the ruched fabric. Japanese textile designers are amongst the most exciting pioneers in fashion's most scientific field, pushing the practical and aesthetic boundaries of material. Hishinuma's training at the Issey Miyake Design Studio gave him a solid background in experimental fabric technology. He launched his own Tokyo-based label in 1984, but not before his freelance work earned him the

New Designer's Prize at Tokyo's Mainichi Fashion Grand Prix. He opened his own studio, specializing in isolated, neck-to-ankle fabric effects. His 1990s collections saw looks of otherworldly chiffon wrapped like crumpled white tissue paper and clipped feathers knitted tightly into a sweater, while in the twenty-first century the designer has explored organic materials and natural dye processes through his label Yoshiki Hishinuma Couture.

► Arai, Isagowa, Milner, Miyake

Yoshiki Hishinuma. b Sendai (JAP), 1958. **'Shibori' technique, spring/summer 1995.** Photograph by Noboru Iwahashi.

Hope Emma

Shoe designer

Emma Hope's shoes are romantic and individual in style, always with a nod to the shapes and detailing of bygone eras. Establishing her company in 1985 after graduating from Cordwainers College in London's East End, Hope began by selling a small range of brocade mules that were worn with Scott Crolla's ornate, antiquarian clothes. Hope's desire is to evoke 'the deliciousness of the first pair of shoes you really wanted', and make them a joy both to wear and behold. Her bespoke and ready-to-wear shoes, which are often covered in delicate detail, such as seed pearls and beads and fine embroidery, are highly coveted in the bridal industry. Hope creates nostalgic shoes, which recall the work of nineteenth-century cobblers such as Pinet. Those made from silk are especially precious, with memories of a time when a lady's foot would rarely meet the pavement.

► Choo, Cox, Crolla, Pinet, Yantorny

Emma Hope. b Portsmouth, Hampshire (UK), 1962. **Brogue courts from spring/summer 2008.** Photograph by Ben Wright.

Horst Horst P.

Photographer

Despite an illustrious career spanning over sixty-five years, photographer Horst P. Horst will forever be linked with his portraiture of the inter-war years. He began by working with George Hoyningen-Huene at *Vogue* in 1932 and, within a few years, had developed an unmistakable fashion style that fused elements of Greek sculpture with the decadent elegance of the time. His early black-and-white images mixed subtle contrast with mood and sensitivity, achieved with carefully positioned lighting that could take three days to perfect. 'I like taking photographs, because I like life,' he once said. Picasso, Dietrich, Dali, Cocteau, Gertrude Stein and the Duchess of Windsor were his friends and the subjects of his portraiture. His work has remained timeless and iconographic – as proved by the singer Madonna who copied his 1939 picture, *Mainbocher's Pink Satin Corset*, for her 'Vogue' video in 1989.

► Cocteau, Coward, Dali, Fonssagrives, Parker, Piguet

Horst P. Horst (Horst Paul Albert Bohrmann). b Weissenfels (GER), 1906. **d** Palm Beach, FL (USA), 1999. **Helen Bennett wears a cape dress by Jean Patou.** French *Vogue*, 1936.   241

Horvat Frank

Photographer

Peering out from between an organic swathe of organza and a milliner's cascade of petals, the model seems to float on a background of racegoers. Male and female, black and white, this 1958 shot for *Jardin des Modes* is an exercise in contrast. Considering its composition, it is perhaps unsurprising that Frank Horvat went on to make his name outside fashion with his photographs of trees. His fashion work in 1960, however, was seminal for fashion photography, using natural make-up and pastoral backdrops rather than the prevailing mood of urban formality. Originally a photojournalist, Horvat's first colour photograph appeared on the cover of the Italian magazine *Epoca* in 1951. His wide-ranging experience benefited his fashion work, adding a broad quality to technically adept images that catch the eye.

► D. Bailey, Givenchy, Milner, Stiebel

Frank Horvat. b Abbazia (IT), 1928. **Givenchy hat, Paris.** *Jardin des Modes*, 1958.

Howell Margaret

Designer

In this gentle fashion image, Margaret Howell's tailored navy shorts resemble those worn in the 1930s. Her clothes blend memories of England with the pleasure of wearing worn-in country clothes. The look was revolutionary when she began in the early 1970s, inspired by nostalgic icons of British style, such as brogues, tweed skirts and her father's gardening mac. Howell's menswear and womenswear collections were launched in 1972, with an emphasis on tailoring. Howell has been so copied that it almost obscures her contribution, but her linen duster coats, shirt dresses, floor-sweeping raincoats and tweed suits for women have an enduring appeal. 'When I started out, I was only thinking about what I wanted,' she told *Vogue*. 'I liked quality and comfort... I was probably responsible for the move towards using men's tailoring tweeds for women's clothes.' In 2007 Howell was awarded a CBE for services to the British Fashion Industry.

► Jackson, Jaeger, De Prémonville

Margaret Howell. b Tadworth, Surrey (UK), 1946. **Cotton sweater and crepe shorts, spring/summer 1992.** Photograph by Koto Bolofo.

Hoyningen-Huene George   Photographer

George Hoyningen-Huene's fashion photographs were inspired by Classical Greek sculpture. He posed his models with props so that they resembled the figures in a frieze. His technique of back- and cross-lighting, to achieve line and volume and to give the models, the clothes and the settings texture and sheen, is unique. During the Russian Revolution, Hoyningen-Huene fled to England and went on to Paris in 1921. He studied painting under André Lhote and began to draw fashion.

After collaborating with Man Ray, he became chief photographer for French *Vogue* in 1926, moving on to New York and American *Vogue*. Hoyningen-Huene worked at *Harper's Bazaar* in New York from 1935 to 1945. He then moved to Los Angeles where he taught photography at the Art Center School and worked on sets and costumes for Hollywood movies.

► Agnès, Blumenfeld, Mainbocher, Morehouse

George Hoyningen-Huene. b St Petersburg (RUS), 1900. **d** Los Angeles, CA (USA), 1968. **Gold reefer jacket by Mainbocher, gloves by Hattie Carnegie.** *Harper's Bazaar*, 1939.

Hulanicki Barbara (Biba) Designer

A woman and child in identical maxi, panne velvet dresses are the essence of the Biba look. Barbara Hulanicki, a fashion illustrator, had dreamed of bringing decadence to the masses. She began with a 'postal boutique' in 1963, opening her first shop, named after her sister, Biba, a year later. It was a treasury of exotic accessories and fabrics and, despite its cheapness, which made it accessible to students and teenagers, dressed stars including Twiggy and Julie Christie. Biba was, in the words of Ossie Clarke, 'Disposable glamour shrouded in purply, mulberry shades...' Hulanicki's style lived somewhere between Art Deco and Art Nouveau: slim, often cut from satin and velvet and highlighted with lean lurex knitwear. In 1973 Biba moved into a department store building. This 'nickelodeon land of Art Deco with potted palms and mirrored hall' only lasted until 1975, but Hulanicki's ideal is still admired.

► Bouquin, Clark, Kamali, Moon, Twiggy

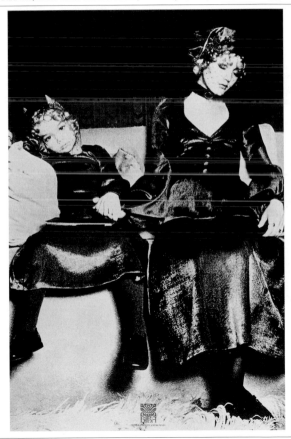

Barbara Hulanicki. b Warsaw (POL), 1936. **Mother and daughter.** Photograph by Sarah Moon, 1969.

Hutton Lauren

Model

Lauren Hutton, with her rare beauty and alluring gap-toothed smile, has graced a record twenty-five *Vogue* covers and countless editorial campaigns. Her most newsworthy career move was the contract she signed with Revlon in 1974. The first of its kind, this exclusive agreement set a precedent for supermodels' fees, changing them from hundreds to thousands of dollars. Over the following ten years Hutton also made a name for herself on screen, her most famous role being *American Gigolo* (1980) with Richard Gere. Born in Charleston, South Carolina, she grew up mainly in Florida and, after dropping out of college, moved to New York where she began modelling to pay for the life of travel she had originally planned. Her return to modelling in the 1990s was a proud achievement for Hutton, who has inspired debate about the size and age of models. Her example, she hopes, will encourage a broader view of beauty.

▶ Armani, Butler & Wilson, C. Klein, Revson, Shrimpton

Lauren Hutton. b Charleston, SC (USA), 1943. **Lauren Hutton.** Photograph by Fred Seidman, 1972.

Iman

Model

A slender sculpture in black velvet and white taffeta, Iman was dubbed Black Pearl for her ebony-black beauty. The contours of her feline figure, boasting a perfect *physique du rôle* to flaunt the 1980s' opulence, ensured that she was a true supermodel of her time. Her exotic presence on the catwalk made her a fetish model for Azzedine Alaïa, Gianni Versace and Thierry Mugler. Born Iman Abdulmajid in Somalia to a diplomat, she studied political science in Nairobi before being discovered by Peter Beard, the photographer who took her into the New York fashion spotlight. A multimillion-dollar contract with Revlon in the late 1970s, as well as her marriage to rock star David Bowie and the launch of her own make-up range (especially devised for black women), have conferred on her almost mythical status among black models, a reputation shared only by Naomi Campbell and Beverly Johnson.

► Alaïa, Bowie, Campbell, Beverly Johnson, Revson

Iman (Iman Abdulmajid Haywood). b Mogadishu (SOM), 1955. **Formal evening gown and feather headdress.** Photograph by Arthur Elgort, 1993.

Inez and Vinoodh

Photographers

Dutch photography team Inez van Lamsweerde and Vinoodh Matadin are among the few practitioners of the early twenty-first century who adeptly straddle the realms of both art and fashion image-making. The duo met in Amsterdam in the early 1980s while studying fashion design at the Vogue Academy. Their creative collaboration began in 1986 and the partners have since built a peerless archive of visionary advertising campaigns, fashion editorials, celebrity portraiture, and original films,

in addition to their oft-exhibited and widely collected artwork. Characterized by the subtle insertion of surrealistic elements into otherwise classic compositions and the digital manipulation of archetypal photographic conventions, Inez and Vinoodh's images are a compelling combination of sophisticated and uncanny. As a result, the photograph's true subject – the fashion – is showcased in a mixture of humour and intrigue.

► N. Knight, Léger, Mert & Marcus, Sims, Tisci

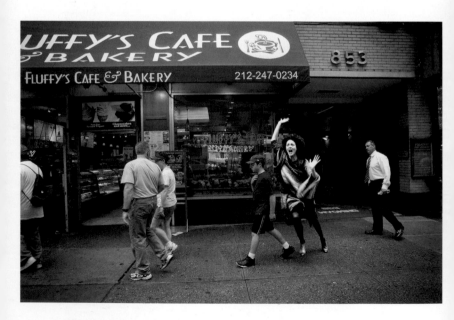

Inez van Lamsweerde. b Amsterdam (NL), 1963. Vinoodh Matadin. b Amsterdam (NL), 1961. Shalom Harlow at 853, 7th Avenue for *Self Service* magazine. 2006.

Irene

This film still from *Seven Sinners* (1940) shows the work of the costume designer known as 'Irene of California'. She started making clothes on the campus of the University of Southern California, where Dolores del Rio became a client. Her connections took Irene into the Beverly Hills sphere, where she became involved with actresses and their personal wardrobes. She moved to Hollywood to continue her trade. From 1942 she took over from Adrian as head costumer at Metro-Goldwyn-Mayer,

making outfits for, among others, Marlene Dietrich and Marilyn Monroe. Her signature style always remained slim, curvy and tailored for daywear; eveningwear, however, was lavish and dramatic, with feathers, frills and sparkle. Here, Marlene Dietrich wears an outfit embellished with the trappings of a romantic vamp: polka-dot veil, net gloves, ostrich-trimmed handbag and chiffon corsage.

▶ Adrian, Head, Louis, Travilla

Irene (**Irene Lentz Gibbons**). b Baker, MT (USA), 1900. d Los Angeles, CA (USA), 1962. **Marlene Dietrich.** Still from *Seven Sinners*, 1940.

Iribe Paul

Illustrator

The simple lines and brilliant colours of Poiret's oriental style are beautifully evoked in this fashion illustration, published a year before the arrival of the Ballets Russes and Bakst in Paris. The 'Hispahan' coat in the centre, made in green cotton velvet, has embroidered Persian palms sharply outlined in bold yellow and white. This coat is framed by two others in shades of yellow and mustard, trimmed with fur. Further contrasts of colour are provided by the dresses visible beneath the coats and by the headwear. With its format of clear, flat areas of colour and the asymmetrical arrangement of the models, the fashion illustration shows the influence of Japanese prints. In order to obtain such jewel-like colours, Iribe used a special technique called the *pochoir* process, whereby a monochrome print was hand-coloured using a series of bronze or zinc stencils, enabling him to capture an image as close as possible to the original.

▶ Bakst, Barbier, Doucet, Gigli, Lepape, Paquin, Poiret

Paul Iribe. b Angoulême (FR), 1883. **d** Paris (FR), 1935. '**Three Coats.**' *Les Robes de Paul Poiret racontées par Paul Iribe*, 1908.

Isogawa Akira

Designer

Against a background of pattern pieces (the building blocks from which fashion takes shape), Akira Isogawa's model wears a vest contructed from bronze jacquard silk. Its seams, brought together as an abstract, asymmetric puzzle, are stitched on the outside, leaving their frayed edges to become part of the exterior decoration. Isogawa left his native Japan for Sydney, Australia, to escape becoming a 'salary man'. He trained in fashion and in 1996 showed his first collection as part of Australian Fashion Week. It was an exotic mélange of Japanese vintage kimonos, delicate and translucent floral-print dresses and modern leather and wool tailoring, all layered together to create a new aesthetic in fashion. The attraction of Isogawa's clothes lies in his passion for fabric. 'I have a connection, a Zen thing with material,' he has said. His delicate handprints, antique fabrics from Japan and form-fitting tailoring make a sharp yet individual statement.

► Arai, Chalayan, Dinnigan, Kobayashi, Lloyd

Akira Isogawa. b Kyoto (JAP), 1964. **Deconstructed bronze brocade top and pinstriped trousers.** Photograph by Eddy Ming, 1998.

251

Jackson Betty

Designer

Square, linen shapes represent the work of Betty Jackson, who is known for her thoughtful balance between fashion and comfort. Consequently, her designs appeal to women whose working and leisure wardrobes tend to be interchangeable – a relaxed, modern concept. She originally wanted to be a sculptor, but instead she freelanced as an illustrator, before turning her attention to fashion in 1973, working for Wendy Dagworthy and then at Quorum. Jackson and her husband, David Cohen, founded their own company under her name in 1981. The core of her easy, fluid collections consists of boldly coloured, simple and versatile shapes; a style that allows elements of high fashion to be represented without compromising her notion that fashion belongs to women of any age. As a member of the advisory panel to the British Fashion Council's Model Health Inquiry, she has been involved in the 'size zero' debate.

▶ P. Ellis, Howell, Pollock, V. Wang

Betty Jackson. b Bacup, Lancashire (UK), 1949. **Linen shirt and drawstring trousers.** Photograph by Tony McGee, American *Vogue*, 1984.

Jacobs Marc   Designer

The irreverent and charismatic New Yorker, Marc Jacobs has become a key figure in fashion. As creative director of luxury empire Louis Vuitton, and his own successful namesake label, Jacobs is a brand in his own right. The one-time designer for Perry Ellis, and Parsons The New School for Design graduate, Jacobs moved to Vuitton in 1997, introducing pop and kitsch elements to its traditional image; described as 'deluxe hip' by journalist Suzy Menkes. Jacobs is a master of collaboration for Vuitton, he has commissioned artists and designers, such as Steven Sprouse, Takashi Murakami, Yayoi Kusama and Richard Prince to assist in his witty update of a brand steeped in tradition and history. His tongue-in-cheek approach carries through to his own label, particularly in his advertising campaigns, which feature photographs by Juergen Teller, playfully toeing the border between art and fashion with commercial success.

► Ford, Grand, Lagerfeld, Teller, Vuitton

Marc Jacobs. b New York (USA), 1963. **Marc Jacobs spring/summer 2009 catwalk show.**

Jacobson Jacqueline & Elie (Dorothée Bis)   Designers

Fun, funky knitwear was the key to the Dorothée Bis style. Their 'total look' often incorporated knitted tights and hats and unconventional layering such as skirts over trousers or, as seen here, thigh-clinging shorts worn with over-the-knee socks. Jacqueline and Elie Jacobson founded the label with the desire to create wearable versions of high-fashion styles, producing clothes that were ideal for the youth-inspired period of short-lived fashion trends in the 1960s. The label was always commercially minded, reflecting their backgrounds in the fashion trade (in the 1950s, Jacqueline owned a childrenswear shop and Elie worked as a wholesale furrier). Each decade they defined the key looks, from knitted maxi coats and skinny-rib sweaters in the 1960s, to voluminous layering in the 1970s and tight, shoulder-padded graphic knits in the 1980s.

► Khanh, Paulin, Rykiel, Troublé

Jacobson. Jacqueline. b Lens (FR), 1928; **Elie, b** B⋯ ⋯ ⋯ ⋯), 1925. **Hooded poncho and shorts.** Photograph by Peter Knapp, French *Elle*, 1970.

Jaeger Dr Gustav

Designer

Dr Gustav Jaeger, a German dress reformer who believed that animal hair made the most healthy fabric, stands erect, wearing close-fitting, woollen breeches. Unlikely as it seems, Jaeger inspired a classic British label that was patronized by George Bernard Shaw and Oscar Wilde. The company was founded in 1883 by Lewis Tomalin, the London businessman who translated and published Jaeger's thoughts. Tomalin went on a health crusade to convert the public to the benefits of wearing wool next to the skin as advocated by the doctor from Stuttgart, securing his rights and name. It wasn't until the 1920s that fashion was embraced by Jaeger, and then it was used to popularize the appeal of 'healthy' materials through a style that came to represent British, dependable design. Today the Jaeger brand is a dominating presence in the mass-market having been transformed for the contemporary fashion industry.

► Benetton, Burberry, Creed, Howell, Muir, Topshop, Wilde

Dr Gustav Jaeger. b Börg am Kocher (GER), 1832. d Stuttgart (GER), 1917. Dr Gustav Jaeger. c.1880.

James Charles

Designer

Charles James was working for Elizabeth Arden when he created the couture dress that is the sculptural centre of this John Rawlings photograph. Every James dress was a *tour de force* of sculptural imagination; the pyramid shape on the left and the black-and-white figure on the right confirm his penchant for sculpture. The evening dress (*c.*1944) anticipates the postwar silhouette, especially that of Christian Dior's New Look. A corseted bodice emphasizes the supported bust and narrowed waist, while the flaring fabrics just below the waist float out from the body to construct fictive hips that make the waist seem even slimmer. Irascible and self-destructive, James couched his designs in pseudo-systems and supposed geometries, but made his name as the maker of the extravagant concoctions that defined the conservative picturesque in post-Second World War fashion.

► Arden, Beaton, Fath, Scaasi, Steele, Weber

Charles James. b Sandhurst, Berkshire (UK), 1906. **d** New York (USA), 1978. **Draped duchesse satin couture gown.** Photograph by John Rawlings, 1944.

James Richard

Tailor

Actor Edward Atterton is laid out in a 'whodunnit' spread for *Elle*, much to the entertainment of the tourists. The photographer, David LaChapelle, maximizes the tongue-in-cheek appeal of Richard James' lilac suit. Since 1976, when he launched his label, James has been regarded as the 'light player' of Savile Row, using vivid colours instead of greys and eccentric checks rather than traditional tweed. His choice of such fabrics gave British tailored menswear a contemporary feel, drawing comparisons with Tommy Nutter and his contemporaries. James sums up his approach, stating that, 'Many of the suits made along the row are beautiful but bland. We are trying to add a youthful spirit and excitement, while maintaining the propriety that Savile Row stands for.' In 2001 he won the Menswear Designer of the Year at the British Fashion Awards and has more recently added underwear, leisurewear and fragrance components to the brand.

▶ Cox, LaChapelle, Nutter, P. Smith

Richard James. b Ely, Cambridgeshire (UK), 1953. **Edward Atterton wears lilac wool suit and woven stripe shirt.** Photograph by David LaChapelle, British *Elle*, 1996.

257

Jantzen Carl

Designer

Swimming champion Johnny Weissmuller poses poolside in a pair of 'Jantzens', the world's first elasticized trunks. Invented by knitwear designer Carl Jantzen, who experimented with the machines that made sweater cuffs, this innovation prompted the world to stop merely 'bathing' and start 'swimming'. Jantzen founded the Portland Knitting Co with John and Roy Zehntbauer in 1910. Their heavy wool sweaters, socks and gloves, produced on a few knitting machines and sold from the company shop, were phenomenally successful. The trunks soon became known as 'Jantzens', and the company changed its name accordingly in 1918. Three years later, the Red Diving Girl motif was added. Jantzen's early designs were unisex (although women wore theirs with stockings), but the developments resulted in streamlined swimwear for women. By 1925 Jantzen was one of the first clothes companies to export its work.

► Gernreich, Knight & Bowerman, Lacoste

Carl Jantzen. b Aarhus (DK), 1883. d (USA), 1939. **Johnny Weissmuller wears wool tanksuit, Olympic Games.** 1924.

Jinteok

Designer

Jinteok is known for simple designs crafted from luxurious fabrics that meld traditional elements of her cultural heritage with Western influences. Here, she uses Chinese red silk for an apron dress. Its bodice and hem are decorated with naturalistic forms in the tradition of oriental silk garments. The underskirt, cut from roughly assembled denim, lends this potentially glamorous garment a rustic, hobo feel. Such subtle themes, inspired mainly by nature, are evident throughout her collections.

Since she opened her first shop in Seoul in 1965, Jinteok has played a pioneering role in contemporary fashion in her native country, South Korea. She founded the Seoul Fashion Designers Association, which encourages young Korean designers, and presented her womenswear collection on the catwalks in Paris for the first time in 1994. Her established prestigious brands are Jinteok and Françoise.

► Arai, Kim, Rocha

Jinteok (Jin Teok). b (KOR), 1938. **Red embroidered gown, spring/summer 1995.** Photograph by Marcio Madeira.

Johansson Jonny (Acne)   Designer

An acronym for 'Ambition to Create Novel Expression', Acne was founded in Stockholm in 1996 by Jonny Johansson and three colleagues with the desire to create a lifestyle brand that addressed various forms of creative output. Starting production with a limited 100-pair line of denim jeans, the collective's projects have expanded to include a film company, men's and womenswear, children's toys, furniture and various collaborations including a denim-based capsule collection with Lanvin's Alber Elbaz in 2008. The brand's unmistakably modern Swedish silhouette, warm colour palette and quirky detailing stems from its firm foundation in wardrobe basics. The collective also publishes *Acne Paper*, an elegant biannual magazine with features on art, fashion, photography, culture, design and architecture. The magazine reinforces the pervasive creative philosophy that is representative of the brand throughout all facets of their endeavours.

► Elbaz, Gustafson, Philo, A. Wang, Warhol

Jonny Johansson. b Umeå (SWE), 1969. **Acne autumn/winter 2012.**

John John P.   Milliner

Although this outfit is heavily accessorized, the pieces are so carefully matched that at first glance they are barely noticeable, camouflaged against the co-ordinated clothing. During the 1930s no fashionable outfit was complete without matching hat, gloves, shoes and bag. At that time, New York's accessory designers were moving into the limelight, and John P. John was one of America's top proponents. Also known as Mr John, he had a career in Hollywood for fifty years, working with Adrian and Travis Banton. With Frederic Hirst he formed the John-Frederics label, creating perfectly co-ordinated outfits. This picture shows how a puff-sleeved, tartan shirt and cream skirt is complemented with formal accessories, including a matching bag. The cream broad-brimmed hat is covered in black net and tones with the gloves. Unusually, a long band hangs from the hat, encircling the blouse and literally pulling the outfit together.

► Adrian, Banton, Daché, Simpson

John P. John. b Munich (GER), 1902. d Los Angeles (USA), 1993. **Veiled panama hat, plaid blouse and pocket book.** Photograph by Horst P. Horst, 1939.

Johnson Betsey

Designer

'Fashion is all about having fun and these are clothes to have fun in,' says Betsey Johnson, whose attitude to fashion is summed up by the cartwheels she performs on the runway at her shows. Best known for her brightly coloured prints, she started designing in 1965 and her imaginative designs took full advantage of the new synthetics and mini-lengths. Her dresses were decorated with shower-ring hems and her fluorescent underwear came in tennis ball cans. Johnson also sold dresses in kit form for the wearer to arrange as she wanted. It was a dress with a ten-inch, extended collar that made her name. Worn by British actress Julie Christie, it sold in the tens of thousands. Her career was launched by New York's Paraphernalia boutique, a champion of youth fashion in the 1960s. In 2002 she joined the American Fashion Walk of Fame and in 2009 she received the National Arts Club Medal of Honor for Lifetime Achievement in Fashion.

► Bailly, Foale, Rabanne, Rhodes

Betsey Johnson. b Hartford, CT (USA), 1942. **Betsey Johnson in her design studio, New York.** Photograph by Harry Benson, 1982.

Johnson Beverly

Model

Beverly Johnson has a place in fashion history, not only as the first black model to be featured on the cover of American *Vogue*, but also for paving the way for black women the world over to feel part of the fashion industry. Johnson began modelling while a student at Northeastern University in Boston, receiving assignments for *Vogue* and *Glamour* despite having no portfolio. Fashion editors were impressed by her fresh beauty. When Scavullo photographed her for the *Vogue* cover in August 1974, the magazine was taking a chance. Little did they know that its circulation for that month would double. Johnson said at the time, 'The participation of black models...is unjust in proportion to the amount of money that is put into the industry by black people.' Her career spanned the 1970s and early 1980s and also included film roles, records and two books.

► Iman, Nast, Scavullo, Turbeville

Beverly Johnson. b (USA), 1953. **Beverly Johnson.** Photograph by Francesco Scavullo, American *Vogue*, 1974.

Jones Grace

Model

Grace Jones poses for a Polaroid taken by her friend Antonio Lopez in his bathroom. Jones, with her Amazonian figure and shorn hair, was the antithesis of femininity. The daughter of a Pentecostal minister, she rebelled against her strict upbringing and pursued a modelling career in Paris at a time when her theatrical attitude perfectly suited the extremes of 1970s fashion. As she said, 'Glitter? Uh-huh. Platform shoes? Yeah... It was sort of old Hollywood star stuff.' Fashion centred on the flashy nightclub scene at Paris's Club Sept, where Jones partied every night. Together with friend Jerry Hall, Jones brought outrageous performance to modelling and, as a result, created a second career for herself. In the 1980s she turned to music, cultivating an aggressive look of razor sharp, angular, leather clothes and a razored quiff to clothe her image as a modern diva.

► Alaïa, Antoine, Antonio, Grand, Iman, Mugler, Price

Grace Jones. b Spanish Town (JAM), 1948. **Grace Jones.** Photograph by Antonio López, 1980.

Jones Kim

Designer

Macho enough to look after himself, but clearly not likely to go for long without washing, the beautiful boy in the launderette sums up Kim Jones's design sensibility. The Londoner's innate appreciation of the demands of menswear – smart but not effeminate, youthful yet mature – enabled him to breathe new life into old brands, including Umbro, Alfred Dunhill and now Louis Vuitton. Graduating from Central Saint Martins in 2001, Jones stood out at his first London Fashion Week collection in 2003 with his unique mix of sportswear, denim and splashes of ethnic influence. In 2011 artistic director Marc Jacobs hired him at Louis Vuitton as style director of menswear, bringing an East London edge to the Paris fashion and luxury industry. Jones's blend of sports, travel and tailoring, and assimilation of wide influences, such as the Masai blankets in his first Vuitton collection, made him the perfect choice for the modern face of the brand.

▶ Central Saint Martins, Jacobs, Simons, Vuitton

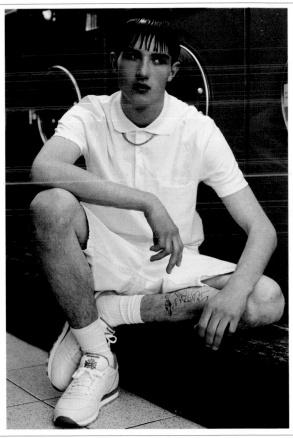

Kim Jones. b London (UK), 1979. **Louis Vuitton menswear autumn/winter 2012 resort collection.** Photograph by Jeff Hahn, *Used* magazine.

Jones Stephen

Milliner

The model L'Wren Scott camps it up for Mario Testino's camera. On her head she wears a miniature topper by milliner Stephen Jones, known for his innovative, witty and gregarious hats. Boaters, caps and bowler hats have all been reduced to create millinery caricatures. He was a central figure in London's New Romantic movement in the early 1980s, making hats for his friends Steve Strange and Boy George. In 1984 his work was noticed by Jean Paul Gaultier and Thierry Mugler, who both asked him to design hats to accessorize their collections, making him one of the first British milliners to work in Paris. Jones has since collaborated with a succession of international fashion designers. As with the shoe designer Manolo Blahnik, his work as an accessory designer lends itself to collaborative ventures because of its sympathy with the clothes, as well as a sharpness that makes it a punchy punctuation mark.

► D. Bailey, Blow, Galliano, Gaultier, Testino, Treacy

Stephen Jones. b West Kirby, Merseyside (UK), 1957. **Top hat worn by L'Wren Scott.** Photograph by Mario Testino, *Harpers & Queen*, 1988.

Jourdan Charles

Shoe designer

In the 1930s, Charles Jourdan was the first shoe designer to advertise in fashion magazines. In the 1970s, his dramatic advertisements, such as the one below, were photographed by Guy Bourdin and became legendary. Bourdin lent the shoes wit and mystery by placing them in surreal scenes, making them components of a larger story. Here, two women are escaping over a wall, leaving three of their platform sandals behind. Jourdan had introduced low-priced diffusion lines to his handmade collection after the Second World War. He sold simple designs in a multitude of colours and fits, for a developing ready-to-wear business. In 1958 Maxime, a low-heeled, square-toed court shoe with a satin bow, became his best-selling style. In the 1960s, a collaboration with André Perugia added a touch of glamour, but Jourdan's collaboration with Guy Bourdin remains the most exciting impression of his work.

▶ Bourdin, Hardy, Oldfield, Perugia

Charles Jourdan. b Bourg-de-Péage (FR), 1883. **d** Romans-sur-Isère (FR), 1976. **Summer sandals.** Photograph by Guy Bourdin, 1974.

Kamali Norma

Designer

In the tradition of American fashion, Norma Kamali formed an entire wardrobe from utilitarian material. When she launched her own range of clothes, Kamali created a fashion phenomenon by using sweatshirt fleece fabric for clothes such as leggings, kick skirts and wide-shouldered dresses. Her outfits addressed a problem felt by millions of American women: how could they get away with comfort when fashion dictated structure and ostentatious formality? She was also one of the first to

offer the unitard. Kamali's fashion career began in 1968, when she opened a boutique with her husband Eddie in New York. At the time, she was an air stewardess and sourced many European fashions, particularly from Biba in London. In 1978, after her divorce, Kamali set up OMO (On My Own) and her new-found independence was reflected in her clothes, which have continued to provide a modern response for modern women.

► Campbell, Hechter, Hulanicki, Karan

Norma Kamali. b New York (USA), 1945. **Sweatshirt collection, spring/summer 1980.** *Women's Wear Daily.*

Kane Christopher   Designer

One thing that is always certain with Christopher Kane is his individual focus on a particular theme that hits fashion sideways. His signature style is embellishment, details that are head-turningly new, as in this dress where he explores his fascination with dinosaur scales and apes' leather tunics, taking inspiration from films such as *Planet of the Apes* (1968) and *One Million Years BC* (1966). It is a dress composed of a variety of circles of chiffon that ripple like scales around the model, oscillating to a short leather skirt trimmed with tiers of marabou. The dress displays Kane's genius for construction, each panel intricately meeting the next with three-dimensional geometric-precision cutting. The collection drew widespread praise from both fashion critics and the fashion public alike, selling out on Net-A-Porter.com within twenty-four hours of launching. Kane won the British Fashion Council British Collection of the Year in 2009.

► Central Saint Martins, Deacon, Katrantzou, Saunders

Christopher Kane. b Newarthill, Scotland (UK), 1982. **Minidress with marabou trim, spring/summer 2009.**

Karan Donna

Designer

'What do I need? How can I make life easier? How can dressing be simplified so that I can get on with my own life?' Donna Karan's own thoughts could be running through the head of this 'first woman president'. Professional wearability dictates Karan's work. Her first collection was a wardrobe of separates based around the 'body' – a practical, leotard with poppers at the crotch. Karan also aims to flatter the normal woman and only designs clothes that she would wear herself.

Karan trained with Anne Klein, taking over the design with Louis Dell'Olio when Klein died. Karan's fidelity to Klein's easy-to-wear never waned, but in the 1990s she became increasingly interested in spiritual philosophies, and began producing looser, more sensual clothing. In 1994 she launched popular diffusion brand DKNY, and in 2000 Karan sold her company to the LVMH group, but remains chief designer of the brand.

► Dell'Olio, A. Klein, Maxwell, Morris

Donna Karan. b New York (USA), 1948. **'In Women We Trust' advertising campaign.** Photograph by Peter Lindbergh, 1992.

Katrantzou Mary   Designer

Since graduating in 2008 from London's Central Saint Martins, with a BA degree in textile design, Mary Katrantzou has become instantly recognizable on the international fashion stage for her complex and elaborate digital prints. Seen here in a rich editorial by photographer Erik Madigan Heck, Katrantzou's autumn/winter 2011 is no exception. Her signature deeply intricate and kaleidoscopic repeat patterns reference any number of decorative sources from interiors and bank notes to antique artefacts. Here the saturated hues harmonize with the startling patterns of Katrantzou's designs, creating an exquisite mix of photography and illustration where the interior blends with the clothes. Winner of the Emerging Talent Award at the British Fashion Awards in 2011 and the Young Designer of the Year at the 2012 *Elle* Style Awards, Katrantzou has been recognized as an influential technical and graphic innovator.

► Erdem, Kane, Pilotto, Saunders, Williamson

Mary Katrantzou. b Athens (GR), 1983. **Printed trompe-l'oeil dress, autumn/winter 2011 collection.** Photograph by Erik Madigan Heck.

Kawakubo Rei (Comme des Garçons) Designer

The distressed bricolage of this knitted ensemble from 1984 is a fierce rebuttal to the body-conscious, sexy, silhouette of the 1980s. Thus the sensation caused by Rei Kawakubo's Paris debut in 1981 with fellow Japanese Yohji Yamamoto. Presenting garments influenced by little more than the cloth, thread, structure and ingenuity of their own creation, Kawakubo sought to release fashion from its endless cycle of historical references, and to create a wardrobe striking and unconstrained in the way they moved. Her deconstructed sensibility has made her one of the most influential figures in fashion. Comme des Garçons, under her direction, has since become a groundbreaking retailer, sending collections on tour to locations that included Ljubljana, Helsinki and Singapore in the form of 'guerrilla' stores. The touring shops culminated in the 2004 launch of Dover Street Market in London, the first of her high-fashion, multi-brand stores.

► Lindbergh, Margiela, Miyake, Takahashi, Vionnet, Watanabe

Rei Kawakubo. b Tokyo (JAP), 1942. **Knitwear, autumn/winter 1984.** Photograph by Peter Lindbergh.

Kélian Stéphane

Shoe designer

A pair of bronze sandals epitomizes the work of one of France's most enduringly fashionable shoe designers. Basket-woven leather has been a feature of Kélian shoes since Georges and GérardKéloglanian opened a workshop to design and manufacture classic men's shoes in 1960. In the mid-1970s, Stéphane entered into partnership with his two older brothers, bringing a new fashion spirit to their traditional shoe company. In subsequent collections, he continued to feature the specialist weaving techniques used by his brothers, but modernized the designs and introduced a panoply of shimmering colours into the palette. Stéphane presented his first collection of women's shoes in 1977 and the opening of the first of many international boutiques followed a year later in Paris. Kélian is known for his design collaborations with fashion designers and other cobblers, including Martine Sitbon and Maud Frizon.

► Frizon, Jourdan, Sitbon, Steiger

Stéphane Kélian (Stéphane Kéloglanian). b Romans-sur-Isère (FR), 1942. **Basket-weave sandals, autumn/winter 1997.** Photograph by Roberto Badin.

Kelly Patrick

Designer

Shining out amidst the backstage chaos are symbols that characterize one of the most exuberant designers of the 1980s. A committed Francophile, Patrick Kelly describes the Eiffel Tower in rhinestones for a black dress, uses it for clunking gilt earring charms and even on high-heeled shoes. Journalist Bernadine Morris noted Kelly's 'collection of lively, unpretentious clothes that made fashion look like fun...an unforced feeling of happiness'. His work always contained an element of the theatrical and his catwalk shows combined the largesse of a rural Southern American culture with the camp bravado of Moulin Rouge entertainment. Affordable ready-to-wear clothing was gaily decorated with buttons, and black rag dolls, once a sign of oppression, were festooned over a coat. Between 1985 and 1989, Kelly seemed an irrepressible force for dynamic fashion, involving young people and black experience.

► W. Klein, Moschino, Parkinson, Price

Patrick Kelly. b Vickysburg, MI (USA), 1954. **d** Paris (FR), 1990. **Backstage.** Photograph by William Klein, 1987.

Kennedy Jacqueline

Icon

Ladylike but youthful, formal but fashionable, the 'Jackie' style caught America's attention and made the young woman a fashion icon. This picture illustrates Jackie's trademarks: the simple coat, the white gloves, the hair by Kenneth. In 1961 Oleg Cassini became her designer, telling her that she could only wear his clothes – although she would occasionally consult with Diana Vreeland at *Harper's Bazaar*. In return, Cassini created a wardrobe for the First Lady. It had a pared-down elegance and an informal spirit that was unusual. She rarely wore patterns and stuck to simple shapes: sleeveless, boxy shift dresses with matching coats and accessories. Halston was her milliner, creating her famous style. Jackie always wore gloves and rarely wore jewellery, except for occasional pearls. As with her clothes, Jackie liked her shoes 'slender...but not exaggerated – no tricky...business – timeless and elegant'.

► Cassini, Daché, Lane, Pulitzer, Vanderbilt, Vreeland

Jacqueline Kennedy. b New York (USA), 1929. **d** New York (USA), 1994. **'Raja' coat in dupion silk by Oleg Cassini.** Photograph by Art Rickerby, *Life*, 1962.

Kenneth

Hairdresser

In 1963, an article in American *Vogue*, entitled 'The Kenneth Club', described the lengths to which women would go for an appointment with the hairdresser Kenneth Battelle. He attended to Jackie Kennedy's bouffant bob, copied across America. He created the perfect domed bobs on Veruschka and Jean Shrimpton for *Vogue* covers when Diana Vreeland was editor. She called it the 'Dynel period' because of the enormous quantities of synthetic hair that were used for ever more elaborate wigs and extensions. Famously, in Tahiti, they used Dynel not just on the models but on a real white horse to create a fairy-tale ponytail. However, for Kenneth, the cut rather than the dressing was the most important element to a hairstyle: his teased and backcombed precision bobs defined an era. 'I defy a woman to wear a Courrèges dress without really great make-up and a hairdo,' he is quoted as saying.

► Antoine, Kennedy, Shrimpton, Veruschka, Vreeland

Kenneth (**Kenneth Battelle**). **b** New York (USA), 1927. **Bouffant bob.** Photograph by Art Kane, American *Vogue*, 1962.

Kenzo

Designer

Her layered, prairie cottons swing to life; an earthy, retrospective look that dominated much of the mid-1970s. The dress and jacket use the Victorian details such as a fitted bodice and billowing sleeves caught into deep cuffs. Kenzo Takada, its designer, opened his first shop in Paris in 1970. Since it was decorated with jungle prints, he called it Jungle Jap, a name that soon became popular with young, fashionable models looking for fresh, spirited clothes. Inspired mostly by traditional Japanese shapes,

Kenzo's early, highly desirable collections included easy-to-wear smocks, tunics, oriental blouses and wide-legged trousers. They were predominantly made from cotton and quilted. Kenzo also specialized in knitwear, which was added to the cottons to produce an eclectic, comfortable look. Kenzo Takada retired from the house in 1999. The new co-creative directors of Kenzo are Humberto Leon and Carol Lim.

► Ashley, Ettedgui, Leon & Lim, Matsuda

Kenzo (Kenzo Takada). b Hyogo (JAP), 1939. **Tiered floral print dress, Spain.** Photograph by Peter Knapp, 1973.

Keogh Lainey

Designer

Naomi Campbell wears an intricately knitted dress which is light as air, clingy and revealing. 'Lainey's knitwear,' said Hamish Bowles in American *Vogue*, 'challenges all one's preconceptions of the woolly jumper.' Knitting is one of Ireland's oldest cottage industries and although Keogh's style is modern – with details such as the quirky, asymmetric hem and shoulder – this dress is also ethereal and romantic. The emerald green conjures up images of mermaids and fishing nets. Lainey Keogh says her hand-knitted clothes are 'like food or sex: intimate and personal'. This poetic sensibility is her signature; she claims to have discovered her talent through knitting a jumper for her lover. She loves the 'exquisite feeling of the lightest textures against the skin' and her fabrics are created using cashmere and iridescent chenille. In 2010 Ireland issued a set of stamps honouring six contemporary Irish designers. Lainey Keogh was one of them.

► Campbell, Kobayashi, Macdonald

Lainey Keogh. b Dublin (IRE), 1957. **Lace knitwear, autumn/winter 1997.** Photograph by Chris Moore.

Kerrigan Daryl

Designer

A Daryl K dress is hitched up in a movement that corrects a predicament known as the 'Daryl dip'. Daryl Kerrigan's problematic but highly fashionable strapless tops, worn with tomboyish hipster trousers, blend sportswear with tailoring for women who aren't ready to commit to a suit. She studied fashion at the National College of Art and Design in Dublin, before moving to New York in 1986. Kerrigan was determined to design the perfect pair of jeans. Her boot-cut, hipster jeans, dubbed 'low riders', were partly inspired by a pair of 1970s hip-huggers she had found in a vintage warehouse. The jeans were to make her name and become the mainstay of her collections, alongside her stretchy tube tops, drawstring nylon skirts and zip-up jersey sweat-jackets. She says 'Women want something new and don't want to feel like they're dressing in a period play.'

► Demeulemeester, Farhi, Lang

Daryl Kerrigan. b Dublin (IRE), 1964. **Strapless dress.** Photograph by Jon Mortimer, 1998.

Khanh Emmanuelle   Designer

'Haute couture is dead,' proclaimed Emmanuelle Khanh in the 1960s. Her French street fashion paralleled Mary Quant's during the 'youthquake' movement. Her radical designs, tightly modelled on the curves of the body, drew inspiration from the pop scene. A former model for Balenciaga and Givenchy, Khanh reacted against the stiff sophistication of 1950s couture by reflecting and modernizing the loose, feminine frame of the 1930s. Her relaxed style, shown here, was a mixture of low-waisted culottes, fitted jackets with narrow shoulders and dog-eared collars. These flattering innovations were adapted from her earlier knitwear for Missoni, Cacharel and Dorothée Bis. Her own label, created in 1972, echoed the ethnic look of the period in Romanian hand embroidery and peasant-style dresses. Khanh represented the young face of French fashion, together with Christiane Bailly and Paco Rabanne.

► Antonio, Bailly, Ettedgui, Jacobson, Quant, Rosier

Emmanuelle Khanh. b Paris (FR), 1937. **Ready-to-wear womenswear.** Illustration by Antonio López, French *Elle*, 1967.

Kim Christina (Dosa)

Designer

In an installation presented at The Music Museum (Il Museo della Musica) in Bologna, Dosa's delicate textiles hang ethereally from the ceiling in this stunning setting. Lightness and delicacy are words that could consistently describe the work of Christina Kim – the designer behind the label – with a practice fundamentally inspired by traditional and ethnic textiles. Launching the brand in 1983, Kim was born in Korea but has lived much of her life in Los Angeles. The Dosa philosophy was born when her t'ai chi teacher's traditional Chinese jacket caught her eye and inspired her to make a similar one in a heavy, washed linen. Kim has since perfected the art of melding simple shapes, inspired by her Korean heritage, with fabrics from diverse cultures, in a palette of soothing, often iridescent colours. Mindful of the environment, Kim also uses the by-products of the clothing manufacturing process for home accessories.

► Jinteok, Matsuda, Zoran

Christina Kim. b Seoul (KOR), 1957. **'Life of Jamdani' exhibition at Il Museo della Musica in Bologna, Italy, 2008.** Photograph by Studio Pym.

Kirkwood Nicholas

Shoe Designer

A graduate of Cordwainers, the prestigious college for the study of footwear (now part of the London College of Fashion), Nicholas Kirkwood creates striking forms that are underpinned by his skilled craftsmanship. He launched his own label in 2005 and opened his London boutique in 2011 with a collection dedicated to the late artist Keith Haring. It was Haring's bold shapes that Kirkwood captured in his 'power stretch' boot mounted on roller skates and encrusted with Swarovski crystals. As well as being the dazzling highlight of the collection, the roller skate boot sums up both the extravagance and the street culture that epitomized the 1980s. His eye-catching pop- and art-influenced designs have led to successful collaborations with Peter Pilotto, Erdem and Rodarte. In 2010 he won the Accessory Designer Award at the British Fashion Awards, the same year he was appointed creative director of Italian footwear label Pollini.

► Blow, Erdem, Pilotto, Treacy

Nicholas Kirkwood. b Münster (GER), 1980. **Keith Haring roller skate boots, 2011.**

Klein Anne

Designer

A belted, white playsuit over a long-sleeved T-shirt epitomizes every practical detail used by Anne Klein. Klein only just missed inventing American designer sportswear. Following the pioneers of the 1930s and 1940s – McCardell, Leser, Maxwell *et al* – she came to represent the ethos of contemporary sportswear, creating clothes that suited modern women. Beginning with her work at Junior Sophisticates in 1948, she always thought in terms of carefree and casual forms, soft materials (especially jersey for evening), mixable separates (for sensible wardrobe-building) and forgiving tunics and outer wraps. Her bodysuits and derivations from active sportswear determined the basic canon of American designer sportswear in the 1950s and 1960s. Klein's lead was followed by Donna Karan and Louis Dell'Olio who both excelled (and still do in Karan's case) at fashion that is friendly towards a multitude of figure shapes.

▶ Dell'Olio, Leser, McCardell, Maxwell, Rodriguez

Anne Klein. b New York (USA), 1923. **d** New York (USA), 1974. **Cream shorts suit.** Photograph by Kourken Pakchanian, American *Vogue*, 1972.

Klein Calvin

Designer

Lauren Hutton wears a simple blouson jacket, mannish pleated trousers cinched with a silk tie, and a clean, white top. The styles may have changed but the adjectives have followed Calvin Klein's work through three decades and come to define the versatility of modern fashion. In the 1970s, Klein produced branded jeans, thereby creating the modern-day designer label as a branding tool. Klein is also known for his clever marketing (from Brooke Shields purring 'Nothing comes between me and my Calvin's', to the pin-up, billboard posters for his men's and women's underwear in the 1980s) and is often credited as being the designer most in tune with the Zeitgeist. The brand portfolio now includes a variety of lines including Calvin Klein Jeans and Calvin Klein Underwear. Klein sold the company to conglomerate Phillips-Van Heusen in 2003 but in the same year brought in Francisco Costa as creative director of womenswear, Calvin Klein Collection.

► Baron, Coddington, Hutton, Moss, Turlington, Weber

Calvin Klein. b New York (USA), 1942. **Lauren Hutton wears cream.** Photograph by Francesco Scavullo, American *Vogue*, 1974.

Klein William

Photographer

The viewer always has the best seat in the house for Klein's spectacle. In a 1960 meeting of Roberto Capucci dresses on the Piazza di Spagna in Rome, Simone d'Aillencourt almost steps into the viewer's lap; Nina de Vos, walking the other way, looks back as if to notice that the two dresses are so Op Art and so alike. Only the 'chance' presence of the guy on the Vespa tells us that this is the street and not a commissioned runway. Klein exalted the artifice of a fashion photograph, defying many of his contemporaries in the 1950s, who preferred naturalism or its simulation. Klein sought the startling effect. Later a film-maker, Klein let out some of his fashion contempt in the satirical film, now a fashion legend, *Qui êtes-vous, Polly Magoo?* (1966). Klein appeared to care little about the dresses; he was always a maker of eccentric, visual melodramas.

► Capucci, Courrèges, Fontana, Kelly, Paulette

William Klein. b New York (USA), 1928. **Black-and-white dresses by Roberto Capucci.** American *Vogue*, 1960.

Knight Nick   Photographer

Devon, the young model, looks vulnerable and fragile. She is scarred, her face transformed by make-up artist Topolino. Although her stance and expression are aggressively defiant, the image is a deeply disturbing vision by photographer Nick Knight. It is fashion photography *in extremis*. 'If you want reality, look out of the window,' says Knight. Like many 1990s photographers, he manipulates his images to heighten their impact. His photographs, which have appeared in *Vogue* and *i-D*, usually have a fairy-tale aspect to them, often contrasted with disturbing touches of violence, as here. They focus on form as well as fashion, as demonstrated by the geometric shapes in this image. His unconventional view of beauty has led him to photograph a size 14 model for *Vogue* and a septuagenarian for a Levi's advertising campaign. He is also the founding director of SHOWstudio.com, an online platform for fashion photography and film.

► McQueen, SHOWstudio, Strauss, Topolino

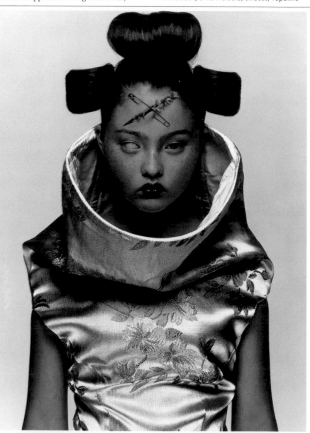

Nick Knight. b London (UK), 1958. **Brocade cowl dress by Alexander McQueen.** 1996.

Knight Phil & Bowerman Bill (Nike)   Designers

The famous 'Swoosh' tick is the designer logo of the sportswear market. One of Nike's two founders, Phil Knight, was a middle-distance runner at the University of Oregon. He founded Blue Ribbon Sports in 1971 and soon after began manufacturing his own range, which he named Nike after the Greek winged goddess of victory. Much of the key to Nike's success lies in the marketing of its image, with advertisements that push the brand rather than the product. The company's slogans, including 'Just Do It', are unapologetically uncompromising; Nike was criticized by the Olympic Committee for its 'You don't win silver – you lose gold' advertisements. Taking advantage of the sportswear-as-streetwear trend, Nike produces fashion-conscious designs in limited editions that have since become collectors' items, displaying an increasingly technical and technologically innovative approach to products in both of these markets.

► D. Beckham, Crawford, Dassler, Hechter, Lacoste

Phil Knight. b Portland, OR (USA), 1938; **Bill Bowerman. b** Portland, OR (USA), 1911. **d** Fossil, OR (USA), 1999. **Allyson Felix models Nike Pinnacle collection.** 2013.

Kobayashi Yukio

Designer

This photograph by the legendary photographer of New York's drug culture, Nan Goldin, was taken in 1996 as part of a series entitled *Naked New York – Nan Goldin meets Yukio Kobayashi*. Kobayashi had been designer of the Matsuda menswear line since 1983, and took on the role of chief designer of womenswear in late 1995. This photograph is from the autumn/winter 1996 Matsuda collection and was taken to capture its 'raw energy and artistic foundation'. Kobayashi is unusual in his mission to create clothes that break free of conventional style and offer an 'ageless' and 'genderless' alternative, using highly developed sewing and decorative techniques, such as 'needle punch' and quilting. 'From my perspective,' he says, 'fashion and art are inseparable...both need to be nurtured and developed to ensure they prosper over time'. Here translucent prints on bare skin simulate intricate tattoos.

▶ Isogawa, Keogh, Matsuda

Yukio Kobayashi. b Niigata (JAP), 1951. **Yukio Kobayashi for Matsuda, autumn/winter 1996.** Photograph by Nan Goldin.

Kors Michael

Designer

Michael Kors' aspiration is to design clothes that can be both shown off and worn for everday life. Kate Moss wearing this strapless, black outfit on a racing track and holding a helmet bearing the US flag epitomizes his style: it is sexy, fun and practical. Kors had two career aims as a child – to be a movie star or a fashion designer. He chose fashion and studied it briefly, but learnt his trade by working at a boutique where he eventually became a designer. He established his label in 1981, incorporating menswear in 1990. Kors' clothes are minimalistic in shape and luxurious to touch. He layers his silhouette and uses luxury fabrics, preferring cashmere, kid leather, silk and organza over cheaper alternatives. In 1998 he also began designing for deluxe French house Céline, a parallel to Marc Jacobs' move to Louis Vuitton. His autumn/winter 2003 collection was the last he designed for Céline.

► Céline, Eisen, Jacobs, Mizrahi, Moss, Richardson, Tyler

Michael Kors. b New York (USA), 1959. **Kate Moss wears stretch tube top and pedal pushers.** Photograph by Terry Richardson, *Harper's Bazaar*, 1997.

LaChapelle David

Photographer

'I love drama and outrageousness. I love crazy scenes,' says LaChapelle, who creates an unforgettable interpretation of John Galliano's outfits for his two 'Milkmaids' here. When he was young, his mother organized elaborately staged photographs, 'In the family albums we look like the Vanderbilts. My mom remade her reality through snapshots.' Their move from conservative Connecticut to the brashness of Carolina encouraged LaChapelle to 'celebrate the artificial'. He left home at fifteen and moved to New York where he worked as a busboy at the legendary New York nightclub, Studio 54 – 'a big influence...all that pop imagery'. He met Andy Warhol at a Psychedelic Furs concert and was employed by him at *Interview*. 'For me, taking photographs, planning them and working on them, is a big escape,' he says. LaChapelle likes his subjects to be equally dramatic. 'Exhibitionists make the best models.'

► Galliano, R. James, Vanderbilt, Warhol

David LaChapelle. b Hartford, CT (USA), 1963. **'Milkmaids.'** *Stern*, 1996.

Lacoste René

The French tennis star, René Lacoste, launched his polo shirt in 1933, six years after he had earned the nickname 'le crocodile' for winning a crocodile-skin suitcase in a bet. 'A friend drew a crocodile,' he said, 'and I had it embroidered on the blazer I wore on the courts.' His polo shirts were the first example of sportswear as fashion. The Lacoste empire now includes leisure-, golf- and tennis-wear. As such, it was a precursor to the sportswear phenomenon that accelerated throughout the century.

Lacoste's crocodile, one of the most famous fashion emblems, is sold across the world to brand-conscious youth. When logo mania boomed in the 1980s, it became a major label, worn from Laos to Liverpool; it was in this city that Casuals – working-class football supporters – began wearing upmarket labels such as Lacoste as an emblem of personal success. Lacoste remains a prominent brand in the sports and lifestyle market.

► Dassler, Jantzen, Knight & Bowerman

René Lacoste. b Paris (FR), 1904. d Saint Jean-De-Luc (FR), 1996. **René Lacoste wears blazer with a crocodile motif.** 1927.

Lacroix Christian   Designer

This printed leotard, smattered with beading and worn with grandiose jewellery, epitomizes Christian Lacroix's role as an ornate antidote to monochrome power dressing. His grandfather, a dandy who lined his suits with green silk, inspired Christian's love affair with the eighteenth century, introducing him to Madame de Pompadour and Louis XIV. An *ancien régime* opulence influences much of his work, which is also coloured by his southern French roots. Having designed for Hermès, Lacroix joined Patou in 1981. His 1984 couture collection for that house injected life back into the couture scene. Lacroix opened his own house in 1987 and became wildly famous for his fearless styles. He sold the company to the LVMH conglomerate in 1993, who in turn sold it to the Falic Group in 2003. During the global recession in 2009 the house was put into administration. Lacroix continues to design, collaborating with Desigual in 2011.

▶ Etro, Gigli, Hermès, Patou, Pearl, Pucci, Testino

Christian Lacroix. b Arles (FR), 1951. **Marie Sophie wears printed and embroidered catsuit.** Photograph by Mario Testino, 1990.

Lady Gaga

Icon

For her third costume change of the night, Lady Gaga was stitched into a dress made of raw beef for the 2010 MTV Video Music Awards in Los Angeles. Nicola Formichetti, fashion director of Lady Gaga's creative team Haus of Gaga, conceptualized the dress (and matching boots, clutch and fascinator). Visual sensation has played a pivotal role in the pop megastar's global domination. Born in 1986, Stefani Germanotta grew up in New York City and attended an uptown all-girls Catholic school –

only to take a stage name and make her mark with racy performances on the downtown club scene where she gathered many devoted fans before taking the world by storm. Her unforgettable outfits include a nude leotard embellished with translucent bubbles and a jacket made of Kermit the Frogs (typically of Gaga, neither outfit included trousers) as well as Alexander McQueen's futuristic armadillo high heels.

▶ Blow, Formichetti, Galliano, Guinness, G. Jones, Warhol

Lady Gaga (Stefani Joanne Angelina Germanotta). b New York (USA), 1986. **Lady Gaga at the MTV Video Music Awards, 2010.**

293

Lagerfeld Karl   Designer

Lagerfeld once stated, 'Energy should always be new. There is no old energy. You cannot stock energy. You can for electricity, but not for creativity.' And as such the designer has frequently redefined himself and fashion alike over the course of a highly productive career. An avid devourer of art and culture, Lagerfeld began his career at the house of Balmain, with stints at Chloé, Fendi and eventually Chanel where he re-invigorated the house. Taking Coco Chanel's traditional leitmotifs – the tweed suit for example – and turning them into design features, has made Chanel the luxury empire it is known as today. Also a celebrity in his own right, Lagerfeld has become famous for his outrageous quotes ('The iPod is genius. I have 300!') and signature black slim-fitted silhouette, which is finished off with a severe white collar and ponytail. The designer remains one of the most important and influential creative forces in contemporary fashion.

► Balmain, Chanel, Fath, Fendi, Léger, Lenoir

Karl Lagerfeld. b Hamburg (GER), 1938. **Chanel ready-to-wear autumn/winter 2005.** Photograph by Olivier Hostlet.

Lalique René Jules

Jewellery designer

A gold and diamond tourmaline dragonfly brooch displays Lalique's precise copying techniques and delicate pictorial detailing. Master goldsmith René Lalique led the Art Nouveau jewellery movement of the 1890s, and later became a premier glass-maker. Unconventionally, Lalique worked with materials for their aesthetic value rather than their preciousness. Decoration was the purpose of the pieces and elaborately ornate hair combs were especially popular. Many of the pieces had references to nature, such as insects, animals or flora, and many featured pictorial scenes, such as a forest clearing, with a single pearl suspended below. Often impractically large in order to increase the visual impact, the pieces were favoured by extroverts such as Sarah Bernhardt. Lalique moved into glass jewellery in the 1920s and 1930s, creating all-glass rings, and pendants on silk cords.

► Bulgari, Tiffany, Winston

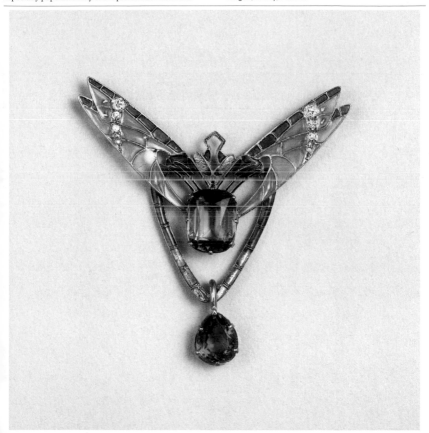

René Jules Lalique. b Aÿ (FR), 1860. **d** Paris (FR), 1945. **Diamond tourmaline pendant brooch.** *c.*1900.

Lancetti Pino

Designer

Two models tread Pino Lancetti's catwalk. Their richly detailed gowns serve to reinforce their sleek-haired conspicuousness, a style that belongs to the wealthy society for which he caters. Both dresses fall from raised waistbands and are accessorized with co-ordinating wraps to maintain their decorum. Initially a painter, Lancetti became involved in fashion when he moved to Rome and began sketching 'for fun' for the couturiers there. In 1963 he launched a seminal 'Military Line'

collection that transferred the uniform into fashion. His designs, unsurprisingly, tended to be painterly, their inspiration ranging from Modigliani to Picasso to Impressionism. The look was often 'folksy', using soft, printed fabrics. Even the Military Line showed ethnic touches within the braiding. Lancetti avoided the trappings of the international fashion world and was best known in Japan and Italy. He retired from couture in 2001.
► Lapidus, McFadden, Scherrer, Storey

Pino Lancetti. b Bastia Umbra (IT), 1935. **d** Rome (IT), 2007. **Gilded evening dresses**. *Women's Wear Daily*, 1977.

Lane Kenneth Jay

Jewellery designer

Dubbed 'the undisputed king of costume jewelry' by *Time* magazine, Kenneth Jay Lane believes every woman has the right to look glamorous – no matter what her income or status. Lane eschews the elitist stance of many designers. Early in his career, he designed shoes for Christian Dior, where he worked under the tutelage of Roger Vivier. By 1963 Lane had decided costume jewellery was his future and spent his spare time covering cheap plastic bangles with stripes, patterns and crystals. He was celebrating the possibilities of non-precious materials. Lane would place demonstrably artificial plastics next to glass approximations of diamonds. This has been an enduring formula that was widely copied in the 1980s and 1990s. His clients, all of whom were famous for their real jewels, have included Jackie Kennedy, Elizabeth Taylor, Babe Paley, Barbara Bush and Joan Collins.

► Butler, Kennedy, Leiber, Paley, Vivier

Kenneth Jay Lane. b Detroit, MI (USA), 1932. **Paulette Stone.** Photograph by Norman Eales, 1967.

Lang Helmut

Designer

A theatrical headdress, worn with plain vests, epitomizes the work of Helmut Lang, one of the most sought-after designers of the 1990s. Technology and fabrics that are rarely made from natural fibres are joined in his collections. Lang's keywords were 'urban', 'clean' and 'modern', reflecting a downbeat style that is instantly recognizable. He described his clothes as conveying, 'the sort of anonymous status that the truly knowing admire'. Lang launched his own label in 1977, with his first Paris show in 1986 an immediate success, affording him a cult status. The essence of his design ethos is to create a simple silhouette that is then made more complex with textural combinations – sheer/opaque, shiny/matte – and flashes of bright colour. After nearly three decades of success, Lang retired from fashion in 2005 and continues to work as an artist. The label was relaunched in 2006 with Michael and Nicole Colovos as creative directors.

► Capasa, Kerrigan, Sander, Teller, Tennant

Helmut Lang. b Vienna (AUS), 1956. **Kirsten Owen wears feather headdress.** Photograph by Juergen Teller, 1997.

Lanvin Jeanne

Designer

The waisted, full-skirted dress was a speciality of Jeanne Lanvin, as the mannequin and the sketches on the floor attest. Famous for her frocks that recalled earlier times, Madame Lanvin promoted romantic clothes when other couturiers such as Vionnet, Chanel and Jean Patou were modernizing with their vertical aesthetic. Opening her *maison de couture* just before the First World War, Lanvin was already fifty-one when the war ended. Rather than initiate revolutionary trends, she clung to that era –

designing on the lines of the full skirt of 1915–16 with only slight adjustments. Madame Lanvin was also famous for her mother/daughter outfits and for introducing, in 1926, a line of menswear. The house changed hands several times after being taken over by L'Oréal in the 1960s. It is the oldest fashion house in operation and continues to flourish into the twenty-first century with the appointment of Alber Elbaz as creative director in 2001.

► Abbe, Arnold, Castillo, Crahay, Elbaz, Grès, Poiret

Jeanne Lanvin. b Brittany (FR), 1867. d Paris (FR), 1946. **Jeanne Lanvin with mannequin in her Paris studio.** 1921.

Lapidus Ted

Designer

Ted Lapidus and his model Lilo pose for Eve Arnold backstage at his winter show in 1977. Lilo wears a typically romantic, crepe georgette dress by Lapidus. Despite its heavy embroidery and beading, it is a relaxed shape that is dressed down with a peasant neckline and a tiered skirt – details usually found on daywear. Lapidus's design education began with an engineering diploma taken in Tokyo in 1949, but he was inspired by his Russian tailor father to take up fashion instead. Using the principles learnt from both disciplines, Lapidus attracted a reputation as a master of pattern-cutting. Inspired by his experience of high technology in Japan, he felt that it was important to integrate science with fashion. Consequently, he became involved with mass-manufacture at the same time as applying his precision techniques to his couture collections.

► Arnold, Lancetti, McFadden

Ted Lapidus (Edmond Lapidus). b Paris (FR), 1929. **d** Cannes (FR), 2008. **Ted Lapidus with Lilo wearing a beaded dress.**
Photograph by Eve Arnold, French *Vogue*, 1977.

Laroche Guy

Designer

Guy Laroche's career began at a hat maker's in Paris, then in New York, on Seventh Avenue. On returning to Paris, he found employment in the *maison de couture* of Jean Dessès. His successful apprenticeship encouraged him to open his own house in 1957. Laroche was renowned for his mastery of cutting and tailoring. His early work was influenced by the architectural cutting of Cristóbal Balenciaga, but he later gave that formality a lively freshness, cultivating popularity with younger women – this meant diversifying his couture business by moving into ready-to-wear in 1960. Laroche is remembered from that time for lending an almost girlish attitude to formal clothes – especially with his empire-line dresses with material gently gathered into raised waistbands. In the following decade, his trouser suit, itself a symbol for liberated women, was required wearing.

► Dessès, Fath, Miyake, Paulette, Valentino

Guy Laroche. b La Rochelle (FR), 1923. **d** Paris (FR), 1989. **Tweed suits and woollen accessories.** Photograph by Chris Moore, 1971.

Lauder Estée

Cosmetics creator

The Estée Lauder look from 1961 is a constructed scheme using shading, lighting and lashings of liquid eyeliner. Lauder, who founded her company in 1946, was one of the queens of New York cosmetics. Born there, she was the daughter of a well-to-do Hungarian mother and Czechoslovakian father. Her interest in skincare was inspired by her Uncle John, a dermatologist, who, when he came to stay in America, admonished her for washing her face with soap. With him, the family set up a laboratory and produced creams that became favourites with their friends and friends of friends. The real business began when Lauder was invited to sell the products at a Manhattan salon. Lauder encouraged women to buy scent for themselves and was one of the first names to develop a full range of cosmetics. The company is now a giant, encompassing other brands: Aramis, Clinique, Prescriptives, Origins, Aveda and Bobbi Brown.

► Brown, Dovima, Factor, Horst, Revillon

Estée Lauder (Josephine Esther Mentzer). b New York (USA), 1906. **d** New York (USA), 2004. **Estée Lauder make-up.**
Photograph by Horst P. Horst, American *Vogue*, 1961.

Lauren Ralph

Designer

A Californian ranch is the setting for Ralph Lauren's advertisement from 1988. His vision, conjured by Bruce Weber, is of a measured, monied society that has a home in Connecticut and a ranch in Pasadena. Lauren, apart from being one of the most famous fashion product designers in the world, is a clever marketing man; a purveyor of a Waspish, all-American lifestyle, dressing every aspect of it, from exotic travel to business suits for Wall Street. Since 1968, when he launched his menswear label, Polo, Lauren has created a brand that is known throughout the world and clothes that are status symbols. His style, borrowed from vintage clothing, evolved from a desire to give new relevance to nostalgic elegance. It was an aesthetic summed up in the films *The Great Gatsby* (1974) and *Annie Hall* (1977), for which Lauren worked on the actors' wardrobes. In later years, he has made the look his own.

▶ Abboud, Brooks, Hilfiger, Weber

Ralph Lauren. b New York (USA), 1939. **'Polo' advertising campaign, Pasadena.** Photograph by Bruce Weber, 1988.

Léger Hervé

Designer

These rainbow dresses, formed from hand-stitched elastic bandages, are little more than extended swimsuit shapes. Hervé Léger learned his craft working with Karl Lagerfeld, designing swimwear first for Fendi, then Chanel. His forte is remoulding the body and Léger is more concerned with perfecting the female form than he is about passing trends. He claims that the woman he designs for is, 'fed up with the vagaries of fashion. She does not give a damn about trends, she refuses to be a feminine clothes hanger.' His use of stretchy bands for his 'bender dresses' means his clothes are often compared with those of Azzedine Alaïa, but Léger arguably pioneered the glamorous simplicity and uninterrupted line of the 'body-con' (body-conscious) look of the '80s, and his name is synonymous with the look. The label is now known as Hervé Léger by Max Azria after it was acquired by the BCBG Max Azria group in 1998.

► Alaïa, Chanel, Inez and Vinoodh, Model, Mugler

Hervé Léger. b Bapaume (FR), 1957. **Joanna.** Photograph by Inez and Vinoodh, 1995.

Leiber Judith

Accessory designer

A glittering Judith Leiber evening bag has been the focus of Hollywood outfits since the 1960s. Despite its high-voltage sparkle, the example carried by Elizabeth Hurley is understated. 'I like to do things that look crazy, yet are practical,' says Leiber, who sent First Lady Hillary Clinton a bag modelled on Socks, the White House cat. Ladybirds, teddy bears, fruit and Fabergé eggs have all been fashioned into such rhinestone whimsies. Though Leiber was offered a place to read chemistry at London's King's College in 1939, the Second World War forced her to stay in her native Budapest, where she was apprenticed to a master handbag maker. Leiber moved to New York in 1947, starting her own business in 1963. Her handbags are collected by customers such as American social queen Pat Buckley, who displays them as works of art. Leiber is less reverent about her own work, saying, 'The bag is really an object to be worn.'

▶ Butler, Lane, Mackie, V. Wang

Judith Leiber. b Budapest (HUN), 1921. **Liz Hurley with diamanté minaudière and Hugh Grant.** 1997.

Lelong Lucien

Designer

The sleeves of this black, silk velvet evening gown are intricately cut in the style of a medieval robe, with pointed cuffs that swoop like swallows' wings. The gown closely follows the shape of the figure, moulding the waist and the hips before widening into a skirt that flows softly into a train, like the outspread feathers of a bird's tail. The birdlike character of the dress is associated with the imagery of Surrealism, the dominant art movement of the 1930s. Lelong, who opened his own couture house after the First World War, was president of the Chambre Syndicale de la Couture Parisienne from 1937 to 1947. He persuaded the occupying Germans to allow French couture houses to remain in Paris rather than be transferred to Berlin or Vienna. Through his efforts, at least one hundred fashion houses were kept running throughout the Occupation of Paris from 1940 to 1944.

► Balmain, Chéruit, Dessès, Givenchy, Hoyningen-Huene

Lucien Lelong. b Paris (FR), 1889. **d** Danglet (FR), 1958. **Black, silk velvet gown.** Photograph by George Hoyningen-Huene, French *Vogue*, 1934.

Leon Humberto & Lim Carol   Designers

Like its Olympic namesake, Opening Ceremony distinguishes itself as an enterprise with global interests and influences. The brand was founded in 2002 in Soho, New York, by Humberto Leon and Carol Lim, who met as students at UC Berkeley in Los Angeles, and has since become a digital and retail tourist destination for the achingly hip. As early adopters for online shopping and editorial content, Leon and Lim have expanded Opening Ceremony with a 'multinational approach to retail',

drawing inspiration from any number of sources and collaborating with creatives such as Chloë Sevigny, Spike Jonze, Rodarte and, more recently, Yoko Ono. They have proven themselves, not only as business-savvy retailers, but also as successful designers since taking over as creative directors of the house of Kenzo in 2011, injecting a youthful sensibility into the fashion brand traditionally known for its dynamic use of colour and print.

▶ Kenzo, Lerfel, Mulleavy, Richardson

Humberto Leon. b Los Angeles, CA (USA), 1975; **Carol Lim. b** Los Angeles, CA (USA), 1975. **Opening Ceremony spring/summer 2011 modelled by Lindsey Wixon.** Photograph by Terry Richardson, 2010.

Leonard

Hairdresser

For one of Leonard's striking hair designs, a hairpiece is looped under the chin and caught in a hand-painted hair slide by Pablo and Delia. Leonard's extreme colouring techniques were developed by him for Stanley Kubrick's *2001: A Space Odyssey* (1968). 'I had to push things as far as they would go,' says Leonard. 'The coloured hair, the crazy colours, the unnatural ones, they started there.' His work was innovative and directional in the 1960s and 1970s: he cut The Beatles' mopheads and when Justin de Villeneuve delivered his young prodigy Twiggy to Leonard for a haircut, he made the best business move of his life. Leonard, who had started out with de Villeneuve on a Shepherd's Bush Market fruit barrow, asked Twiggy to model a new haircut invented by him. After eight hours of snipping, a talent honed during his training with Vidal Sassoon, Twiggy's waifish crop was born and so was her career.

► The Beatles, Mesejeán & Cancela, Sassoon, Twiggy

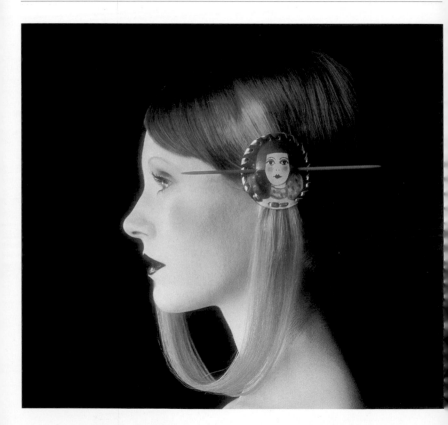

Leonard (**Leonard Lewis**). **b** London (UK), 1938. **Hair coloured by Leonard.** Photograph by Barry Lategan, 1970.

Lepape Georges

Illustrator

These 'Fashions of Tomorrow' most certainly live up to their name. Poiret's pantaloon gowns, illustrated here by Georges Lepape, were considered shocking at the time, but anticipated the move towards greater physical freedom in women's fashion. This illustration is one of the plates from *Les Choses de Paul Poiret vues par Georges Lepape*. The sculptural simplicity of Lepape's illustrations captures perfectly the silhouette of Poiret's clothes. Poiret was the first couturier to relate fashion successfully to the other arts and was innovative in commissioning the artists Georges Lepape and Paul Iribe to compile limited-edition albums of his designs. Lepape contributed illustrations to *La Gazette du Bon Ton*, a folio of fashion news and drawings in the twentieth century, and regularly appeared on the cover of *Vogue* in the 1920s. Lepape was instrumental in bringing art movements such as Cubism into the realm of fashion.

► Barbier, Benito, Drian, Iribe, Poiret

Georges Lepape. b Paris (FR), 1887. **d** Bonneval (FR), 1971. **'Fashions of Tomorrow.'** From *Les Choses de Paul Poiret vues par Georges Lepape*, 1911.

Lerfel Sarah (Colette)

Retailer

One of the first-ever concept stores, Colette has remained one of the coolest – thanks to Sarah Lerfel, the creative director and co-founder. Opening in 1997, the expansive, streamlined space is credited with bringing hipsters back to ultra-posh central Paris and continues to draw in savvy tourists from around the world. Its name is not a salute to the twentieth-century novelist, but a reference to Lerfel's mother and store co-founder, Colette Rousseaux. Reflecting Lerfel's ever-changing tastes in fashion, food, art and design, the ground floor displays sneakers, artsy magazines and a curated selection of music, while upstairs on the first level there is a pricey ready-to-wear section. Lerfel's social connections facilitate Colette's renowned collaborative projects, which include the issue of exclusive Hermès foulards and a pop-up Chanel shop where the artist Fafi customized purchasers' quilted bags with special drawings.

► Kawakubo, Lagerfeld, Leon & Lim, Richardson

Sarah Lerfel. b Paris (FR), 1976. **The Colette store on rue Saint-Honoré, Paris.** 2012.

Leroy Véronique   Designer

Véronique Leroy was once described as 'the unchallenged reigning queen of the Paris sexy-tack scene'. This sportswear-meets-eveningwear outfit is typical of Leroy's flirtation with bad taste. Her method is to use recently outmoded references. She used gilt chain and nylon mesh at a time when the memories of their misuse in the hands of the mass market were still fresh. The chain, a reference to Chanel's handbag handles, suspends an Op Art patchwork of artificial sportswear fabrics. These thrift store-inspired collections dabble in different themes, each one rich in its potential for anti-taste, including *Charlie's Angels*, Pop Art and science fiction. Before starting her own label, Leroy worked with Alaïa, who taught her how to handle synthetics, and Martine Sitbon from whom she learned about the rock-chick market. Her brand has evolved in the new millennium, opening her first store in Paris in 2005 and showing at Paris fashion week.

► Hemingway, Inez and Vinoodh, Sitbon

Véronique Leroy. b Liège (FR), 1965. **Blue halterneck dress.** Photograph by Christophe Kutner, British *Elle*, 1995.   311

Lesage Albert

Embroiderer

This bolero jacket, embroidered with a parade of elephants, is from Schiaparelli's 'Circus' collection of 1938. Not since Poiret had a fashion designer shown such an instinctive flair for the use of embroidery, making it a glamorous adjunct to haute couture. Collaborating with the celebrated Maison Lesage, which had been founded in 1922 by Albert Lesage (*maître brodeur*) and in particular with his son, François, Schiaparelli designed her collection especially to offset the sumptuous embroidery. Her basic silhouette of wide shoulders and neat waist enabled Lesage to adorn her jackets with embroideries that enhanced her whimsical dreams. Maison Lesage, renowned for its jewel-studded embroidery, let loose all the capriciousness of Schiaparelli's Surrealism. Karl Lagerfeld later collaborated with the house for Chanel for many years, and when François Lesage died, in 2011, Hubert Barrière was appointed the new head of Maison Lesage.

▶ Balenciaga, Givenchy, Saint Laurent, Schiaparelli, Yantorny

Albert Lesage. b Paris (FR), 1888. **d** Paris (FR), 1949. **'Circus', elephant embroidery for Schiaparelli.** 1938.

Leser Tina   Designer

A cute, teenager outfit of turned-up denim jeans and striped cotton shirt epitomizes the freshness of American fashion after the Second World War. Tina Leser was among the new wave of designers unique to American culture who concentrated on sportswear as fashion. Her clothes, designed for a manufacturer (until 1952 when she formed her own company), were informed by everyday shapes such as play-suits, sarong dresses, smocks, swimsuits and shrug-on jackets, but they were almost always influenced by a more formal aesthetic, as is evident here. Leser's mother was a painter, and the designer studied art, painting, design and sculpture in Philadelphia and Paris. Leser moved to Honolulu and opened a boutique in 1935, relocating to New York in 1942. During the 1950s she designed cropped and harem pants before any other designers; she is also thought to have been the first designer to make dresses from cashmere.

► Connolly, A. Klein, McCardell, Maxwell, Simpson

Tina Leser (Christine Wetherill Shillard-Smith). b PA (USA), 1910. **d** Sands Point, NY (USA), 1986. **Mexican cotton shirt and denim jeans.** Photograph by John Rawlings, *Harper's Bazaar*, 1951.

Lester Charles & Patricia

Designers

A golden, hand-pleated silk dress is set against antique fabrics. It recalls the Delphos style designed by Fortuny eighty years earlier, but it is the work of designers Charles and Patricia Lester, who were unaware of his work when they started their experiments in the 1960s. Years of research go into the techniques used by the Lesters: designs are burnt out of velvet to form devoré and others are hand-painted to produce unique cloth that is used for tunics, dresses and robes. The historical perception of these techniques has an attraction that sets their work apart from the less enduring elements of high fashion. Consequently, it has been used for opera productions and for the film adaptation of Henry James' novel *The Wings of a Dove*, in which Helena Bonham Carter wafts around pre-First World War Venice. Her pleated silk dresses and velvet coats, however, were taken from the Lesters' 1990s collection.

► Fortuny, McFadden, V. Wang

Lester. Charles. b Banbury, Oxfordshire (UK), 1942; **Patricia. b** Nairobi (KEN), 1943. **Gold pleats.** Photograph by Alex Chatelain, British *Vogue*, 1985.

Levine Beth

Shoe designer

Freedom of movement and freedom from the conventions of footwear are provided by Beth Levine's innovative stocking boots. All Levine's shoes gave the potential for motion, from the elasticated sole of her Spring-O-Lator mule, to the aerodynamic curves and rounded 'rock-a-bottom' sole of her Kabuki pumps, the prototype for which was carved from a teak salad bowl (a shape later reinvented by Vivienne Westwood for her 'rocking horse' platforms). Levine was known for her sexy, stretchy boots, including pairs made for Nancy Sinatra who sang 'These Boots Were Made for Walking'. She conjured imaginative heels, from a rolled scroll shape to chunky cuboid blocks, and favoured unconventional materials such as Astroturf and frog skin. Originally untrained in shoe design, Levine pushed the physical possibilities of footwear – her high-heeled 'topless' shoe was a satin sole stuck to the foot using spirit gum.

▶ Ferragamo, Parkinson, Westwood

Beth Levine. b New York (USA), 1914. **d** New York (USA), 2006. **Suede boots.** Photograph by Sir Norman Parkinson, American *Vogue*, 1969.

Ley Wolfgang & Margaretha (Escada)   Designers

The affectations of this image are stereotypical of the 1980s: strong-shouldered siren with sharp, glittery skirt, big hair and bigger attitude. What Escada meant for women far surpassed their angst-ridden boundaries as working mothers and wives – it symbolized the triumph of ostentatious glamour at a time when image dominated substance, and even taste. Launched in 1976 by Wolfgang and Margaretha Ley, Escada was aptly named after a winning racehorse. Their sexy, chiselled suits, leopard-print blouses and nautical-striped sweaters, all offset with gold buttoning and braid, eulogized a 'bourgeois chic' look. It was a hugely popular style. Wealth was counted in sequins, which were applied to every surface – even sweaters were taken out of their casual context with a smattering of sparkle. With Todd Oldham hired as creative consultant in 1994, Escada took a fresh approach and embraced the spirit of the times.

▶ Féraud, N. Miller, Norell, Oldham

Ley. Wolfgang. b GA (USA), 1937. **Margaretha. b** Västernorrland (SWE), 1933. **d** Berlin (GER), 1992. **Sequined sweater and skirt for Escada.** Photograph by Albert Watson, 1984.

Liberman Alexander

Photographer / Art director

Alexander Liberman photographs Christian Dior, Bettina Ballard, fashion editor of American *Vogue*, and Despina Messinesi, also from *Vogue*, in the early 1950s. This image, taken during one of the legendary Sundays that a few privileged people spent at the French couturier's country house, bears witness to the intimate relationship that Liberman had with the fashion world for almost six decades. After working for Lucien Vogel on *Vu*, a photo-journalism magazine published in Paris, Liberman moved to New York, where he became art director of *Vogue* in 1943. In 1962 he was appointed editorial director of all Condé Nast's publications, thus acquiring a unique insight into every aspect of the fashion journalism trade. He maintained that its appeal lay in providing the viewer with a ticket of escape from her surroundings, 'into the heaven of fashion and the unbelievable nirvana of luxe and elegance.'

► Abbe, Chanel, Dior, McLaughlin-Gill, Nast

Alexander Liberman. b Kiev (RUS), 1912. **d** Miami Beach, FL (USA), 1999. **Bettina Ballard, Christian Dior, Despina Messinesi and Bettina Ballard's husband.** 1950.

Liberty Arthur Lasenby Retailer

Just as the work of Liberty has reflected the times ever since it was founded in 1875, this lawn dress, speckled with flowers, was perfectly in tune with the mood of its age. It is bright, simple and, with its co-ordinated accessories, captured young British fashion (and the Rolling Stones). It was designed by The Ginger Group, a label founded in 1963 by Mary Quant, the quintessential fashion designer of the 1960s. She was one of the leading lights of 'Swinging London', a term coined by the

American *Time* magazine in 1964, the date of this dress. Arthur Lasenby Liberty's department store went on to specialize in fine fabrics such as lawn – a lightweight cotton material printed with floral motifs. In its history, Liberty has both reflected and contributed to sartorial changes, from the costume associated with the Aesthetic Movement of the 1880s to the fashion revolution of the 1960s.

► Bousquet, Fish, Muir, Parkinson, Quant, Sassoon, Wilde

Arthur Lasenby Liberty. b Chesham, Buckinghamshire (UK), 1843. **d** Lee Manor (UK), 1917. **'How to Kill Five Stones with One Bird.'** Photograph by Sir Norman Parkinson, *Queen*, 1964.

Lindbergh Peter

Photographer

This photograph of 1990 gathers the reigning supermodels in their off-duty uniform of bodies by Giorgio di Sant'Angelo and Levi's jeans. Peter Lindbergh's name is closely intertwined with those of Naomi Campbell, Linda Evangelista, Tatjana Patitz, Christy Turlington and Cindy Crawford, who partly discovered their singularity through him. The image's stark, grainy quality reveals his trademark lack of artifice and calm directness, rooted in the unadorned greyness of the industrial scenes of his childhood in Germany. He was twenty-seven when he used a camera for the first time. Ever since, his photographs have appeared in every major fashion magazine. The key influence that classical portraiture plays on Lindbergh gives his work a timeless allure. As Karl Lagerfeld said, 'His photographs will never be regarded with any condescending emotion in thirty or forty years' time.'

► Campbell, Crawford, Demarchelier, Evangelista, Karan, Kawakubo

Peter Lindbergh (Peter Brodbeck). b Duesburg (GER), 1944. **Naomi, Linda, Tatjana, Christy and Cindy.** British *Vogue*, 1990.

Lloyd Alison (Ally Capellino)   Designer

Alison Lloyd describes her work as 'something which is fashionable, but which doesn't go out of fashion very quickly'. Lloyd and fellow Middlesex Polytechnic graduate Jono Platt set up Ally Capellino – the name, they thought, was Italian for 'little hat'; to their amusement they later discovered that it means 'little head' – in 1979, launching a womenswear (and subsequent menswear and childrenswear) line in 1980. Moving the business solely into accessories in 2000, Lloyd's design philosophy of simple textiles and materials, high-quality craftsmanship and functional design, carries through to today. With a clever use of bright colours and wearable, enduring shapes Lloyd's covetable bags have become popular amongst cyclists and fashion folk alike. Over an illustrious career Lloyd has collaborated with London's Tate Gallery, Apple products, and in 2010 a 30-year retrospective of her work was shown at the Wapping Project in London.

► Arai, Von Etzdorf, Isogawa

Alison Lloyd. b London (UK), 1956. **Ally Capellino autumn/winter 2012.** Photograph by Agnes Lloyd-Platt.

Loewe Enrique

Accessory designer

Supple, lavender leather distinguishes a strapless dress modelled on a handbag by Loewe, which has created such bags since 1846. Loewe, fabled for its ability to make animal skin behave as fabric, was founded in the Calle del Tobo area of Madrid, a centre for leather artistry, where Enrique Loewe sold snuff boxes and purses alongside his bags. As a company, Loewe entered the fashion sphere in 1947 when it acquired the rights to sell Christian Dior's New Look in Spain. By the 1960s it had begun to design its own fashion collection, one that used the company's proclivity for draping and gathering, as well as producing classic working shirts in suede. In 1997, Loewe modernized its image by appointing Narciso Rodriguez as its house designer. In 2001 Rodriguez was replaced by Jose Selfa, and subsequently designer Stuart Vevers became creative director in 2007.

► Hermès, Rodriguez, Vuitton

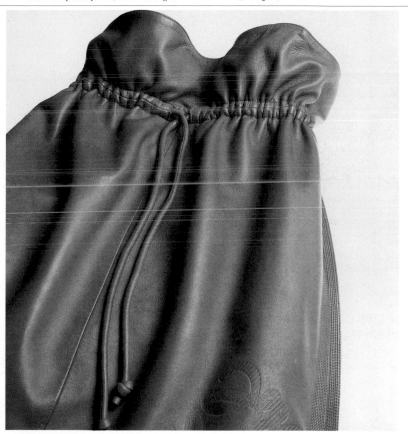

Enrique Loewe. b (GER), 1829. d (SP), 1919. **Lavender leather dress, autumn/winter 1983.** Photograph by Rafael Roa.

Louboutin Christian   Shoe designer

Embroidery, ribbon and blue mosaic heels: a jumble of shoes reveals Louboutin's love of creating fantasies. His seductive shoes, with trademark red soles, are inspired by tropical birds, flowers and gardens. He describes them as a cross between 'a work tool or weapon and an *objet d'art*', and individual commissions are intensely personalized. Love letters, petals, locks of hair and feathers have been encased within his heels. His obsession began in 1976 when, aged ten, he visited a Parisian museum. Far from being inspired by its contents, *bébé* Louboutin couldn't forget the impression made on him by a huge, red high heel worn by another visitor. A meeting with French shoe master Roger Vivier changed his outlook. 'I never thought to do it as a job,' he said. Catherine Deneuve, Inès de la Fressange and Princess Caroline of Monaco would be barefoot without him. In 2012 he was the subject of an exhibition at the Design Museum, London.

► Blahnik, Ferragamo, Jourdan, Pfister, Vivier

Christian Louboutin. b Paris (FR), 1963. **Christin Louboutin autumn/winter 1998.** Photograph by Mark J. Curtis.

Louis Jean

Designer

'There NEVER was a woman like Gilda!' was the caption above Rita Hayworth's picture on the poster from the 1946 film. Sheathed in a satin dress by Jean Louis, she played a seductive *femme fatale*. The bodice that supports Hayworth's body hides an intricate construction of boning and padding, although she maintained that it stayed up 'for two good reasons alone'. Having started his career as a sketch artist for Drecoll, Jean Louis moved to New York where he designed for Hattie Carnegie. He brought the drama of his film work to a couture business that excelled at creating lavish gowns. The potency of this made Hayworth America's dream mistress and her wardrobe the blueprint for sexy, yet illusory dresses, which is still followed today. Hayworth later sadly reflected on her broken relationships with men, saying, 'Every man I ever knew had fallen in love with Gilda and woken up with me.'

► Carnegie, Galanos, Head, Irene

Jean Louis (Jean Louis Berthault). b Paris (FR), 1907. **d** Palm Springs, CA (USA), 1997. **Rita Hayworth in *Gilda*.** Photograph by Bob Coburn, 1946.

323

Lutens Serge

Make-up artist

Every element of this surreal advertisement for Shiseido was created by Serge Lutens, from the make-up and styling to the photograph itself. Lutens grew up wanting to be an artist. School bored him and he spent all his spare time performing makeovers on his friends, then taking their pictures with a Kodak Instamatic. In 1960 he met his partner, Madeleine Levy, and together they launched a 'test salon' in Paris for make-up, hair, jewellery and furniture. In 1968 he was invited to look after the

image and product creation of Christian Dior cosmetics, leaving to join Shiseido in 1980. Lutens does not regard his images as schemes that should (or even could) be copied by women. Fantastical in the extreme, they have the surreal spirit of Salvador Dalí's fashion work. He advocates that women should develop their own creative effects with make-up, whether they want to look natural or artificial.

► Nars, Page, Topolino, Uemura

Serge Lutens. b Lille (FR), 1942. **'Absolutely Amazing' campaign for Shiseido.** Photograph by Serge Lutens, 1998.

McCardell Claire

Designer

Claire McCardell, who pioneered American sportswear, conceived this empire-silhouette 'baby dress' in 1946. The black wool jersey, suggesting an update of Chanel's little black dress, used nonchalant tying in the manner of the casual lifestyle design she championed. Tying and wrapping were not only apt for the active woman, but they also accommodated the inexact sizing and fit of ready-to-wear apparel. Cultivating such traits in soft, relatively inexpensive garments, McCardell made clothing that

had a loyal following among women who wanted independence from corporeal restrictions or dictates from Paris. Instead, versatile separates and the use of materials from menswear, lingerie and childrenswear promised an adaptable, flexible lifestyle akin to the garment itself. Projecting her own desires into design, McCardell never forgot a woman's need for pockets. Her speciality was leisurewear, including playsuits and swimwear.

▶ Cashin, Dahl-Wolfe, Karan, Leser, Maxwell, Steele

Claire McCardell. b MD (USA), 1905. **d** New York (USA), 1958. **Drawstring dress.** Photograph by Louise Dahl-Wolfe, *Harper's Bazaar*, 1946.

McCartney Stella

Designer

An embroidered satin evening dress bears the *richesse* associated with traditional French fashion, but the proportions belong to the modern age. Chloé showed the first collection by Stella McCartney (selected as head designer of the house in 1997 at only twenty-five, her appointment was seen by some as a precocious one) in the opulent setting of the Opéra Garnier in Paris. McCartney had worked previously for Lacroix and was influenced by finds made in London's Portobello Market where she would gather antique buttons and vintage clothes. Her skill in tailoring is attributable to a short apprenticeship with Edward Sexton, a Savile Row tailor. As testament to her solidified reputation McCartney was asked to design the Team GB uniforms for the London 2012 Olympic Games in collaboration with Adidas. She was also awarded an Order of the British Empire (OBE) in the 2013 New Year's Honours list.

► Aghion, The Beatles, Dassler, Moss, Philo

Stella McCartney. b London (UK), 1971. **Miniature satin evening dress for Chloé.** Photograph by Perry Ogden, 1998.

McCollough Jack & Hernandez Lazaro   Designers

Craftsmanship and attention to detail, demonstrated here in Proenza Schouler's spring/summer 2012 collection, has come to define the work of the New York-based duo. Splashes of colour with exquisite, silhouette-conscious tailoring sums up their refined aesthetic. Jack McCollough and Lazaro Hernandez met at New York's prestigious Parsons The New School for Design where, in 2002, they formed Proenza Schouler (named after the maiden names of the pair's mothers). Their first collection was an instant hit and New York high-fashion retailer Barneys bought the entire range. The brand quickly established itself as a leading name on the American fashion scene, collecting the inaugural CFDA Vogue Fashion Fund award in 2004. In 2008 Proenza Schouler launched a shoe collection, followed swiftly by a handbag collection, of which the 'PS1' satchel (named for the New York school system) has become a classic.

▶ Kane, Leon & Lim, Mouret, Mulleavy, Rodriguez, A. Wang

Jack McCollough. b Tokyo (JAP), 1978. **Lazaro Hernandez. b** Miami, CA (USA), 1978. **Backstage at Proenza Schouler spring/ summer 2012.** Photograph by Chris Moore.

McDean Craig

Photographer

Model Guinevere, wearing nothing but artfully undone hair and make-up by Eugene Souleiman and Pat McGrath, appears from behind traditional wallpaper in an advertisement for Jil Sander. That this photograph is representing a fashion and make-up company would make it surreal, except that this is an example of selling a mood rather than a product. McDean's work appeared in the 1990s at a time when his realist photography stood out against the fashion for photographs that presented a limited number of scenarios. He has said, 'I want to appeal to everyone, not just the fashion world,' but it is primarily those in fashion who appreciate his work, which is subtly challenging. It is modern and each photograph, deliberately accidental, is stark and voyeuristic, seemingly capturing a dream-like moment. McDean is part of the neo-realism school dubbed 'Heroin Chic' by US President Bill Clinton in 1997.

► Berardi, McGrath, Sander, Sitbon, Souleiman

Craig McDean. b Nantwich, Cheshire (UK), 1964. **Guinevere van Seenus in Jil Sander's spring/summer 1996 campaign.**

Macdonald Julien

Designer

With hairstyle and make-up to match, Jodie Kidd wears a tight-fitting sheath of gossamer-fine yarns and beading that decorates her body like calligraphy. Seductive and opulent, Julien Macdonald's work takes the girlishness out of knitwear. He spins out fiery fantasies like this from his trusty knitting machine. Karl Lagerfeld, who hired him as knitwear designer for Chanel in 1996, declared to *Vogue*, 'Julien plays with his machine like Horowitz plays on his Steinway.' While regarded as a master of innovation, he pays homage to the traditional craft, making it modern by using fluorescent yarns and luminous mohair (an idea sparked by metallic Nike trainers). Macdonald graduated from the Royal College of Art in 1996 and designed knitwear for Alexander McQueen and Koji Tatsuno. He founded his own label in 1997 and in 2001 he succeeded Alexander McQueen as creative director at Givenchy, a post he held until 2004.

► S. Ellis, Givenchy, Keogh, Lagerfeld, Tatsuno

Julien Macdonald. b Merthyr Tydfil, Glamorgan (UK), 1972. **Jodie Kidd wearing a red knitted dress.** Photograph by Sean Ellis, 1998.

McFadden Mary

Designer

While Mary McFadden will probably always be remembered principally for her pleated dresses *à la* Fortuny, she has not only made outfits for Grecian maidens, but has also brought global artistry to the comfort of easy sportswear. Hand-painted skirts, dresses and jackets are informed by McFadden's acute awareness of international design traditions, with a special leaning towards Southeast Asia and Africa. Textile scholarship and crafts luxury are, however, mediated by McFadden's unerring sense for modern comfort and poise. Inspired by decorative traditions and her pleasure in textiles, McFadden has rendered both Klimt and the *Book of Kells* in sumptuous coats, seized details from Portuguese tiles and understood the rich batiks of Southeast Asia. She straddles the art-to-wear movement and the pragmatic fashion industry. Likewise her clothing strikes an urbane formality for daywear and a wearable ease for evenings.

► Fortuny, Lancetti, Lapidus, Lester

Mary McFadden. b New York (USA), 1936. **Finely pleated dress and throw.** Photograph by Pierre Scherman, *Women's Wear Daily*, 1977.

McGrath Pat

Make-up artist

Pat McGrath heightens the dramatic potential of make-up by using it as a brilliant focus, isolating dense blocks of colour in a parody of one accepted scheme. Here, red lipstick is the single feature on an otherwise undecorated face. In a customary twist on the *i-D* cover (established with the magazine's inception in 1980), model Kirsten Owen's eye is shrouded by her hat. Her fiery mouth is the dominating focal point. McGrath, in partnership with hairdresser Eugene Souleiman, works with Steven Meisel, Paolo Roversi and Craig McDean to push the boundaries of beauty, and her directional vision has featured in catwalk shows by Prada, Comme des Garçons and Dolce & Gabbana. Her innovation has released make-up from the framework of facial contours since her patterns of colour are daubed seemingly randomly. *Vogue* called her the most influential make-up artist in the world, McGrath continues to work as beauty director at *i-D* magazine.

► McDean, Page, Roversi, Souleiman, Toskan & Angelo

Pat McGrath. b Northampton, Northamptonshire (UK), 1966. **Kirsten Owen on the cover of *i-D*, 'The Supernatural Issue', May 1998.** Photograph by Paolo Roversi.

Mackie Bob

Designer

Mackie offers a rhinestone cowgirl, a marvel in swinging fringe and bold motion and dressed in his signature style (reminiscent of the all-singing, all-dancing films of old Hollywood). Coming to fame as a television designer for *The Sonny and Cher Comedy Hour* (1971–74) and *The Carol Burnett Show* (1967–78), Mackie presented a hyperbolic form of showbiz glamour that was effective, even at television scale, in conveying large-screen and Las Vegas opulence and extravaganza. It was a tour de force achieved by letting the dress, or a few dresses, serve as the embodiment of a grandiloquence. By the advent of MTV, Mackie was too much associated with old-style theatricality to be popular there, but he was responsible for establishing brilliant costume for the medium of television. This was his contribution to fashion, the championing of beading and sequins for gowns, swimwear and loungewear.

► Leiber, N. Miller, Norell, Oldham, Orry-Kelly

Bob Mackie. b Monterey Park, CA (USA), 1940. **Black fringed, beaded dress.** Photograph by Steven Klein, British *Vogue*, 1988.

McKnight Sam

Hairdresser

Three women wear gamine hairstyles by Sam McKnight. The 'extreme gelled girls' illustrate his highly polished, sharply defined work. This sleek look, achieved by his 1920s-inspired styles, equals the make-up for dramatic effect, thus providing a fine balance. 'Hair is like clothes', says McKnight, 'you should look as though you wear it with ease, that's the sexiest hair.' He is known for nonchalant glamour, and it was this he gave to Diana, Princess of Wales, when, on a shoot for *Vogue* in 1990,

she asked him, 'What would you do if you had a free rein with my hair?'. 'Cut it short,' was McKnight's reply. And he did, becoming the architect of her later, modernized look. Trained in a salon that eschewed electrical appliances, he learned to create uncontrived hairstyles and still maintains that hair should not look forced. A woman, he believes, should always look approachable and should never risk fashion at the expense of her comfort.

► Antoine, Diana, Pita

Sam McKnight. b New Cumnock, East Ayrshire (UK), 1959. **Extreme Gelled girls.** Photograph by Arthur Elgort, Italian *Vogue*, 1993.

333

McLaren Malcolm

Designer

Malcolm McLaren delivers his manifesto wearing the rubber clothes sold in his shop, Sex, for the film, *The Great Rock 'n' Roll Swindle* (1978). A maverick entrepreneur and music aficionado, McLaren is credited with shaping the punk movement. In 1971 he and his partner, Vivienne Westwood, took over the running of a vintage shop, Let It Rock. Within three years they were selling bondage and fetish clothing, renaming the shop Sex in 1975. Its graphic anti-monarchy and pseudo-porn images by Jamie Reid caused outrage (the shop was regularly raided by police). The same year McLaren managed a US band, whose pre-punk music inspired him to return to the UK to form his own band. The Sex Pistols was cast from customers and named after the shop. The band was effectively a public relations exercise that exploded; McLaren later confessed, 'Punk was just a way to sell trousers.'

▶ Van Beirendonck, Rotten, Westwood

Malcolm McLaren. b London (UK), 1946. **d** New York (USA), 2010. **Malcolm McLaren wears rubber all-in-one.** *The Great Rock 'n' Roll Swindle*, 1978.

McLaughlin-Gill Frances   Photographer

This picture could be placed in any year since the one it was taken: 1948. The subject, Carol McCarlson, dries herself on a Florida beach; it is a picture that uses the blur of her oscillating towel to lend a naturalness for which its photographer is known. In 1941, Frances McLaughlin-Gill and her twin sister, Kathryn, entered a photography competition in *Vogue*. Both were finalists and Kathryn landed a job with *Vogue* photographer Toni Frissell. It was she who recommended that Frances should

be introduced to her art director Alexander Liberman. He hired McLaughlin-Gill in 1943 and she came to illustrate the lives of the new young market for *Glamour* and *Vogue*, making relaxed depictions of real scenes the context for the burgeoning teenage and American sportswear markets. McLaughlin-Gill also added a spirit of informality to the stiff, grown-up couture of the 1950s.

► Campbell-Walter, Dessès, Frissell, Griffe, Shrimpton

Frances McLaughlin-Gill. b New York (USA), 1919. **Carol McCarlson on the beach, St Augustine, Florida.** American *Vogue*, 1948.

McQueen Alexander   Designer

London-born Alexander McQueen followed a trajectory of success after graduating from Central Saint Martins in 1992, with his entire collection – 'Jack the Ripper Stalking his Victims' – bought by fashion patron, and friend, Isabella Blow. His highly articulate, decorative approach to beauty could perhaps be attributed to his early training on Savile Row where he perfected his impeccable technique and ability to draw with his scissors. 'Eclectic, verging on the criminal' is how he described his work, exploring deeply emotive themes of history and nature. 'Highland Rape', a 1996 collection, dressed women in bloodied, tattered lace dresses, with savagery usually close to the surface. His work for Givenchy from 1996 to 2001 showed glimpses of a more mellow McQueen. A comprehensive exhibition of his work entitled 'Alexander McQueen: Savage Beauty' was shown at the Metropolitan Museum of Art, New York in 2011.

▶ Blow, Burton, Chalayan, Galliano, Givenchy, N. Knight

Alexander McQueen (Lee McQueen). b London (UK), 1969. **d** London (UK), 2010. **McQueen cutting in his studio.** Photograph by Nick Waplington, published in *The Horn of Plenty*, 2009.

Madonna

Icon

A very real master of fashion's seasonal about-face, Madonna has a unique and dynamic propensity for continually reinventing herself. Her impact as a vocalist and fashion icon in the early 1980s was undeniably heightened by the timely introduction of the new TV channel MTV. But it was her ability to assume various, often controversial, personas with each new video release that set her apart from other artists. She has variously embraced lace and torn denim, a trashy, sexy, punky image for the release of her premier album in 1983; a glamorous, blonde Marilyn Monroe lookalike in 'Material Girl' in 1986; and a sophisticated persona as Eva Perón in the film *Evita* (1997), wearing 1940s-inspired couture. Madonna continues to court controversy and explore her chameleon style into the new millennium, reigning supreme in outfits by Riccardo Tisci and a Philip Treacy headdress at the 2012 Superbowl celebrations.

▶ Baron, Galliano, Gaultier, Lady Gaga, Pita, Testino, Versace

Madonna (Madonna Louise Ciccone). b Detroit, MI (USA), 1958. **Madonna wears pink basque by Jean Paul Gaultier.** 1990.   337

Maier Tomas

Designer

In a witty tribute to Alfred Hitchcock's *The Birds* (1963), a glamorous blonde moves through the city clutching her Cabat bag. The woven leather, logo-less sack bag helped save the Italian accessories house Bottega Veneta from bankruptcy when Tomas Maier took over as creative director in June 2001. Maier introduced the Cabat in his first season and it remains a bestseller. Hired by Tom Ford, German-born Maier successfully transformed the company into a modern lifestyle brand, encompassing clothing, furnishings, luggage, watches and jewellery. Dedicated customers can even stay in a Bottega Veneta suite at the Park Hyatt, Chicago, or the St Regis hotels in Rome and Florence. At Bottega Veneta, Maier honed the skills he developed at Hermès and Sonia Rykiel: high-quality materials and craftsmanship married with functionality and timeless design. In doing so, he reinvented the brand as a dominating force in the luxury market.

► C. Bailey, Ford, Hermès, Rykiel, Vuitton

Tomas Maier. b Pforzheim (GER), 1957. **Bottega Veneta spring/summer 2011 campaign.** Photograph by Alex Prager, 2010.

Mainbocher

Designer

During the 1940s, Natalia Wilson (Mrs John C. Wilson, Princess Paley) was manager of Mainbocher's New York salon and his main *vendeuse*. She often posed for fashion magazines wearing his clothes, in this case a sumptuous evening outfit that would have been worn to a dinner party or to the theatre. Mainbocher was celebrated for his lush evening suits, which consisted of a long dark skirt and contrasting jacket decorated with trimmings such as fur. With the distinctive beauty of Natalia

Wilson modelling these suits, Mainbocher won acclaim and went on to become the first American designer to open a *maison de couture* in Paris. Mainbocher's earlier career had included sketching for *Vogue*. Like many others, he was influenced by Madeleine Vionnet's bias-cutting technique a method he used for the Duchess of Windsor's wedding dress.

▶ Hoyningen-Huene, Ricci, Vionnet, Windsor

Mainbocher (Main Rousseau Bocher). b Chicago, IL (USA), 1890. **d** New York (USA), 1976. **Princess Natalia Paley.** Photograph by Louise Dahl-Wolfe, American *Vogue*, 1944.

Maltézos Madeleine & Carpentier Suzanne   Designers

The anonymity of the design team who created this dress is testament to their desire to remain on the conservative side of fashion, at a time when colleagues were using shocking innovation as an advertisement for their houses. Upon the retirement of the legendary Madeleine Vionnet, two of her staff (Mad Maltézos and Suzie Carpentier) established a new fashion house. After the Second World War, Mad Carpentier was known for luxurious dresses and coats favoured by a restrained clientele not likely to go to the 'hot' fashion houses such as Dior, Fath or even Balenciaga. Rather, what Mad Carpentier distilled was an essence of the past, harking back to Art Deco and the streamlining of the 1920s and 1930s. Dresses were demure and coats elegant and comfortable. They were also more or less timeless and nameless, recognized mainly by New York's garment district, Seventh Avenue, which copied their saleable good taste.

► Connolly, Morton, Simpson, Vionnet

Madeleine Maltézos and **Suzanne Carpentier**. (Active 1940s–1950s.) **Shawl-collared dress.** French *Vogue*, 1949.

Mandelli Mariuccia (Krizia) Designer

Sharp pleats are thrown into black-and-white relief, capturing an atmosphere of drama and amusement, which conveys almost a circus mood in Mariuccia Mandelli's design for her company Krizia. There is a strong sense of architecture expressed in the geometric lines formed by the pleats of the outfit. When the wearer moves, these pleats form a rolling wave. Mandelli explained her distinctive style thus, 'There is often a sense of architecture in my clothing...one of my collections was inspired by the Chrysler Building.' Krizia, named after Critias, a Greek politician and poet commemorated in one of Plato's dialogues, was formed in Milan in 1951. Noted for her experimental construction and irreverent approach to glamorous clothes, Mandelli featured in the exhibition 'Fashion, Italian Style' at the Museum of the Fashion Institute of Technology, New York in 2003.

► Capucci, Ferré, Miyake, Venet

Mariuccia Mandelli. b Bergamo (IT), 1933. **Pleated lamé frills.** Photograph by Giovanni Gastel, 1998.

Man Ray

Photographer

Photographer Man Ray was one of the central figures in the Surrealist movement in Paris. He was fascinated by women's lips as objects of desire. Other artists and fashion designers have ventured to portray the lips of Surrealism: Dalí designed a sofa modelled on Mae West's lips, Saint Laurent created a 'Lip Dress' and Elsa Schiaparelli used lips as a pocket (the hand inserted between them). In 1921 Man Ray left New York for Paris, where he took up photography to finance his painting.

An introduction to Poiret, who was looking for a different sort of photographer, brought him into fashion, a field that united his experimentation with a commercial product. In the 1920s his work for *Vogue* and *Harper's Bazaar* extended fashion photography from posed formality into the sphere of collaborative art. He asserted that, 'inspiration, not information, the force that binds all creative acts' is at the root of great fashion.

► Bernard, Blumenfeld, Dalí, Hoyningen-Huene

Man Ray (Emmanuel Radnitsky). b Philadelphia, PA (USA), 1890. **d** Paris (FR), 1976. **Lips on Lips.** 1930.

Maramotti Achille (MaxMara)   Designer

'For us to be considered fashionable would be very dangerous,' said MaxMara's former managing director, Luigi Maramotti. 'It is not chic for a woman to move violently from one way of dressing to another.' MaxMara is the epitome of Italian fashion: good quality and cut, in classic styles, while managing to interpret trends in a wearable way. The camel-coloured wrap coat shown here is pure cashmere, and although the design seems pared down, attention to detail is impeccable. One of Italy's largest and oldest fashion companies, MaxMara was founded in 1951 by Doctor Achille Maramotti, a lawyer turned dressmaker. His first collection consisted of just two outfits: a suit and an overcoat. This brevity of design has always been MaxMara's signature, and the collections still focus on these key items of tailoring. In 2005 Maramotti left the company in the hands of his three children, Maria Ludovica, Luigi and Ignazio.

► Beretta, Meisel, Paulin, Venturi

Achille Maramotti. b Reggio nell'Emilia (IT), 1926. **d** Albinea (IT), 2005. **Linda Evangelista wears MaxMara camel coat.**   343
Photograph by Steven Meisel, 1997.

Marant Isabel   Designer

Since launching her label in 1994, Isabel Marant's signature style has been Parisian gamine chic. With the opening, in 2012, of her stores in New York and Los Angeles she extended this theme, looking at Americana for her cowboy-inspired autumn/winter 2012 collection 'Arizona Muse'. The collection applied Western-style detailing – floral embroidery, snap studs, denim and fine lace – to Marant's classic boyish, but effortlessly feminine silhouette, mixing French tomboy with bohemian elements. It is a formula that has made her a retail success with 13 stores worldwide and a collection of loyal clientele from actress Kirsten Dunst to Beyoncé. The executive committee of the Fédération Française de la Couture nominated Marant as a new member of the association in 2003, thus formally marking her acceptance by the doyens of French fashion.

► Johansson, W. Klein, Moss, Sims, Sitbon

Isabel Marant. b Paris (FR), 1967. **Arizona Muse, Isabel Marant autumn/winter 2012 campaign.** Photograph by David Sims.

Margiela Martin

Designer

Martin Margiela's cigarette-sleeve jacket reoccurs throughout his work, revealing the classic tailoring skills that underpin his conceptual, avant-garde output since his first presentation in 1989. A graduate of the Royal Academy of Fine Arts in Antwern, Margiela worked for Jean Paul Gaultier in 1985 before launching his own label. Margiela's influence on the fashion industry is profound and subversive; maintaining relative anonymity and presenting all collections as the work of the Maison, each garment is signed with the infamous four white stitches. 'Couture' tops were stitched from military surplus socks; dresses made out of lining silk with seams left unfinished. Behind it all was a deep respect for traditional couture and an academic fascination with the inner workings of garment construction. In 2002 Maison Martin Margiela was sold to the Italian Diesel group. Margiela himself quietly stepped down from the label in 2009.

► Demeulemeester, Gaultier, Hermès, Kawakubo, Van Noten

 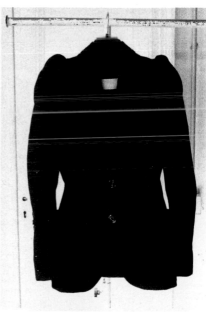

Martin Margiela. b Louvain (BEL), 1957. **Cigarette sleeve jacket.** Photograph by Ronald Stoops, 1989.

Märtens Dr Klaus (Dr Martens) Shoe designer

In a stunning duality of purpose the Dr Marten ('DM') boot has been a symbol of aggressive, anti-fashion cults for three decades. It is also worn by most uniformed, establishment figures. It began life as an orthopaedic aid. Designed in 1946 by Klaus Märtens, a Bavarian doctor who had broken his foot while skiing and wanted something to relieve the pain, the boot was an overnight success. In 1959 the British bootmaker R. Griggs was granted permission to use Märtens' air-cushioned sole on his steelcapped workmens' boots; the compound was changed to granular PVC (resistant to fat, oil, acids and petrol) and has remained unchanged ever since. The 'Famous Footwear AirWair, with bouncing soles' was born. In the mid-1960s, the eight-eyelet boot in black or cherry red became a uniform for skinheads; in the 1980s, DMs became an essential part of British 'street style' when they were worn with a pair of Levi's jeans.

► Cox, Jaeger, McClaren, Strauss

Dr Klaus Märtens. b Braunschweiz (GER), 1915. **d** (GER), 1988. **Policeman and skinhead wear Dr Martens, Southend, UK.** 1980.

Massenet Natalie (Net-A-Porter)   Retailer

As former fashion editor for *W*, *Women's Wear Daily* and *Tatler*, Natalie Massenet's concept in founding Net-A-Porter was to create an online magazine where current designer collections could be purchased directly from the pages of its editorial features. Launched in 2000, Net A-Porter was a pioneer in integrating editorial content and e-commerce into a single medium with widespread accessibility. Credited by *Vogue* as 'revolutionizing the way we buy designer clothes', the website quickly became the world's premier online luxury fashion destination for women. In 2009 the Net-A-Porter Group expanded to include The Outnet and later Mr Porter, the first online editorial and retail menswear destination. In 2010, Massenet sold the Net-A-Porter Group to Richemont, but she remains executive chairperson. Today the Net-A-Porter Group Limited employs more than 2,000 people in London, New York, Shanghai and Hong Kong.

► Kane, Lerfel, SHOWstudio, Style.com

Natalie Massenet. b Los Angeles, CA (USA), 1965. **Editorial spread from the Net-A-Porter iPad magazine.**

Matsuda Mitsuhiro   Designer

Mitsuhiro Matsuda arranges a variety of woven linens for an outfit that hardly resembles clothes at all. The fabrics themselves dominate the image, with checks and stripes loosely woven to form a semi-transparent material. Matsuda is one of the early greats in the tradition of Japanese fashion design that carried successfully over to a Western tradition and sensibility. In the 1980s, his clothes were whimsical and romantic in the British style, often taking their inspiration from the costumes of historical England. Yet he maintained a practicality and wearability in his tailoring that was androgynous and sexy. His menswear was directional and elements of it were used for his womenswear. Matsuda's father worked in the kimono industry and it was with that garment that he and his contemporaries, Kenzo and Yohji Yamamoto, examined the principle of Western clothes.

► Kenzo, Kim, Kobayashi, Y. Yamamoto

Mitsuhiro Matsuda. b Tokyo (JAP), 1934. **d** Tokyo (JAP), 2008. **'Madame Nicole.' Mixed linens, spring/summer 1996.**
Photograph by Mitsuhiro Matsuda.

Matsushima Masaki

Designer

'Fashion is necessary but I think it is of secondary importance,' says Masaki Matsushima. His suits for men and women show both sides of this argument at once. Inherently they deal with the pinstripe tradition, lending them a sober quality, and yet they have a fashion edge that is sharpened with broad shirt collars and a flamboyant buttonhole. But Matsushima feels that these styling touches are down to the individual who will make the clothes their own. 'I am trying to create a mass image,' continues Matsushima. 'That is why I don't think that creation means to force the designer's own personality on the people.' Matsushima graduated from Tokyo's famous Bunka Fashion College in 1985. He designed costumes for conceptual singer Ryuichi Sakamoto and launched his own label. His clothes are by turns highly technical and instrumental in promoting the notion of conceptual streetwear.

► Bartlett, Dolce & Gabbana, Newton

Masaki Matsushima. b Magoya (JAP), 1963. **Reworked pinstripe suits.** Photograph by Satoshi Saikusa, 1998.

Maxwell Vera

Designer

'Buy a Share in America' declare the wartime posters, and Americans did – even in fashion. During the Second World War, European fashions, in particular those from Paris, were not available, so America turned to its own designers. Vera Maxwell was one who came to the fore at this time. Her separates – simple shapes in humble fabrics – adhered to wartime restrictions as well as being conscious of the pressures and new-found responsibilities of women workers. Maxwell often reinterpreted men's workwear shapes – this jacket is based on a man's lumberjack shirt. In 1970, Maxwell discovered Ultrasuede, which was to become a durable yet sophisticated staple for women's tailoring, championed especially by Halston. In 1974 she designed her first Speed Suit – an elasticated dress that could be quickly slipped down over the head for busy women. It was a precursor to Donna Karan's ethos a decade later.

► Dahl-Wolfe, Halston, Karan, A. Klein

Vera Maxwell. b New York (USA), 1903. **d** Rincon (PR), 1995. **Co-ordinated day suit.** Photograph by Louise Dahl-Wolfe, *Harper's Bazaar*, 1942.

Mazzilli Tiziano & Louise (Voyage)

Designers

Wrinkled velvet ribbon sewn onto the neckline of a sheer T-shirt signifies the work of Voyage, designed to look like antiques or cast-offs and yet recognizable as expensive garments to those in the know. Made from silk, linen, velvet and taffeta, each garment is hand-dyed or hand-painted and washed mixing colours in the same haphazard way, Founder Tiziano Mazzilli and his wife Louise fostered the label's image as an exclusive and expensive one. In 1991 they opened Voyage on London's Fulham Road. 'Our philosophy is to be unique,' says Mazzilli. 'We don't want to please everyone.' And they don't. Each visitor to the boutique was obliged to ring a bell, and undergo scrutiny before being allowed in, an example of fashionable exclusion surpassed only by a later move to introduce membership cards. Despite this Voyage went into liquidation in 2002. Louise and her children, Rocky and Tatum, created Year Zero London.

► Von Etzdorf, Oudejans, Williamson

Mazzilli. Tiziano. b Udine (IT); **Louise. b** Brussels (BEL). **Velvet-trimmed T-shirt and cutwork pink skirt.** Photograph by Howard Sooley, *Joyce*, 1997.

Meisel Steven

Photographer

Steven Meisel's picnic illustrates a collection by Dolce & Gabbana. The sunny lighting contradicts the cold, dull background, giving the picture a surreal edge. Meisel calls himself 'a reflection of my times'. It is a phrase that equally applies to his work. His strength is as an image-maker, both in terms of his own image, and that of the designers' work he photographs and the models whose careers he has transformed – Meisel discovered Linda Evangelista and Stella Tennant. He has a sensitivity

towards clothes and is able to adapt to each garment he photographs, 'I am always influenced by the philosophy of the particular couturier whose dress I am photographing.' American and Italian *Vogue* are Meisel's biggest arenas. In one Italian edition he was given thirty pages to depict a single story: a fact that makes him the undisputed emperor of fashion image-making.

► Dolce & Gabbana, Enninful, Evangelista, Garren, Gigli, Tennant

Steven Meisel. b New York (USA), 1954. **'Early Fall Picnic in Dolce & Gabbana.'** Italian *Vogue*, 1998.

Menkes Suzy

Editor

As fashion editor of the *International Herald Tribune* in Paris since 1988, Suzy Menkes is a familiar sight – with her trademark trouser suits, vintage jackets and pompadour hairstyle – in the front row of fashion shows. While studying dressmaking in Paris, Menkes attended her first couture show at Nina Ricci, stimulating an interest in high fashion, which led to an illustrious career including fashion editorships of the *Evening Standard*, the *Daily Express* and *The Times*. In addition to reporting on international collections for the *International Herald Tribune*, she covers a gamut of subjects, from reviewing fashion exhibitions to interviewing leading designers and figures in the luxury market. Menkes is highly respected in the fashion industry for her incisive, fair and balanced reporting and also for her flair and elegant style. Menkes holds the *Légion d'honneur* and was awarded an OBE for services to journalism in 2005.

► Blow, Hartnell, SHOWstudio, Windsor, Wintour

Suzy Menkes. b Beaconsfield, Buckinghamshire (UK), 1943. **Menkes drinking tea during her 'In Fashion' interview with SHOWstudio's Alex Fury.** September 2011.

Mert & Marcus

Photographers

Cryptic, dark narratives often suffuse the sensuous and beautiful images of photography team Mert Alas and Marcus Piggott. In this image they conjure up a scene of intense melodrama: Natalia Vodianova floats, her face barely breaking the surface of the water in a composition that, according to the artists, was designed to evoke the 'psychological state of drowning'. In rich, seductive tones, the hyper-real trademark of their images is evident. With backgrounds in classical music and graphic design,

Turkish Alas and Welsh Piggott combined forces in London in 1994. After showing their work to *Dazed & Confused* magazine and securing a cover, the fashion assignments started to roll in. Characterized by an emphasis on feminine beauty and power and exploration of the human psyche, they are masters of post-production; every detail that goes into their work is significant, resulting in highly articulate and confident image-making.

► Bourdin, Enninful, Grand, Meisel

Mert Alas. b Ankara (TUR), 1971. Marcus Piggott. b Bangor, Wales (UK), 1971. Natalia Vodianova in 'Sleep No More' for *W* magazine, styled by Edward Enninful. 2012.

Mesejeán Pablo & Cancela Delia (Pablo & Delia)   Designers

The flower power youth revolts from Paris to San Martín and the resurgence of artisan crafting paved the way for Pablo and Delia's fantasies. Inspired by Lewis Carroll's stories, this shirred, floral-printed cotton top with a layered tulle, flower-shaped headband heralds the bloom of naïveté as a lifestyle. The mood of the times was summarized in Pablo Mesejeán and Delia Cancela's 1966 Manifesto, which proclaimed, 'We love sunny days, the Rolling Stones, tanned bodies, the *young savage look*, pink and baby blue, happy ends.' Upon the arrival in London in 1970 of these two art students from Buenos Aires, British *Vogue* instantly featured a cover with Jean Shrimpton in their trademark rainbow-coloured, painted leather dress. Pablo and Delia's clothes were usually accompanied by their own dream-like illustrations of wizards and fairies wearing their creations. Since Pablo's death, Delia has concentrated on painting and illustration.

► Coddington, Gibb, Leonard, Shrimpton

Pablo Mesejeán. b Buenos Aires (ARG), 1937. **d** Paris (FR), 1986; **Delia Cancela. b** Buenos Aires (ARG), 1940. **'Petal' hat and shirred dress.** Photograph by Barry Lategan, British *Vogue*, 1972.   355

De Meyer Baron Adolph   Photographer

In balletic pose, Baron de Meyer's subject displays layers of opulent lace trimmed with silk satin ribbon. Her peignoir and dress are backlit to give them and her a luminous glow in a hugely romantic portrait of femininity. De Meyer's fashion photography was founded in the *belle époque* before the First World War. Having spent his childhood in Paris and Germany, he entered London's fashionable society at the end of the nineteenth century. He was hired by Condé Nast in 1914, becoming *Vogue*'s first full-time photographer and later moving to *Harper's Bazaar* in 1921. With their halos and fragile clothes, his subjects appeared too delicate to participate in vigorous modern life, which included swimming, tennis, golf and the Charleston, and his style was replaced by dynamic experiments in movement. De Meyer left *Harper's Bazaar* in 1932, his place taken by Martin Munkacsi and his invigorating look.

► Antoine, Arden, Boué, Nast, Reboux, Sumurun

Baron Adolph de Meyer. b Paris (FR), 1868. **d** Los Angeles, CA (USA), 1949. **Romantic chiffon dress.** American *Vogue*, 1922.

Miller Lee

Photographer

A model, with her painted nails, lipstick, coiffed hair and bias-cut dress, is a tantalizing vision for the service-women she parades for. One stretches her arm to feel the cloth, the wearing of which, for most, would have been an impossible dream. Her unconscious touch renders the model as unreal as the image she projects. American photographer Lee Miller is known for her poignant photographs taken during the Second World War as a member of the London War Correspondents' Corps.

During this time she also worked for *Vogue*. Her captivating photograph shows that Paris couture had lost none of its power during the war, and the city was well positioned to re-establish itself as a fashion leader. In the late 1920s Miller was a model, photographer and writer for *Vogue* in New York. In 1929 she moved to Paris, where she lived and worked with Man Ray and was friendly with Picasso and the Surrealists.

▶ Arnold, Bruyère, Dalí, Man Ray

Lee Miller. b Poughkeepsie, NY (USA), 1907. **d** Chiddingly (UK), 1977. **Service women at a fashion salon, Paris.** 1944.

Miller Nolan

Designer

Nolan Miller, architect of the extravagant *Dynasty* look that defined the shameless glamour and camp of 1980s fashion, sits surrounded by the show's female stars. His studio generated twenty-five to thirty such outfits every week – with just two days to discuss a wardrobe and five days to create it. His 'bitch' wardrobe for Joan Collins (Alexis Colby), who wears a gleaming column of pink sequins here, was modelled on that worn by Joan Crawford in the 1940s. Her shoulders are exaggerated with vast outcrops of fuchsia ruffles. Next to her, Diahann Carroll (Dominique Devereaux) and Linda Evans (Krystle Carrington) also bear the inflated, squared-off shoulder line that was associated with masculine power. Miller moved to Hollywood in the hope of dressing glamorous women by becoming one of cinema's legendary costume designers. He arrived too late for that but was in time to bring glamour to the small screen.

▶ Banton, Bates, Burrows, Mackie

Nolan Miller. b Burkbarnette, TX (USA), 1935. **Nolan Miller and his female cast.** *Dynasty*, 1985.

Milner Deborah

Designer

Deborah Milner's clothes are sculptural fantasies that defy the term 'fashion'. Indeed, this gauzy, full-length black coat featuring Milner's signature – a superb sweeping cowl neck and intricate textiles – could probably stand alone in an art gallery. Milner says, 'My work ranges from the avant-garde to the quite classic.' One of her former tutors describes her as having, 'revived the art of couture by adapting her skills to work with everyday materials'. These include net, tape, film and coated wire. Milner had a strict Methodist upbringing and countered it by enrolling at art college where she discovered fashion. She began with a small couture studio in 1991, specializing in one-off, avant-garde fashion pieces for, among others, milliner Philip Treacy, who used them as foils for his climactic headgear. Here, his ergonomic glittered ellipse equals Milner's semi-sheer coat for drama.

▶ Hishinuma, Horvat, S. Jones, Treacy

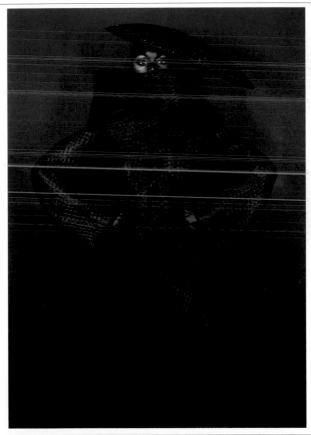

Deborah Milner. b Walton-on-Thames, Surrey (UK), 1964. **Gauze coat.** Photograph by Mark Mattock, *i-D*, 1997.

Missoni Ottavio, Rosita & Angela   Designers

1971 or 2008? We rely on modern photography and styling for the answer because the enduring popularity of Missoni's colourful knitwear in basic shapes means their clothes have changed little over the years. Their strength and appeal lies in their simple beauty. Colour is the key to the Missoni look. The distinctive, flecked 'flame dye' effect is achieved by only partly immersing the yarn in the dye to leave a white mark or to allow the colour of the yarn to show through. Ottavio and Rosita Missoni met at the 1948 Olympics in London, where Ottavio was competing in the 400-metre hurdles, wearing the team tracksuit that had been designed by his own small knitwear company. They married and their first collection was presented in Milan in 1966. In 1997 Ottavio and Rosita handed the business over to their daughter, Angela, who has inherited the Missoni sensibilities.

► Maier, Prada, Rykiel, Testino

Missoni. Ottavio (Tai). b Ragusa (SYR), 1921; **Rosita. b** Golasecca (IT), 1931; **Angela. b** Milan (IT), 1958. **Chevron vest and striped cardigan, spring/summer 1998.** Photograph by Mario Testino.

Miyake Issey

Designer

Peeking through torn tissue, a vivid pink shirt is displayed as though it were an installation. The process of folding a length of polyester, twisting it tightly, then treating it with heat is a technique trademarked by the innovative designer Issey Miyake, whose highly dynamic work is characterized by vividly coloured, layered silhouettes. Miyake started his career in Paris with the likes of Guy Laroche and Givenchy, and eventually worked for Geoffrey Beene. He returned to Japan in 1970 to set up his design studio in Tokyo. Miyake is a member of Japan's fashion elite, alongside Rei Kawakubo and Yohji Yamamoto; his clothes are admired and worn by artists and architects alike, so much so that his diffusion lines Pleats Please and A-POC have also received critical acclaim. Miyake is now one of the co-directors of 21_21 Design Sight, with designer Dai Fujiwara taking his place as creative director of the Miyake Design Studio in 2006.

▶ Arai, Givenchy, Hishinuma, Kawakubo, Mandelli, Y. Yamamoto

Issey Miyake. b Hiroshima (JAP), 1938. **Pleats Please pink shirt.** Photograph by Kazumi Kurigami, 1995.

Mizrahi Isaac

Designer

Isaac Mizrahi, wearing his customary headband, is photographed in his New York studio with model Amber Valletta, who is laid out on his pattern-cutting table. Beyond the scorching colour of her dress, designed for spring 1995, there is a rainbow of cottons stored on the wall and an intense mix of shades represented on a rail of samples behind them. They are all evidence that Mizrahi is not a designer afraid of colour – Pacific blue, cartoon yellow, bubblegum pink. 'I love Technicolor –

it's wildly beautiful,' he says of his untrammelled taste in sunshine colours. He marries vibrant, unusual materials with shapes long used for American sportswear. This sense of comedy in his work and personality was aired in a docufilm, *Unzipped*, which followed the creation of his autumn/winter 1994 collection. It comes from his training at New York's High School for the Performing Arts prior to his entry into fashion.

► Beene, Kors, Moses, Oldham

Isaac Mizrahi. b New York (USA), 1961. **Mizrahi with Amber Valletta.** Photograph by Gilles Bensimon, American *Elle*, 1995.

Model Philippe

Milliner

Complex hats, such as this sculpted headpiece formed from interwoven, red velvet segments, have put Philippe Model at the forefront of French accessories design since 1978. It was then he left school and started his business from scratch by making haute couture hats. Shortly afterwards, Model was awarded the title *'Meilleur ouvrier de France'* (finest craftsperson in France), a coveted prize for excellence which dates back to the Middle Ages. He moved to the heart of French fashion in the early 1980s, after working with Jean Paul Gaultier, Claude Montana and Thierry Mugler for whom he accessorized avant-garde collections. Model doesn't limit his work to millinery – he is also a shoe designer whose neat, elasticated shoes became widely copied. Similar in idea to Hervé Léger's 'elastic bandage' dresses, they are formed from strips of stretch material and display a practical design talent.

▶ S. Jones, Léger, Montana, Mugler, Paulette, Underwood

Philippe Model. b Sens (FR), 1956. **Spiral hat.** Photograph by Satoshi Saikusa, *Harpers & Queen*, 1988.

Molinari Anna

Designer

Setting up her brand Blumarine in 1977 with her husband, Gianpaolo Tarabini, Anna Molinari is a name synonymous with the provocative feminity illustrated in this image. In this editorial, model Trish Goff fulfils both by wearing a sheer shirt, brief satin shorts and a snowy tailored jacket for cooking. Molinari's work deals with creating sexy clothes, often using a formula that marries brief hemlines with sheer fabrics with delicate detailing. She initially produced knitwear, a selection of which remains in the form of sweater-girl shapes trimmed with diamantés – a signature look for the designer. Attracting a following of ultra-feminine women, her more romantic medium uses flouncy dresses, tutus and tops decorated with ruffles, frills and bows, which are always just decent. Now the company is divided into three brands: Blumarine, Blugirl and Anna Molinari, continuing in the romantic aesthetic in which Molinari has made a name for herself.

▶ Dell'Aqua, Dinnigan, Ferretti, Thomass, Versace

Anna Molinari. b Carpi (IT). (Active 1970s–) **Trish Goff.** Photograph by Pamela Hanson, American *Vogue*, 1995.

Molyneux Captain Edward

Designer

A romantic look back to the silhouette worn by the Empress Josephine during the First Empire (1804–15) characterizes this evening dress. The empire-style dress has a high waistline, a square-cut neckline, short, puffed sleeves and rich embroidery. A draped, floor-length stole tapering into a train and long gloves completes the regal look. Such aristocratic grandeur made Molyneux a favourite fashion designer among royalty, society women and film stars. Princess Marina, Duchess of Kent, was one of his most famous and elegant clients. Trained under Lucile (Lady Duff Gordon), who in the early twentieth century designed empire-style gowns, Molyneux nevertheless walked a fine line between romantic revival and modernity. He was a fashion designer with a reputation for exquisite taste based on purity of line and cut. Christian Dior was known to have preferred Molyneux to any other couturier.

► Balmain, Dior, Duff Gordon, Griffe, Stiebel, Sumurun

Captain Edward Molyneux. b London (UK), 1891. **d** Monte Carlo (MON), 1974. **Embroidered satin, empire-line dress.** Photograph by François Kollar, 1939.

Montana Claude   Designer

Aggressive jackets cut from leather epitomize Claude Montana's extreme style. Broad-shouldered, para-military shapes accentuated with epaulettes and cinched waists have dominated his work, the most powerful using leather, since his own label was launched in 1979. Montana understands a simple Constructivist shape with its straight, uncompromising lines and uses extreme styling in the way Pierre Cardin did in the 1960s. He relishes the act of 'building' his designs and was widely respected for those he created for Lanvin haute couture from 1989 to 1992. Montana's career began in London, when he ran short of money on a visit and started designing jewellery, which was then featured in *Vogue*. After a year, he returned to Paris to work for the leather firm MacDouglas. In the 1980s his work symbolized a movement of women's fashion that dressed them as super-heroines.

▶ Flett, Model, Mugler, Steiger, Viramontes

Claude Montana. b Paris (FR), 1949. **Embroidered, white and gold leather outfits for Idéal Cuir**. Photograph by Alain Larue, *L'Officiel*, 1980.

Moon Sarah

Photographer

A Sarah Moon photograph is almost always a dreamy, soft-focus trip back to the fashion mood of the 1920s and 1930s. When she photographed the Pirelli Calendar in 1972, it was a groundbreaking event: not only was she the first woman to do so (she was chosen to pacify objections from the feminist movement), but she was also the first to show fully exposed breasts. Moon spent much of the 1960s as a fashion model, but towards the end of that decade turned to photography. Her first assignment was an advertising campaign for Cacharel, which led to editorial work for *Nova*, *Vogue*, *Harper's Bazaar* and *Elle*. Subsequent advertising campaigns for Biba cosmetics summed up the fashion mood of the early 1970s. Moon has since moved beyond the constraints of fashion and into the sphere of fine art photography. Her work has remained muted, somewhat surreal, and always beautiful.

► Bousquet, Dinnigan, Hulanicki, Williamson

Sarah Moon. b Paris (FR), 1941. **Katia wears Enrica Massei.** *The Frankfurter*, 1997.

Morehouse Marion   Model

The photographer Edward Steichen once declared that, 'Good fashion models have the qualities inherent in a good actress.' For Steichen, Morehouse was 'the best fashion model I ever worked with'. Fashion in the 1920s demanded a sleek and willowy silhouette, and Marion Morehouse had that archetypal figure. This, together with her commanding presence and seemingly effortless elegance, made her the ideal fashion model for the period. As Steichen said, 'She transformed herself into the sort of woman who really would wear that gown.' Morehouse was also frequently photographed by some of the other great photographers who began working in the 1920s, such as Horst P. Horst and George Hoyningen-Huene. She married the writer e. e. cummings, and later in her career also took up photography.

► Chéruit, Horst, Hoyningen-Huene, Steichen

Marion Morehouse. b (USA), 1906. **d** New York (USA), 1969. **Marion Morehouse wears bias-cut satin dress.** Photograph by Cecil Beaton, 1929.

Mori Hanae

Designer

The radiant daylight catches Hanae Mori's favourite model Hiroko en route to her wooden pagoda retreat. Her bird-like frame, veiled in a tissue-soft, silk organza caftan printed with daisies, echoes Mori's restrained elegance and Japanese aesthetic. Kimono silk printed with cherry blossoms and butterflies, produced by Mori's husband Kei, Japanese asymmetry and obi belting are all indicative of her respect for her cultural heritage. Invariably balancing this with Western styling, Mori's feather-light creations are consistent and sensible, never enslaved to the dictates of fashion. A graduate in Japanese literature, Mori went back to college after her marriage and two sons to learn the fundamentals of dressmaking. She designed costumes for Japanese film and theatre, before setting up shop at Tokyo's shopping haven Ginza in 1955. She was admitted to Paris's Chambre Syndicale de la Couture in 1977.

► Hirata, Kenzo, Scherrer, Snowdon

Hanae Mori. b Yoshika (JAP), 1926. **Silk caftan.** Photograph by Snowdon, British *Vogue*, 1972.

Morris Robert Lee

Jewellery designer

Three twisted, sterling silver bangles represent the sculptural work of Robert Lee Morris. The filing marks and beaten indentations lend them the natural spirit for which Morris is known. He says, 'I adore natural forms. I am a student of anatomy,' and his designs forge elements of nature into a variety of objects, ranging from Africa-inspired breastplates to a lipstick holder for Elizabeth Arden. Morris has used cork, rubber, granite and silicone in his work, but when New York's Fashion Institute of Technology staged a twenty-five-year retrospective for Morris's work, it was titled 'Metalmania'. His use of stark, urban metals brought him close to Donna Karan, whose cultivated designs are an ideal backdrop for dramatic modern jewellery. Their work in the mid-1980s, often pairing navy fabric with elegant gold cuffs, created a uniform for white-collar women who wanted to escape the Baroque excesses of that period.

▶ Arden, Barrett, Karan, Perretti

Robert Lee Morris. b Nuremberg (GER), 1947. **Sterling silver Orbit bangles.** Photograph by Wolfgang Ludes, 1998.

Morton Digby

Designer

'Fashion is indestructible,' proclaimed British *Vogue*
when it published this photograph by Cecil Beaton as
London was bombed during the Second World War. Digby
Morton provided leadership in British fashion during
the war years. He specialized in tailored tweed suits. The
example in this photograph has a hip-length jacket and
a slightly flared skirt just covering the knees. Morton
took the severity and masculinity out of the tailored suit.
In 1928 he joined the house of Lachasse, quickly gaining

recognition for his suits in exquisitely shaded tweeds,
designed to be worn with silk blouses. He left in 1933
to start his own couture business and was succeeded at
Lachasse by Hardy Amies. Morton was a member of
the Incorporated Society of London Fashion Designers,
a group of leading couturiers that promoted the British
fashion industry in the face of wartime restrictions.

► Amies, Beaton, Cavanagh, Creed, French, Maltézos & Carpentier

Digby Morton. b Dublin (IRE), 1906. d London (UK), 1983. **Grey tweed suit.** Photograph by Cecil Beaton, British *Vogue*, 1941.

Moschino Franco

Designer

Typical of Franco Moschino is this cheeky mockery of haute couture where, just for a second, the silhouette of a military jet is accepted as a couture hat in the grand French style. Moschino believed that fashion should be fun and he demanded laughs with the slogans he applied to clothes and advertising: 'Waist of Money' and 'Warning: fashion shows can be damaging to your health'. That his protest became fashion itself was testament to the garments they adorned: chic formal suits and evening dresses. As a boy, Moschino would go into his father's iron foundry and create images in the dust on the walls. He went on to study art and worked for Gianni Versace until 1977. In 1983 he launched the Moschino label. After his death in 1994, each garment was sold with a manifesto stating that environmental concern is 'the only true fashion trend'.

► Kelly, Steele, G. Versace

Franco Moschino. b Abbiategrasso (IT), 1950. **d** Milan (IT), 1994. **Silhouette of a Moschino Couture! cocktail dress, 1988.** Photograph by Fabrizio Ferri.

Moses Rebecca · Designer

A cartoon figure reclines in a classic bikini that represents Rebecca Moses' starting point for every piece of clothing: colour. The walls of her Italian studio are covered with plastic envelopes, each containing colour swatches in the form of materials, flowers and paper. They turn up on her cashmere sweaters with names such as 'Frozen Cranberries' and 'Robin's Egg'. The clothes she forms owe nothing to transient fashion trends. 'I'm not saying fashion should stay still, but it should stop for long enough to consider the needs of modern men and women... I was fed up with fashion. There was just so much clothing out there.' She refers to her clothing as 'mobile style' that can 'travel' between daywear and eveningwear, summer and winter and from outfit to outfit. She is a member of the Council of Fashion Designers of America and of the Italian National Chamber of Fashion. She is the author of *A Life of Style*, published in 2010.

▶ Biagiotti, Jacobs, Mizrahi

Rebecca Moses. b New York (USA), 1956. **Magenta bikini.** Illustration by Rebecca Moses, 1998.

Moss Kate   Model

Every so often a special face appears, a face that changes the way we perceive beauty and that challenges our tastes. Kate Moss was 'discovered' aged fourteen at JFK Airport, New York. Sarah Doukas, owner of Storm modelling agency in London, felt 'she was going to be special'. Kate Moss became the Twiggy of the 1990s; young and fresh, she symbolized the triumph of naturalness over artifice. Labelled a 'superwaif', her rise to fame coincided with the grunge phenomenon that celebrated an anti-designer look of uncoordinated clothes worn with rock-star attitude. Calvin Klein's unisex perfumes were one of the first products to literally bottle this attitude and make it a commercial product, leaving Kate Moss as the obvious choice of model. In addition to her modelling work, she has also designed a clothing line for Topshop and handbags for Longchamp.

► Day, Hilfiger, C. Klein, Kors, Sims, Topshop

Kate Moss. b London (UK), 1974. **'cK be' advertising campaign for Calvin Klein.** Photograph by Richard Avedon, 1997.

Mouret Roland

Designer

London-based French designer Roland Mouret became a celebrity overnight when he launched his iconic 'Galaxy' dress in his spring/summer 2006 collection. Its low-cut square neckline, soft shoulder and nipped-in waist create an hourglass silhouette reminiscent of the figure-hugging dresses worn by actresses in films of the 1940s. It became an instant icon, worn by an array of Hollywood A-list stars including Rachel Weisz, Demi Moore, Cameron Diaz and Dita Von Teese – a dress with a cinematic feel for a new generation of starlets. The precision of the cut, combined with lining the bodice with a bust-shaping power mesh, enables the dress to sculpt the body, following Mouret's mantra that, 'dresses are for undressing'. In addition to heading his fashion house based in Mayfair, London, in 2011 Mouret was appointed creative director at Robert Clergerie in Paris.

▶ V. Beckham, Berardi, Erdem, Saunders, Williamson

Roland Mouret. b Lourdes (FR), 1962. **'Galaxy' dress worn by Dita von Teese.** 2006.

Mugler Thierry

Designer

Thierry Mugler's photograph of his corset and latex trousers conjures up the themes of Aryan vamp and Pop Art dominatrix. Running through his work is a sexy 'anatomical vision' of moulded silhouettes, hand-span waists and exaggerated shoulders that have influenced Azzedine Alaïa and Hervé Léger. 'It's all about looking good, helping the silhouette,' Mugler memorably informed Kim Basinger in Robert Altman's *Prêt à Porter* (1994). Mugler made his first outfit for a female friend at the age

of fourteen. Joining a ballet company, he moved to Paris at nineteen and in 1973 launched his own label. Mugler's vision has been unswerving. Each season jackets are cut, padded and stitched to create his cartoon-like ideal, a theme that also runs through his superhero menswear. Mugler re-shapes the body using seam and fabric – an uncompromising and total vision. In 2010 Nicola Formichetti became the creative director of the house.

▶ Bergère, Formichetti, S. Jones, Léger, Model, Montana

Thierry Mugler. b Strasbourg (FR), 1948. **Shaped bustier and latex pants.** Photograph by Thierry Mugler, 1996.

Muir Jean Designer

The minimalism of Jean Muir's jersey tunic and matching culottes presents a stark silhouette on Joanna Lumley (Muir's model in the 1970s). Simplicity was Muir's signature. She said, 'I am a traditionalist with a sense of evolution.' She inspired the respectful address 'Miss Muir', and always wore navy. Geraldine Stutz, president of Henri Bendel in New York, called her, 'the most outstanding dressmaker in the world'. After working at Liberty, she designed for Jaeger, before setting up her own company in 1966. She made the 'little nothing' of a black dress a classic. But her designs were often deceptively simple – jackets could contain up to eighteen pattern pieces. The understated elegance of Muir's wearable designs have made them timeless classics. As the designer herself said, 'When you have found something that suits you and never lets you down, why not stick to it?'

► Clark, Liberty, Rayne, G. Smith, Torimaru

Jean Muir. b London (UK), 1933. **d** London (UK), 1995. **Joanna Lumley wears jersey tunic and culottes in Jean Muir's apartment.** Photograph by Michael Barrett, 1975.

377

Mulleavy Kate & Laura (Rodarte)   Designers

In spring 2005 sisters Kate and Laura Mulleavy left their native California for New York with no more than a handful of designs. Within a week they had touted their collection to every major buyer and fashion editor in the city. A favourite of both critics and collectors, Rodarte – named for their mother's maiden name – presents a whimsical femininity and meticulous emphasis on detail. Delicate fabrics such as lace and soft chiffon exist side by side with stiffer brocades and metallics in a harmony painstakingly choreographed by the designers. The Mulleavys have stated, 'Our work is often a study of balance, in which volume, construction, and colour have a complex interplay that we carefully control.' In 2009 Rodarte received the coveted Womenswear Designer of the Year award. In 2010 the designers elegantly traversed the divide between high fashion and popular appeal when they collaborated on the costumes for the film *Black Swan* (2010).

► Erdem, Katrantzou, Leon & Lim, McCollough & Hernandez

Mulleavy. Kate. b Aptos, CA (USA), 1979; **Laura. b** Pasadena, CA (USA), 1980. **Rodarte autumn/winter 2012.** Photograph by Autumn de Wilde.

Munkácsi Martin

Photographer

With her head high and arms swinging, Martin Munkácsi's subject is the personification of fashion liberation as she strides from the shadows into sunshine. Her bias-cut dress, blurred and flowing in the wake of her motion, moves with her body rather than restraining it. It is free of any detail that will date it and the sash is carelessly tied around her natural waist. It is this real-life spirit of spontaneity that Munkácsi brought to fashion photography when he joined *Harper's Bazaar* in 1932,

encouraged by his mentor Alexey Brodovitch. As well as showing clothes in motion, thereby better describing the real potential of fabric once it is placed on the body, he shot fashion from new angles, giving the impression of a scene snapped rather than posed. Munkácsi's subjects always had a purpose beyond being a beautiful clothes horse, whether they were running on the beach or, as is shown here, enjoying an unaccompanied evening stroll.

▶ Brodovitch, Burrows, De Meyer, Snow

Martin Munkácsi (Mermelstein Márton). b Cluj-Napoca (ROM), 1896. d New York (USA), 1963. **Marion Davies, San Simeon, California.** *Harper's Bazaar*, 1934.

Nars François

Make-up artist

Photographed by François Nars, Karen Elson wears his signature make-up. Nars uses dense pigments to create rich blocks of colour. Against a snowy base, he isolates the eyes and lips with a striking, abstract method. 'The runway is my sketchpad,' says Nars who, like Bobbi Brown and Frank Toskan, belongs to a circle of make-up artists who have created signature make-up lines. For them, the catwalk is a public laboratory on which new directions are born. His company was formed on the catwalks of Versace and Karl Lagerfeld, with vivid Technicolor schemes that became the blueprint for each seasonal look. His work draws inspiration from a variety sources, from *King Kong* to Elsa Schiaparelli. Amongst his lines are a dark chocolate lipstick formulated to match the giant ape's fur, and 'Schiap' is an exact match of Elsa Schiaparelli's classic shocking pink. He has also made a name for himself as a photographer for *Vogue* and *Elle*.

► Dolce & Gabbana, Lutens, Schiaparelli, Toskan & Angelo

François Nars. b Biarritz (FR). (Active 1980s–) **Karen Elson.** Photograph by François Nars, 1997.

Nast Condé

Publisher

In one sideways glance, the Countess Divonne makes the first-ever photographic cover of *Vogue*. Her romantic pose and its artful styling preceded today's charismatic fashion covers. Following his 1909 purchase of *Vogue*, Condé Nast's transformation of the American social magazine into a high-class fashion glossy heralded a new era in international magazine publishing, starting with Baron de Meyer becoming the first full-time fashion photographer in 1914. With his editor, Edna Woolman Chase, Condé

Nast exerted strict control at *Vogue*, and gave Carmel Snow and Alexander Liberman their first glimpses of fashion editorship and art direction respectively. Such a controlling policy did not always work: it fuelled Diana Vreeland's sacking in the 1960s, and caused *Harper's Bazaar* to poach De Meyer in 1921. Nast then hired Edward Steichen, Cecil Beaton and *Harper's Bazaar's* Christian Bérard, sparking a long-standing feud.

▶ Coddington, Liberman, De Meyer, Snow, Tappé, Wintour

Condé Nast. b Montrose, CO (USA), 1873. d New York (USA), 1942. **First *Vogue* cover.** Photograph by Harry McVickar, 1893.　　381

Newton Helmut   Photographer

The Scandinavian model Vibéké wears a superlative pinstriped suit and *crêpe-de-chine* blouse by Yves Saint Laurent. Shot at night on a Parisian street, her hair is slicked to her head in the sexually ambiguous manner of Garbo and Dietrich, and she holds the cigarette as a man would. It is a scene conjured by Helmut Newton, whose work is always charged with sexual themes. Preferring statuesque, Teutonic women, he places his subjects on the line between pornography and fashion photography –

this is a tame, but nonetheless powerful example of Newton's highly provocative work. His employment of ring-flash photography lends a menacing mood to his scenarios, which have inspired debate for decades: does he objectify women, or does he empower them? In 2003 he donated his photo collection to the Prussian Cultural Heritage in his native Berlin, establishing the Helmut Newton Foundation.

► Matsushima, Palmers & Wolff, Saint Laurent, Teller

Helmut Newton. b Berlin (GER), 1920. **d** Los Angeles, CA (USA), 2004. **Tailored Yves Saint Laurent suit.** French *Vogue*, 1975.

Propriety, the Norell hallmark, was never more evident than when all-over sequins, verging on the vulgar, were framed by his application of them on a gown of classic lines. An added layer of shimmer, perhaps an evening sweater, was justified as being warm protection for the shoulders on a wintry or Second World War night. From joining Hattie Carnegie in 1928 until his death in 1972, Norell was an important figure in American fashion design and his work personified New York style. Norell's success resided in his simple silhouettes and pragmatism in the fickle world of late-day and evening dresses. With wool jersey dresses for evening, beaded sweaters matched to evening dresses and, later, trouser suits, Norell applied the ethos of sportswear to more formal times of day. His uncanny capacity was to foster a comfortable, easy glamour that he achieved chiefly through an enduring fix on the 1920s.

► Carnegie, Ley, Mackie, Parker

Van Noten Dries

Designer

Dries Van Noten's sensational menswear show for autumn/winter 2012 saw models in vividly decorated silhouettes flanked by artists painting a giant, graphic mural. The graphic patterns that ran the length of the catwalk were a collaboration between the Dutch artists Gijs Frieling and Job Wouters, providing the backdrop for the slim 1960s cut of Van Noten's trademark tailoring. Van Noten has a knack for showmanship; previous runways have been carpeted in gold leaf, backed with a spectacular wall of fresh flowers or transformed into a giant table for a pre-show dinner. He gained initial publicity as a member of the eponymous 'Antwerp Six': a group of early 1980s graduates from the Royal Academy in Antwerp. In both his menswear and womenswear Van Noten's most recognizable signature is his extraordinary flair for fine patterned textiles and prints, styled expertly with classic European tailoring.

► Bikkembergs, Demeulemeester, Margiela, Prada, Thimister

Dries Van Noten. b Antwerp (BEL), 1958. **Dries Van Noten menswear autumn/winter 2012.** Photograph by Chris Moore.

Nutter Tommy

Tailor

Mick Jagger marries Bianca Perez Morena de Macias at the town hall in St Tropez in 1971. He wears a suit by Tommy Nutter, the man who opened the doors of Savile Row to a new generation (and also cut both John Lennon's and Yoko Ono's wedding suits). After studying architecture, he had answered an advertisement for a salesman at the Savile Row tailors G. Ward and Co. In 1969 he opened Nutters in Savile Row. His three-piece suits were styled with narrow, square shoulders, wide lapels, tight waists, tightly crotched flared trousers, and waistcoats. Charming and shy, Nutter was a frontman for the company which, employing master cutters and tailors, made the Savile Row bespoke suit fashionable again. In 1976 he left the company and joined tailors Kilgour French and Stanbury. He is still remembered with affection and respect by the tailors of Savile Row. 'He was a modern stylist,' said one. 'He brought fashion here.'

► The Beatles, Fish, Gilbey, R. James, Liberty, T. Roberts

Tommy Nutter. b London (UK), 1942. d London (UK), 1992. **Mick and Bianca Jagger on their wedding day, St Tropez.** 1971.

Oldfield Bruce

Designer

Bruce Oldfield reclines next to his black silk crepe evening dress. The bodice is ruched with gold lamé and the mannequin wears shoes by Charles Jourdan; together they present a collaboration of deluxe fantasy. Oldfield once claimed, 'I can make any woman look better. That's what I do.' His starry clientele has ranged from aristocrats to soap queens; the Princess of Wales to Joan Collins. The glamour could hardly be further removed from Oldfield's childhood in a Dr Barnardo's home. His foster mother

was a seamstress and it was from her that Oldfield first developed his interest in fashion. He presented his first collection in London in 1975. His shop opened in 1984, attracting a strong following from the 'ladies who lunch'. Suzy Menkes, who selected his design as the Dress of the Year in 1985, praised 'his skills as a dressmaker, his belief in cut, line and silhouette, his standards of workmanship and his conception of women'.

► Diana, Jourdan, Price

Bruce Oldfield. b London (UK), 1950. **Bruce Oldfield with a gold lamé and black silk crepe dress.** Photograph by Nick Briggs, 1985.

Oldham Todd

Designer

Todd Oldham sits with one of fashion's more exotic muses – his grandmother Mildred Jasper. 'Granny's always been a huge inspiration to me. She does exactly what she wants, with great irreverence.' Sitting for *Harper's Bazaar*, Mildred wears Oldham's hot pink, quilted satin jacket, which comes close to being a boudoir robe. His family have long been connected to his career, which began at the age of fifteen when he turned a K-Mart pillowcase into a sun dress for his sister. Oldham always risks kitsch to achieve his distinctive style. Quirky colour combinations and textures are used for his down-home Texas style of flash and panache. Oldham creates a kaleidoscope of decorative pastiche for his own collection and, to a slightly lesser extent, for Escada, a label for whom he became a consultant in 1994. He has also branched out into writing, with *Todd Oldham: Without Boundaries* and *Suits: The Clothes Make the Man*.

► Eisen, Ley, Mackie, Mizrahi, De Ribes

Todd Oldham. b Corpus Christi, TX (USA), 1961. **Todd Oldham and grandmother.** Photograph by Gus Van Sant, *Harper's Bazaar*, 1997.

Orry-Kelly

Designer

Orry-Kelly's hand-sewn, decorative costumes made him one of Hollywood's great designers, alongside Travis Banton and Adrian. On his first Hollywood movie, Orry-Kelly worked with Bette Davis and they formed a partnership that was to last for fourteen years. Orry-Kelly understood Davis's need for the drama in her wardrobe to match, but not overshadow, that of her on-screen acting. They only fell out once when the studio insisted she be glamorized for *Fashions of 1934* (1934), which she hated.

The life and soul of many showbiz parties, Orry-Kelly was also a prima donna and an alcoholic. But his time with Warner Brothers ended on a high note after he dressed Ingrid Bergman in simple classics for *Casablanca* (1942), before being drafted into the army. He later freelanced, winning Oscars for Marilyn Monroe's sexy glamour in *Some Like It Hot* (1959) and Leslie Caron's colourful costumes in *An American in Paris* (1951).

► Adrian, Banton, Mackie, Stern

Orry-Kelly (John Kelley). b Kiama (ASL), 1897. **d** Hollywood, CA (USA), 1964. **Marilyn Monroe wears diaphanous beaded dress.** Still from *Some Like It Hot*, 1959.

Oudejans Marie-Anne   Designer

Each season, Marie-Anne Oudejans produces dresses in just a few simple shapes but in many different fabrics and colours. The story of her label, Tocca, is similar to that of Lilly Pulitzer who, in the 1960s, became famous for her printed dresses. Oudejans was originally a stylist who wore her own cotton dresses on fashion shoots; the supermodels who saw them begged for their own copies. Claudia Schiffer, Helena Christensen and Naomi Campbell were photographed wearing the dresses and customers started calling stores trying to find out how to buy them. 'It became a fashion by chance,' says Oudejans. Her dresses are unapologetically pretty and are cut from cotton or silk sari fabrics with a girlish quality that sits apart from mainstream fashion. In 2002 she launched a range of accessories.

▶ Dinnigan, Mazzilli, Pulitzer, Williamson

Marie-Anne Oudejans. b (NL), 1964. **Helena Christensen wears a pink embroidered dress.** Photograph by Niall McInerney, 1994.

Owens Rick

Designer

At Rick Owens's autumn/winter 2008 'Stag' collection, models with dishevelled, unkempt hair strode out in his exquisitely tailored black creations that Owens himself described as 'glunge' – glamour plus grunge. It is highly theatrical with its array of unconventional shapes and imagery of dark sensibility. And yet in spite of its look of toughness and severity, it is not only a pop culture style but also glamorous high fashion, supple and eminently wearable. After studying at the Otis College of Art and Design in Los Angeles, Owens took pattern-making and draping courses at Los Angeles Trade Technical College and began his own label in 1994. He started to receive attention when a photograph of Kate Moss wearing one of his fitted leather jackets appeared in French *Vogue*. His first collection was shown during New York Fashion Week in September 2002, winning the Council of Fashion Designers of America Emerging Talent Award that year.

► Ackermann, Demeulemeester, McDean, Pugh

Rick Owens. b Porterville, CA (USA), 1961. **Autumn/winter 2008 'Stag' collection.** Photograph by Craig McDean.

Ozbek Rifat

Designer

Rifat Ozbek visited North Africa, India and his own Turkish roots for this eclectic, delicate outfit. A gauze cardigan is heavily braided and trimmed with cording. Underneath, a dress is embroidered with flowers and the raised waistband dotted with silver beads. Since setting up his own label in 1984, Ozbek has been inspired by the clothing and decoration of a variety of cultures, from American Indian and South African Ndebele to Eastern European gypsy and Haitian voodoo. Brought up in Britain, Ozbek initially worked with the seminal 1970s designer Walter Albini in Italy, before moving back to London to work for Monsoon. He has been heavily influenced by London street fashion. Before moving his business to Milan in 1991, Ozbek designed his 'New Age' collection. Using white and silver, it revealed a new-found purity in his work. In 2010 he launched a new business in the UK, called Yastik.

► Abboud, Albini, Hendrix, Oudejans

Rifat Ozbek. b Istanbul (TUR), 1953. **Embroidered jacket and dress.** Photograph by Gilles Bensimon, British *Elle*, 1989.

Page Dick

Make-up artist

Model Annie Morton sits in her apartment bare-faced and with dishevelled hair. The image is *deshabille* in the extreme. Make-up artist Dick Page did nothing to disturb her early morning beauty. Using this pre-shoot image, he contests the idea of what constitutes beauty, saying, 'There is no such thing as natural make-up. As soon as there is make-up on the face it is not natural.' This is the key to Page's ethos. While effecting transformations by giving skin a shiny surface, he rejects further artificiality and won't use make-up that regulates and reduces women to a uniform beauty – on one occasion even leaving spots as an 'undeniable part of the woman underneath'. Page's iconoclastic methods are unique in a business designed to sell make-up. However, he was a champion of the 'greasy, glossy' direction of make-up in the 1990s, a movement that, bizarrely, accelerated the sale of make-up. In 2007 he was named artistic director of Shiseido cosmetics.

► Brown, Day, Lutens, McGrath

Dick Page. b Gosport, Hampshire (UK), 1964. **Annie Morton in her apartment.** 1996.

Paley Babe

Icon

Babe Paley liked to look flawless; her clothes – twinsets, to-the-knee skirts and crisp blouses – always had to be just so. Here she decorates an exacting two-tone dress with an armful of costume jewellery in the style of another paragon of personal style, Coco Chanel. Truman Capote commented, 'Babe Paley only had one fault: she was perfect; otherwise, she was perfect.' Another friend, the socialite Slim Keith, called her style 'perfection in an era of casual convenience'. Paley was born Barbara Cushing

into a middle-class family, with two elder sisters. All of the Cushing girls were trained by their socialite mother to snare wealthy husbands, which they did. Babe's second marriage was to Bill Paley, chairman of CBS. As a fashion editor of American *Vogue* in the 1940s, she was an arbiter of style and appeared in America's best-dressed list fourteen times. Her look is best described as effortless chic, achieved at great effort.

► Chanel, Horst, Lane, Parker

Barbara Paley. b Boston, MA (USA), 1915. **d** New York (USA), 1978. **Babe Paley.** Photograph by Horst P. Horst, American *Vogue*, 1946.

Palmers Walter & **Wolff** Reinhold (Wolford)   Hosiery designers

Nadja Auermann wears a pair of semi-opaque tights that were specially created for this photograph. In her right hand she holds a Polaroid, the chosen film of a voyeur, of herself in a provocative pose. The Wolford company, founded by Walter Palmers and Wolff Reinhold, operates from the small Austrian town of Bregenz, and creates four collections of hosiery and bodywear every year. For its 1996 advertising campaign to promote no-seam, 'second-skin' tights (which took four years to develop),

Wolford chose photographer Helmut Newton, who places his subjects in a steely sexual context. Wolford has been associated with hosiery since 1949. The patronage of Vivienne Westwood, Helmut Lang, Christian Lacroix and Alexander McQueen, as well as devoted, style-conscious women around the world, has elevated Wolford to its position as the preferred hosiery of the fashion industry.

► Alaïa, Audibet, Karan, Newton

r Palmers. b Vienna (AUS), 1903. **d** Vienna (AUS), 1983. **Reinhold Wolff. b** Hard (AUS), 1905. **d** Hard (AUS), 1972.
Neon' tights. Photograph by Helmut Newton, 1996.

Paquin Jeanne   Designer

It is five o'clock and Mme Paquin's salon is crowded with *vendeuses* (without hats) showing clients (with hats) bolts of fabric from which they will order their dresses. At the centre of the room one models a fur-trimmed gown for two ladies, one of whom is examining the embroidery on its skirt. Mme Paquin founded her own haute couture house in 1891. She was appointed President of the Fashion Section of the Paris Exposition Universelle of 1900 and promoted spectacular displays of fur. It

was from this time that fur appeared as a trimming or accessory in the collections of leading couturiers. Mme Paquin also made exotic and brilliantly coloured garments, blending her superb tailoring with drapery inspired by Iribe and Bakst. As *soignée* as her models, Mme Paquin was the first couturier to achieve international fame, establishing further couture salons in London, Buenos Aires and Madrid.

► Boué, Doucet, Gibson, Poiret, Redfern, Rouff

Jeanne Paquin. b Île Saint-Denis (FR), 1869. d Paris (FR), 1936. 'Cinq Heures chez Paquin.' Painting by Henri Gervex, 1906.

Parker *Suzy*

Model

One hand holding a cigarette, the other thrown behind her head – both bear witness to Suzy Parker's reputation as someone who could never sit still. With high cheekbones, green eyes and red-gold hair, she became the most famous model of her generation, photographed extensively by, among others, Horst and Richard Avedon. It was while watching her sister Dorian Leigh model for Irving Penn in 1947 that Suzy was first discovered. Later she was taken on as the face of Revlon and of Chanel No. 5

(Coco Chanel became her friend and godmother to her daughter Georgia). Although Suzy secretly married the playboy journalist Pierre de La Salle in 1955, it did not last and she later married the actor Bradford Dillman, for whom she put her modelling career aside for marriage and motherhood. She was introduced to photography by Robert Capa and for a while was listed as a Magnum photographer.

► Avedon, Bassman, Chanel, Horst, Norell

Suzanne (Suzy) Parker. b Long Island City, NY (USA), 1932. **d** Montecito, CA (USA), 2003. **Suzy Parker.** Photograph by Lillian Bassman. *Harper's Bazaar*, 1963.

Parkinson Sir Norman   Photographer

Sir Norman Parkinson evokes the breathtaking thrill of Paris first seen from the air in this editorial picture taken in 1960. He was a realist who took fashion photography outdoors. After the Second World War, he embarked upon a successful career in fashion photography for *Vogue*, pioneering the use of colour. Parkinson had a feeling for the essentials of fashion, to which he brought great urbanity, charm and sophisticated wit. In colour and composition, his fashion photographs have often been compared to the paintings of John Singer Sargent. He was the official photographer for the wedding of Princess Anne and Captain Mark Phillips in 1973 and photographed the Queen Mother on her eightieth birthday in 1980. His wife, Wenda Parkinson, was a celebrated fashion model, whom he often photographed. Together they brought the new cosmopolitan spirit of intercontinental jet travel to the pages of *Vogue*.

► Avedon, D. Bailey, Fratini, Kelly, Levine, Stiebel

Parsons The New School for Design

From Tom Ford to Donna Karan, Marc Jacobs and Alexander Wang, Parsons has trained some of the most prestigious names in fashion. Building on its earlier incarnation as the New York School of Fine and Applied Art, Parsons The New School for Design brings a unique New York slant to fashion education. Established in 1904 by its namesake Frank Alvah Parsons, Parsons is credited with the birth of Seventh Avenue, the epicentre of American fashion. McCardell's Popover dress, Karan's capsule wardrobe, Alexander Wang's slouchy T-shirts: these garments changed main street, combining urban cool with retail savvy, continuing in the tradition of modern American dressing. In 1970, Parsons joined The New School, reinforcing an emphasis on progressive thinking, sustainability and constant questioning of the place of fashion in the world.

► Central Saint Martins, Ford, Jacobs, Karan, A. Wang

Parsons The New School for Design. est. New York (USA), 1896. **The Sheila C. Johnson Design Center, Parsons The New School for Design, New York City.** Photograph by Bob Handelman.

Patou Jean

Designer

Jean Patou's dress is influenced by two art movements: Art Deco and Cubism. Purity of line, a key element of Art Deco, was the hallmark of Patou's style. He also took inspiration from Cubism, creating sharp, geometric shapes and patterns in his fabrics. He worked closely with the textile firm Bianchini-Férier (where Raoul Dufy was under contract in the 1920s), in his search for materials that would best adapt to his design philosophy of simplicity and a streamlined, uncluttered silhouette.

His long-waisted dresses with their luxurious designs were constantly described in the fashion magazines of the time as 'chic' and were worn by actresses such as Louise Brooks, Constance Bennett and Mary Pickford. Long strings of pearls and fur-trimmed coats added embellishment and also enhanced Patou's precision of cut. Tennis player Suzanne Lenglen was also dressed by Patou, setting a fashion for sleeveless jumpers.

► Abbe, Benito, Bohan, Eric, Frizon, Lacroix, Lanvin

Jean Patou. b Normandy (FR), 1887. **d** Paris (FR), 1936. **Sequined dress.** Photograph by Laure Albin Guillot, *c.*1927.

Paulette

Milliner

Lush silk roses adorn the brim of a summer hat by Paulette, who was one of France's leading milliners for thirty years. She began creating hats in 1921, and set up her own millinery salon in 1939 at the start of the Second World War. These straitened circumstances were to bring out her most creative talents, just as Ferragamo was forced to experiment with plastics. Paulette reinvented the turban, which became a symbol of wartime practicality, by accident. When cycling she would wrap her head, a simple solution that turned into the biggest fashion for a decade. The theme developed, with draped veils and fabric often featuring in her work. Paulette went on to create work for Chanel, Pierre Cardin, Ungaro, Mugler and Laroche, demonstrating the versatility and wide-ranging appeal of her designs – helped by Philippe Model, who trained with her.

► Barthet, W. Klein, Laroche, Model, Mugler, Talbot, Ungaro

Paulette (Paulette de la Bruyère). b Le Tours (FR), *c.*1900. **d** (FR), 1984. **Barbara Mullen wears hat decorated with roses.**
Photograph by William Klein, 1956.

Paulin Guy

Designer

In 1987 the baby-doll grew up in the hands of Guy Paulin. The pin-tucked, big-pocketed, girlish style becomes womanly with its floral print reduced to a few scattered petals. An admirer of Claire McCardell, Guy Paulin's easy-going, vibrant style consciously blended office formality with the no-nonsense detailing of American sportswear. Fired by a two-year training with Jacqueline Jacobson at Dorothée Bis, he took his passion for knitting to New York in 1968, where he shared rails with Mary Quant and Emmanuelle Khanh at the boutique chain Paraphernalia. Having freelanced for MaxMara, he replaced Karl Lagerfeld as designer at Chloé in 1983. Paulin had a reputation for pleasing women with his brand of French chic and his intention was always to create clothes that would boost the wearer's self-esteem.

▶ Jacobson, Khanh, Lagerfeld, Lenoir, Maramotti

Guy Paulin. b Lorraine (FR), 1945. d Paris (FR), 1990. **Baby-doll dress**. *Women's Wear Daily*, 1988.

Mr Pearl

Designer

A child wears a garment designed to reduce an adult's circumference to that of a child. It is the highly crafted work of Mr Pearl, the man who made the corset a fashion item. Called the best corsetier in the world by Vivienne Westwood, he is famous for his own corseted eighteen-inch waist. Pearl left South Africa in the early 1980s for London and the costume department at the Royal Opera House, where his interest in the art of corsetry was aroused. He was inspired by photographs of the clothes of his great-grandmother, who was a couturier during the *belle époque*. As he said, 'The world used to be a more interesting place visually and I wanted to bring some of that visual stimulus back.' Pearl has worked on collections for Thierry Mugler, Christian Lacroix, John Galliano and Alexander McQueen. He reached celebrity status when he created the corset worn by Victoria Adams for her marriage to David Beckham.

▶ V. Beckham, Ellis, Galliano, Lacroix, McQueen, Mugler

Mr Pearl (Mark Erskine-Pullen). b (UK), (Active 1990s–.) **Black beaded corset.** Photograph by Sean Ellis, *The Face*, 1996.

Penn Irving

Photographer

Model Jean Patchett becomes an exercise in graphic perfection under the lens of a photographer whose work defined haute couture in the 1950s. The power and simplicity of Irving Penn's images made him the Balenciaga of fashion photography – a designer whose work was often shot by Penn. Penn invests his subjects – a model, a still-life or even a sleeve – with a strong presence. He said, 'The camera is just a tool, like a wrench. But the situation itself is magical. I stand in awe of it.' His black-and-white photography of the 1940s and 1950s captured the grandeur and drama of haute couture. Of couture, he said, 'When I am working with the haute couture I think again and again of the beauty of women and the magic of Paris.' His work was exhibited in some thirty shows worldwide during his lifetime and he continues to inform the world of photography even after his death, with an archive of his work held at the Art Institute of Chicago.

► Brodovitch, Dovima, Fonssagrives, Vreeland

Irving Penn. b Plainfield, NJ (USA), 1917. **d** New York (USA), 2009. **Jean Patchett.** American *Vogue*, 1950.

Peretti Elsa

Jewellery designer

Like so many of Elsa Peretti's designs, this seemingly
molten silver cuff, with its smooth, tactile lines, was
inspired by her love of organic forms; in this case, the
irregular contours of bones. A renowned craftswoman,
Peretti creates jewellery and home accessories with
a unique rhythmic sense of the natural world. She seizes
the figurative essence of something as simple as a bean or
a teardrop and translates it into a beautiful, sculptural,
timeless piece of body art. She presented her inaugural

pieces alongside Giorgio di Sant'Angelo's collection in
1969 and later designed for Halston. Her other designs,
sold by Tiffany & Co, have included the famous Peretti
'Open Heart' pendant and 'Diamonds by the Yard' –
a simple chain interspersed with diamonds that became
a classic worn by Liza Minnelli in the 1970s and in the
1990s by Naomi Campbell, who threaded hers through
her navel ring.

► Halston, Hiro, Di Sant'Angelo, Tiffany, Warhol

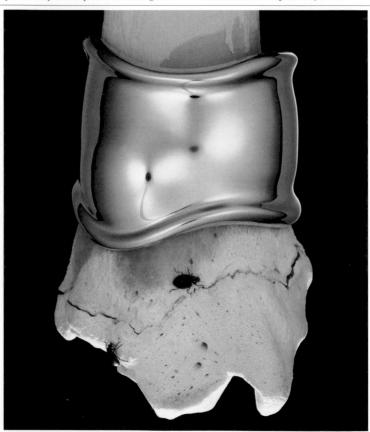

Elsa Peretti. b Florence (IT), 1940. **Silver 'Bone' cuff.** Photograph by Hiro, 1989.

Perint Palmer Gladys

Illustrator

With its deft pen strokes and blocks of pastel colour, Gladys Perint Palmer's simple catwalk illustration resonates with fluidity and movement, accurately capturing not only Yves Saint Laurent's couture gypsy but also the women watching her. Like a cartoonist, Perint Palmer's work gives a humorous insight into the catwalk world. Subtle exaggerations, such as the model's extended neck that creates an imperious air, are just one step removed from reality. The close attention of Chanel's former model Inès de la Fressange, wearing a red jacket in the foreground, adds to an ambience that only a camera can record faithfully. Each picture is a microcosm of a show, illustrating the spirit of a collection and that of the spectators. Perint Palmer belongs to a tradition that is as old as fashion presentations. Sketch artists were once the only way for collections to reach the wider public before the clothes did.

► Chanel, Saint Laurent, Vertès

Gladys Perint Palmer. b Budapest (HUN), 1947. **Yves Saint Laurent catwalk show.** 1992.

Pertegaz Manuel

Designer

Henry Clarke's great attribute as a fashion photographer was his precision in defining a fashionable image, showing here how this haute couture coat was cut and how it hung. He has made the brilliantly tiled walls of the Villa Rosa, an elegant Madrid restaurant, the perfect backdrop for Manuel Pertegaz's vivid green, paper taffeta evening coat. Falling to mid-calf, it has an oval-necked shoulder yoke and three tie-fastenings. The most distinctive feature is its tent shape, flaring widely from the shoulders. One of the great Spanish fashion designers, Pertegaz earned a reputation for formal designs in the grand manner from his start in the early 1940s. The tent silhouette was first launched in 1951 by Pertegaz's compatriot, Balenciaga. Together they built up Spain's reputation for couture. In 1968 Pertegaz opened his Madrid boutique, selling couture, and in the 1970s launched a ready-to-wear collection.

► Balenciaga, Clarke, Grès, Saint Laurent

Manuel Pertegaz. b Olba (SP), 1917. **Green taffeta evening coat.** Photograph by Henry Clarke, British *Vogue*, 1954.

Perugia André

Shoe designer

This decorative boot, based on turn-of-the-century spats, was the perfect complement to the attention-grabbing designs of Elsa Schiaparelli. Schiaparelli was a brilliant colourist. Shocking pink, which she made the predominant colour in the world of fashion in the late 1930s and throughout the 1940s, was her famous trademark. The sheer expanse of the surface of this boot, in black suede with a pink platform, enabled André Perugia to capture the essence of fantasy that was so much in accord with Schiaparelli's own creations. Despite its size, the boot was easy to walk in. Perugia understood balance, scale and the engineering of footwear, having been an apprentice at his father's shoe business in Nice prior to opening his own shop there when he was only sixteen. In 1920, he established his own salon in Paris. Perugia also designed footwear for Poiret, Fath and Givenchy, as well as Schiaparelli.

▶ Fath, Jourdan, Poiret, Schiaparelli, Talbot, Windsor

André Perugia. b (FR), 1893. **d** Cannes (FR), 1977. **Buttoned boot with scalloped edging for Elsa Schiaparelli.** 1939.

Pfister Andrea

Shoe designer

With 'Martini dry', a sunshine yellow sandal, Andrea Pfister evokes the cocktail culture of the mid-1970s. Its heel is shaped to resemble a martini glass embellished with a slice of lemon; a surreal object that demands attention. Pfister treats his shoes as a centrepiece rather than a distant accessory, and the foot, for him, is the start of the human body rather than its end. In 1964, having trained as an art historian, he moved to Paris to design footwear collections for Jean Patou and Lanvin. He moved on to design his own collections, which became known for their humour; Pfister has appliquéd snakeskin penguins to the side of a boot, decorated the heel of a wedged mule with a three-dimensional frolicking sea lion and wrapped a black suede boot with clasping hands. The tradition of fantasy footwear in the twentieth century remained vigorous – from Perugia's pink platforms to Pfister's leather martini glass.

▶ Ferragamo, Lanvin, Louboutin, Patou

Andrea Pfister. b Pesaro (IT), 1942. **'Martini dry' kid sandal.** Photograph by Joël Garnier, 1975.

Philo Phoebe

Designer

Phoebe Philo studied design at Central Saint Martins where she gravitated to the minimalist tendencies of designers such as Jil Sander and Helmut Lang. In 1997, a year after graduation, she began working as Stella McCartney's design assistant at Chloé, succeeding her as creative director in 2001. She stayed at Chloé until 2006 and in 2008 was appointed creative director at Céline. This photograph taken by Juergen Teller for the spring/ summer 2011 campaign for Céline shows her signature style of colour-blocking, clean lines and contemporary minimalism. Her loose-fitting silhouette and minimal make-up allies well with Teller's style of photography with its raw, over-exposed quality. Philo states, 'what I love is this idea of a wardrobe,' summing up her approach, which takes classic pieces and cleverly reworks them for the luxury market – a formula that has been hugely influential since her appointment at Céline.

► Aghion, Lang, McCartney, Sander, Teller, Tisci

Phoebe Philo. b Paris (FR), 1973. **Daria Werbowy wears a pair of striped sports trousers for Céline spring/summer 2011 campaign.** Photograph by Juergen Teller.

Piguet Robert

Designer

Horst has photographed Robert Piguet's outfit in a
Surrealist manner. At first glance, we see the sitter
wearing a well-cut bodice with the emphasis focused
on the white sleeve. Ms Zelensky's other sleeve becomes
a shadow, together with her Tyrolean hat and skirt.
Horst has created an illusion for the designer. Having
trained with Redfern and Poiret, Piguet understood the
decorative importance of the hat, and has used it here
as a witty punctuation mark to his garment. Piguet's

work was admired for its uncluttered yet flamboyant
shapes, an element greatly supported by contributions
from talented freelance designers, including Dior and
Balmain before the Second World War and Bohan after.
Here, it is represented by the sleeve with its head raised
to meet Ms Zelensky's cheekbone. The purity of Piguet's
outfit is simplified further by Horst's impeccable style.

► Balmain, Bassman, Bohan, Castillo, Galanos, Horst

Robert Piguet. b Yvedon (FR), 1901. **d** Paris (FR), 1953. **Doris Zelensky wears puff-sleeved jacket.** Photograph by Horst P.
Horst, 1936.

Pilati Stefano

Designer

After Tom Ford's departure from the house of Yves Saint Laurent, the relatively unknown assistant to Ford, Stefano Pilati, was chosen to helm the legacy of the great Saint Laurent. Successfully bringing the house into the new millennium with an understated but decisive elegance, Pilati gave Ford's Saint Laurent bohemian vixen of the Rive Gauche a simpler, more composed sexiness. The Milanese Pilati – who originally trained as a land surveyor, a career path that he gave up – began his career in fashion at the house of Cerruti. In keeping with the style of modern Italian luxury, Pilati's elegant silhouette often favours starkly simple and elemental materials: wool, silk and silver, with expert flashes of colour. This new direction proved successful for the house of YSL. After ten years, Pilati parted ways with the house, moving to Ermenegildo Zegna in 2012.

► Ford, Ghesquière, Philo, Saint Laurent, Simons

Stefano Pilati. b Milan (IT), 1965. **Yves Saint Laurent spring/summer 2011.** Photograph by Chris Moore.

Pilotto Peter & De Vos Christopher (Peter Pilotto)

Peter Pilotto and Christopher De Vos – the two designers behind the label Peter Pilotto – met in 2000 while studying at the Royal Academy of Fine Arts in Antwerp. Now based in London, the young label is known for its modern, bold silhouettes that are illustrated with bright colour and maximal-prints inspired by recurring patterns in nature, decor and technology, seen here in their autumn/winter 2012 collection. The digitally printed illustration on the fabric (a modern interpretation of a jacquard-style pattern) works with the sporty design and detailing; the puffa-jacket style with zip and toggles is a contemporary take on the high fashion genre. Peter Pilotto is at the forefront of a London fashion movement, having innovated and reinvented textile technology, producing hyperreal prints united with soft, sculptural shapes.

► C. Bailey, Erdem, Kane, Katrantzou, Kirkwood

Peter Pilotto. b Wörgl (AUS), 1977; **Christopher De Vos. b** Tripoli (LIB), 1980. **Peter Pilotto autumn/winter 2013.**

Pinet François

Shoe designer

The dainty flower design and distinctive Louis heel of this delicate, white satin boot – a finer version of the lowish, wasp-waisted heel worn in the reign of King Louis XV of France – are typical of the designs by the French shoemaking firm Pinet. Established in 1855 by François Pinet, the Paris company soon became known for creating elegant footwear for the most fashionable members of society, shoes that would be worn underneath the grand gowns by Charles Worth. Shoemaking was a family concern for Pinet; he had learnt his craft from his father and, when he retired in the early years of the twentieth century, his son took over and continued to expand the firm, opening shops in Nice and London. Roger Vivier later supplied designs to this prestigious firm, which has become known for demonstrably expensive shoes, such as women's court shoes entirely covered with rhinestones and animal-skin footwear for men.

► Hope, Pingat, Vivier, Worth, Yantorny

François Pinet. b Château-le-Vaillère (FR), 1817. d (FR), 1897. **Women's embroidered boot.** Photograph by Elisabeth Eylieu, 1867.

Pingat Emile

Designer

This navy faille day dress from the 1870s, with its frills, ruching and cut velvet bodice, recalls the grandeur of Emile Pingat's work. He was a contemporary of Charles Frederick Worth, the father of haute couture. They were rival couturiers, with their names mentioned together in the guidebooks for female tourists visiting Paris in the second half of the nineteenth century. His own fashion house flourished from 1860 to 1896. He was known preeminently as a couturier who created fashions of delicate contrasts and for a perfect harmony of proportion, evocative of the current ideal of femininity. His striking ball gowns captured the fantasy and romance of the great festive occasions in Paris during the Second Empire and the Third Republic. Together with Worth, his creations reflected the fashionable silhouette and aesthetic of the Parisian world of haute couture from the mid- to late nineteenth century.

► Boué, Pinet, Reboux, Worth

Emile Pingat. b (FR), 1820. **d** (FR), 1901. **Blue faille and silk velvet day dress.** *c.*1870s.

Pipart Gérard

Designer

Arlette Ricci, granddaughter of the couturière Nina, wears a luxurious astrakhan coat cinched with an elastic belt – an ironic conceit that displays modern use of a deluxe garment. It is the work of Gérard Pipart for the house of Nina Ricci, once described as a 'never too haute' designer. Pipart joined the house in 1964 after the departure of Jules-François Crahay. His education had been conducted in the houses of the great couturiers Balmain, Fath, Patou and Givenchy; consequently he creates simple Parisian chic rather than chasing seasonal trends. Pipart is also true to the tradition of maintaining 'house' styles, those which women can order each season with few alterations beyond a change of fabric. He never learned to cut fabric so he is unusual in working from precise drawings and making amendments straight onto the toiles. Pipart's style is one of conservative beauty that eschews gimmickry.

▶ Balmain, Crahay, Fath, Givenchy, Patou, Ricci

Gérard Pipart. b Paris (FR), 1933. Arlette Ricci wears belted astrakhan coat for Nina Ricci. Photograph by Peter Knapp, 1976.

Pita Orlando

Hairdresser

Model Shalom Harlow's hairstyle accurately reflects Orlando Pita's aesthetic approach, where, while creativity and subversion are critical elements, beauty still remains a priority. 'A hairstyle may be stunning, but I will have failed if it doesn't make a woman beautiful,' says Pita. Often informed by ethnic or traditional techniques, such as the Hasidic *payos* on the Jean Paul Gaultier catwalk and African-American braidings in videos for Madonna, one of his most loyal clients, Pita finds an ideal ground for experimentation in the diva, who allows him to break away from all stereotypes. 'There's no room for fantasy in the salon,' he says when asked why he concentrates on editorials and catwalk shows appearing in pages from *Vogue* and *Vanity Fair* to *i-D*. Pita, who vehemently resists shampooing hair in the belief that its own sebaceous secretions have a natural cleansing function, has even used toilet rolls as curlers to achieve some of his Surrealist styles.

► Gaultier, McKnight, Madonna, Meisel, Testino

Orlando Pita. b Havana (CU), 1962. **Shalom Harlow.** Photograph by Mario Testino, *Harper's Bazaar*, 1994.

Platt Lynes George

Photographer

With her face turned away from George Platt Lynes' camera, the reclining figure presents herself as a living model in an art gallery setting. The drape of her *crêpe-de-chine* dress mirrors that on the dress of her companion and the wavy print snaking along her body is a reminder of that fabric's propensity for liquid movement. These gowns, by Gilbert Adrian, are presented as vaguely Surrealist *objets* by a photographer who followed that movement, explored during a friendship with Jean Cocteau. Platt Lynes started to publish his fashion work in *Town* and *Harper's Bazaar* in 1933 and became director of *Vogue*'s Hollywood studio in 1942. His later life was spent photographing male nudes (Platt Lynes was a charismatic, openly gay member of New York's artistic community). These, it is said, set precedents for the work of Herb Ritts and Bruce Weber, who apply simplicity and the artistic merit of a sinewy male physique to their work.

► Adrian, Ritts, Weber

George Platt Lynes. b East Orange, NJ (USA), 1907. **d** New York (USA), 1955. **Adrian's 'Magic' draped silk dresses.** British *Vogue*, 1947.

Poiret Paul

Designer

The scope of Paul Poiret, the 'Sultan of Fashion', is illustrated in this line-up of models influenced by the Ballets Russes. In 1909 he introduced a fluid style of dress, inspired by the French *Directoire* and orientalism but also the sumptuous splendour in which he lived and worked. He gave fashion a theatrical spin by throwing lavish fêtes at his *maison de couture*, where the *beau monde* of Paris would wear Poiret-designed costumes – which became fashion overnight. He added a new dimension to fashion by parading his mannequins in the gardens of his house, at racecourses and on tours of Europe and the United States. Poiret opened his own salon after serving an apprenticeship under Doucet and working for Worth. He was one of the most creative fashion designers of the twentieth century, revolutionizing fashion design, reviving fashion illustration, establishing a school for the decorative arts and even diversifying into perfume.

► Bakst, Barbier, Brunelleschi, Erté, Iribe, Lepape

Paul Poiret. b Paris (FR), 1879. **d** Paris (FR), 1944. **Poiret's mannequins.** *L'Illustration*, 1910.

Pollock Alice

Designer

The model sweeps down the catwalk in Pollock's crepe evening dress. Unadorned but for neat front buttoning, the design combines simplicity with femininity in keeping with the avant-garde of the 1960s. Challenging convention, Pollock created fluid and comfortable eveningwear. She opened Quorum, a wholesale and boutique business in London's King's Road, becoming the first to employ Ossie Clark, a stalwart of the 1960s Chelsea scene. Their designs often used fabrics designed by Celia Birtwell, Clark's wife. Together they produced clothes renowned for their sensuality – evident in deep necklines and wasp waists and in their luxurious trademark fabrics of crepe, chiffon, satin and close-fitting jersey. More than a designer, Pollock was an iconoclastic force in Britain's emerging fashion world who encouraged Clark and Birtwell, amongst others, to 'do their thing'.

► Birtwell, Clark, Jackson, Porter

Alice Pollock. b (UK), 1942. **White crepe dress.** Photograph by Annette Green, British *Vogue*, 1970.

Porter Thea

Designer

A printed voile headdress is weighted with gold embroidery and bugle beads. Under it the model wears exotic make-up: kohl applied inside the lower lid, emerald eye shadow and ruby nail varnish. Her kaftan top is made from a patchwork of rough Madras cotton and co-ordinating, semi-sheer voile. It all evokes the mixture of Middle Eastern influences that surrounded Thea Porter as she grew up in Damascus and later in Beirut. Porter took her international style to London's Soho in the 1960s where she opened a shop on Greek Street. It sold her own interpretation of Eastern clothing to an artistic clientele that included Elizabeth Taylor and Barbra Streisand. Porter concentrated on clothes that had an illusory element removed from real life: impressive robes embroidered with Arabic designs and evening dresses cut from silk brocade.

▶ Bouquin, Gibb, Hulanicki, Pollock, Rhodes

Thea Porter. b Damascus (SYR), 1927. **d** London (UK), 2000. **Eastern kaftan and headdress.** Photograph by Barry Lategan, British *Vogue*, 1975.

Del Pozo Jesús   Designer

Jesús del Pozo adds substance to a drifting, cotton voile dress by piping its vertical seams. A natural, simple shape, it is a poetic garment, which becomes the focus of a dream-like image photographed in heightened colour by Javier Vallhonrat. Strong colour and simple shape is the backbone of del Pozo's style, which has also cross-hatched a vibrant, melon slip dress with bold painted stripes. Del Pozo trained as an engineer, abandoning the discipline to study furniture design and interior decorating, before moving into painting, the influence of which is clear in his work; this dress resembles a sweep of paint. Del Pozo moved on once more, opening his first menswear store in 1974. Two years later his collection was being presented in Paris and worn by women who admired his soft, colourful menswear. Encouraged, he started to present womenswear in 1980.

► Dominguez, Sybilla, Vallhonrat

Prada Miuccia

Designer

The intelligence behind the label Prada belongs entirely to Miuccia Prada. Inheriting her grandfather's leather luggage business in the 1970s, Prada revamped the label by introducing innovative fabrics and design, pioneering the lightweight nylon backpack embraced by the fashion cognoscenti and legion counterfeiters. Focusing on freedom of definition, rather than sex appeal, Prada's experimentation with 1970s furnishing fabrics heralded the 1996 'geek chic' look. She has commented, 'I never dress according to how beautiful I look, but always on my imagination'. Prada developed a line that is brave in spirit, controversial and desired above almost any other label. In 2004, she was awarded the Council of Fashion Designers of America International Award. In 2012 she was celebrated at the Metropolitan Museum of Art's exhibit 'Schiaparelli and Prada: Impossible Conversations'.

► Fendi, McGrath, Van Noten, Souleiman, Steele

Miuccia Prada. b Milan (IT), 1949. **Miuccia Prada photographed by Brigitte Lacombe.** 2005.

De Prémonville Myrène Designer

The jacket is given a dramatic cut by Myrène de Prémonville for a feminized business suit. Its long-line shape is softened with pockets that follow its curving hem. The shoulders are encircled with a strap that mimics an off-the-shoulder gown. De Prémonville's first designs for her own label in the late 1980s were a response to what she felt was missing from her own (and other women's) wardrobes. In the tradition of other female designers, such as Carven and Margaret Howell, de Prémonville started to design for her own needs. The results were sculpted, sassy suits that used unusual colour combinations, bright graphic appliqués and contrasting trims. She also designed a pair of classic black stirrup trousers because, as she says, 'No one else's felt comfortable.' By the early 1990s, de Prémonville had found an audience of working women who appreciated her meticulous attention to detail.

► Howell, Marant, De Tommaso

Myrène de Prémonville. b Hendaye (FR), 1949. **Day suit with banded yoke.** Photograph by Philippe Costes, 1984.

Presley Elvis

Icon

Presley's hip-thrusting style spoke eloquently to a new American phenomenon: the teenager. Wearing a loosely cut suit, black shirt and half-mast tie, he is the image of a young man who has rejected the formalities of dress of the older generation. This new, essentially working-class image scorned established ideas about status and redefined male attractiveness as youthful and overtly sensual. Presley started out as a truck driver and in 1953 recorded a few songs for Sun Records. Within five years he had made nineteen hit records and starred in four blockbuster movies. His hip gyrations would turn girls to jelly, earning him the nickname 'Elvis the Pelvis'. He was also known as 'The Hillbilly Cat', a reference to the 'hip cats' of the black jazz tradition – the song 'Blue Suede Shoes' denotes a cool dandyism synonymous with a certain black style.

► Bartlett, The Beatles, Dean, Hendrix

Elvis Presley. b Tupelo, MS (USA), 1935. **d** Memphis, TN (USA), 1977. **Elvis Presley.** *c.*1957.

Price Antony

Designer

Antony Price is photographed with Jerry Hall, his friend and model. She wears a peplum dress of metallic and red French silk lace placed over lamé, an outfit worn for a benefit show in 1985. 'It wasn't the chicest or most subtle garment,' Price explains, 'but when Jerry moved under the lights she looked like a Siamese fighting fish in a vast blue tank.' It is a theatrical example of his potent eveningwear, designed, as he once said, by a man for a man. Price and Hall met when she was seventeen and modelling a blue

mermaid frock for the cover of a Roxy Music album. In 1968 Price had designed a groundbreaking menswear show; its nostalgic 1930s and 1940s statement became a blueprint for the intellectual glam of Roxy Music. Launching his own label in 1979, Price consolidated his reputation for corseted super-heroine evening gowns made for 'women who go to serious parties'.

▶ G. Jones, Kelly, Mackie, Oldfield

Antony Price. b Bradford, West Yorkshire (UK), 1945. **Antony Price with Jerry Hall.** Photograph by Richard Young, 1986.

Pucci Emilio

Designer

A skier is frozen in flight above a model wearing a classic Pucci design: a boldly patterned and brightly coloured jacket with slim ski pants is typical of Emilio Pucci, the Marchese di Barsento, scion of an old aristocratic Tuscan family. He was a member of the Italian Olympic ski team and, after photographs of him on the slopes wearing his own designs appeared in *Harper's Bazaar*, he was invited to create winter clothes for women to be sold in New York. In 1951 he established his own fashion house in his Palazzo Pucci in Florence. His 'palazzo pyjamas' in non-crushable, silk jersey were worn by Grace Kelly, Lauren Bacall and Elizabeth Taylor, and became a jet-set uniform. Pucci's iconic swirling patterns, based on medieval Italian banners, captured the psychedelic mood of the 1960s. Christian Lacroix and Matthew Williamson are among the major designers who have worked for the label since Pucci's death.

► Ascher, Galitzine, Missoni, Pulitzer

Emilio Pucci. b Naples (IT), 1914. **d** Florence (IT), 1992. **Ski jacket.** Photograph by Peter Beard, American *Vogue*, 1964.

Pugh Gareth

Designer

For his spring/summer 2007 ready-to-wear collection, British designer Gareth Pugh transformed his models into otherworldly creatures on an inflated, billowing runway. Every centimetre of skin was hidden under futuristic materials – mostly in black, shaped into geometric structures – and topped with sculptural hairstyles. Pugh's fashion week presentations are often driven by performance – stemming perhaps from his background as a costume designer for the English National Youth Theatre. After graduating from Central Saint Martins, Pugh's darkly carnivalesque debut show made its mark with a ballooned-out puffa-coat and a preference for fierce females, garnering the soft-spoken couturier comparisons to eccentric compatriots John Galliano and Alexander McQueen. Filmmaker Ruth Hogben collaborates with Pugh on films that play during his shows, giving his visionary fashions a fitting digital-age presentation.

► Deacon, Demeulemeester, Galliano, McQueen, Owens

Gareth Pugh. b Sunderland, Tyne and Wear (UK), 1981. **Black, open-knit dress with sculptural PVC sleeves, from spring/summer 2007 collection.** Photograph by Chris Moore.

Pulitzer Lilly

Designer

The 'Lilly' dress, worn here by Rose Kennedy and her granddaughter Kathleen, suited every age. Like Pucci, Pulitzer found one style of pattern and kept with it. Her simple, summer shift dresses came in bright, colourful, floral cottons. Living in Florida's Palm Beach, Pulitzer knew what would make the perfect vacation-wear and she always claimed, 'The great thing about the Lilly is that you wear practically nothing underneath.' This wealthy resort area lent her clothes a certain cachet and her squiggly signature was on every dress. She had originally made one for herself to wear when, as a rich but bored housewife, she began selling freshly squeezed orange juice on the beach in 1959. The original dresses were made from cheap-and-cheerful cotton from Woolworths. She started selling her dresses on her stall and the 'Lilly' became an overnight success. John Fairchild dubbed it a 'little nothing' dress.

► Kennedy, Oudejans, Pucci

Lilly Pulitzer. b Roslyn, NY (USA), 1931. **Rose Kennedy with granddaughter Kathleen.** *c.*1960s.

Quant Mary · Designer

Grace Coddington wears a jersey dress inspired by a footballer's strip. Fresh and youthful, Mary Quant's work democratized fashion, bringing an affordable version of couture to young working women. In 1955 Quant and her husband, Alexander Plunket-Greene, opened Bazaar, a Chelsea boutique that sold clothes that expressed an anti-establishment sentiment. The pair had met at art school and together they were members of a new society of design entrepreneurs that included Terence Conran and Vidal Sassoon. From 1962 Quant's hemlines were raised until, in 1964, skirts arrived at the era-defining mini length. It was dubbed the 'gymslip of the permissive society' and Mary Quant wore one at Buckingham Palace when collecting her O.B.E. in 1966. Her look also used matching pantyhose, inspired by dance rehearsal outfits. Ease, exercise and stretch: these elements add up to the foundations of modern fashion.

► Charles, Coddington, Courrèges, Khanh, Liberty, Paulin, Rayne

Mary Quant. b London (UK), 1934. **Grace Coddington wears a Mary Quant Ginger Group mini dress.** 1967.

Rabanne Paco

Designer

Aluminium discs and panels linked by wire using pliers have replaced conventional fashion created by threads and needles in this space-fantasy costume. Rabanne studied architecture at the École des Beaux-Arts in Paris but turned to fashion, supplying plastic buttons and jewellery to Givenchy, Dior and Balenciaga. Opening his own fashion house in 1966, it was his architectural training combined with the impact of space and space travel in the 1960s that inspired Rabanne to create such startling new styles. His space-age fashions using alternative, experimental materials were important in pushing aside the traditional parameters of what were acceptable clothes to wear on the street. Other fashion designers who travelled the space-age fashion route in the 1960s were Pierre Cardin, André Courrèges, Rudi Gernreich and Yves Saint Laurent.

► Bailly, Barrett, Dior, Gernreich, Betsey Johnson

Paco Rabanne. b San Sebastián (SP), 1934. **Aluminium chainmail dress.** Photograph by Gunnar Larsen, 1966.

Rayne Sir Edward

Shoe designer

'Ladies Day at Ascot. It simply mustn't rain,' reads the caption to this playful image. Rayne's lemon-yellow court shoes, striped with nylon mesh, are flirting with masculine polished riding boots and Oxford brogues. Impeccably crafted in myriad colours, from the day japonica pink to the evening jewelled jade, Rayne's shoes dressed Britain's well-heeled. Granted the Royal Warrant for Queen Elizabeth, the Queen Mother, Rayne designed for Princess Elizabeth's wedding trousseau in 1947, draping her sandals in ivory silk with seed pearls. The family-owned business, H&M Rayne, was founded by his grandparents in 1889. Edward Rayne joined the company in 1940, taking over in 1951. He collaborated with couturiers Hardy Amies and Norman Hartnell, while still keeping his eye on prevailing trends. Both Jean Muir and Mary Quant lent their talents to Rayne's fashion profile by designing youthful footwear.

▶ Amies, Hartnell, Muir, Quant, Vivier

Sir Edward Rayne. b London (UK), 1922. d Bexhill, East Sussex (UK), 1992. 'Jaress' yellow shoe with mesh toe. 1963.

Reboux Caroline

Milliner

Caroline Reboux was a milliner who excelled at structured simplicity. She avoided decoration and ornamentation. She liked working with felt – a strong and malleable material that she cut and folded on her clients' heads. For Mlle Conchita Montenegro, the milliner decorated the hat very simply with a lotus plant motif that reflected the line of the hat. This style of hat also complemented the tailored yet dramatic ensemble. Reboux designed hats for many couturiers and, later

in her career, had a special relationship with Madame Vionnet, whose classicism matched her own. In the 1860s, Caroline Reboux's individual style caught the eye of Princess Metternich, who was credited with introducing Worth to the Empress Eugénie. She was soon making hats for the Empress and by 1870 she was established in the centre of fashionable Paris at 22 rue de la Paix, where she worked until her death.

► Agnès, Barthet, Daché, Hartnell, Pingat, Windsor

Caroline Reboux. b Paris (FR), 1830s. **d** Paris (FR), 1927. **Hat trimmed with broderie anglaise.** Photograph by Baron de Meyer, American *Vogue*, 1919.

Recine

Hairdresser

A visual artist first and foremost, Recine blurs the immutable division between art and commerce in a way that few hairstylists have managed to do. Using the head as a vehicle for sculptures constructed from found objects, he innovatively integrates materials into his designs that transcend the traditional sphere of hairdressing. Early in his career, he secured a window display project for famed department store Henri Bendel in his home city of New York. Soon after, he was enlisted by celebrated hairstylist Jean Louis David, relocating to Paris to fine-tune his craft. Building an impressive portfolio of editorial and advertising commissions, today he is a frequent collaborator of fashion and fine art photographers alike, including Mario Sorrenti, Peter Lindbergh and Paolo Roversi. Recine's designs have also been instrumental in constructing the iconic and imaginative style of influential cultural figures such as Lady Gaga.

► Lady Gaga, Lindbergh, Roversi, Sorrenti, Soulemain

Recine (**Bob Recine**). **b** CT (USA), 1958. **Ingrid Mask.** Photograph by Robbie Fimmano, 2007.

433

Redfern John

Designer

Mary Garden, the celebrated Scottish opera singer, wears a town dress made of pleated Rajah silk with a matching cape and a lace blouse. It evokes the fashionable silhouette of the *belle époque*: a high-necked, full bodice that gives a pouched effect, over a deep, tightly constricted waist. The skirt is cut straight at the front and filled out by pleats and extra fabric at the back that extends into a train. This style of dress became known as the S-bend. It reflected the taste for Art Nouveau. Redfern began as a ladies' tailor in Cowes on the Isle of Wight. The success of his tailored garments, especially his yachting costumes, led to his becoming a couturier, designing fashionable clothes for royalty, singers and actresses. In 1881 he established fashion houses in London and Paris, followed by branches in Edinburgh and New York. Redfern closed his houses in 1920.

► Boué, Von Drecoll, Gibson, Paquin

John Redfern. b Cowes, Isle of Wight (UK), 1853. **d** 1929. **Town dress of pleated Rajah silk and lace.** 1905.

De la Renta Oscar   Designer

Carla Bruni looks as though she owns, and plays, the grand piano on which she is perched, in keeping with the de la Renta image: sophisticated, lavish, grown-up. The svelte black bodice, which sweeps into a softly gathered skirt, is finished with flat bows on the shoulder. Known for ornamentation and feminine silhouettes, de la Renta has cultivated clients among the rich and beautiful with whom he socializes. Originally training with Balenciaga, de la Renta went on to design for Elizabeth Arden in New York, where his idealism of European glamour was applied to conventions of American dressmaking. In 1993 he returned to Europe to design Balmain couture, bringing his distinctive silhouettes: flattering dresses and sophisticated suits, with a special gift for dress-up and evening glamour. He received the Council of Fashion Designers of America Designer of the Year Award in 2000 and 2007.

► Alfaro, Arden, Balenciaga, Balmain, Roehm, Scaasi

Oscar de la Renta. b Santo Domingo (DOM), 1932. **Carla Bruni wears black cocktail gown.** Photograph by Arthur Elgort, 1992.   435

Revillon Théodore, Albert, Anatole & Léon (Revillon Frères)   Designers

Louise Dahl-Wolfe shoots a shawl-collared, sealskin cape draped around the shoulders like a wash of black ink; it is an image of a woman coated in wealth. The pioneers of this sort of fur fashion, the Revillon brothers – Théodore, Albert, Anatole and Léon – treated the pelt like silk, cutting it skilfully a century earlier. Were it not for their aristocratic father's neck-saving decision to change his name from Count Louis-Victor d'Argental during the French Revolution, such coats might not have existed.

Louis-Victor had already taken fur beyond its practical use as a provider of warmth with much-coveted juxtapositions of exotic furs such as ocelot, chinchilla and Arctic fox, making Paris the fur capital of the world. On his death, the firm, renamed Revillon Frères by his four sons, became the first French global company with trading posts across Canada and Siberia and a museum opened in their name.

► Dahl-Wolfe, Fendi, Lauder

Revillon. Théodore. b Paris (FR). d (FR), 1920; Albert. b Paris (FR). d 1887; Anatole. b Paris (FR). d (FR) 1916; Léon. b Paris (FR). d (FR), 1915. (Active 1840s–1910s.). Seal cape. Photograph by Louise Dahl-Wolfe, *Harper's Bazaar*, 1956.

Revson Charles (Revlon)

Cosmetics creator

Sassy and liberated, Shelley Hack – the 'Charlie Girl' – strides across the page wearing a trouser suit and an expression that says, 'I've got it all.' Revlon captured the mood of a new generation of independent women with the image of its scent, Charlie, in the 1970s. Revlon was founded in 1932 by brothers Charles and Joseph Revson and a chemist named Charles Lachman. Charles Revson had the marketing brain. When Elizabeth Arden referred to him as 'that man' (because she thought he copied her ideas), he created a line of men's cosmetics named 'That Man'. Success, however, was founded on opaque-coloured nail polish that supplanted clear tints and introduced women to matching nail and lip colour. They started with Fire and Ice, a strong red, with the ad slogan, 'There's a little bit of bad in every good woman.' Revson said he wanted his models to be like 'Park Avenue whores – elegant, but the sexual thing underneath'.

▶ Arden, Factor, Hutton, Venturi

Charles Revson. b Somerville, MA (USA), 1906. **d** New York (USA), 1976. **Shelley Hack modelling for Revlon's 'Charlie' perfume.** Photograph by Albert Watson, c.1974.

Rhodes Zandra

Designer

Zandra Rhodes once said that she tried to achieve an ageless exoticism. As such, she is an original; her trademarks were slashed silk tatters, abstract beading, handkerchief points, squiggle prints, tulle crinolines and pleated fabrics edged with ruffles. The 'Conceptual Chic' collection of 1977, shown here, brought street-style to couture using embroidered rips and safety pins as jewellery. Her dresses used techniques that are still seen as subversive: exterior seams and 'winking' holes revealing erogenous zones and semi-sheer jersey. 'We were determined to live in a world of today, making it all ourselves, creating our own environment, a perfect world of plastic, perfectly artificial,' she recalled. She cited Edith Sitwell as her inspiration. Her own image – multi-coloured hair and statement make-up – contributes to her aura of outrageousness. In 2003 she founded the Fashion and Textile Museum, London.

► Clark, Rotten, Sarne, G. Smith, Williamson

Zandra Rhodes. b Chatham, Kent (UK), 1940. **'Conceptual Chic' punk jersey dresses.** Photograph by Clive Arrowsmith, 1977.

De Ribes Jacqueline   Designer

In a pose of fragile elegance, the Comtesse Jacqueline de Ribes gazes out in a stark, black velvet dress, its rigorous cut softened only by a gentle froth of silk cloqué. Dubbed the 'Most Stylish Woman in the World' by *Town and Country* magazine in 1983, the Comtesse was already appearing on the international best-dressed lists by the age of twenty-five, having consistently worn haute couture all her life. Because of a family history of French aristocratic wealth – which suggested fashion design was beneath her station – her longing to become a designer was not fulfilled until she was well into her forties.

An innate sense of good taste meant success for her first collection in Paris and America in 1983. It catered for women of her ilk, who admired its aura of discreet grandeur and slender lines adorned by extravagant though simple shoulder detail. In 2010 the designer was made a Chevalier of the *Légion d'honneur*.

▶ Von Furstenberg, De la Renta, Roehm

Comtesse Jacqueline de Ribes. b Paris (FR), 1931. **Jacqueline de Ribes, Paris.** Photograph by Victor Skrebneski, 1983.

Ricci Nina

Designer

In this advertisement from 1937, a slimline suit, the jacket trimmed with fur, is placed in the context of Nina Ricci's world; the centre of which was the Place Vendôme in Paris. Unlike her contemporaries Coco Chanel and Elsa Schiaparelli, Nina Ricci did not set trends; instead, she concentrated on providing clothes for wealthy society women of a certain age, whose aim was to appear feminine, elegant and beautiful. It was a tradition that was continued by Jules-François Crahay and then by Gérard Pipart, both of whom respected Ricci's original tenet. She opened her Parisian couture house in 1932 and, with the help of her son Robert Ricci, rapidly established a reputation as a true couturière. She worked by draping fabric directly onto the body, gathering and tucking to emphasize her clients' attributes and disguise their imperfections. Olivier Theyskens was creative director from 2006 to 2009. He was replaced by Peter Copping.

► Ascher, Crahay, Frizon, Hirata, Mainbocher, Pipart, Theyskens

Nina Ricci. b Turin (IT), 1883. **d** Paris (FR), 1970. **Fur-trimmed jacket and skirt.** Illustration by Pierre Mourgue, 1937.

Richardson Terry   Photographer

As a friend of photographer Terry Richardson, actress and style icon Chloe Sevigny is a frequent subject of his work. Here Sevigny captures the dauntless sexuality that – often controversially – typifies his photographs. But Richardson's popularity has yet to wane. Former New York gallery owner Jeffrey Deitch once referred to him as, 'one of the more charismatic figures in downtown culture', an opinion seemingly reinforced by his persistently high volume of assignments. Raised in California, Richardson

inherited his artistic eye from his father Bob Richardson, also a fashion photographer. Characterized by raw eroticism and a stark palette, Richardson's photography is often conflated with his licentious public persona and inability to discern where the work ends and the man begins. In Richardson's estimation, it makes little difference, 'I think all your work is personal,' he stated. 'It's your life.'

► Leon, Meisel, Sorrenti, Teller, Testino

Terry Richardson. b. New York City (USA), 1965. **Chloe Sevigny for *Out* magazine, 2012.** Photograph by Terry Richardson.

Ritts Herb

Photographer

Using his customary talent for black-and-white photography, Herb Ritts makes a drama out of Gianni Versace's already arresting dress. The funnel of black fabric, and that worn by the model, create startling geometric shapes that contrast with her pale skin and the desert backdrop. Born into a wealthy Los Angeles family in 1952, Herb Ritts lived next door to Steve McQueen and was exposed to a world of sophisticated beauty by his mother, an interior decorator. Photography started as a hobby, with portraits of friends and landscapes. In 1978 a picture he had taken on the set of Franco Zeffirelli's remake of *The Champ* was used by *Newsweek*. A friend, male model Matt Collins, introduced Ritts to Bruce Weber and fashion photography. Ritts's style was sexy and powerful, often homo-erotic and always fascinated by the texture of skin. He also directed numerous influential and award-winning music videos and commercials.

▶ Platt Lynes, Sieff, Versace, Weber

Herb Ritts. b Los Angeles, CA (USA), 1952. **d** Los Angeles, CA (USA), 2002. **Tatjana Patitz wears Versace.** *Le Mirage*, 1990.

Roberts Michael   Illustrator

Recalling the collage work of Henri Matisse, Michael Roberts accurately depicts Azzedine Alaïa's sculptural Sphinx dress. Bands of white paper emulate the elastic bands in Alaïa's trademark creation; a black paper silhouette accentuates these bands' curvaceous effect. Using a naïve, 'child-like' illustrative technique, Roberts keeps an outsider's perspective, while his humorous treatment hints at a deep knowledge of fashion's intricacies. A fashion writer, stylist, photographer, illustrator, video director and collagist, Roberts pokes fun at fashion icons. His outrageous sense of style and venomous pen found their way through his appointments at *The Sunday Times* in 1972, society magazine *Tatler* in 1981 and at British *Vogue* and the *New Yorker* magazine. His provocative vision was acutely exemplified when, for an 'April Fool' issue of *Tatler*, he transformed designer Vivienne Westwood into Margaret Thatcher.

► Alaïa, Antonio, Ettedgui, Gustafson, Westwood

Michael Roberts. b Aylesbury (UK), 1947. **'Azzedine's Sphinx.'** Paper collage, 1991.

Roberts Tommy (Mr Freedom)   Designer

Photographer Clive Arrowsmith puts Tommy Roberts' work into its kitsch Americana context for *Vogue* in 1971. The stretchy wrestler's dungarees are appliquéd with a bubblegum-pink satin heart and worn over a colour-blocked T-shirt. The grinning baseball team seals the story. This was fun fashion for the pop generation at a time when *Vogue* asked the question, 'Is bad taste a bad thing?' Designer Tommy Roberts was Mr Freedom, a man with an eye both for design and for the gap in the market. His cheerful T-shirts and tightly cut trousers were also decorated with camp symbols of 1930s and 1940s Hollywood – Mickey Mouse and Donald Duck adorned iconoclastic clothing for both sexes. In 1966 Roberts opened Kleptomania, a hippie emporium near London's Carnaby Street, which was followed in 1969 by Mr Freedom, on the King's Road. It sold a fast-moving style that never took itself too seriously.

► Fiorucci, Fish, Nutter

Tommy Roberts. b London (UK), 1942. **d** London (UK), 2012. **Dungarees with pink appliqué heart.** Photograph by Clive Arrowsmith, British *Vogue*, 1971.

Rocha John

Designer

Creative yet commercial, John Rocha says, 'Sex never comes into it. I'm interested in beauty more than anything else.' Here, his organza dress printed with vast orchids is thrown into relief by Pat McGrath's abstract cobalt-blue make-up. The dress is designed to stand proud of the body, creating a see-through sheath shadowed with flowers. Despite the hot mood of this picture, it is Irish references that often influence Rocha's work. Natural fabrics, including linen, wool and sheepskin, are given the colours of a Celtic landscape: soft moss green, stone, slate grey. Rocha describes his clothes as 'free in spirit...a bit gypsy'. This description also fits the Portuguese-Chinese designer who moved from Hong Kong to London to study fashion. His Celtic-inspired end-of-year show was spotted by the Irish Trade Board who invited him to work in Dublin, where he has lived since 1979. His daughter, Simone, has followed in his footsteps as a designer.

► Eisen, Kim, McGrath, Watanabe

John Rocha. b Hong Kong (HK), 1953. **Organza print dress.** Photograph by Steven Klein, *Frank*, 1998.

Rochas Marcel   Designer

Marcel Rochas oversees the fitting of a dress, conducted by his wife Hélène, who pins and tucks the skirt into the New Look shape – a curvaceous silhouette that Rochas was credited with presaging in his film work for Mae West. In 1946 he launched the *guêpière*, a long-line strapless brassiere which enclosed the hips – a foundation garment that was to train figures for a decade. Counting Jean Cocteau and Christian Bérard among his friends, and with the encouragement of Poiret, Rochas opened his own couture house in 1925. He started to create black-and-white dresses that featured a white collar – one of which is photographed here. His creative innovations often featured a strong shoulder line, an element that Rochas considered 'a sign of the feminine'. Olivier Theyskens was creative director of the house of Rochas from 2002 to 2006, and in 2008 Marco Zanini took on the role at the fashion house.

▶ Bérard, Cocteau, Dior, Givenchy, Theyskens

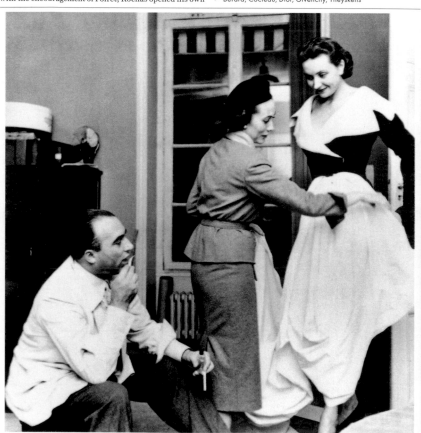

Marcel Rochas. b Paris (FR), 1902. **d** Paris (FR), 1955. **Marcel and Hélène Rochas with model.** 1944.

Rodriguez Narciso   Designer

Cerruti, for whom he designed this dainty, embroidered bodice, gave Narciso Rodriguez his first international platform as a designer of minimal fashion. However, it was the creation of a wedding dress that really brought his name to general attention. In 1996 Carolyn Bessette married John F. Kennedy Jr wearing one of Rodriguez' rigorously simple, bias-cut sheath dresses. 'I made a wedding dress for a really good friend and [it] brought a lot of attention to the work I was doing,' he said afterwards. Rodriguez learned the power of understatement while working for a succession of design houses, each of whose philosophy is based around clean, modern, luxurious and wearable clothes: Anne Klein, Calvin Klein (where he met Bessette) and TSE, a design label specializing in cashmere. In 1997, Rodriguez launched his own label in Milan and was appointed to design for the luxurious Spanish label Loewe.

► Cerruti, Ferretti, A. Klein, C. Klein, Loewe

Narciso Rodriguez. b NJ (USA), 1961. **Embroidered bodice and skirt for Cerruti.** Photograph by Carter Smith, *Harper's Bazaar*, 1997.

Roehm Carolyne

Designer

Carolyne Roehm, photographed at a gala event held by Bill Blass, is her own best advert. When she launched her own deluxe, ready-to-wear business in 1984, it was her tall, whippet-thin frame that starred in the glossy adverts and sold her feminine clothes. 'I wasn't so gung ho on the idea of being in the ads,' she said. 'I was told it would be a tremendous advantage.' And so it was. Roehm sold her society clothes to rich women who were either like her or wanted to be like her. She has been described as both 'driven' and 'highly organised' and it is these qualities that led her to Oscar de la Renta, for whom she worked for ten years as designer, house model and muse. Roehm mixes luxury with a practical awareness. Garments cut from lavish fabrics, such as a full-length, duchesse satin evening skirt, will be worn with a cashmere sweater to simulate the feel of sportswear.

► Blass, De la Renta, De Ribes, V. Wang

Carolyne Roehm. b Kirksville, MI (USA), 1951. **Satin cocktail dress.** Photograph by Daniel d'Errico, *Women's Wear Daily*, 1991.

Rosier Michèle   Designer

A mountain takes on the look of another planet for the backdrop to Michèle Rosier's space-age sportswear. The model's bug-eyed goggles and silver boots amplify the drama of Rosier's foil ski jacket and pants. Together with her contemporary Christiane Bailly, Rosier was a major player in France's burgeoning ready-to-wear market. With her young, accessible response to haute couture, she helped boost the export of French *prêt-à-porter* five-fold between 1962 and 1970. Rosier spent her childhood with her mother, publisher Hélène Gordon-Lazareff, in the United States, where the youth-orientated style was a formative influence. Rosier began her career as a writer for *New Woman* and *France-Soir*, but quit journalism to found V de V (Vêtements de Vacances) in 1962 with Jean-Pierre Bamberger. Rosier's use of sportswear fabrics, such as nylon fleece, paved the way for their adoption as part of everyday fashion clothing.

► Bailly, Bousquet, Khanh, W. Smith

Michèle Rosier. b Paris (FR), 1929. **Quilted ski jacket and pants for V de V.** Photograph by Eugene Vernier, British *Vogue*, 1966.   449

Rotten Johnny

Icon

Created by Malcolm McLaren and styled by Vivienne Westwood, the Sex Pistols were a promotional tool for the pair's punk-defining London's King's Road shop, Sex. Johnny Rotten, lead member of the group, pronounced, 'The kids want misery and death. They want threatening noises, because that shakes you out of your apathy.' This uniform was designed as the sartorial equivalent. It was antipathetic to every dress code before it; even the individual protest clothes worn by hippies had proclaimed a mood of utopian collectivity, but punk was invented to alienate every other element of society by using sex and bondage as its themes. Rotten was surprised himself when Westwood gave him a rubber shirt to wear on stage saying, 'I thought it was the most repulsive thing I'd ever seen. To wear it as a piece of clothing rather than as some part of a sexual fetish was hilarious.'

► Cobain, Hemingway, McLaren, Rhodes, Westwood

Johnny Rotten (John Lydon). b London (UK), 1956. **Johnny Rotten wears tartan bondage trousers.** *c.*1977.

Rouff Maggy

Designer

The East provides the inspiration for this evening gown. Rouff has incorporated Japanese influence into superlative modern tailoring: the long, loose pendant sleeves recall those of a kimono. Like Poiret and Bakst before her, Rouff has infused her design with a feel for the exotic, the Orient. She has achieved a perfectly cut European gown. By using the bias-cutting technique, this dress takes on an almost seamless appearance, with a sweep of unbroken fabric reaching from the bodice to the cuff's hem. Rouff began her career as a fashion designer at Drecoll, where her mother, Madame de Wagner, was head designer. But it was Jeanne Paquin who was her main inspiration. Rouff founded her own fashion house in 1929, rapidly gaining a reputation for ravishing eveningwear and also for sportswear. In 1937 she opened her salon in London where her Parisian gowns were shown to her British clientele.

▶ Agnès, Bakst, Von Drecoll, Paquin, Poiret

Maggy Rouff. b Paris (FR), 1876. **d** Paris (FR), 1971. **Evening dress with cut sleeves.** Photograph by George Hoyningen-Huene, 1935.

Roversi Paolo

Photographer

Paolo Roversi describes Kirsten Owen, his favourite model, as 'somewhere between an angel and a demon', which is how he captured her in this photograph taken for a Romeo Gigli campaign. Gigli, a long-term collaborator of Roversi's, believes the photographer, 'succeeds in seizing a fleeting moment, a tremor of emotion which projects the women themselves into a timeless dimension'. Roversi's illusory work stands alone among late twentieth-century fashion photographers. He left his native Italy for Paris in 1973, and by the end of the decade had developed a distinctive style using double exposure and Polaroid film. Roversi's images are poetic, romantic and painterly, and by turns demure and slightly demented. He describes them as 'a very intense exchange', an attempt to 'capture a lot of their soul, a little of their personality'.

▶ Ferretti, Gigli, McGrath, McKnight

Paolo Roversi. b Ravenna (IT), 1947. **Kirsten Owen models for Romeo Gigli.** 1987.

Royal Academy of Fine Arts   School

Fantastical but historically informed toiles are exhibited on mannequins lining the corridor of the Fashion Department at Antwerp's Koninklijke Academie (or Royal Academy as it is better known), evidence both of the school's reputation for encouraging creative originality and its insistence on hands-on technical excellence. Despite the school's avant-garde reputation, its students are expected to be as skilled in traditional draughtsmanship, pattern design and tailoring as they are in developing a compelling fashion story. Nestled in the gothic Antwerpen streetscape, the Academy's reputation has flourished since it rose to prominence in the mid-1980s as the alma mater of talents such as Dries Van Noten, Martin Margiela and Ann Demeulemeester. Like designer Walter Van Beirendonck, director of the Fashion Department since 2006, many also return to the school to teach.

▶ Van Beirendonck, Demeulemeester, Margiela, Van Noten

Royal Academy of Fine Arts (Koninklijke Academie voor Schone Kunsten). est. Antwerp (BEL), 1663 (fashion department founded 1963). **Students in the fashion studios at the Royal Academy of Fine Arts.** Photograph by Tim Stoops.   453

Rubinstein Helena

Cosmetics creator

'Life Red comes to life on your lips' claims Helena Rubinstein's fresh-faced advertisement from the 1940s. The healthy image promoted by Rubinstein's make-up and skin creams was born in a laboratory. She had wanted to study medicine but, denied her chance, left Poland to live with an uncle in Australia. She started to sell a face cream, Creme Valaze, brought from home to protect her complexion from the sun. A successful small skincare school followed and when one of her seven sisters joined her, Rubinstein studied with the best European dermatologists. Her white-coated approach to cosmetics resulted in several innovations, including the first skin cream to use male and female hormones in an attempt to delay the process of ageing. Her artistic credentials were also impeccable – in Paris she became friend and patron to Matisse, Dufy, Dalí and Cocteau.

► Cocteau, Dalí, Dufy, Lauder

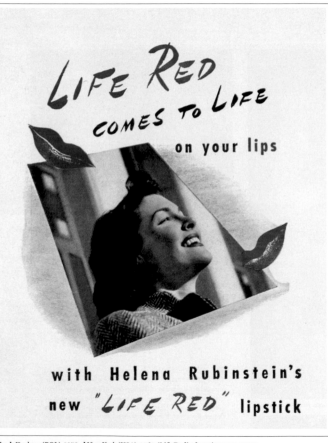

Helena Rubinstein. b Krakow (POL), 1870. **d** New York (USA), 1965. **'Life Red' advertisement.** 1940.

Rykiel Sonia

Designer

During a salon presentation, Sonia Rykiel's tailored knitwear is exemplified by cardigan coats and dresses accessorized with sequined roses and gold belts. Her attitude to the grand feasibility of knitted wool was explained when she said, 'Just as one woman looks fantastically erotic naked...another can seem the same in a polo-neck sweater.' The 'Queen of Knits' began designing in 1962 when she was pregnant and unable to find any soft sweaters. Rykiel's style of chic separates is typically French. She calls her clothes *'le nouveau classicisme'*, their slim line owing much to the 1930s. fluid jersey, wide trousers and raglan-sleeve sweaters in muted colours are her trademarks; her Lurex knitwear is sophisticated enough for evening. 'I love knit,' Rykiel says, 'because it is very magical. You can do so many things with just a thread.' In 2008 she was the subject of an exhibition held at Musée de la Mode et du Textile, Paris.

► Albini, Jacobson, Turbeville

Sonia Rykiel. b Paris (FR), 1930. **Knitted co-ordinates.** 1974.

Saint Laurent Yves

Designer

A vulnerable and androgynous Yves Saint Laurent is captured by his friend, photographer Jeanloup Sieff, in an image that made advertising history. In this controversial approach to branding, Yves Saint Laurent paved the way for the cult of the designer that we now take for granted. He introduced masculine tailoring for women, using military uniforms and variations on the tuxedo or 'Le Smoking', and brought street styles and peasant costume to high fashion. Saint Laurent has often referred to art, basing some designs on paintings by Mondrian, Matisse and Picasso, but always put a modern twist on the historical icons. Saint Laurent said, 'Like Proust, I'm fascinated most of all by my perceptions of a world in awesome transition.' Great fashion is about cutting those moments of transition out of cloth. He once described what he did as 'minor art' but later added 'maybe it is not so minor after all'.

► Deneuve, Dior, Ford, Newton, Pilati, Sieff

Yves Saint Laurent. b Oran (ALG), 1936. **d** Paris (FR), 2008. **Yves Saint Laurent models for the Pour Homme campaign.**
Photograph by Jeanloup Sieff, 1971.

Sander Jil

Designer

Sander began her career as a fashion journalist, but moved into fashion design. In 1968 she opened a boutique in Hamburg and five years later was showing on the catwalk. Sander perceived a need for understated clothes with a sense of quiet self-confidence, but which would provide the wearer with the ultimate in fit, quality and modernity. It was a prophetic vision: today her clothes have become the byword for an ultra-modern, androgynous sensuality that is as uncompromisingly technical as it is beautiful. Her simplicity must not, however, be confused with classicism. As Sander told *Vogue*, 'A classic is an excuse, because one is too lazy to contrast the spirit of the time.' She rejects the clichés of femininity for the refinements found in the architecture of men's suits. Sander handed over the reins of the company to the designer Raf Simons in 2005, but returned to the role of creative director in 2012.

► Capasa, Lang, Margiela, Philo, Simons, Sims

Jil Sander. b Wesselburen (GER), 1943. **Angela Lindvall wears silk shirt and tweed trousers.** Photograph by David Sims, 1998.   457

Di Sant'Angelo Giorgio   Designer

Veruschka's body is barely covered by a chain bikini by Giorgio di Sant'Angelo. Her hair is wrapped with gold lamé and her body encircled with gold chains. The 1960s was a decade devoted to the cult of youth and Sant'Angelo designed to make women aware of their bodies. Born in florence, he trained as an architect and studied art, ceramics and sculpture, before winning an animation fellowship with Walt Disney in Los Angeles. In the early 1960s, he moved to New York and worked as a textile designer, where his talent was spotted by Diana Vreeland, the flamboyant editor of American *Vogue*. She sent him to Arizona with an array of materials, scissors and Veruschka to 'invent' clothes for a spread in her magazine, of which this design is an example. In later life Sant'Angelo found new customers with his wrapped, stretchy Lycra clothes designed according to the same principles. John Galliano and Marc Jacobs have cited him as an influence.

► Bruce, Lindbergh, Peretti, Veruschka, Vreeland

Giorgio di Sant'Angelo. b florence (IT), 1936. **d** New York (USA), 1989. **Veruschka wears gold chain bikini.** Photograph by Franco Rubartelli, American *Vogue*, 1968.

Sarne Tanya (Ghost)

Designer

A fine georgette fabric, traced over with a print titled 'Ice River', is slashed into an asymmetrical dress, of its season but at the same time unique to one label. Regardless of their style, changing every season, Ghost's dresses are machine-washable, a practicality not usually associated with high fashion. Tanya Sarne, founder and figurehead at Ghost, came up with the idea of developing a fabric that is hardy, yet sensuous against the skin. The result was a material woven mainly from viscose yarns and derived from specially grown soft woods. This is put through an intensive process of boiling and dyeing in an unusual palette of colours. This costly and time-consuming activity gives it a unique crepe-like texture and density. Such garments have longevity and require minimal attention. Ghost's signature fabrics are used for everything from vests to complicated gowns, making them popular for women who travel, or for more formal occasions.

► Clark, Dell'Acqua, Dinnigan, Rhodes, Tarlazzi

Tanya Sarne. b Southgate (UK), 1945. **'Ice River' printed georgette dress.** Photograph by Niall McInerney, 1997.

Sassoon Vidal

'Hair is nature's biggest compliment and the treatment of this compliment is in our hands. As in couture, the cut is the most important element.' Vidal Sassoon's words explain the reasons for his simplified, Bauhausian haircuts that freed women from weekly beauty-parlour visits and the tyranny of curlers, lacquered shapes and other hair constriction. Sassoon's cuts – the geometric, the wash-and-wear perm, the bob (cut on a horizontal plane) and the Nancy Kwan – were low-maintenance, high modernism. Belonging to the generation of The Beatles and Swinging London, Sassoon took the cult of the natural to hair and elevated the role of the hairdresser, working in partnership with designers such as Mary Quant and Rudi Gernreich. He was more recently the subject of a retrospective exhibition held at Somerset House, London in 2012.

▶ The Beatles, Coddington, Gernreich, Leonard, Liberty

Vidal Sassoon. b London (UK), 1928. **d** Belair, Los Angeles (USA), 2012. **Grace Coddington models Vidal Sassoon's five-point haircut.** Photograph by David Montgomery, 1964.

Saunders Jonathan   Designer

It is behind the scenes that designers work out their inspirations and ideas to put together a collection that makes a catwalk show what it is. In creating his spring/summer 2013 show, Jonathan Saunders drew inspiration from a Michael Clark performance, where the costumes of the dancers were bisected into different colours, and Op Art, especially the work of its great originator, Victor Vasarely. Saunder's explains 'colour always drives me and I love the balance of colours in Vasarely's work.' His resulting collection, shown during London Fashion Week, was full of colour, fluidity and movement. Bias-cut dresses with asymmetrical panels, black-and-white stripes and chevrons referenced disco apparel. Jonathan Saunders has worked with Alexander McQueen, Christian Lacroix at Pucci and Phoebe Philo at Chloé. He was awarded the Lancôme Colour Design Award in 2002 and has also achieved two British *Vogue* covers in 2004 and 2012.

▶ Katrantzou, Lacroix, McQueen, Philo, Pilotto, Pucci

Jonathan Saunders. b Rutherglen (UK), 1977. **Backstage at Jonathan Saunders spring/summer 2013.** Photograph by Rebecca Thomas.

Scaasi Arnold

Designer

When Barbra Streisand went on stage to collect the Academy Award for her Best Actress role in *Funny Girl* (1969) in a barely opaque, sequinned Arnold Scaasi pant suit, both actress and designer caught the world's attention. Having originally trained with couturier Charles James, Scaasi left in 1956 to set up his own label, specializing in evening clothes for socialite functions. Scaasi was the first designer to do the snappy matching coat and dress look for evening, favouring large 'grand entrance' prints and silhouettes. In 1958 his polka-dot evening dress was the first formal evening outfit to end above the knee. He opened his couture salon in 1964, producing short evening dresses and spectacular ball gowns for New York's elite, from celebrities to first ladies. 'I am definitely not a minimalist designer!' said Scaasi. 'Clothes with some adornment are more interesting to look at and more fun to wear.'

▶ Deneuve, C. James, De la Renta, Schuberth

Arnold Scaasi. b Montreal, QC (CAN), 1931. **Barbra Streisand with her Academy Award for *Funny Girl.*** 1969.

Scavullo Francesco   Photographer

The model Antonia plays a tourist in an epic fashion scene shot in the populated chaos of a Hong Kong marketplace, directed by the photographer Francesco Scavullo. Her flight bag crashes into her silk dress, oriental make-up and hat, dramatizing the outfit and dressing Antonia for her role. Scavullo's obsession with photography began at an early age: at nine he was making home movies and much of his early work has a filmic quality. He began his career at American *Vogue* and spent three years with Horst, before going to work on the new teenage magazine *Seventeen*. Scavullo's passion for photographing beautiful women was harnessed by American *Cosmopolitan*, whose unapologetically sexy covers he began to photograph in 1965. But his lasting legacy to fashion photography was undoubtedly his technical knowledge, particularly his use of diffused lighting designed to flatter the greatest 'cover' faces.

▶ Deneuve, Fonssagrives, C. Klein, Turlington

Francesco Scavullo. **b** Staten Island, NY (USA), 1929. **d** New York (USA), 2004. **Antonia, Hong Kong.** 1962.   463

Scherrer Jean-Louis

Designer

This fantasy world of a Botticelli woman rising from a shell serves as the ideal medium for the revelation of a silk-chiffon dress with a waterfall collar and butterfly cape. Its luxurious yet dramatic qualities adorn Jean-Louis Scherrer's refined classicism. Scherrer moved into haute couture when, after the petrol crisis in the 1970s, he provided the wives of affluent Arabs with longer, covered-up fashions that satisfied the modesty requirements dictated by Islamic laws, while also proclaiming their wealth. Parisian ballrooms have witnessed Scherrer's sumptuous embroideries and glittering silks since he started as Christian Dior's assistant, after an accident finished his career as a dancer at the age of twenty. After Dior's death and the choice of Saint Laurent as his successor, Scherrer left and opened his own business in 1962.

► Lancetti, Mori, Ungaro

Jean-Louis Scherrer. b Paris (FR), 1936. **Print dress and straw hat.** Photograph by Angus McBean, *Harpers & Queen*, 1989.

Schiaparelli Elsa

Designer

Is the woman wearing this 'Desk Suit', designed by Elsa Schiaparelli in 1936, going to the office or the beach? The suit features a vertical series of true and false pockets, embroidered to look like desk drawers with buttons for knobs. Dress designing for Schiaparelli was an art, and this suit is based on two Surrealist drawings by Salvador Dalí entitled 'City of Drawers' and 'Venus de Milo of Drawers'. Flourishing in the 1920s and 1930s, Surrealism reacted against the rational and formal real world, and substituted instead fantasy and a dream world. It had a particular influence on Schiaparelli during the 1930s, and the designer's smart, sophisticated, witty clothes took the fashion world by storm. She commissioned some of the best artists of the period, such as Salvador Dalí, Jean Cocteau and Christian Bérard, to design fabrics and embroideries for her.

► Banton, Cocteau, Lesage, Man Ray, Nars, Perugia, Prada

Elsa Schiaparelli. b Rome (IT), 1890. **d** Paris (FR), 1973. **'Desk Suit.'** Photograph by Cecil Beaton, 1936.

Schiffer Claudia

Model

In one of her most famous photographs, Claudia Schiffer becomes a sex kitten. Shortly after being discovered in a discotheque in 1987, Schiffer secured the Guess? advertising campaign and subsequently became one of the most sought-after models in the world. She has appeared on the covers of more than 500 magazines (including *Vanity Fair*, which, at the time, had an editorial policy that usually refused to place any model on its cover). As a member of the supermodel troupe, she represents natural blonde beauty – a modern, healthy look that dates back to Cheryl Tiegs. She modelled for *Sports Illustrated*'s swimwear issue in 1998, opening up the pin-up market for models. This became a lucrative avenue for women such as Schiffer and Cindy Crawford whose beauty had a general appeal. She launched Claudia Schiffer Cashmere in 2011.

► Crawford, Thomass, Von Unwerth

Claudia Schiffer. b Rheinberg (GER), 1970. **Guess? Jeans publicity campaign, 1989.** Photograph by Ellen von Unwerth.

Schön Mila

Designer

This 1968 photograph, which features a perfectly cut, Mila Schön, white wool suit, represents several of the designer's signatures. Schön's favourite fabric was double-faced wool; she was a perfectionist who worked within a classical structure, to exacting specifications, and she also created modernist garments. She came from a family of wealthy Yugoslavian aristocrats who had fled to Italy to escape Communism. In 1959, Schön launched her business. She had gained her love of fashion as a couture customer at Balenciaga, and within her clothes can be seen his austerity of cut, together with the influences of Dior and Schiaparelli. By 1965, Schön had developed her own style and began showing on the catwalk. Construction of her tailoring is highlighted by its very simplicity – making details out of seams and darts. In 2008, the year of her death, a tribute event '50 Mile Schön: lines, colours, surfaces' was held at the Palazzo Reale, Milan.

► Cardin, Cashin, Courrèges

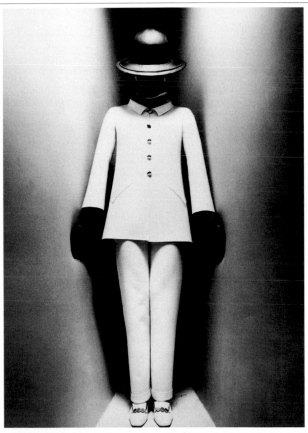

Mila Schön. b Trau, Dalmatia (CRO), 1916. **d** Alessandria (IT), 2008. **Benedetta Barzini wears double-face trouser suit and hat.** Photograph by Ugo Mulas, 1968.

Schuberth Emilio Designer

A ruched taffeta, puff-ball gown, inspired by a late eighteenth-century shape, flaunts a tiered underskirt decorated with a filigree print. The underlying flamenco theme is given cachet by the length of black ribbon adorning the model's chignon. As one of Rome's top couturiers in the 1950s, Emilio Schuberth was also one of the first to present his collection on the Italian catwalks in 1952. His signature touch, of undercutting serious evening crinolines with unexpectedly baroque embroidery, attracted the early fashion paparazzi, who were drawn to his double-sided skirts, which metamorphosed into capes strewn with appliquéd flora. Schuberth often created fantastical skirts decorated with rows of foaming tulle and dotted with silk flowers. His only known training was twenty years of atelier work within his own house prior to 1952, earning him an elite clientele, which included the Duchess of Windsor.

► Biagiotti, Fontana, Scaasi, Windsor

Emilio Schuberth. b Naples (IT), 1904. **d** Rome (IT), 1972. **Ruched taffeta evening gown.** Photograph by G.M. Fadigati, 1955.

Schuman Scott

Photographer

Stylish young men- and women-about-town want to be noticed – and we want to look at them. From this simple realization Scott Schuman forged a career that changed the fashion world. His pioneering blog, *The Sartorialist*, began in September 2005, after he quit his day job to look after his daughter. Inspired by street photography greats such as August Sander and Bill Cunningham, Schuman brought the genre into the digital age, photographing anyone in New York City whose clothes caught his eye.

Schuman's attention to quirky details, be it creased jeans, playful layering or an unusual tailoring feature, combined with a sense of style and brevity, and his perfectly framed photographs began to attract hits. His merchandising acumen helped build the brand, with a first book of photographs from the site becoming a bestseller, and he developed a flourishing parallel career as a photographer for brands including DKNY, Gap and Burberry.

► Burberry, Cunningham, Fisher, Style.com

Scott Schuman. b Indianapolis, IN (USA), 1968. New York, August 2010. Photograph by Scott Schuman.

SHOWstudio

Website

Founded in 2000 by fashion photographer and filmmaker Nick Knight, SHOWstudio is an innovative platform focused on commissioning and broadcasting collaborative creative projects to fashion enthusiasts via the web. The website's goal is to construct a more expansive vision of the fashion industry than previously permitted by more traditional media. Relying predominantly on moving image and live-streaming content, SHOWstudio offers a uniquely contemporary platform for fashion industry and art world creatives to engage audiences with their work. Of his objectives in establishing the site, Knight stated, 'SHOWstudio is based on the belief that showing the entire creative process – from conception to completion – is beneficial for the artist, the audience and the art itself.' Notable collaborations with leading figures in the fashion world have included John Galliano, Lady Gaga, Björk, Comme des Garçons, Thierry Mugler and Rodarte.

► Galliano, N. Knight, Lady Gaga, McQueen, Style.com

SHOWstudio. Founded 2000. **Models in SHOWstudio gallery space, Bruton Place, London.** 2011.

Shrimpton Jean

Model

Although Jean Shrimpton had been modelling for a few years when she was pictured here, she retained a quality that prompted her to say, 'I was as green as a salad,' of the day she joined London's Lucie Clayton modelling school in 1960. Later that year she was on a shoot for a cornflakes advertisement when she met the photographer David Bailey. 'Duffy was taking her picture against a blue background,' recalled Bailey. 'It was like her blue eyes were just holes drilled through her head to the paper behind. Duffy said, "Forget it – she's too posh for you," and I thought, "We'll see about that".' In the course of her affair with Bailey, Shrimpton became a sex icon and top model; 'the Shrimp' was born. Shrimpton's gawky, urchin style was perfect for Courrèges' space-age look and Quant's mini. When the couple appeared in American *Vogue* editor Diana Vreeland's office, she exclaimed, 'England has arrived!'

► D. Bailey, Kenneth, McLaughlin-Gill, Mesejeán & Cancela

Jean Shrimpton. b Buckinghamshire (UK), 1942. **Jean Shrimpton in Epping Forest.** Photograph by Frances McLaughlin-Gill, *Harper's Bazaar*, 1965.

Sieff Jeanloup

Photographer

Astrid wears a black pillbox hat by Halston and silk crepe gown by Bill Blass. Jeanloup Sieff said of this photograph, 'She had an aristocratic profile and a very inspiring back.' For Sieff fashion photography was always about more than the simple representation of clothing. Instead, his work reflects his passion for beauty and form. 'The simple pleasure of rendering certain shapes, those maddening lights...' he said of his predominantly black-and-white images. Born in Paris to Polish parents, Sieff received

a camera for his fourteenth birthday. By 1960, after a brief spell at French *Elle* and the Magnum picture agency, he was living and working in New York taking fashion pictures for *Harper's Bazaar*. His fame grew quickly, as did his disdain for fashion. In 1966 he returned to Paris where he remained until his death, occasionally dabbling in fashion, but mostly staying true to his passion for capturing moments that cannot recur.

► Blass, Halston, Ritts, Saint Laurent

Jeanloup Sieff. b Paris (FR), 1933. **d** Paris (FR), 2000. **'Astrid's back.'** Palm Beach. *Harper's Bazaar*, 1964.

Simons Raf

Designer

Model Yannick Abrath is cocooned inside a furry Prussian-blue coat with giant lapels, topped off with a hooded wool hat resembling a vast back-to-front baseball cap. So often in his eponymous menswear collections, Simons is interested in a play of contrasts: the outsized garments of skate culture translated by refined tailoring; the proportions of street met with high fashion; the energy of youth sitting shyly in the uniform of manhood. After studying industrial design in Genk, Simons became aware of the work of designers such as Martin Margiela and saved to move to Antwerp. Launching his label in 1995, his intelligent, street-inflected silhouette had a huge impact on the style of the decade. In 2005 Simons became artistic director of Jil Sander and over a period of seven years refined a vivid, luxurious modernism for the label. A move to Dior in 2012 saw him revelling in a prettier, more feminine direction, in keeping with the label's history.

▶ Dior, Galliano, K. Jones, Margiela, Sander

Raf Simons. b Neerpelt (BEL), 1968. **Yannick Abrath wears Raf Simons autumn/winter 2012.** Photograph by Pierre Debusschere.

Simpson Adele

Designer

From Mrs Eisenhower to Mrs Carter, Adele Simpson's conservative versions of the current trends have delighted the wives of many leading US politicians. Her clothes, which could be co-ordinated into complete wardrobes, proved practical and suitable for the active and exposed lives of her clients. The ensemble shown illustrates this: though not a suit, the slim skirt and asymmetrically fastening jacket could easily match other elements of Simpson's collections. The first American designer to treat cotton seriously as a fashion fabric, she used this fibre for street dresses and full-skirted evening gowns. Cotton was also used in one of Simpson's most celebrated creations: a 1950s chemise dress with attached belts which could be tied at the front or the back. Reputedly one of the highest-paid designers in the world at the age of twenty-one, she bought her own company in 1949.

► Galanos, Leser, Maltézos & Carpentier

Adele Simpson. b New York (USA), 1903. **d** Greenwich, CT (USA), 1995. **Formal day suit.** Photograph by John Rawlings, 1947.

Sims David

Photographer

The stark, gritty images of dynamic photographer David Sims' early work have evolved into the slick – although still subversive – fashion images that appear regularly on the pages of *Harper's Bazaar*, *Vogue* and *W*. Perhaps it is these qualities, not typically associated with fashion, which emerge from his early work for magazines like *The Face* and *i-D*. Beginning his career in the early 1990s, after working as assistant to photographers like Robert Erdman and Norman Watson, Sims began working with stylist Melanie Ward and models Kate Moss and Emma Balfour. Together they helped to pioneer the grunge look, which gave them all an international platform with major fashion magazines. Sims always tries to push the boundaries of the fashion image; bold, graphic and sometimes alien or other-worldly, are just some of the words that describe his creative sensibility.

▶ Day, Grand, McDean, Moss, Sander

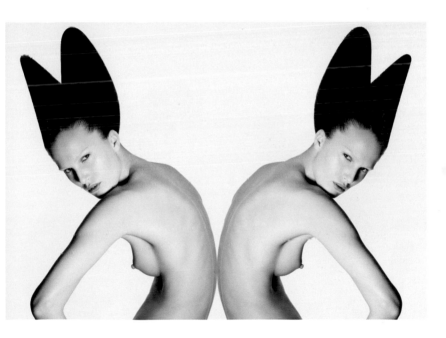

David Sims. b Sheffield (UK), 1966. *LOVE* magazine presents a special hair project by Guido Palau, spring/summer 2010.   475

Sitbon Martine

Designer

Wearing a splash-printed dress by Martine Sitbon, Stella Tennant crouches next to a surreal arrangement of wild animals. Sitbon herself started out as the wild child of French fashion, influenced by the rock scene inhabited by the Rolling Stones and the Velvet Underground (whose music was used as backing music for her first collection). As a teenager, Sitbon's early fashion education was gained in the flea markets of London and Paris, as has been the case for many designers before and since. Her passion for the English scene stayed with her as she worked first as a stylist, then as a designer. The art of pulling a look together from many inspirations is at the centre of Sitbon's style. In the mid-1980s she became known for feminized menswear, in particular fitted tail coats worn with slim trousers – suits inspired by those hanging on flea market rails.

► Kélian, Lenoir, Leroy, McDean, Tennant

Martine Sitbon. b Casablanca (MOR), 1951. **Stella Tennant wears devoré dress.** Photograph by Craig McDean, 1997.

Slimane Hedi

Designer

Hedi Slimane entered the fashion limelight in 1996 while designing the Yves Saint Laurent Rive Gauche Pour Homme line, where he first developed his unmistakable pencil-slim silhouette. A wild success, the aesthetic earned him considerable respect from the fashion critics during his tenure as creative director at Dior Homme (2000 to 2007) and has continued to dominate menswear well into the new millennium. Slimane breathed new life into the genre by combining elements of street style with linear, minimalist tailoring. Skinny trousers are worn with cropped jackets and open-neck shirts. For clothes very much of their time, the vast majority of Slimane's models were young men street-cast or hand picked from the indie music scene; here, Girls frontman Christopher Owens models Slimane's debut collection at Saint Laurent Paris (formerly Yves Saint Laurent) – in 2012 Slimane was appointed creative director of the fashion house.

► Lagerfeld, Pilati, Saint Laurent, Simons

Hedi Slimane. b Paris (FR), 1968. **Saint Laurent autumn/winter 2012 campaign featuring Christopher Owens.**
Photograph by Hedi Slimane.

Smith Graham

Milliner

A floral confection balances a formal hairstyle and co-ordinates with a powder-pink dress. It is a ceremonious hat made for the English season by Graham Smith who is noted for his royal millinery. He believes that a hat should appear to be part of the wearer, with particular emphasis on silhouette and scale. His lightweight, delicate textures create a hat that is showy yet well-mannered. Educated at the Royal College of Art, Smith's graduation collection achieved such acclaim that he was immediately appointed milliner at Lanvin-Castillo in Paris. In 1967 Smith launched his own label, at the same time collaborating with designers Jean Muir and Zandra Rhodes. Smith specializes in traditional styles, best shown by his designs for Princess Diana and the Duchess of York in the 1980s (he believes the Royal Family has saved British millinery). He is a master of balance and proportion, determined not to forsake flattery for fashion.

► Castillo, Diana, Muir, Rhodes

Graham Smith. b Bexley (UK), 1938. **'Small head, tiny roses, black-and-white chic'.** Photograph by Henry Clarke, British *Vogue*, 1965.

Smith Sir Paul

Designer

Paul Smith, the quintessentially British designer – now with more than 250 stores worldwide – opened his first shop in his hometown of Nottingham in 1970. His brand combines tailoring tradition with a sense of humour, characterized by unique detailing and an unexpected combination of materials and tradition. Smith playfully works with classic shapes cut with a fashionable edge in a skilful use of colour and prints. Smith's shops remain an inspiring mix of luxury and humour, selling anything from high-fashion brogues to vintage books and limited-edition prints and toys. It is this inspired eccentricity and a mind fine-tuned for business that has, unusually for a British company, turned Smith's label into a global luxury brand, showing in both London and Paris Fashion Week. Smith retains a watchful eye remaining as both designer and chairman of the company.

► Cox, R. James, Van Noten, Nutter, Stephen

Sir Paul Smith. b Nottingham (UK), 1946. **Paul Smith spring/summer 2013.** Photographed by Sir Paul Smith, 2012.

Smith Willi   Designer

A jumpsuit, with functional zip, tie belt, large patch pockets and cuffed sleeves became extraordinary in the hands of Willi Smith, who decided to cut it out of silver-coated cloth in 1973. As a freelance designer he was already exploring the concept of putting fun into function. Then, in 1976, Smith launched his label Willi Wear. It produced well-priced, young, easy-to-wear, easy-to-care-for separates that brought designer fashion to a wider market. He used mainly natural fabrics and cut them with room for movement. For both men and women, Smith plugged the gap between jeans and, the stiff, formal clothes that meant nothing to the age group he was addressing. It was a market he was proud of, saying that he didn't design clothes for the Queen but for those who wave at her as she passes. Smith's style was founded on the concept of separates, at a time when the idea of traditional office dressing was being challenged.

► Bartlett, A. Klein, Rosier

Willi Smith. b Philadelphia (USA), 1948. **d** New York (USA), 1987. **Metallic jump-suit.** Photograph by Nick Machalaba, *Women's Wear Daily*, 1974.

Snow Carmel

Editor

The chic image of Paris is achieved through Louise Dahl-Wolfe's graceful composition of a model controlling her excitable poodles against a backdrop of the Sacré Cœur. Part of an illustrated fashion story, the picture accompanied Snow's 1955 Paris report for *Harper's Bazaar*, which concentrated largely on Balenciaga's and Dior's new silhouettes. Well before the rest of the press understood him, Carmel Snow was applauding Balenciaga's clean, sculptural lines, and she christened

Christian Dior's New Look purely by accident in a letter to the designer. She was a major presence as American *Vogue*'s fashion editor, and then at *Harper's Bazaar* from 1932; it was said that if a dozing Snow awoke during a showing, the outfit appearing to her would be a hit. For twenty years of her editorship-in-chief, *Harper's Bazaar* mixed crisp fashion reportage with fresh visuals by Martin Munkacsi, Louise Dahl-Wolfe and Salvador Dalí.

► Balenciaga, Bassman, Brodovitch, Dahl-Wolfe, Dior, Vreeland

Carmel Snow. b Dublin (IRE), 1887. d New York (USA), 1961. **Tunic and curled hat by Balenciaga.** Photograph by Louise Dahl-Wolfe, *Harper's Bazaar*, 1955.

Snowdon

This 1957 fashion shoot by Lord Snowdon, then Antony Armstrong Jones, for *Vogue* shows a new approach: the picture is infused with the energy inherent in the run-up to the 1960s. In fact, Snowdon's spontaneous moment was staged – the tumbling champagne glass was suspended on a clear thread and the model's thrilled greeting an act of theatre. He recalled, 'I made the models move and react, putting them in incongruous situations or performing incongruous feats. I made them run, dance, kiss, anything but stand still. Each sitting became a short story or miniature film strip.' This was the beginning of the language of contemporary fashion photography, a new naturalism and reality within artificial confines. In 1960 Armstrong Jones married Princess Margaret, prompting Cecil Beaton to call him 'the Cinderella of our time'.

► Avedon, Beaton, Fish, Mori

Snowdon (Antony Armstrong Jones, 1st Earl of Snowdon). b London (UK), 1930. **Champagne glasses.** British *Vogue*, 1957.

Sorrenti Mario

Photographer

Did housework ever look so sexy? Italian-born, New York-raised photographer Mario Sorrenti was a model himself before he took the world of photography by storm, but it was his intimate black-and-white photograph of a naked Kate Moss, his then-girlfriend, for Calvin Klein's Obsession perfume campaign that propelled him to instant fame in 1993, aged only twenty-one. Since then, the self-taught photographer has worked for most of the biggest names in fashion. With campaigns for Prada

and Yves Saint Laurent, and editorial shoots for *Vogue*, *W* and *V* magazine, Sorrenti has gone from strength to strength, establishing himself as a powerful figure in the industry. In 2012 he was commissioned to create the prestigious Pirelli Calendar, showcasing twelve models and actresses, including Kate Moss and Lara Stone, against the sparsely beautiful landscape of Corsica.

► C. Klein, Moss, Richardson, Testino

Mario Sorrenti. b Naples (IT), 1971. **Lara Stone for *V* magazine.** 2007.

Souleiman Eugene

Hairdresser

Eugene Souleiman's chignon is an amalgamation of traditional hairdressing and modern styling. The feathered hairpieces make an avant-garde foil for this rococo gown by Valentino. London-born Souleiman forges his own path through the world of hairdressing, often working with make-up artist Pat McGrath. Frequently contentious, he once – in defiance of their expressive outfits – sent models along Prada's catwalk with belligerently unstyled hair, a typically contrary idea. Playful experiments with hair textures, using hairpieces and unexpected materials have helped Souleiman to reinvent the discipline, making him one of the hairdressers who have made the manipulation of hair an indivisible element of fashion. In 2012 he collaborated with the artists Dinos and Jake Chapman on an exhibition at the Saatchi Gallery, London, entitled 'The Art of Chess', where he individually styled the hair of each chess figure.

▶ McDean, McGrath, Prada, Recine, Valentino

Eugene Souleiman. b London (UK), 1961. **Taffeta gown.** Photograph by Craig McDean, Italian *Vogue*, 1998.

Sprouse Stephen   Designer

A design-school dropout, Sprouse arrived in New York in 1972 and soon made all the connections he needed for a career in fashion. Debbie Harry introduced him to Andy Warhol who introduced him to Halston who took him on as an assistant. But Sprouse's artistic interests distracted him and he and Halston parted company. In 1984, the photographer Steven Meisel persuaded him to launch his own label. Warhol's influence was always obvious – from Sprouse's silver showroom to his claim that Edie Sedgwick was his 'favourite meteor'. In 1997, when he relaunched his label, he used Warhol's artwork as prints on dresses. (Sprouse had exclusive rights to use the famous Pop Art images in clothing designs.) His work in the 1980s was largely influenced by the pop music scene: cut-out minidresses were printed with video images, Day-Glo 'hip hop' style graffiti was sprayed onto dresses. In 2001 Sprouse designed graffiti logo bags for Louis Vuitton.

► Halston, Jacobs, Meisel, Vuitton, Warhol, K. Yamamoto

Stephen Sprouse. b OH (USA), 1953. **d** New York (USA), 2004. **'Partytime' tank and sequined skirt.** Photograph by Rainer Hosch, *i-D*, 1998.

485

Steele Lawrence

Designer

Working on the lingerie theme, with a pin-tucked, chiffon camisole worn over a satin petticoat skirt, Lawrence Steele demonstrates his love of luxuriously simple clothes. His restraint is inspired by the work of Charles James and Claire McCardell. Born in Virginia, Steele had a military upbringing that took him to different cities throughout the United States, as well as Germany and Spain. Elements of this upbringing have been worked into his collections, including direct references such as epaulettes applied to the shoulders of shirts and jackets. Steele trained with Moschino in Milan, before moving on to Miuccia Prada's then relatively new womenswear line. He brought it forward with his simple, modern style, which blends American and European influences, then left in 1994 to continue his development under his own label.

► C. James, McCardell, Moschino, Prada

Lawrence Steele. b Hampton, VA (USA), 1963. **Pin-tucked camisole with skirt.** Photograph by Miles Aldridge, 1998.

Steichen Edward

Photographer

Gloria Swanson confronts the camera head-on. She wears a cloche, the tight-fitting, helmet-like hat that was the characteristic fashion headwear of the 1920s. In 1963, Edward Steichen recalled the circumstances surrounding the taking of this photograph; he and Gloria Swanson had a long session, with many changes of costume. At the end of the session, he took a black lace veil and hung it in front of her face, causing her hat to mould to her head and give a streamlined appearance. Her eyes dilated and

her look was that of a leopardess lurking behind leafy shrubbery watching her prey. Steichen, a thoroughly modern fashion photographer, was noted for his settings, which conveyed atmosphere and structure anchored to current fashions – a mood he took to *Vogue* in 1923. His working relationship with the model Marion Morehouse was the first such collaboration between mannequin and photographer.

► Barbier, Daché, Morehouse, Nast

rd Steichen. b Luxembourg (LUX), 1879. d West Redding, CT (USA), 1973. **Gloria Swanson.** Photograph by
Steichen, American *Vogue*, 1924.

Steiger Walter

Shoe designer

For Walter Steiger, the composition of a shoe is just as important as the aesthetic appeal of its exterior. Distinctive designs have been those with heels like many-sided cones or with triangular structures – an approach that was particularly popular in the 1970s and 1980s. Swiss-born Steiger followed family tradition by undertaking an apprenticeship in shoemaking at the age of sixteen, after which he found employment at Bally in Paris. He moved to London in the early 1960s, where he designed lavish shoes under the Bally Bis label, as well as for Mary Quant. He also opened a successful studio in 1966 but felt Paris more appropriate for his first shop, which he opened in 1973. The sophistication of Steiger's highly innovative shoe construction met the demands of several couturiers with whom he subsequently collaborated, including Karl Lagerfeld, Chanel, Chloé, Montana, Oscar de la Renta and Nina Ricci.

► Bally, Kélian, Lenoir, Montana, De la Renta, Ricci

Walter Steiger. b Geneva (SW), 1942. **Heeled pump.** Photograph by Sheila Metzner, American *Vogue*, 1984.

Stephen John

Tailor

Photographed with his dog Prince, John Stephen wears the pristine suit, with Italianate 'Bum-freezer' jacket, of a late 1950s buck. Known as the 'Million Pound Mod', Stephen revolutionized the way menswear was sold when he opened Carnaby Street's first swinging boutique in 1958. He would watch his teenage customers for inspiration – when he noticed them fluffing up their collars as they tried jackets on, he realized they were looking for wider lapels, which he produced and sold by the thousand. Stephen introduced extravagant details into the dusty realm of menswear, including flares, fly-fronted shirts inspired by dress shirts and suits cut from tweed treated with a lustrous finish. He had an early understanding of how quickly fashion would begin to change over the following decades and would not commit himself beyond eight weeks ahead, saying, 'In this world, change is violent. Anything can happen in two months.'

► Fish, Gilbey, P. Smith

n **Stephen. b** Glasgow (UK), 1934. **d** (UK), 2004. **John Stephen and Prince.** *Daily Mail*, 1957.

Stern Bert

Photographer

Bert Stern was the last person to photograph Marilyn Monroe, seen here wearing Christian Dior. This stroke of luck made him world famous and left the world with a series of sensitive portraits that transcend the duty of fashion photography. Stern taught himself photography while working as art director for the American magazine *Mayfair*, 'I was always moving around and reframing things in front of me.' His desire to capture the perfect image led him to a career in commercial photography, where he worked on print advertisements for Pepsi-Cola, Volkswagen and, most famously, Smirnoff. His 1955 picture of a martini glass in front of one of the pyramids at Giza became legendary, as did his image of Lolita wearing heart-shaped glasses for the 1962 film. He worked on fashion and portraiture throughout his career, photographing the most famous and most beautiful women of the time.

► Arnold, Dior, Orry-Kelly, Travilla

Bert Stern. b New York (USA), 1929. **Marilyn Monroe wears Dior.** British *Vogue*, 1962.

Stewart Stevie & Holah David (Body Map)   Designers

The revolutionary style of Stevie Stewart and David Holah – the duo behind the innovative and influential label Body Map, founded in 1982 – helped turn British fashion on its head. Their unconventional designs focused on contouring and covering the body with printed stretch jersey incorporating details such as cut-outs and stretchy stripes, 'rebelling against the conservative, the bland, striving for excitement'. In 1984 British choreographer Michael Clark launched his own dance company uniting the classical ballet of his training with a more complex, contemporary sensibility – a heady mix of rock and fashion. Clark's close collaboration with Body Map was in keeping with this aesthetic, their designs proving to be the perfect match for Clark's groundbreaking style of dance. In 1987 Body Map won a Bessie Award for their costumes for the Michael Clark Company. Stewart continues to work with Clark.

► Bowery, Bowie, Boy George, Ettegui, Westwood

Three women are snapped by Norman Parkinson en route to an Ascot race meeting. They are dressed and hatted by Stiebel in his romantic style, with their vast cartwheel hats dominating soft, feminine dresses with hemlines that stop eight inches from the ground. As a favoured designer of society women, Stiebel carefully considered his accessories, regarding them as part of his total look. Stiebel studied architecture at Cambridge before being encouraged to enter fashion by Norman Hartnell. Having served as an apprentice at Reville & Rossiter, he became an accomplished British fashion designer and a member of the Incorporated Society of London Fashion Designers, together with Hartnell, Hardy Amies and Edward Molyneux. Stiebel also dressed actresses and members of the British Royal Family, including Princess Margaret for whom he designed the going-away outfit for her marriage to Anthony Armstrong Jones.

► Amies, Hartnell, Horvat, Molyneux, Parkinson

Victor Stiebel. b Durban (SA), 1907. **d** London (UK), 1976. **Dresses and 'Cartwheel' straw hats.** Photograph by Sir Norman Parkinson, *Harper's Bazaar*, 1938.

Storey Helen   Designer

Helen Storey has loved texture since childhood. Here she applies sequins to leggings with the intention of glamorizing what, at the end of the 1980s, was a basic garment usually cut from black Lycra. Her womenswear had the intention of putting forward a new mood of aggressively sexy feminism. Her bras were decorated with dangerously sharp gemstones and her metal minidresses and black patent leather chaps were equally challenging. 'Clothes made by women don't deny what's underneath – we dress the essence, not the male-inspired dream,' Storey said of this work. She trained with Valentino and Lancetti, both designers famous for their feminine sensibilities. After a partnership with designer Karen Boyd in the 1980s, Storey continued her explorations alone. In 1996, she collaborated with her sister to produce a sci-art project, *Primitive Streak*, which used magnified human structures as a basis for textile designs.

► Lancetti, Rosier, Valentino

Helen Storey. b London (UK), 1959. **Sequined leggings.** Photograph by Eamonn J. McCabe, British *Elle*, 1990.

Strauss Levi

Designer

A septuagenarian teacher invites her young audience to grapple with its preconceptions in an advertisement for Levi Strauss. 'I wish I had invented blue jeans,' Yves Saint Laurent once said. 'Jeans are expressive and discreet, they have sex appeal and simplicity – everything I could want for the clothes I design.' The real inventor was Levi Strauss, a Jewish-Bavarian immigrant pedlar who followed the Gold Rush to sell his goods. When his customers asked for trousers, he cut up tents to make them. In 1860 Strauss discovered an equally tough fabric called *serge de Nîmes* (denim), from France. Jeans were named after the Genoese sailors' trousers on which the original 501 style was based. First brought to Europe by GIs during the Second World War, jeans were glamorized by the 1950s rebels James Dean and Marlon Brando. In the 1980s, a pair of Levis worn with Dr Martens shoes became the enduring uniform for an entire generation.
► Benetton, Dean, Fisher, Hechter, N. Knight

Levi Strauss. b Bavaria (GER), 1829. **d** San Francisco, CA (USA), 1902. **'Josephine, 79, teacher, Colorado'** wears **501 jeans.** Photograph by Nick Knight, 1996.

Style.com

Even Condé Nast, owner of fashion bibles *Vogue* and *W*, did not want to enter the digital world alone. So when, in September 2000, the corporation announced that it was going to dip its toes into digital, it founded *Style.com* with the upmarket US department store Neiman Marcus. The idea was simple: the fashion-conscious would be drawn to the site for up-to-the-minute news, gossip and trends in the fashion world – traditional editorial content in a digital format. Continuing in the style of a fashion publication, Condé Nast brought in executive editor Nicole Phelps from *Elle* in 2004, with Dirk Standen joining her the following year as editor in chief. Shaping solid editorial content – comprehensive show reviews and trend reports – *Style.com* has established itself as an essential reference point, enlisting contributors such as *The Sartorialist*'s Scott Schuman, later replaced by Canadian Tommy Ton in 2009 as street-style reporter.

► Grand, Nast, Schuman, Wintour

Style.com. est. New York (USA), 2000. **Home page featuring Marc Jacobs' spring/summer 2013 collection.**

Sui Anna

Designer

Nadja Auermann appears on Anna Sui's catwalk as Greta Garbo in sequins, trilby and boa. The key to Sui's look is the eclectic way she mixes her clothes, rather than the individual garments themselves. As shown here, she has a modern take on most fashion periods. This retro-reworking is typical of 1990s fashion, and Sui's versions are more wearable than many. She attended Parsons School of Design in New York and worked as a stylist – a skill that can be appreciated in the way she brings a look together from several directions. While studying, she teamed up with a classmate, photographer Steven Meisel. She also worked briefly as a designer in a sportswear company, before setting up on her own in 1981, after Macy's began stocking her designs. Her inspiration comes from some forty years of magazine cuttings, stored away in what she calls her 'Genius Files'.

► Garbo, Garren, Meisel

Anna Sui. b Dearborn Heights, MI (USA), 1955. **Nadja Auermann wears a sequined sweater and boa.** Photograph by Chris Moore, 1995.

Sumurun

Model

When Edward Molyneux left Lucile to open his own haute couture house in 1919, he hired Vera Ashby as his head mannequin. He named her Sumurun, the 'Enchantress of the Desert', and she became the highest-paid model in Paris (crowds would gather to see her enter and exit the Molyneux establishment). She was photographed by Baron de Meyer and drawn by Drian. This photograph shows Vera in the Molyneux studio dressed for the *Coucher du Soleil* (sunset) ball. Inspired by her exotic, oriental look, Molyneux created a harem dress of silver tissue worn under a sleeveless tunic of gold lamé. He concealed electric bulbs in the ruby jewels that decorated her outfit. As the house lights were dimmed, she pressed a button to light up her outfit, causing men to whoop and cheer. After retiring, Vera became a *vendeuse* at Molyneux, later moving to Norman Hartnell where she was appointed *vendeuse* to the Queen.

► Drian, Hartnell, Molyneux, De Meyer

Sumurun (Vera Ashby). b London (UK), 1895. **d** Victoria, BC (CAN), 1985. **Sumurun wears costume by Molyneux.** Photograph by Jean Desboutin, 1921.

Swinton Tilda

Icon

Tilda Swinton wears outfits as if they were a character, infusing them with the same eloquent tension that she brings to her film roles. In this image by Craig McDean, her angular pose echoes the sculptural form of the dresses stacked on her slim frame, but her ambiguous expression transforms this geometrical composition into something more suggestive and complex. A star of art cinema, notably in roles for Derek Jarman and in Sally Potter's *Orlando* (1992), Swinton rose to popularity after a succession of award-winning roles. 'I would rather be handsome for an hour,' Swinton once told an interviewer, 'than pretty for a week.' Otherworldly, androgynous, with her hair cut in a boyish crop and her cream-pale face, she seems not to play fashion's game, and in so doing has become an object of fascination. Swinton is regularly cited as a muse to designers (including Haider Ackermann), photographers and artists alike.

► Ackermann, Lanvin, McDean, Viktor & Rolf

Tilda Swinton (Katherine Mathilda Swinton). b London (UK), 1960. **Swinton poses for** *Another* **magazine shoot, spring/summer 2009.** Photograph by Craig McDean

Sybilla

Designer

'Travelling Clothes' is the title of this image by Javier Vallhonrat of Sybilla's autumn/winter 1989 collection. The incongruous title reflects the designer's Spanish sense of humour – these clothes are suited to a walk in the rain rather than international travel. Sybilla creates surreal designs and marries opposites in her work: extravagance with subtlety, humour with elegance. Here, a coat has the spirit of both a traditional belted trench coat and an opera coat by her fellow countryman Cristóbal Balenciaga.

Sybilla grew up in Madrid and moved to Paris in 1980 to work at Yves Saint Laurent's couture atelier. After one year she dismissed Paris as too snobbish and cold, returning to the fun and laid-back atmosphere of her home city. In 1983 she launched her own label and swiftly became renowned for her use of soft colours and quirky, sculpted shapes in her clothing, shoes, bags and, latterly, furniture.

▶ Toledo, Vallhonrat

Sybilla (**Sybilla Sorondo-Myelzwynska**). **b** New York (USA), 1963. **'Travelling Clothes', 1989.** Photograph by Javier Vallhonrat.   499

Takahashi Jun (Undercover)   Designer

The model with her face lost in the light is an apt metaphor for the designer Jun Takahashi and his label, Undercover, which he founded in 1990. It's fair to say that the reclusive Japanese designer has an on-off relationship with the catwalk, returning to the Paris shows for autumn/winter 2011 after an absence of three years. Like his mentor, Rei Kawakubo of Comme des Garçons, Takahashi takes a classic garment and deconstructs and reshapes it with imaginative flair. His spring/summer 2005 show featured the 'Tree Branch Coat', an asymmetrical red trench with branches sprouting from the torso. But he knows how to make clothes to sell, introducing his high-end cult status to streetwear with a running range for Nike, launched in 2010: the Nike x Undercover Gyakusou (*gyakusou* means 'running in reverse' in Japanese). In 2012 he designed for the Japanese mass retailer Uniqlo, releasing a Uniqlo Undercover collection UU.

► Kawakubo, Knight & Bowerman, Watanabe, Y. Yamamoto

Jun Takahashi. b Kiryu (JAP), 1969. **Purple cape of 'skull' rosettes, spring/summer 2007.** Photograph by Yoshie Tominaga.

Talbot Suzanne

Milliner

'Talbot would send us out to dine in public looking as exotic as the Wicked Queen in *Snow White* – easily the most chic vamp the films have ever evolved.' The caption that accompanied this picture takes us into Suzanne Talbot's charmed world. Talbot had long since died (her own powers being at their peak in the 1880s) but her spirit lived in the house's close alliance with the fashion world. The Talbot premises were part of the rich fashion map of Paris in the 1920s and 1930s, which included those of hairdresser Antoine, couturières Chanel and Schiaparelli and shoe designer André Perugia. This black silk jersey hat, embellished with a golden spike and embroidery, included a veil. Such theatrical French millinery was greatly admired by the American market. With Paulette, Mme Agnès and Lilly Daché, who moved to New York having trained at Talbot, it was a house whose work moved in parallel with the fashions for clothes.

► Agnès, Antoine, Daché, Hoyningen-Huene, Paulette, Perugia

Suzanne Talbot. (Active 1880s–1900s.) **Embroidered, silk jersey hat for Bergdorf Goodman.** Photograph by George Hoyningen-Huene, *Harper's Bazaar*, 1939.

Tappé Herman Patrick

Designer

Mary Pickford, 'America's Sweetheart', wears the wedding dress chosen for her marriage to Douglas Fairbanks. It was originally made by Herman Tappé for Natica Nast, Condé's daughter, to wear for a *Vogue* sitting published in 1920. Tappé had been upset that he should be asked to make it in such a tiny size, but that was before Pickford had seen and selected it for her high-profile nuptials. The silk tulle wrap, worn over a plain, strapless dress, is trimmed with ruffles edged with silk organdie. Elsewhere, the tulle is formed into rows of tight gathers. Wedding dresses, and those for bridesmaids, formed the core of Tappé's exclusive, expensive work. He was known as the Poiret of New York for his individual and mysterious style. His was a romantic, feminine view, and he became a creator of robes de style – quixotic dresses based on costumes found in paintings.

► Emanuel, De Meyer, Nast, Poiret

Herman Patrick Tappé. b Sidney, OH (USA), 1876. **d** (USA), 1954. **Organdie dress with ribbon-banding and matching bonnet.** Photograph by Baron de Meyer, American *Vogue*, 1920.

Tarlazzi Angelo   Designer

An asymmetric, taffeta evening dress perfectly details Angelo Tarlazzi's well-recognized skill: blending Italian imagination with French chic. Its bodice, caught on one shoulder, flows into a point, moving over a contrasting skirt. Tarlazzi abandoned his studies in political science to pursue a career in fashion design. He worked at the house of Carosa for a number of years, before leaving Rome for Paris to become an assistant at Jean Patou. By the late 1960s he was freelancing between Paris,

Milan, Rome and New York, during which time he was affiliated with Laura Biagiotti. It was a mix that formed his appreciation of the international market. By 1972 he was back at Patou but this time as artistic director, a high-status position he held until he launched his own ready-to-wear label in 1977. Tarlazzi's garments are amply cut from soft fabrics and often use such asymmetric drapes.

► Biagiotti, Patou, Sarne

Angelo Tarlazzi. b Ascoli Piceno (IT), 1945. **Taffeta evening dress.** Photograph by Jean-François du Sel des Monts, *L'Officiel*, 1980.

Tatsuno Koji   Designer

Dress? Costume? Sculpture? Amid the acceleration backstage, the models stand motionless in orchestrated coils of fine mesh, trimmed with rows of flowers. Like sculptural relief, these lyrical compositions reflect Tatsuno's synthesis of modern technology and folkcraft. He has spent his career experimenting with rare craft techniques, initially from his bespoke tailoring establishment in London's Mayfair and now from his small gallery at the Palais-Royal in Paris. Completely self-taught in the most English art of tailoring, Tatsuno arrived in London as an antique art dealer in 1982. He co-launched the design label Culture Shock, based on the 1980s temperament of avant-garde Japanese fashion. Disillusioned by what he calls the 'corrupt and ephemeral', Tatsuno went on to pursue a more cerebral approach to fashion, developing his label in 1987, financially backed by Yohji Yamamoto.

► W. Klein, Macdonald, Y. Yamamoto

Koji Tatsuno. b Tokyo (JAP), 1964. **Backstage at Koji Tatsuno's catwalk show.** Photograph by William Klein, 1992.

Teller Juergen

Photographer

Iris Palmer lies flat; her underwear, designed as a covering, is made superfluous by the camera's angle – an example of the 'sexual fashion photography' that Juergen Teller feels allies his work to that of Helmut Newton. For him models should never be regarded as clothes horses, rather they should be represented as the people they are. Consequently, Teller shoots clothes as part of an image rather than its focus. Primarily he is a diarist recording the lives of those he works and lives with, resulting in sometimes uncomfortable real-life documentary moments of those working in fashion. His uncompromising style is also non-judgmental and Teller doesn't prettify those lives. Originally encouraged by Nick Knight, Teller is first and foremost an art photographer, however, his reportage work has created distinctive fashion imagery for Marc Jacobs, Katharine Hamnett and Helmut Lang in addition to many high-profile fashion magazines.

► Day, Hamnett, Jacobs, N. Knight, Lang, Philo, Richardson

Juergen Teller. b Erlangen (GER), 1964. **Iris Palmer in Katharine Hamnett campaign.** 1997.

Tennant Stella

Model

The six-foot figure of Stella Tennant is dressed here in Helmut Lang. Despite her model figure and superlative skin, Tennant's edgy looks originally fell outside the usual parameters for models, defying the traditional stereotype and succeeding because of that defiance. The art student who had pierced her own nose on a railway platform was propelled into modelling after being photographed by two leading photographers: as one of London's 'It' girls by Steven Meisel, and as the granddaughter of the Duke and Duchess of Devonshire by Bruce Weber. Called the 'antithesis of the supermodel', Tennant was nevertheless picked up by Karl Lagerfeld for Chanel. Her slouching, tomboy demeanour on the catwalk made the bouncing, pouty attitude of other models look passé. What she brought, and continues to bring, to fashion is 'cool'.

▶ S. Ellis, Lagerfeld, Lang, Meisel, Sitbon, Weber

Stella Tennant. b Chatsworth (UK), 1971. **Helmut Lang T-shirt and tiered skirt.** Photograph by Sean Ellis, American *Vogue*, 1998.

Testino Mario   Photographer

Nadja Auermann pulls her T-shirt from under her skirt. In doing so she exposes her legendary legs for Mario Testino, or 'Super Mario' as he is nicknamed. 'Fashion is all about making a girl look sexy,' he says, and it is his ability to orchestrate this mood that has made his photographs so powerful. In the case of his advertising images for Gucci, Testino imbues overtly sexy clothes with a dramatic quality, placing his models in the glamorous world in which he himself lives. He has photographed the most famous and iconic women of the late twentieth century, including Madonna, a friend, who was his model for an advertising campaign for Versace Atelier. Testino used his talent for best representing the women he adores when he became the last person to photograph Diana, Princess of Wales. Those pictures, which use a relaxed reportage style, are regarded as the most flattering and modern taken in her later life.

► C. Bailey, Diana, Ford, S. Jones, Missoni, Versace, Westwood

Mario Testino. b Lima (PER), 1954. **Nadja Auermann.** French *Glamour*, 1994.   507

Theyskens Olivier

Designer

Establishing his eponymous label to immediate success at just twenty years old, Belgian-born Olivier Theyskens has gone on to collaborate with high-end artists, such as Madonna, and became creative director at Rochas in 2002. To Rochas he brought his expert cutting and aesthetic of dark, feminine fragility to haute couture, completely redefining the Parisian couture house. In 2006 Theyskens was awarded Best International Designer by the Council of Fashion Designers of America, the same year he became artistic director of Nina Ricci. In 2010 Theyskens took a new direction, joining strengths with Andrew Rosen, CEO and founder of Theory, to create the line Theyskens' Theory; here his design approach, the elegant tension between masculine and feminine sensibilities, found a new home. That year Theyskens was also appointed as artistic director of the global Theory brand.

► Ghesquière, Madonna, Ricci, Rochas, Tisci

Olivier Theyskens. b Brussels (BEL), 1977. **Model Marte Mai Van Hasster at the fittings for Theyskens' Theory spring/ summer 2013 collection.** Photograph by Julien Claessens and Thomas Deschamps, 2012.

Thimister Josephus Melchior   Designer

Surrounded by patterns and fabric, Josephus Thimister and his team work on a collection for Balenciaga, the label for which he designed from 1992 to 1997. Thimister was perceived by some as the natural heir to Cristóbal Balenciaga, sharing the pure vision of the Spanish designer often described as the Picasso of the fashion world. After one collection French *Elle* said, 'Balenciaga probably clapped in his grave.' Thimister used his detailed archives to create religiously simple clothes which have been called 'neo-couture' for their modern attitude. Educated at Antwerp's Royal Academy of Fine Arts, the training ground for Martin Margiela, Ann Demeulemeester and Dries Van Noten, Thimister describes his clothes, now designed under his own label, as being about 'light, fabric and shadow'. In his first collection, he studiously avoided fuss, cutting thirty dresses from black or blue-black fabric.

► Balenciaga, Demeulemeester, Margiela, Van Noten, Vandevorst

Josephus Melchior Thimister. b Maastricht (NL), 1962. **Josephus Thimister in his apartment.** Photograph by Christoph Kicherer, *Elle Decoration*, 1997.

Thomass Chantal

Designer

Photographed against the masculine background of American footballers, Chantal Thomass's tartan-lined jacket flies away to reveal a co-ordinating bustier. Providing frilly, coquettish underwear and outerwear for every Lolita or Vargas Girl in France, Thomass describes her designs as 'provocative, but not vulgar'; it is a delicate distinction and a line she treads carefully. Thomass did not train as a designer but began her fashion career in 1966 by opening a boutique, Ter et Bantine, in partnership with her husband. It sold tantalizing, flirtatious clothes and enjoyed patronage from Brigitte Bardot, among others. In 1975 the pair founded the Chantal Thomass label and designed a clothing range. Thomass trimmed jackets and evening dresses with lace but her name will forever be connected to lacy underwear, nightwear and stockings that combine fashion and sensuality.

▶ John-Frederics, Molinari, Schiffer

Chantal Thomass. b Malakoff, TX (USA), 1947. **Bustier and grey skirt suit.** Photograph by Bill King, French *Vogue*, 1982.

Thornton Justin & Bregazzi Thea (Preen)   Designers

Thornton and Bregazzi are the husband and wife team behind the label Preen founded in 1996. Renowned for their distinctive brand of deconstructed chic, their spring/summer 2013 collection was a patchwork of print and minimalism. Their inspiration was *Buffalo 66* (1998), the cult American film starring Vincent Gallo and Christina Ricci; as they explain, 'it was the toughness of his snakeskin boots to her sweet femininity that we tried to capture.' This was seen in the controlled and refined insertions of reptilian and snakeskin prints in striking asymmetrical garment compositions, demonstrating Preen's mastery in balancing form with fabric. This sheer, airy, diaphanous dress is a collage of printed textures on delicate cotton voile. This ultra-sleek splicing and crispness of detail has become a signature for the designers.

► Berardi, Kane, Pilotto, Pugh

Justin Thornton. b Isle of Man (UK), 1969. **Thea Bregazzi. b** Isle of Man (UK), 1968. **Backstage at Preen's spring/summer 2013 show at The Natural History Museum, London.** Photograph by Nick Dorey.   511

Tiffany Charles Lewis   Jewellery designer

Audrey Hepburn's role as Holly Golightly in the film *Breakfast at Tiffany's* (1961) made the jewellery store, whose clients have included Queen Victoria, even more famous. In this photograph, Hepburn wears a Givenchy dress and the priceless 'Ribbon' necklace made by Jean Schlumberger, the celebrated Parisian jeweller, who worked for Tiffany & Co from the 1950s until his death in 1987. The centrepiece of the necklace, which is made from eighteen-carat gold, platinum and white diamonds, is the Tiffany diamond, bought by founder Charles Lewis Tiffany in 1877 for $18,000. Rather than selling it, Tiffany placed it in the window of his New York store. Charles's son, Louis Comfort Tiffany, Elsa Peretti and Paloma Picasso continued to keep Tiffany at the forefront of jewellery design. It is regarded as a fashion-friendly company for its broad range – providing both grandeur and delicate, modern pieces.

► Cartier, Givenchy, Lalique, Peretti

Charles Lewis Tiffany. b New York (USA), 1848. **d** New York (USA), 1933. **Audrey Hepburn wears the Tiffany 'Ribbon' necklace at a press reception for *Breakfast at Tiffany's*.** 1961.

Tisci Riccardo

Designer

Hubert de Givenchy's muse and ideal of feminine beauty was Audrey Hepburn, who became a close friend and wore his classic cuts both on and off the screen. Givenchy's retirement in 1995 led to a quick succession of designers: John Galliano, Alexander McQueen and Julien Macdonald, landing in the hands of Italian Riccardo Tisci in 2005. With Tisci, the house of Givenchy had a new designer, a new muse and a new way of thinking, he says, 'My way of showing is very melancholic. People call me a gothic designer. I don't think I am. I love romanticism and sensuality.' And his friend and muse, Mariacarla Boscono, 'represents the reincarnation of my woman' who translates that vision, shrouded in a severe black-and-white silhouette, reflecting his Italian Catholic heritage and firm belief in spirituality. Under Tisci, Givenchy has become a byword for an immediately recognizable style of dark, edgy femininity.

▶ Ghesquière, Givenchy, Inez and Vinoodh, Owens

Riccardo Tisci. b Taranto (IT), 1974. **Mariacarla Boscono models Givenchy autumn/winter 2005 campaign.** Photograph by Inez and Vinoodh.

Toledo Isabel

Designer

Latin flavour, surreal lines and futuristic content define Isabel Toledo's radical fashions sewn in the tradition of couture. Toledo, who speaks of herself as a seamstress rather than a fashion designer, creates in the manner of couturières such as Madeleine Vionnet and Madame Grès. Like them, she does not start from a flat sketch, but envisions clothing in three dimensions, always bearing a shape in her mind – usually a circle or a curved line. 'I love the maths behind the romance,' she says of her so-called liquid architecture's craftsmanship. The crepe jersey that forms the body of this dress is suspended by the armholes and anchored at the hem (unseen) by a construction of lace, net, wool and felt; the effect is like that of water slowly pouring into a barrel. Toledo's husband, Ruben, known for his whimsical fashion illustrations, manages the business side of the New York-based company and acts as her creative alter ego.

► Grès, Sybilla, Vionnet

Isabel Toledo. b Camajani (CU), 1961. **Matte jersey 'Infanta' dress, spring/summer 1992.** Photograph by Ruven Afanador.

De Tommaso Carmen (Carven)   Designer

This immaculate striped cotton dress is designed specifically for a petite figure. The vertical lines that appear from pin-tucks above and below the waist will lengthen the figure while the dainty detail of bows and reversed stripes accentuate the hand-span waist. Carmen de Tommaso started designing because she was unable to find the clothes she wanted – in her case those that would fit her tiny figure. She studied architecture before founding the house of Carven in Paris in 1937 (a modification of her first name). With her architectural training, de Tommaso excelled at adjusting the accessories to the exact proportions of her clientele. The dress below is an example of intelligent problem-solving – a vital aspect of good fashion design. She diversified and enjoyed a successful career creating and marketing perfumes, of which 'Ma Griffe' is the most enduring.

► De Prémonville, De la Renta

Carmen de Tommaso. b Châteauroux (FR), 1909. Carven's 'Ma Griffe' dress. 1945.

Topolino

Make-up artist

Conceptual make-up artist Topolino lists his influences as 'street, insects, nature, space, fairies, circus, cartoons and life', and his style as 'trashy trendy, fantasy but chic', which sums up this photograph. When asked about his technique, Topolino replied, 'It is more about imagination than technique.' Here, that imagination conjures nails embellished with rose thorns and lacquered. The lips are half-coloured by feathered pencil lines. These methods are examples of the way Topolino explores the potential of make-up and uses it to accessorize fashion – in this case a fake fur jacket that begs such aggressive touches. He taught himself the art of make-up because of his interest in fashion, and began working in 1985. He has produced startling and influential catwalk work for designers Alexander McQueen and Philip Treacy. In 2002 his book, *Make-up Games*, a stunning collection of his most spectacular work, was published.

► Colonna, N. Knight, McQueen, Treacy

Topolino. b Marseille (FR), 1965. **Nails decorated with rose thorns.** Photograph by Norbert Schoerner, French *Glamour*, 1994.

Topshop

Retailer

Topshop is a name synonymous with British fashion. Launched in the basement of a department store in 1964, the brand was once associated with affordable kitschy clothes. In the 1990s Topshop gained a new lease of life with retail guru Jane Shepherdson overseeing its transformation into the youthful fast-fashion empire it is today. In 2007 Kate Moss created a capsule collection, a partnership that lasted four years, launching the brand in the US market. Topshop continues to be a leader in the genre under managing director Mary Homer, fostering creative talent through support of the British Fashion Council, which runs the NEWGEN initiative, as well as directing innovative collaborations with emerging design talent such as JW Anderson, Simone Rocha, Gareth Pugh and Christopher Kane. Topshop's flagship at London's Oxford Circus has since become an iconic destination, for tourists and the fashion-minded alike.

► Benetton, Fisher, Kane, Moss, Net-A-Porter, Pugh

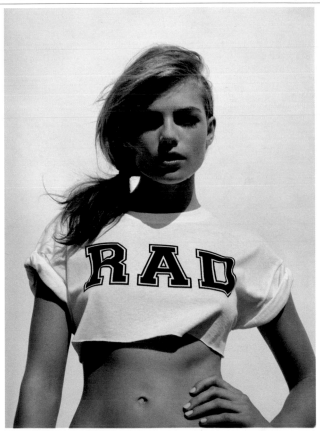

Topshop. est. London (UK), 1964. **Rosie Tapner models Topshop.** Photograph by Alasdair McLellan.

Torimaru Gnyuki (Yuki)

Designer

Jersey flows like water from a halter-neck bodice by Gnyuki Torimaru, formerly known as Yuki. He studied architecture, before becoming a textile engineer, an occupation that has dominated his work since. His love of vivid colour, purity and fluidity has remained a constant in Torimaru's work. He developed them to their fullest potential after discovering, in 1984, a luxurious non-crease polyester that could maintain long-lasting pleats. Using intricate pleating techniques, he created ever-more fantastical designs. Japanese-born, Yuki made London his permanent home in 1964, having worked for Norman Hartnell and Pierre Cardin, and launched his own label in 1972. He soon enjoyed a degree of fame for his one-size hooded or draped jersey dresses, often inspired by monastic garb. His dramatic cut often uses panels cut on a full circle – a luxurious technique that gives a garment the maximum fullness that can be achieved without seaming.

► Burrows, Muir, Valentina

Gnyuki Torimaru. b Miyazaki-Ken (JAP), 1940. **Jersey halter-neck dress. Late 1970s.** Photograph by Richard Davis.

Toskan Frank & Angelo Frank (M.A.C)

Cult beauty brand M.A.C began in 1985 when hairdresser Frank Angelo and make-up artist Frank Toskan met. Initially launching a long-wearing foundation to meet the harsh demands of film and stage work, the theatrical motivations of M.A.C ('Makeup Artist's Cosmetics') remain a strong element of the company to this day. Creative collaborations over the years span musicians, fashion designers, icons and artists alike; including Cindy Sherman, Daphne Guinness and Lady Gaga. Here Frank Toskan is joined by drag queen RuPaul and singer K.D Lang for their iconic 'Viva Glam' collection: a line that donates all proceeds to their AIDS campaign. Ever sassy, excessive and unconventional, M.A.C's beauty colourscape, from the futuristic space tramp, glammed-up drag queen to sun-buffed naturalist, has promoted the notion of make-up as complete freedom of expression, forging these philosophies into a successful global brand.

► Apfel, Guinness, Lady Gaga, McGrath, Nars, Recine, Uemura

Frank Toskan. b Trieste (IT), 1950; Frank Angelo. b Montreal, QC (CAN), 1947. d Coral Gables, fl (USA), 1997. 'Viva Glam' lipstick advertisement. 1996.

Tran Hélène

Illustrator

A sedate, navy pyjama suit by Hardy Amies and crisp, organza shirt and skirt by Alistair Blair are put into a pastoral English scene by Hélène Tran. This was one of a series of images that illustrated the social summer season of 1987. Tran's easy, loose technique characterizes rich clothes and their languid wearers with broad washes of watercolour and baroque curls. Details such as Manolo Blahnik's shoes and sandals are picked out with fine brushwork. The picture recalls the social commentary by artists such as Marcel Vertès, who captured social situations in a way that photography cannot. Tran studied illustration at the École Supérieure d'Art Graphique in her native city, Paris. Her dramatic and often humorous illustrations have been published in British and American *Vogue* and *La Mode en Peinture*. Tran has also illustrated for clients, including Jean Patou and Roger Vivier.

▶ Amies, Blahnik, Blair, Vertès, Vivier

Hélène Tran. b Paris (FR), 1954. **Outfits by Hardy Amies and Alistair Blair.** *Harpers & Queen*, 1987.

Travilla William

Designer

In one of film history's most famous moments, Marilyn Monroe's halter-neck dress is whipped into action over a city grille in the steamy comedy *The Seven Year Itch* (1955). The dress was designed by William Travilla, a favourite of Monroe's, who designed the costumes for eleven of her films. This dress is an adaptation of classical Grecian robes, with pleats mimicking draping and a bodice shaped by a criss-cross tie. It actually came off the peg and remains a best-seller – resurrected every couple of years by retailers who are still profiting from its sexy allure. Travilla's appeal was his ability to flatter figures, including Marilyn's healthy hips and chest. His traditional assertion that 'femininity is the strongest weapon a woman can have' took him on to design the wardrobe for the early 1980s soap opera *Dallas*, in which the characters did indeed wield their womanliness like instruments of medieval battle.

► Head, Irene, Stern

William Travilla. b Avalon, CA (USA), 1920. **d** Los Angeles, CA (USA), 1990. **Marilyn Monroe wears her famous white pleated dress.** Still from *The Seven Year Itch*, 1955.

Treacy Philip   Milliner

Demonstrating his fastidious attention to detail, Philip Treacy makes the final, crucial, adjustments to the arrow-like plumes of a creation worn by singer and fashion icon Grace Jones. Discovered by the late Isabella Blow, Treacy began his career in 1990 in a basement in Belgravia, London. Since then he has become the milliner of choice for the biggest names in fashion, including Alexander McQueen, Karl Lagerfeld, Valentino, Ralph Lauren and Donna Karan among others. In 2000 he became the first person to present a Paris haute couture show dedicated to millinery. He has created hats for various films including the *Harry Potter* franchise and designed for the likes of Daphne Guinness, Naomi Campbell, Lady Gaga and Madonna. More than 30 of his hats were worn at the wedding of Prince William and Kate Middleton in 2011. He has been awarded the title of British Accessory Designer of the Year at the British Fashion Awards five times.

► Blow, Burton, Guinness, G. Jones, Lady Gaga, McQueen

Philip Treacy. b Ahascragh (IRE), 1967. **Treacy trims a hat on the head of Grace Jones.** Photograph by Kevin Davies, 1998.

Tree Penelope

Model

Cecil Beaton photographs Penelope Tree's elfin face, an extraordinary one that made 'The Tree' a match for 'The Twig' in the 1960s. She was the rebellious daughter of a rich and serious-minded family who were disappointed in Penelope's original decision to embark on a career as a model. When she was first shot at thirteen by Diane Arbus, her father, a British multimillionaire, vowed he would sue if the pictures were published. By the time Diana Vreeland sent her to Richard Avedon, she was seventeen and her father had relented. David Bailey described Penelope as 'an Egyptian Jiminy Cricket'; in 1967 she moved into his flat in London's Primrose Hill, which became a hang-out for spaced-out hippies who, Bailey recalls, would be 'smoking joints I had paid for and calling me a capitalist pig!' In 1974, Bailey and Tree split up and she moved to Sydney, Australia, far away from the focus of the fashion photographer's camera.

► Avedon, D. Bailey, Beaton, Shrimpton, Verushka, Vreeland

Penelope Tree. b London (UK), 1950. **Penelope Tree.** Photograph by Sir Cecil Beaton, 1967.

Trigère Pauline

Designer

The structured tailoring on show here explains why, in *Breakfast at Tiffany's* (1961), Patricia Neal's character, an uptight girlfriend wearing Pauline Trigère, nearly proved a match for Audrey Hepburn's youthfully elegant outfits by Hubert de Givenchy. She represented grown-up and urban New York fashion. Born and trained in the family business of dressmaking in Paris, Trigère arrived in New York in 1937. After working with Travis Banton at Hattie Carnegie, Trigère opened her own business in 1942.

Over fifty years later, she would demonstrate how she cut into luxury fabric directly from the bolt onto the mannequin to awestruck fashion students. Her cutting was sure, emphasizing wrapping and tying in the French tradition of magnificent scarves and idiosyncratic knottings. Trigère was the best model for her fashion: urban chic in luxury fabrics, coats robust and flowing, and rhinestone bras.

► Banton, Carnegie, Givenchy

Pauline Trigère. b Paris (FR), 1912. **d** New York (USA), 2002. **Leopard-print turban and crimson coat.** Photograph by Karen Radkai, American *Vogue*, 1959.

Troublé Agnès (agnès b.)   Designer

With her simple clothes, swept-back hair and classic black sunglasses, this model is the epitome of Parisian chic. The stripy black-and-white T-shirt shown is reminiscent of Jean Seberg's in *Breathless* (1960), and the simple style of Left Bank beats. 'I don't like the word "fashion"; I say I design clothes,' says agnès b. Her neutral-coloured wardrobe staples: crisp white shirts, plain knitwear and pared-down (often black) tailoring have survived precisely because they pay very little attention to fashion. She worked as a junior fashion editor at *Elle* magazine in France, and as a stylist at Cacharel and Dorothée Bis. She opened her first shop in 1975, during an eccentric era of flared trousers and platform shoes. From the outset, her designs, based on utilitarian clothing, such as workman's blue overalls and undershirts, found a place as fashion's antidote. She has received much recognition including the *Légion d'honneur*.

► Bousquet, Farhi, Jacobson, Marant

Agnès Troublé. b Versailles (FR), 1941. **Black-and-white striped top.** Photograph by Darzacq, 1997.

Turbeville Deborah

Photographer

Models Isabelle Weingarten and Ella Milewiecz become part of Deborah Turbeville's dreamscape. A typical shot, it depicts motionless subjects who pose in a group but without relating to one another. Turbeville's career path was a tortuous journey through fashion – an experience that gave her a deep understanding of clothes. Having arrived in New York in 1956, she worked as a model and moved on to assist designer Claire McCardell. She then turned to magazines, becoming a fashion editor for

Mademoiselle. In 1966 she changed course again and became a freelance photographer for *Harper's Bazaar* after being inspired by a talk given by Richard Avedon. By 1972 she was working for the cult magazine *Nova* in London. Her haunting style was very different from other fashion photography of the time and yet it was intriguing rather than alienating.

► Avedon, McCardell, Rykiel

Deborah Turbeville. b Medford, MA (USA), 1938. **Isabelle Weingarten and Ella Milewiecz.** 1978.

Turlington Christy

Model

Christy Turlington's beauty is a versatile one. Here Francesco Scavullo makes hers a cover face in the traditional sense. But equally, she has personified nude, unaffected beauty – representing Calvin Klein's fragrances since 1987. While modelling relies on the arts of lighting, make-up and retouching, few women are able to achieve a perfect look through self-awareness; Turlington is one such woman. She told *Vogue*, 'I know how to make every part of my body appear different than it actually is.

I can make my eyes and my lips appear bigger by putting my chin down... You can manipulate everything for photography.' Called 'the most beautiful woman in the world', she feels it's all down to her full, symmetrical lips: 'I have gotten most of my advertising contacts because of them.' She made an easy transition from the haute glamour of the 1980s to the relaxed simplicity of the following decade and has a skincare line called Sundari.
▶ Ferre, C. Klein, Lindbergh, Scavullo, Valentino

Christy Turlington. b Oakland, CA (USA), 1969. **Christy wears Gianfranco Ferre.** Photograph by Francesco Scavullo, 1988.

Twiggy

Model

Twiggy poses next to her mannequin lookalikes. It was the only way to replicate her powerful figure at a time when the whole world wanted to have a part of her magic. Lesley Hornby had come from the suburbs of London. At fifteen she met Nigel John Davies, then a hairdresser. He reinvented himself as Justin de Villeneuve and Lesley as 'Twig', later Twiggy. Just as it took a haircut to launch Linda Evangelista's career as a supermodel, twenty years earlier the potential of Twiggy's gamine charm

was unlocked with a haircut by Leonard. With her elfin crop and teenage figure, Twiggy became the icon of young fashion and the first model to grow into a media personality, albeit a startled one. In response to one journalist's assertion that she earned more than the prime minister, she could only giggle, 'Do I?' Twiggy 'retired' at the age of nineteen.

► D. Bailey, Evangelista, Foale & Tuffin, Shrimpton

Twiggy (Lesley Hornby). b London (UK), 1949. **Twiggy with mannequins by Adel Rootstein.** Photograph by J. Drysdale, 1966.

Tyler Richard   Designer

Model Irina wears a shrunken, three-piece suit by Richard Tyler. Finding success when Hollywood discovered his meticulous tailoring, Tyler became well known late in life, winning an award for best newcomer at forty-six. His fashion career, however, has been his life's work. He learned his craft from his seamstress mother and trained as a tailor. He built his career designing stage clothes for Elton John, Cher and Diana Ross. A change of direction in the mid-1980s led to Tyler launching a menswear range with business partner and soon-to-be wife Lisa Trafficante. This was followed in 1989 by womenswear. Both collections became successful through Tyler's reputation as a master cutter. 'I have no ego. All I have is my skill,' he says. Part of his catwalk show was featured in the film *Head over Heels* (2001). In 2006 he appeared as a guest on the TV programme *Project Runway*, which focuses on fashion designers.

▶ Alfaro, Dell'Olio, Kors

Richard Tyler. b Melbourne (ASL), 1947. **Irina Pantaeva wears black three-piece suit.** Photograph by Chris Moore, 1995.   529

Uemura Shu

Cosmetics creator

With his design philosophy *'bien être'* (a sense of well-being), Shu Uemura freed the face from the shifting dictates of transient fashions and developed a notion of the inner sense of beauty, reflecting a mood of introversion and lack of artifice. Originally a hairdresser, Shu Uemura became a make-up artist to stars such as Shirley MacLaine and Frank Sinatra in 1950s Hollywood. He raised the standard of make-up and made it into an art form, using superior cosmetics as his palette and the finest beauty tools as apparatus. These he stocked in his aesthetically modern Beauty Boutiques, which resembled art supply stores, and heralded a cosmetics-counter revolution in the 1980s. After three decades, the natural style of his cosmetics, in soft, muted colours and distinct transparent packaging, is still relentlessly modern and very much a hallmark of twentieth-century design.

► Bandy, Bourjois, Factor, Lutens, Nars

Shu Uemura. b Tokyo (JAP), 1928. **d** Tokyo (JAP), 2007. **Shu Uemura making up a model's face.** Photograph by Morozumi, 1983.

Underwood Patricia

Milliner

The familiar stetson is given a modern twist: straw braid instead of suede, a wider brim and modest curve to create a feminine and elegant shape. The particular cock of the brim remains, hinting at the provocation the cowboy hat was noted for. Subtle yet interesting manipulations of traditional hat shapes are characteristic of Underwood's millinery designs. Relying completely on shape and proportion, rather than fussy ornamentation, her hats are noted for their spartan modesty that makes them into one-statement sculptures for the head. 'A simplicity of design avoids the pitfalls of a hat becoming a distraction on the wearer,' she says. British-born Underwood moved to New York in 1967 after a brief tenure at Buckingham Palace as a secretary. Her understated aesthetics fit the New York look, where she works with designers Bill Blass and Marc Jacobs who mirror her modernist, abstract forms.

► Blass, Jacobs, Model, Sui, Treacy

Patricia Underwood. b Maidenhead (UK), 1948. **Black straw stetson.** 1991.

Ungaro Emanuel   Designer

This minidress by Ungaro shows him to be in touch with the flower power mood of the late 1960s and demonstrates his love of delicate fabric and surface detail. Yet the acute sense of cut remains. The son of an Italian tailor, Ungaro's favourite toy at six years old was his father's sewing machine and he became a tailor at fourteen. In 1955 he moved to Paris and was introduced to Balenciaga by Courrèges. He joined the Spaniard's house in 1958 and stayed for six years. Having learnt the master's rigorous attitude to cut, he opened his own couture business in 1965 with simple, bold garments such as blazers worn with shorts. Four years later, along with Cardin and Courrèges, Ungaro created a new nudeness in French fashion, but by the 1970s his style had softened. His 1980s eveningwear used vivid florals cut and ruched to form extremely ladylike, grown-up versions of his girlish dresses from 1969.

► Audibet, Balenciaga, Cardin, Courrèges, Paulette

Emanuel Ungaro. b Aix-en-Provence (FR), 1933. **White, floral, trellis appliqué, lace dress.** Photograph by Peter Knapp, 1969.

Von Unwerth Ellen

Photographer

Wearing towering heels, stockings, silk underwear and corset, model Iris Palmer presents a traditionally provocative figure. Many observers are surprised to find that von Unwerth, the photographer, is a woman. She encourages her subjects to look sensual and her success stems from the fact that she projects these images from a female perspective. 'The models love to look sexy,' she says. 'They all like to be photographed in that way.' Von Unwerth 'discovered' the supermodel Claudia Schiffer in 1992 when she photographed her for Guess? Jeans. She has also famously created advertising images for Wonderbra, Katharine Hamnett and Gianfranco Ferré. Von Unwerth left her native Germany in 1974 to begin a modelling career in Paris, becoming a photographer ten years later. She has grown to be a key image-maker through her editorial work for *Vogue*, *The Face*, *Interview* and even *Playboy*.

► Hamnett, Schiffer, Teller

Ellen von Unwerth. b Frankfurt (GER), 1954. **Iris Palmer.** *The Face*, 1996.

Valentina

Designer

Madame Valentina, photographed here in triplicate, wears her own design: a dinner dress with a jewelled belt and collar. The dress was made in jersey – a material that swathes and clings to the figure, creating a sculptured look. The strong rosy-red colour provided an uninterrupted line, another key feature of the Valentina style. Colour to intensify line is enhanced by the fluid green cowl draped around her high-piled, chignon hairstyle and caught up in a belt. The whole aura is that of a Byzantine emperor's consort. The grand manner of Madame Valentina was rooted in her Russian heritage, even though she moved to Paris during the Russian Revolution and then to New York in 1922, where she set up her own establishment four years later. The costume also has a theatrical air, traceable to Madame Valentina's training for the stage. Her fashionable eveningwear was very popular with actresses.

▶ Grès, Torimaru, Vionnet

Valentina (Valentina Nicholaevna Sanina Schlee). b Kiev (RUS), 1904. **d** New York (USA), 1989. **Madame Valentina wears her jersey dress and cowl.** Photographs by John Rawlings, American *Vogue*, 1945.

Valentino

Designer

The 2008 movie *The Last Emperor* paid homage to Valentino's stunning career, which has spanned forty-five years. His fiery red gowns represent the romance, beauty, femininity and decadence of Rome, the city where he launched his own label in 1960. Valentino worked with Jean Dessès and then Guy Laroche, before becoming a couturier himself. Initially he made gowns for Italian socialites, but in 1968 he caused a sensation when he launched a radical, all-white collection. Jackie Kennedy wore an outfit from the collection when she married Aristotle Onassis. His suave demeanour, impeccable manners and seductive clothes are all about style rather than fashion. In 2006 he was awarded the *Légion d'honneur* for his outstanding contribution to fashion. Valentino announced his retirement in 2007 and held his last haute couture show in 2008.

► Armani, Von Etzdorf, Rodriguez, Ungaro

Valentino Garavani. b Voghera (IT), 1932. **Valentino with models in his signature shade of red.** Photograph by Lorenzo Agius, 2008.

Vallhonrat Javier

Photographer

Almost surreal, this dream-like image softly releases fashion of its social connotations. The model enjoys the company of the dolphins in aquamarine waves coloured with Vallhonrat's customary intensity. In a campaign for John Galliano, in which nature is a source of harmony and fantasy, Javier Vallhonrat frees the clothes from their visual role. Vallhonrat, who has also collaborated with Sybilla, Jil Sander and Romeo Gigli in their advertising campaigns, takes pride in only working for those designers whose creativity will serve as a ground for photographic research. His photographs, he affirms, never document fashion but exploit its creativity to pursue autonomy in photography, which is Vallhonrat's main concern. Having worked for European *Vogues* from 1984 to 1994, he now lectures and exhibits. He made a comeback in 2011, portraying the jeweller Pomellato's celebrity spokeswoman, Tilda Swinton, in an ad campaign of the house.

► Frissell, Galliano, Gigli, Del Pozo, Sander, Sybilla

Javier Vallhonrat. b Madrid (SP), 1953. **Beaded chiffon 'Dice' vest by John Galliano.** 1986.

Valli Giambattista

Designer

Like fellow Italian haute couture master Valentino, Giambattista Valli skilfully splashes a unique shade of red throughout his autumn/winter 2012 haute couture collection. Valli is one of the newest names in haute couture, showing his first collection in Paris in 2011, nearly six years after the founding of his ready-to-wear line. Here Valli's lush crimson dress explodes in a swirl of sculptural ruffles from top to bottom, a palette and silhouette that enhances and celebrates the female form

as he breathes new life into the traditional world of couture. Valli not only draws influence from his Roman roots, but also from his discovery of French fashion through the watercolours of Yves Saint Laurent and the illustrations of René Gurau. Valli honed his skills as an assistant to Roberto Capucci, when he was introduced to the vivid colours and the sculptural beauty of the haute-couture dresses of the Roman master.

► Capucci, Ghesquière, Gurau, Saint Laurent, Tisci

Giambattista Valli. b Rome (IT), 1966. **Backstage at Giambattista Valli haute couture spring/summer 2013.** Photograph by ³ly Nava Archive, *Self Service* magazine.

537

Van Cleef & Arpels

Jewellery designers

This illustrated magazine cover, featuring a faceted ruby and platinum cuff, typifies the Van Cleef & Arpels customer of 1942. Her high turban, squared shoulders and fur wrap are worn with grand jewellery in a defiantly glamorous response to the occupation of Paris. Alfred Van Cleef and his three brothers-in-law, Charles, Julien and Louis Arpels, founded their jewellery company in 1906. They were among the first craftsmen to move into Place Vendôme in Paris, a square now lined with many such jewellery companies. Van Cleef & Arpels introduced exotic themes inspired by the excavation of Tutankhamun's tomb and *chinoiserie*. They used characteristic mixtures of bright precious and semi-precious stones to create jewellery that paralleled the work of Poiret and Paquin. Impeccably chic stars of the screen, such as Marlene Dietrich and Joan Fontaine, were clients of Van Cleef & Arpels.

▶ Paquin, Poiret, Di Verdura

A. Van Cleef. b Paris (FR), 1873. **d** Yvelines (FR), 1938; **C. Arpels. b** Paris (FR), 1880. **d** Le Vésinet (FR), 1951; **J. Arpels. b** Marseille (FR), 1884. **d** Paris (FR), 1964; **L. Arpels. b** Nancy (FR), 1886. **d** Neuilly (FR), 1976. Advert by L. Louchel, 1942.

Vanderbilt Gloria   Designer

'Money is the symbol by which your peers judge you,' said Gloria Vanderbilt complacently. Heiress to one of America's biggest fortunes, Vanderbilt's gold-stitched signature logo on 'designer jeans' summed up the decadence of the disco decade. Here, they are put into the unlikely context of a cocktail party. A one-time actress, writer and poet, Vanderbilt was not a fashion designer, but was approached by Murjani International to license her name to their design of jeans. Vanderbilt was supposedly the company's second choice after Jackie Kennedy. By the early 1980s Vanderbilt's were the best-selling jeans in America. She was mobbed at in-store appearances, and made TV advertisements for 'the jeans that hug your derrière'. She didn't need the money but, she said, 'The only money that means anything to me is the money I make myself.' Her range later extended to dolls, greeting cards, soya-bean desserts, luggage and furniture.

► Adolfo, Von Fürstenberg, Kennedy, LaChapelle

Gloria Vanderbilt. b New York (USA), 1924. **Jeans for Murjani, 1982.** Photograph by John Claridge.

Vandevorst An & Arickx Filip (A.F. Vandevorst) Designers

A model lies curled up on a hospital bed with only her back exposed, a crisp white shirt stitched taut up the spine, a flounce of a pleated skirt and a tangle of dark hair hinting at a hidden narrative. The lacing on her shirt recalls both the spine sutures of Sophie Ristelheuber's surgery photographs and a Victorian corset, or perhaps a straitjacket, yet for all its suggestions of darkness, tragedy and institutionalism, it is disturbingly erotic. Troubling sexuality is stock in trade for An Vandevorst and Filip

Arickx, the designers behind A.F. Vandevorst. Having met in 1987 on their first day at Antwerp's Royal Academy, the couple went on to found their label ten years later to almost immediate acclaim. Their intelligent, beautifully cut womenswear often carries connotations of constraint, be it leather straps or the strictures of a military or medical uniform. The straps and belts are balanced by liquid draping of fine fabrics that has become their trademark.
► Ackermann, Branquinho, Demeulemeester, Margiela

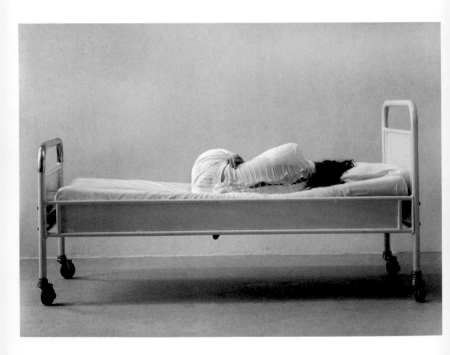

An Vandevorst. b (BEL), 1968; **Filip Arickx. b** (BEL), 1971. **A.F. Vandevorst spring/summer 1999**. Photograph by Ronald Stoops.

Venet Philippe

Designer

A petal-like, organdie collar grazes Jane Birkin's face, extending down her back in a spine of ruffles, the red embroidered polka-dots sprayed like pollen. Venet explored floral themes like this to enliven his imaginative and deft tailoring, the hallmark of his creations. Apprentice to a Parisian couturier at the age of fourteen, Venet went on to work for Elsa Schiaparelli in 1950. Here, he met the young Hubert de Givenchy, who hired him as master tailor for his couture house in 1953. Venet's contributions were extensive during Givenchy's heyday in the 1950s, notably for dressing Audrey Hepburn in the film *Sabrina Fair* (1954) and conceiving her iconoclastic gamine look. He opened his own couture house in 1962, and became known for his tailored coats built on geometric silhouettes and organic lines, such as the triangle-shaped kite coats and oversized capes with dolman sleeves.

► Givenchy, Mandelli, Schiaparelli

Philippe Venet. b Lyon (FR), 1929. **Jane Birkin wears spotted organdie dress.** Photograph by Jean-Jacques Bugat, French *Vogue*, 1972.

Venturi Gian Marco   Designer

A prominent designer in the Italian fashion scene of the 1980s, Venturi based his women's ready-to-wear label on sensuous, masculine tailoring. His dynamic, swingy designs reflected the elevated sportswear look of the time and had a distinctive Milanese feel in their artistic minimalism and architectural fluidity. Venturi was not formally trained in design; instead he majored in business and economics at the University of florence. He then spent many years travelling, embracing rich artistic and cultural Zeitgeists, before working as a designer/stylist. He was quickly noted for his classic, tactile separates in earthbound colours. He launched his own collection in 1979, favouring the bold, feminine look of a modern Louise Brooks dressed in a black snakeskin jacket, animal-printed capri trousers and dark aviator glasses. He entered the millennium with three boutiques in Japan and more than ten franchised fashion sales outlets in New York.

► Maramotti, Revson, Wainwright

Gian Marco Venturi. b florence (IT), 1943. **Jacket and jodhpurs.** *Women's Wear Daily*, 1981.

Di Verdura Fulco

Jewellery designer

Diamond earrings and a gold bracelet are illustrated for 1950s America in a highly original composition. Their designer, whose own vision was equally original, was Fulco Santostefano della Cerda, Duke of Verdura, a widely influential, forward-thinking jewellery designer. Di Verdura worked for Chanel, before opening his own New York shop in 1939. Some of his designs were based on tassels from coats of arms and mariners' knots, but Di Verdura found his greatest source of inspiration in nature, referencing wings, leaves, mermaids, pomegranates and especially shells for motifs. Jewellery designs evoked by nature were typical of his era, but, unlike many of his peers, he was far more experimental and eclectic in his approach. In 1973 he sold his business to his longtime associate, Joseph Alfano. It was bought by Ward Landrigan in 1985, and his son, Nico, became president in 2009, the 70th anniversary of Di Verdura opening his shop.

▶ Chanel, Van Cleef & Arpels, Vreeland

Fulco di Verdura (Fulco Santostefano della Cerda, Duke of Verdura). b Sicily (IT), 1898. **d** London (UK), 1978. **Gold bracelet and diamond earrings.** Photograph by Karen Radkai, American *Vogue*, 1958.

Versace Donatella

Designer

Donatella Versace is pictured here at a New York nightclub with her friend Jennifer Lopez. Blonde since the age of eleven, and the picture of the high-maintenance glamour and brazen sexuality that epitomize the Versace style, Donatella is royalty among the international party crowd. The devoted socializing was good for business. A year later, Lopez wore a Versace creation – the notorious Jungle dress – to the Grammy awards. Slashed to the pubis, its billowing chiffon décolleté magically stopping shy of Lopez's nipples, it turned the actress into a red-carpet sensation and the designer into a force in her own right. Profoundly involved in the Versace label since its foundation in 1978, Donatella was thrust into her role as the label's figurehead, presenting her first collection only months after Gianni's death. She has gradually steered the label's aesthetic from skin-bearing bling to a more refined sexiness.

► Kane, Lady Gaga, Madonna, Richardson, G. Versace

Donatella Versace. b Reggio Calabria (IT), 1955. **Jennifer Lopez and Donatella Versace at a party at the New York club Limelight.** 1999.

Versace Gianni

Designer

'I like to dress egos, if you haven't got a big ego, you can forget it,' said Gianni Versace, who dressed the biggest personalities; here, Madonna, a longtime friend, models his work. Brightly coloured, sexually exuberant and celebrity-endorsed, Versace's clothes brought something of Hollywood glamour back to fashion. His sexy, extrovert designs were worn by the famously rich of both sexes, from rock stars to royalty – Elton John to Diana, Princess of Wales. One Versace dress could make a woman's career (as Elizabeth Hurley found out when she wore his safety-pinned column), and he is credited with fuelling the supermodel phenomenon with his flamboyant, baroque style. It often seemed out of step with modern sobriety, but Versace celebrated the breadth of fashion. He said, 'I don't believe in good taste,' and then created a demure pastel suit for a princess. In 2002 a major exhibition dedicated to him was held at the Victoria & Albert Museum, London.

► Madonna, Molinari, Moschino, Nars, Testino, D. Versace

Gianni Versace. b Reggio Calabria (IT), 1946. **d** Miami, fl (USA), 1997. **Madonna in Versace Atelier advertising campaign.** Photograph by Mario Testino, 1995.

Vertès Marcel

A woman wearing a black, bias-cut gown by Molyneux laments – has someone else also turned up in the same dress? Is her colour scheme hopelessly wrong? (Which might explain the imperious look on the face of her tormentor.) This drawing by Vertès demonstrates his flair for observing both the social life and the fashion of the Parisian *beau monde*. He sketched their foibles and vanities at the same time as illuminating the romantic dress of the period – here a trio of formal, bias-cut gowns

worn with capes or a fichu. Vertès studied drawing and painting at the Academy of fine Arts in Budapest. In 1921 he settled in Paris and his watercolours were exhibited at the Salon des Humoristes in 1925. Vertès' light fashion drawings portrayed high society and high fashion with a seemingly effortless lightness and grace, and were a major contribution to the graphic tradition of *Vogue*.

► Beaton, Delhomme, Molyneux, Tran

Marcel Vertès. b Budapest (HUN), 1895. **d** New York (USA), 1961. **Molyneux evening gowns.** French *Vogue*, 1935.

Veruschka

Model

Rubartelli photographs Veruschka, the woman who put a face to 'hippie deluxe'. Her feathered waistcoat, painted make-up and beads represent fashion from the late 1960s, when her blonde hair and full lips were an ubiquitous element of fashion. From beginning to end, Veruschka's career was an unusual one. Her father, Count von Lehndorff-Steinort, was one of the group that conspired to kill Hitler. 'Little Vera' went on to study art in Hamburg and then Florence, where she was spotted and asked to model at the Palazzo Pitti collections. She became famous for her work with Irving Penn and Diana Vreeland, and for her role in Antonioni's cult film, *Blow Up* (1966). She retired in the early 1970s to do camouflage body art, where she would paint herself to blend in with her background. She described her art as a way of making herself disappear, 'working against my model career'.

▶ Bouquin, Deacon, Kenneth, Penn, Di Sant'Angelo, Vreeland

Veruschka (**Countess Vera von Lehndorff**). **b** Kaliningrad (RUS) (formerly Königsberg, East Prussia), 1939. **Feathered waistcoat.** Photograph by Franco Rubartelli, French *Vogue*, 1970.

Viktor & Rolf

Designers

Dutch duo, Viktor Horsting and Rolf Snoeren met while they were students at the Arnhem Academy of Arts. They graduated in 1992 and held their first haute couture show, based on distortion, reconstruction and layering, in 1993. Viktor & Rolf illuminate the depths of creativity in fashion through presentation; during Paris Fashion Week in 2010, supermodel Kristen McMenamy mounted a rotating carousel, wearing a voluminous coat. As the carousel turned, Viktor and Rolf stripped her of twenty-three layers of clothing, ready to dress the next model like a Russian doll in the clothes they were removing. Among the noteworthy looks were over-sized coats, bustier cocktail dresses, tailored blazers and an array of pleated, geometric silhouettes. Utilitarian, yet sophisticated, the collection gained its 'glamour' credentials through the use of luxurious fabrics, exquisite draping and the employment of unconventional materials like rope and metal.

► Demeulemeester, Margiela, Van Noten, Thimister

Viktor Horsting. b Geldrop (NL), 1969; **Rolf Snoeren. b** Dongen (NL), 1969. **Backstage at Viktor & Rolf's autumn/winter 2012 collection, 'Glamour Factory'.** Photograph by Philip Riches.

Vionnet Madeleine   Designer

Madeleine Vionnet's material does not hang on the models but accompanies them, following natural lines, achieving a modern Grecian silhouette. To get this fluid movement, she dispensed with corsets and used the bias cut, across the grain of the material, to enable it to flow and cling into folds and drapes. To achieve this effect she commissioned fabrics two yards wider than usual. She created her designs on small dolls; those privileged enough to be allowed to watch likened her to a sculptress moulding designs to create these neoclassical dresses. Vionnet, who refused to be called a fashion designer, preferring the title of dressmaker, reached the zenith of her fame in the 1920s and 1930s. Contemporary disciples of this fashion purist include Azzedine Alaïa and John Galliano. In 2009 the Musée de la Mode et du Textile, Paris, held a retrospective exhibition entitled 'Madeleine Vionnet, puriste de la mode'.

► Alaïa, Boulanger, Callot, Hoyningen-Huene, Galliano, Valentina

Madeleine Vionnet. b Aubervilliers (FR), 1876. **d** Paris (FR), 1975. **Bas-relief frieze.** Photograph by George Hoyningen-Huene, French *Vogue*, 1931.   549

Viramontes Tony　　　Illustrator

A waterfall of jersey in scarlet – Valentino's favouite colour – streams down the back of Tony Viramontes' subject. Her skin is a broad stroke of cobalt from naked head to waist-band and the fabric is described with swathes of red gouache. Viramontes worked throughout the 1980s, capturing the vivid, angular attitude of the designers' work he illustrated – in particular Valentino and Montana. He also captured the highly colourful, romantic period of street fashion early in the decade; a time of fashion pirates with their heads wrapped with turbans and bodies decorated with elaborate costume jewellery. Viramontes settled in Venice and Paris, drawn to Europe by his love of fashion and art. Of the artists who inspired him, the most obvious influences were those of Jean Cocteau and Henri Matisse. Viramontes created line drawings similar in intention to Cocteau's figures and blocked them with oil pastel, ink or watercolour.

► Antonio, Cocteau, Montana, Valentino

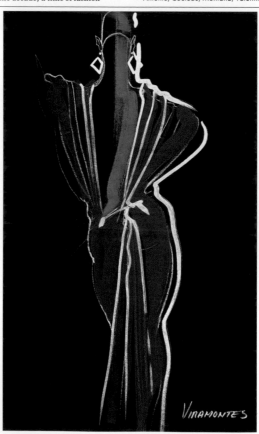

Tony Viramontes. b Los Angeles, CA (USA), 1960. **d** 1988. **Valentino haute couture.** 1984.

Vivier Roger

Shoe designer

This pink satin evening pump, covered with embroidery and encrusted with glass beads and pearls, is as ornate and precious as a piece of jewellery. Roger Vivier's elaborate, sometimes heavily embellished shoes have been described as 'the Fabergé of footwear'. Working at Christian Dior between 1953 and 1963, Vivier has always said, 'My shoes are sculptures.' Indeed, he studied that subject at the École des Beaux-Arts in Paris and is known for innovative heel shapes such as the rhinestone-studded 'ball' heel and the backward-bent 'comma', manufactured in lightweight aluminium alloy by an aeronautical engineering firm. Ava Gardner, Marlene Dietrich, Josephine Baker and The Beatles were all fans of Vivier's shoes. Vivier's shoes are in the collections of the Metropolitan Museum of Art, New York, the Victoria & Albert Museum, London, and the Musée de la Mode et du Textile, Paris.

► Bally, The Beatles, Dior, Lane, Louboutin, Pinet, Rayne

Roger Vivier. b Paris (FR), 1913. **d** Toulouse (FR), 1998. **Pink embroidered shoe with 'Comma' heel, 1963.** Photograph by Jacques Boulay.

Vreeland Diana

Editor

The epitome of a *jolie laide*, Diana Vreeland was the beautiful swan and ugly duckling of fashion, complete with *kabuki*-like make-up. From 1937 to the 1980s, she was an arbiter of style, first as an editor-writer for *Harper's Bazaar* where she is most remembered for her short-lived but legendary 'Why Don't You…' column, which made insouciant suggestions in defiance of Depression-era gloom. Throughout her life, Vreeland had a way with words: her phrases (some sublime, such as 'elegance is refusal') and elegantly turned truisms (such as 'pink is the navy blue of India') have become fashion clichés. From 1962 to 1971, as editor-in-chief of *Vogue*, Vreeland gave the magazine the energy of the jet age and youth, making it a showcase for favoured photographers Richard Avedon and Irving Penn. In 1972 she became consultant to the Costume Institute of the Metropolitan Museum of Art in New York.

► Brodovitch, Coddington, Dahl-Wolfe, Kennedy, Nast, Wintour

Diana Vreeland. b Paris (FR), 1901. **d** New York (USA), 1989. **Diana Vreeland wears Fulco Di Verdura's cuffs.** Photograph by Horst P. Horst, 1979.

Vuitton Louis

Accessory designer

A luxury brand founded on the tradition and history of leisured travel – and the accessories that go with it. Louis Vuitton, the progenitor and namesake, established the name in Paris in 1854 when he saw a general need for high-quality baggage, designing a flat trunk that could be stacked in the cargo hold of transatlantic ships or on the luggage racks of trains. Vuitton's chequerboard 'Daumier' canvas was first introduced in 1888, and the famous monogram – a perennial status symbol – was created in 1886 by Louis' son, Georges. Vuitton's luggage has since been the cornerstone to what is now a global luxury empire known as the LVMH group since it merged with Moët Hennessy in 1987. Today it is the most valuable brand in the luxury market with Marc Jacobs as creative director, overseeing the men's and women's ready-to-wear lines as well as luxury home and lifestyle products.

▶ Gucci, Hermès, Jacobs, Loewe

Louis Vuitton. b Cons-Le-Saunier (FR), 1811. **d** Asnières (FR), 1892. **Mrs Amory Carhart Jr stands by a seaplane, as her Louis Vuitton suitcases are unloaded, New York.** Photograph by John Rawlings, 1954.

Wainwright Janice   Designer

Janice Wainwright brings the outdoors indoors with a pair of moiré taffeta jodhpurs – a widely used theme at the end of the 1970s. Sensuous fabrics cut with a feminine touch were at the centre of her work; here her silk *crêpe-de-chine* shirt is given a fichu tie. Wainwright studied at the Royal College of Art in London, and worked with Sheridan Barnett before founding her own company in 1974. Throughout the 1970s she was known for soft dresses that were often cut on the bias. She produced clothes that, according to *Vogue*, '...obey the first rule of dress which is that clothes must be appropriate'. Wainwright's interest in textiles extended to her involvement with the design and colouring of the fabrics she used. Previous collections include dresses cleverly designed to spiral downwards around the body. Intricate embroidery, appliqué trimmings and accentuated shoulders are other distinctive hallmarks of her style.

► Barnett, Bates, Demarchelier, Venturi

Janice Wainwright. b Chesterfield (UK), 1940. **Plum silk shirt and moiré jodhpurs.** Photograph by Patrick Demarchelier, British *Vogue*, 1980.

Walker Tim

Photographer

Elaborate set design is one of the hallmarks of British photographer Tim Walker's artistic practice. Imaginative and whimsical, his photographs often consist of oversized elements, dwarfing his models within the composition. In this image Walker's characteristic emphasis on production design is beautifully exemplified. Eerie and romantic, a looming skeleton stands in a field of flowers and reaches for the McQueen-sheathed model beneath a darkened sky, in a subtly surreal narrative. Walker began an interest in photography working in the archive of Cecil Beaton at the London Condé Nast library. After studying at Exeter College of Art in London, Walker relocated to New York to assume a position as Richard Avedon's assistant. Walker's photographs have been the subject of multiple exhibitions including a recent retrospective at Somerset House in London, and his portraiture and fashion images continue to be much sought after.

► Avedon, Beaton, Coddington, Deacon, McQueen

Tim Walker. b Guildford (UK), 1970. **'Tim Burton's Tricks & Treats', editorial for *Harper's Bazaar.*** 2009.

Wang Alexander   Designer

The poncho may come and go in fashion, but San Franciscan-born Alexander Wang's 2012 take, made from satin and angora, was more desired than most. Launching his first womenswear collection in 2007, Wang's downtown, 'model-off-duty' look – inspired by the 1990s, French chic and grunge rock – was an instant hit. His studded bags and sporty T-shirts became indispensable. Wang's sports-meets-luxury design inhabits what he calls the 'undone', the gap between refinement and imperfection. In 2008 he won the *Vogue*/CFDA Fashion Fund Award and launched a full womenswear line with menswear not far behind. After opening his flagship store in Soho, NYC, in 2011, Wang chose Beijing as the site of his second store. A fluent Mandarin speaker, he is perfectly placed to storm the Chinese fashion world. In December 2012, after months of anticipation, Wang was announced as the new creative director at Balenciaga.
► Balenciaga, Jacobs, Karan, McCartney, McQueen

Alexander Wang. b San Francisco, CA (USA), 1983. **Satin and angora poncho spring/summer 2012.**

Wang Vera

Designer

A dress never works harder than on Oscar night or when it's worn by a bride. When Hollywood's women or the centrepiece of a wedding emerge from a limousine, they want a dress that will make the audience draw breath. This is what Vera Wang is famous for. She uses rich fabrics such as silk lace and duchesse satin in the tradition of Paris haute couture, and applies them to the simple shapes associated with American sportswear. Wang lives in the society she designs for. Born into New York's Upper East Side, she was forbidden to attend design school, becoming instead *Vogue*'s youngest fashion editor. Having worked for Ralph Lauren, she opened a bridal salon and couture business in 1990. Her appreciation of surface decoration, particularly beading, and the use of net to give the illusion of bare skin have also recommended her for the design of Olympic figure-skating costumes – another career she pursued before design.

► Jackson, Lauren, Leiber, Lesage, Roehm, Yantorny

Vera Wang. b New York (USA), 1949. **Gold brocade couture gown, 1991.** Photograph by Victor Skrebneski.

Warhol Andy

Designer

Andy Warhol began work as an illustrator for fashion companies and magazines such as *Mademoiselle*, growing increasingly aware of the relationship between art, fashion and commerce. He then produced window displays for New York department stores Tiffany's and Bonwit Teller. By the early 1960s, Warhol had reinvented himself as a music and movies impresario and even as a fashion designer. Here two women are hanging out in the Factory, his artist's salon, wearing his slogan dresses.

Warhol began to wear rock-star leather jackets, satin shirts and a silver-sprayed wig and he used the superstar actresses from his films to model paper dresses printed with his Banana paintings. He also became friends with fashion editor Diana Vreeland and designer Betsey Johnson, and in 1969 Warhol launched his experimental style magazine *Interview*, in which he profiled his designer friends Halston and Elsa Peretti.

▶ Bulgari, De Castelbajac, Garren, LaChapelle, Lady Gaga, Sprouse

Andy Warhol (Andrew Warhola). b Pittsburgh, PA (USA), 1928. **d** New York (USA), 1987. **'Brillo' and 'Fragile, Handle With Care'**. Photograph by Ken Heyman, 1962.

Watanabe Junya

Designer

By extending the distances between each model as they tread the perimeter of his square catwalk, Junya Watanabe gives visual silence to his futuristic fashion. Glamour, sound and colour are notably absent; instead, an optical tautology of frugal, white cotton *khadi* presents this complex collection. He graduated from Tokyo's Bunka Fashion Institute in 1984 and joined Comme des Garçons, designing the Tricot line in 1987. As Rei Kawakubo's protégé, his creations reflect the intellectual Zeitgeist of the Japanese maestro. However, he takes a personal approach for his line, Junya Watanabe Comme des Garçons, applying his hand to the futuristic – from cellophane-wrapped neon punks and abstract oriental peasantwear, to poetic stark white. He gives his clothes an irregularity through tucking, pleating and ruching, continuing the spirit of Comme des Garçons in conceptualizing and deconstructing traditional constructs.

► Fontana, Kawakubo, Rocha, Takahashi, Y. Yamamoto

Weber Bruce

Photographer

Chosen by Bruce Weber to represent his work, this photograph shows a girl, fresh and artless, peering from beneath a Charles James gown, itself the very example of constructed beauty. Such human subjects are, however, unusual. His historical paragon is the photographer Leni Riefenstahl, who extolled an exclusive and privileged male body. Weber was the most important photographer of redefined masculinity in the 1980s and 1990s. He created erotic images of muscular, natural bodies. One significant inspiration for Weber is Classical sculpture: his buffed, athletic heroes (seen in Calvin Klein's underwear advertisements) often recall Hellenistic sculpture. The chaos of real life never intrudes or spoils the mood; over the course of two decades his photographs for Ralph Lauren have created a privileged dream world of country houses, polo matches and safaris. He has also turned his hand to film-making and music videos.

► C. James, C. Klein, Lauren, Platt Lynes, Ritts, Tennant

Bruce Weber. b Greensburg, PA (USA), 1946. **Girl beneath vintage dress by Charles James.** 1991.

Westwood Dame Vivienne   Designer

Christy Turlington wears Vivienne Westwood in a photograph by Mario Testino for British *Vogue* in 1993. Westwood regards this outfit as typical of her work, even though it leaves out her waggish references to royalty (crowns set with paste jewels) and historical excess (mini-crinolines and bodices from which the wearer's bosom spills like a milk jelly). When Westwood began her confrontational fashion career in 1970, she would no doubt have laughed at the notion that her clothes would one day appear in an establishment fashion magazine on a famous model. In the intervening years she established herself as the only British designer who could not only explore extremes in dress, but also make sense of them. She did this most significantly with the punk movement during her collaboration with Malcolm McLaren. In 1981 she launched her catwalk collection, continuing her emphasis on eccentricity and subversion.

▶ Barbieri, McLaren, Testino, Turlington

Dame Vivienne Westwood. b Tintwhistle (UK), 1941. **'Anglomania': Christy Turlington wears a bias-cut tartan suit.** Photograph by Mario Testino, British *Vogue*, 1993.

Wilde Oscar

Icon

'A Fashion is a form of dress so unbearable we are compelled to alter it every six months,' said Oscar Wilde in 1884, citing Paris as the centre of sartorial tyranny. This is Wilde photographed in New York in 1882. The picture reflects the writer's campaign for men's dress reform. He wears knee breeches (the artistic alternative to trousers, which he called boring tubes), a smoking jacket (a recent addition to the male wardrobe) and a comfortable, nonconformist soft collar and cravat.

Between 1887 and 1889, he was editor of *Woman's World* magazine, which promoted the aesthetic dress sold at Liberty. By 1890, apart from his green carnation or lily buttonhole, Wilde had decided to wear conventional dress. In *The Picture of Dorian Gray*, he pronounced conventional dress for men to be the most beautiful in the world, stating, 'It is only the shallow people who do not judge by appearances.'

► Coward, Jaeger, Liberty, Muir

Oscar Wilde. b Dublin (IRE), 1854. **d** Paris (FR), 1900. **Oscar Wilde in breeches and a smoking jacket.** Photograph by Napoleon Sarony, 1882.

Williamson Matthew   Designer

In a celebration of a career spanning over 15 years, Matthew Williamson's models wear the signature vividly coloured textiles that made a name for the designer. Here, in full bloom, Williamson's textiles and feminine cutting are brought to life by his brilliant colour palette. He took inspiration from the ethnic dress of his travels to exotic locations such as India, where he learned techniques for the intricate embroidery that features in his work. Williamson originally trained with Zandra

Rhodes, an influence that shows in his choice of unbridled colour combinations and lavish detailing, launching his label in 1996 with a collection of fluid, bias-cut dresses and skirts and cashmere twinsets and a nonchalant glamour. Alongside his own label, the designer took over for a stint as creative director at Emilio Pucci in 2005, before returning to London in 2008 to focus solely on the Matthew Williamson brand.

► Ferretti, Kane, Mouret, Oudejans, Rhodes

Matthew Williamson. b Manchester (UK), 1972. **On set for Williamson's 15-year-anniversary film.** Photograph by Rhys Frampton, 2012.

Windsor Duke & Duchess of   Icons

Together the Duke and Duchess of Windsor symbolized opulence tempered by sartorial restraint. For their wedding day, Wallis Simpson chose a sapphire blue (dubbed 'Wallis' blue), crepe silk dress by Mainbocher, one of her favourite designers. Mainbocher preferred to 'blend mystery rather than to rant and rave with my shears,' and he created an utterly simple, bias-cut dress and jacket that were worn with a matching hat by Reboux. Givenchy and Marc Bohan were other favourites. It was a discreet style that provided an ideal backdrop for her magnificent jewels, many of which were chosen by the Duke. His clothes were equally influential. At university he had championed the flapping trouser legs dubbed 'Oxford bags' and, rejecting the stiff, interlined clothing of his youth, he often flouted convention and pioneered new styles, such as the dark blue, double-breasted dinner jacket.

► Burton, Cartier, Ferragamo, Horst, Mainbocher, Reboux

Duke of Windsor. b Richmond (UK), 1894. d Paris (FR), 1972; Duchess of Windsor. b Blue Ridge Summit, PA (USA), 1896. d Paris (FR), 1986. The Duke and Duchess of Windsor on their wedding day at the Château de Condé, France. 1937.

Winston Harry

Jewellery designer

Elizabeth Taylor wears a suite of diamonds by Harry Winston, the sparkling voltage of which is matched by the glint in her violet eyes for her favourite stone – after which her scent White Diamonds is named. When Marilyn Monroe sang about her favourite rock in *Gentlemen Prefer Blondes* (1953), it was to the 'King of Diamonds' she appealed, 'Talk to me, Harry, tell me about it...' Winston's reciprocal love affair with Hollywood began when he assisted his father in their small Los Angeles

jewellery store. At the age of twenty, he moved back to New York to found his own jewellery business. By the time he had incorporated his firm under his own name in 1932, Winston had become a leading retailer of exclusive diamond jewellery, renowned for using exceptionally large stones. In 1998, the Winston look was encapsulated in a pair of diamond-encrusted Ray-Ban sunglasses, designed for the Oscar ceremony.

► Alexandre, Hiro, Madonna, Tiffany

Harry Winston. b New York (USA), 1896. **d** (USA), 1978. **'Passion' perfume publicity campaign. Elizabeth Taylor wears diamond earrings and collar.** Photograph by Sir Norman Parkinson, 1987.

Wintour Anna

Editor

The most powerful person in fashion is undoubtedly Anna Wintour, editor-in-chief of American *Vogue*. Her influence sends chills through designers vying for attention from the fashion guru. Born in 1949 in London, Wintour left school at sixteen to work in fashion when she landed an assistant role at *Harpers & Queen*, later moving to New York where she swiftly climbed the ranks to take over US *Vogue* in 1988. Among her considerable and far-reaching projects she led an early campaign against AIDS, spearheaded the CFDA/*Vogue* Fashion Fund and fostered a wealth of emerging designers. She has been awarded the OBE and the *Légion d'honneur*, and immortalized in the documentary *The September Issue* (2009) and the film *The Devil Wears Prada* (2006), which features a steely fashion editor played by Meryl Streep and based on Wintour. The muse showed up to the premiere – attired, of course, in Prada.

► Baron, Coddington, Menkes, Nast

Anna Wintour. b London (UK), 1949. **Wintour captured front row in *The September Issue*.** Directed by R. J. Cutler (A&E Indiefilms/Actual Reality Pictures), 2009.

Worth Charles Frederick

Designer

Spangled silk tulle was typical of Worth's work in the 1860s. For Empress Elizabeth of Austria he chose gold to be scattered over her gown – a scheme extended by the golden stars in her hair. The dress's décolleté neckline, which exposes and embraces her shoulders, would be softened with the tulle held lightly around her hips. Winterhalter chronicled the work of Worth through such portraits and painted many similarly graceful compositions of the Empress Eugénie, Worth's most valuable client. The story of modern fashion began when Charles Frederick Worth, a young tailor, arrived at the court of Napoleon III. In his bid to re-establish Paris as the centre of fashionable life, the Emperor stimulated the luxury business and his wife Eugénie patronized it in fabulous style. Under that patronage, Worth drew on the history of costume to create lavish, expensive gowns that raised dressmaking to a new level called haute couture.

► Duff Gordon, Fratini, Hartnell, Pinet, Poiret, Reboux

Charles Frederick Worth. b Bourne (UK), 1825. **d** Paris (FR), 1895. **Empress Elizabeth of Austria wearing spangled tulle.** Painting by Franz Xaver Winterhalter, 1865.

Yamamoto Kansai   Designer

Cartoon graphics and cotton netting were one of the wilder combinations offered by Kansai Yamamoto. Others included lush satin robes and pyjamas appliquéd with huge Japanese figures. Yamamoto married traditional Japanese culture and Western influences, set them to a music beat and put them in the realm of the performing arts. In the 1970s his fashion performance shows were huge events, attracting up to 5,000 people. After training as a civil engineer, Yamamoto left school in 1962 to study English, before moving on to fashion. He designed David Bowie's outrageous costumes for 'Ziggy Stardust' and 'Aladdin Sane' and, in 1975, he began showing in Paris, part of the first wave of Japanese designers who would have an impact on fashion through the following decades. Yamamoto's trademarks are a use of abstract colour sculpted into unique forms, which successfully blend ancient oriental influences with modern sporty themes.

► Bowie, Sprouse, Warhol

Kansai Yamamoto. b Kanagawa (JAP), 1944. **'Kansai' graffiti shirt and mesh skirt.** *Women's Wear Daily*, 1982.

Yamamoto Yohji   Designer

This lean coat represents the traditions of both antique Western tailoring and those of contemporary Japan. In 1981 Yohji Yamamoto presented his clothes to a Western audience for the first time and effectively turned the notion of fashion as structured, sexy and glamorous on its head. Experts were shocked, labelling the collection 'Hiroshima chic'; it was composed of androgynous shrouds in several shades of black, worn with flat shoes, little make-up and a stern expression. But the shock turned to admiration. Yamamoto dropped out of a law degree to work for his widowed mother in her dressmaking shop. He followed this with a fashion degree at Tokyo's Bunka Fashion College, and set up his own label in 1977. He says, 'My clothes are about human beings: they are alive. I am alive.' His vision of women, and later men, as independent, intelligent, liberated artisans has elevated his status to that of a fashion legend.

► Kawakubo, N. Knight, Inez and Vinoodh, Miyake

Yohji Yamamoto. b Yokohama (JAP), 1943. **Red hat and black tail-coat.** Photograph by Paolo Roversi, 1985.

antorny Pietro
Shoe designer

The sumptuous custom-made shoes of Pietro Yantorny survive today as totems of unsurpassed grandeur. The embroidered silk mules were created for rich American socialite Rita de Acosta Lydig. The Turkish-inspired design, alluding to exotic harems, suggests a boudoir slipper, although Lydig may have paired them with one of her gossip-taunting harem dresses. What little is known about Yantorny is partly attributed to a reputation that lasted only a few years, although in that time he enjoyed an international clientele sprinkled with royalty. His lofty aspirations – reinforced by the slogan used in his Parisian salon, 'The world's most expensive custom shoemaker' – did not deter clients, even when orders took two years to arrive. There was reason for their patience: Yantorny made painstaking measurements of each individual in order to make each shoe fit 'like a silk sock'.

► Hope, Lesage, Pinet, V. Wang

Pietro Yantorny. b Calabria (IT), 1874. d Paris (FR), 1936. **Embroidered green silk mules made for Rita de Acosta Lydig, 1914 to 1919.**

Zoran

Designer

Utterly simple, squared black shapes: the name Zoran is associated with minimalism and purity. Elements of his approach to design – mathematical precision-cutting and clean, simple shapes – hark back to his degree in architecture for which he studied in his home town, Belgrade. Zoran moved to New York in the early 1970s, launching his first capsule collection there to wide acclaim in 1977. His first collections were designed around squares and rectangles in silk *crêpe-de-chine*. Unswayed by transient fads of fashion, Zoran prefers to design comfortable clothing with longevity, in sumptuous fabrics, especially cashmere. Using an elemental palette of colours – mainly red, black, grey, white and cream – he also avoids using extraneous decoration. Even the practical details, such as cuffs, collars, zips and fastenings, are hidden away or banished where possible. His clientele has included Isabella Rossellini, Lauren Hutton and Candice Bergen.

► Audibet, Beretta, Chalayan, C. Klein, Y. Yamamoto

Zoran (**Zoran Ladicorbic**). b Belgrade (SER), 1947. **Black outfits.** Photograph by Goe Moe.

Index

Acknowledgements

Authors: Carmel Allen, Tim Cooke, Laura Gardner, Beth Hancock, Rebekah Hay-Brown, Hettie Judah, Sebastian Kaufmann, Caroline Kinneberg, Natasha Kraal, Fiona McAuslan, Alice Mackrell, Richard Martin, Melanie Rickey, Judith Watt and Melissa Mostyn.

The publishers would particularly like to thank Suzy Menkes for her invaluable advice and also Katell le Bourhis, Frances Collecott-Doe, Dennis Freedman, Robin Healy, Peter Hope-Lumley, Isabella Kullman, Jean Matthew, Dr Lesley Miller, Alice Rawsthorn, Aileen Ribeiro, Julian Robinson, Yumiko Uegaki, Jonathan Wolford for their advice. And Lorraine Mead, Lisa Diaz and Don Osterweil for their assistance.

The publishers wish to thank Mats Gustafson for his jacket illustration.

Photographic Acknowledgements

Photograph James Abbe, © Kathryn Abbe: 4; Photograph Randall Mesden, Courtesy Joseph Abboud: 5; © Acne: 260; © Actual Reality Pictures/The Kobal Collection: 566; Photograph Eric Adjani, Sygma/JetSet: 13; © Lorenzo Agius: 535; Photograph Miles Aldridge, Courtesy Lawrence Steele: 486; Photograph Simon Archer: 113; Photograph © Brian Aris, Courtesy Boy George: 80; Courtesy Giorgio Armani: 21; © Eve Arnold/Magnum Photos: 22, 300; Photograph Clive Arrowsmith, Courtesy Zandra Rhodes: 438; Museo di Arte Moderna e Contemporanea di Trento e Roverto: 175; Courtesy Laura Ashley: 24; Associated Press Ltd: 234; © 1978 Richard Avedon. All rights reserved: 26; Photograph Enrique Badulescu: 44; © David Bailey: 28; Courtesy Balenciaga Archives, Paris: 157; Courtesy Bally: 33; © Gian Paolo Barbieri: 38; © Jeff Bark: 18; Courtesy Fabien Baron: 41; Courtesy Slim Barrett: 42; © Michael Barrett: 377; Courtesy Gallery Bartsch & Chariau: 17, 264, 280; © Lillian Bassman: 45, 396; Photograph Peter Beard, Courtesy Vogue, © 1964 Condé Nast Publications, Inc: 426; Photograph Cecil Beaton, Courtesy Sotheby's London: 48, 73, 155, 189, 205, 368, 371, 465, 523; Photograph Cecil Beaton, Courtesy Vogue, © 1952 Condé Nast Publications, Inc: 100; Courtesy Victoria Beckham: 50; Photograph Rebeca Bell, Courtesy Jonathan Saunders: 461; Photograph Bellini, Courtesy Christian Dior: 150; Photograph Gilles Bensimon/Elle NY: 362; Photograph Gilles Bensimon/SCOOP Elle UK: 391; © Harry Benson: 262; © François Berthoud: 60; © Bettmann/Corbis: 93, 462; Courtesy Biagiotti-Cigna, Guidonia/photo Giuseppe Schiavinotto, Rome: 32; Bibliothèque National de France: 105, 418; Bildarchiv Peter W. Engelmeier, Munich. 39, 521; © Billy Nava Archive: 537; Birks Couture Collection, Camrax Inc: 94, 414; Courtesy Manolo Blahnik: 65; Courtesy Bill Blass Ltd. Archives: 67; © Estate of Erwin Blumenfeld: 69; Photograph Jacques Boulay/Musée des Arts de la Mode, Paris: 551; Photograph Guy Bourdin/© Samuel Bourdin: 75, 267; Courtesy Bourjois: 76; Photograph Brian Duffy: 64; © Nick Briggs, 1998: 386; Courtesy Brooks Brothers: 83; Photograph Kelvin Bruce/Nunn Syndication Ltd: 148; Courtesy Burberry: 90; Camera Press Ltd, London: 228; Courtesy Carven: 515; Courtesy Oleg Cassini: 103; Courtesy Cerruti: 108; © Dave Chancellor/Alpha, London: 305; Photograph Walter Chin, reproduced from Bobbi Brown Beauty – The Ultimate Beauty Resource by Bobbi Brown & Annemarie Iverson (Ebury Press, 1997): 84; Photograph Walter Chin, Courtesy Gap: 186; Courtesy Chloé: 9, 326; Christie's Images: 295; Photograph Julien Claessens & Thomas Deschamps, model Marte Mei van Hasster, Courtesy Theyskens' Theory: 508; Photograph John Claridge: 539; Photograph Henry Clarke, Courtesy Vogue Paris: 74, 116; Photograph William Claxton: 209; Photograph Clifford Coffin. Courtesy Vogue, © 1949 Condé Nast Publications, Inc: 121, Photograph Clifford Coffin, Courtesy Vogue, © 1947 Condé Nast Publications, Inc. 207; Courtesy Colette: 310; Photograph Michel Comte, Courtesy Dolce & Gabbana: 152; © Condé Nast Archive/Corbis: 10, 553; © Richard Corkery/NY Daily News Archive/Getty Images: 544; Photograph Bill Cunningham, Courtesy Vogue. Copyright © 1972 Condé Nast Publications, Inc: 7; Photograph Mark J. Curtis: 322; Photograph Louise Dahl-Wolfe, Courtesy Staley-Wise Gallery, New York: 134; Photograph Darzacq, Courtesy agnès b: 525; © Kevin Davies: 68, 522; © Corinne Day: 137; © Pierre Debusschere: 473; © Jean-Philippe Delhomme: 141; © Patrick Demarchelier /Courtesy Harper's Bazaar: 144; Courtesy Parfums Christian Dior: 221; Courtesy Adolfo Dominguez: 153; © Julio Donoso/Sygma /Corbis: 204; Photograph Nick Dorey, model Erjona Ala, Courtesy Preen: 511; Raoul Dufy © Bianchini-Férier (Musée Historique des Tissus): 159; © Arthur Elgort: 11, 35, 114, 247; Photograph Arthur

Courtesy Thom Browne: 85; Photograph Thierry Ledé: 122; Photograph Erica Lennard, model Lise Ryall: 162; © Alexander Liberman: 110, 317; The Library of Congress, Prints & Photographs Division, Toni Frissell Collection: 199; Peter Lindbergh, Courtesy *Harper's Bazaar*: 206; Peter Lindbergh, Courtesy Comme des Garçons: 272; Photograph Peter Lindbergh: 319; Courtesy Agnes Lloyd-Platt/Ally Capellino: 320; Courtesy Loewe: 321; Lisa Lyon, © 1984 The Estate of Robert Mapplethorpe: 86; Courtesy M.A.C: 519; Nick Machalaba/*Women's Wear Daily*: 480; Photograph Andrew Macpherson: 131; Photograph Marcio Madeira: 259; Photograph © Erik Madigan Heck: 6, 145, 271; Photograph Gered Mankowitz © Bowstir Ltd.1998: 233; Photograph Markus & Indrani, art direction GK Reid: 223; Mary Evans Picture Library: 154, 212; Photograph Mitsuhiro Matsuda, 1006 3/8 Madame Nicole ad campaign: 348; Photograph Mark Mattock: 359; Courtesy Max Factor: 176; Photograph Eamonn J. McCabe/SCOOP *Elle* UK: 493; © Craig McDean/Art + Commerce: 390, 498; © Craig McDean: 328, 476, 484; © Tony McGee, London: 252; Photograph Niall McInerney: 389; Photograph Niall McInerney, Courtesy Ghost: 459; Courtesy Malcolm McLaren: 334; © Frances McLaughlin-Gill, New York: 61, 96, 147, 220, 335, 471; © Alasdair McLellan/art partner, model Rosie Tapner: 517; © Steven Meisel/Art + Commerce, art direction Alber Elbaz & Ronnie Cooke Newhouse, models Raquel Zimmerman & Karen Elson, Courtesy Lanvin: 161; © Steven Meisel/Art + Commerce: 165, 213,

352; © Steven Meisel/Art + Commerce, Courtesy MaxMara: 343; Photograph Mert & Marcus, stylist Katie Grand for *LOVE* magazine, Courtesy Katie Grand: 218; © Mert & Marcus/art partner: 354; © Sheila Metzner: 488; Photograph Baron de Meyer: 20; Photograph by Baron de Meyer, Courtesy *Vogue*, © 1922 Condé Nast Publications, Inc: 356; Photograph by Baron de Meyer. Courtesy *Vogue*: 432, 502; © Duane Michals, New York: 225; © Lee Miller Archives: 88, 357; Courtesy Nolan Miller: 358; Photograph Eddy Ming, Courtesy Akira Isogawa: 251; © Ministère de la Culture, France/AAJHL: 128; Mirror Syndication International: 164, 337, 450; Musée de la Mode et du Textile/UFAC: 156; Photograph Jean-Baptiste Mondino, Courtesy Walter Van Beirendonck: 52; Photograph David Montgomery, Courtesy Vidal Sassoon: 460; Photograph Sarah Moon: 77, 367; © Chris Moore: 14, 46, 117, 142, 143, 160, 236, 278, 301, 496, 529, 559; © Christopher Moore Limited (trading as Catwalking) 2013: 109, 210, 327, 384, 411, 427; Courtesy Antonio Berardi/Chris Moore: 56; Courtesy Robert Lee Morris: 370; © Jon Mortimer: 279; Illustration Rebecca Moses, creative direction Deborah Moses, animation & design Detour Design, New York: 373; Courtesy Thierry Mugler: 376; Photograph Ugo Mulas, Courtesy Mila Schön: 467; © Joan Munkacsi, Courtesy Howard Greenberg, NY: 380; Musée de la Mode et du Textile/UFAC: 151, 312, 407; The Museum of Costume and Fashion Research Centre, Bath: 434; The Museum of Modern Art, New York. Gift of the Photographer. Copy print: 487; Courtesy NARS: 380; Courtesy National Portrait Gallery, London:

562; Courtesy Net-a-Porter: 347; © Helmut Newton/Maconochie Photography: 382; Photograph Helmut Newton, Courtesy Wolford: 394; Photograph Fiorenzo Niccoli, Courtesy Roberto Capucci: 98; Courtesy Nike: 287; Photograph Morgan O'Donovan, Courtesy Erdem: 166; © Heathcliff O'Malley/Rex Features: 92; Courtesy L'Officiel: 57, 104, 230, 254, 503; Photograph Perry Ogden: 123; Photograph Kazuo Oishi, Courtesy Gianfranco Ferre: 182; Bill Orchard/Rex Features: 79; © Mike Owen: 193; PA News, London: 226; Photograph Dick Page: 389; Photograph by Kourken Pakchanian, Courtesy *Vogue*, © 1973 Condé Nast Publications, Inc: 202; Photograph by Kourken Pakchanian, Courtesy *Vogue*, © 1975 Condé Nast Publications, Inc: 283; Courtesy Jean Patou: 399; Photograph Irving Penn, Courtesy *Vogue* © 1950 (renewed 1978) by Condé Nast Publications: 190; Photograph by Irving Penn, Courtesy *Vogue*, © 1950 (renewed 1978) Condé Nast Publications, Inc: 403; © Elsa Peretti 1989. Photography by Hiro: 404; Courtesy Gladys Perint Palmer: 405; Photofest, New York: 8, 36, 139, 229, 424; Photograph PICTO: 178; Photograph George Platt Lynes. Courtesy *Vogue*. Copyright © 1947 by the Condé Nast Publications, Inc: 417; © Alex Prager: 338; Courtesy Myrene de Prémonville: 423; © Richard Press/First Thought Films: 132; Courtesy Lilly Pulitzer: 428; Photograph Karen Radkai, Courtesy *Vogue*, © 1959 Condé Nast Publications, Inc: 524; Photograph by Karen Radkai. Courtesy *Vogue*. Copyright © 1958 by the Condé Nast Publications, Inc: 543; Photograph by John Rawlings, Courtesy *Vogue*, © 1947 Condé Nast Publications, Inc: 474; Photograph

Phaidon Press Limited
Regent's Wharf
All Saints Street
London, N1 9PA

Phaidon Press Inc.
65 Bleecker Street
New York, NY 10012

www.phaidon.com

First published 1998
Second edition (revised,
expanded and updated)
published in 2013
This edition © 2014
Phaidon Press Limited

ISBN 978 0 7148 6797 7

A CIP catalogue record for
this book is available from
the British Library.

Jacket illustration by
Mats Gustafson

Printed in China

Abbreviations

ALG = Algeria
ARG = Argentina
ASL = Australia
AUS = Austria
BEL = Belgium
BR = Brazil
CAN = Canada
CHN = China
CI = Canary Islands
COL = Colombia
CRO = Croatia
CU = Cuba
CYP = Cyprus
CZ = Czech Republic
DK = Denmark
DOM = Dominican Republic
EG = Egypt
FR = France
GER = Germany
GHA = Ghana
GR = Greece

HK = Hong Kong
HUN = Hungary
IRE = Ireland
IT = Italy
JAM = Jamaica
JAP = Japan
KEN = Kenya
KOR = Korea
LIB = Libya
LUX = Luxembourg
MAL = Malaysia
MEX = Mexico
MON = Monaco
MOR = Morocco
NL = Netherlands
NZ = New Zealand
PER = Peru
POL = Poland
PR = Puerto Rico
ROM = Romania
RUS = Russia
SA = South Africa

SER = Serbia
SING = Singapore
SP = Spain
SW = Switzerland
SWE = Sweden
SYR = Syria
TUN = Tunisia
TUR = Turkey
UK = United Kingdom
USA = United States of America